A Dictionary of Actors

and of Other Persons Associated with the Public
Representation of Plays in England
before 1642

By

Edwin Nungezer, Ph.D.

Assistant Professor of English in the
University of Oklahoma

AMS PRESS

NEW YORK

Reprinted from the edition of 1929: New Haven

First AMS edition published in 1971

Manufactured in the United States of America

International Standard Book Number: 0-404-04806-4

Library of Congress Catalog Card Number: 75-173803

AMS PRESS INC.
NEW YORK, N.Y.   10003

PREFACE

In this *Dictionary* I have attempted to assemble all the available information regarding actors, theatrical proprietors, stage attendants, and other persons known to have been associated with the representation of plays in England before the year 1642. The resultant sketches, where records are deficient, inevitably suffer from brevity, and where scholarship has failed to clear up obscure problems in stage history, are marred by conjecture. From time to time, of course, fresh details will be added to our store of knowledge; in particular, not a little information remains to be gleaned from unexplored parish registers and court proceedings. Yet the bulk of what we are destined to know of Elizabethan stage folk has doubtless been garnered by the almost countless scholars who, during more than a century and a half of labor, have been diligently searching in the field. It is my hope that the present effort to collect and organize all the discovered facts—now scattered in widely separated places—will be of use to those who seriously concern themselves with the early drama of England.

In order to facilitate reference, I have abbreviated the titles of the most frequently cited works. As a rule, these abbreviations will be clear to students familiar with dramatic literature, or easily understood by a glance at the Bibliography; those which might occasion difficulty are listed below.

Cohn (*Shakespeare in Germany*)
Collier (*History of English Dramatic Poetry*)
Eliz. Stage (Chambers, *The Elizabethan Stage*)
H. D. (Greg, *Henslowe's Diary*)
H.P. (Greg, *Henslowe Papers*)
M.S.C. (Malone Society *Collections*)
Murray (*English Dramatic Companies*)

PREFACE

N.U.S. (*Nebraska University Studies*)
R.E.S. (*Review of English Studies*)
S.P.D. (*Calendar of State Papers, Domestic*)
Warner (*Dulwich Catalogue*)

I desire here to express my thanks to Mr. C. K. Edmonds, of the Huntington Library, who kindly transcribed for me various items from books not otherwise available.

My greatest debt of gratitude, however, I owe to Professor Joseph Quincy Adams, who originally suggested to me this task, who at the outset turned over to me his own extensive collection of notes, and who with sympathetic interest and ever-ready aid encouraged me when the way seemed long and dark.

I have tried hard to attain accuracy; yet the sheer multitude of details, and the inescapable errors that attend the mechanical operations of typing and printing, have, I know, at times defeated my effort. For such mistakes I crave the kindly tolerance of the reader.

Edwin Nungezer

Norman, Oklahoma
August 11, 1928

A DICTIONARY OF ACTORS

A DICTIONARY OF ACTORS

ABYNGDON, HENRY.
Master of the Chapel Royal, 1455–78 (Wallace, *Evolution*, pp. 22 ff.).

ADAMS, JOHN.
As one of Sussex's (Chamberlain's) company, John Adams received payment for the play given at Court on February 2, 1576 (Steele, p. 58). In 1583 he was a member of the Queen's troupe in London, for he is named in a City record that gives the personnel of the company at this time (*Eliz. Stage*, ii. 106). Again in 1588 he is mentioned in a document concerning the Queen's players for the non-payment of 8*s*. 4*d*. subsidy (*M.S.C.* i. 354). He is referred to as a comic actor with Tarlton by the stage-keeper in *Bartholomew Fair* (Induction): "I kept the *Stage* in Master *Tarletons* time, I thanke my starres. Ho! and that man had liu'd to haue play'd in *Bartholomew Fayre*, you should ha' seene him ha' come in, and ha' beene coozened i' the Cloath-quarter, so finely! And *Adams*, the Rogue, ha' leap'd and caper'd vpon him, and ha' dealt his vermine about, as though they had cost him nothing." Adams probably survived Tarlton, who died in 1588. He may have played the clown in *A Looking-Glass for London and England* (not later than 1590), since the clown is sometimes called Adam (Greene, *Plays*, i. 193). He may also have played in *James IV* (*c.* 1591), for Adam, evidently an actor, is mentioned in the part of Oberon (*Ibid.*, ii. 153). The two plays seem to have been acted by the same company, probably the Queen's men (Greg, *H.D.* ii. 153).

ADKINSON, WILL.

Apparently an actor or stage-attendant mentioned in a stage-direction of Beaumont and Fletcher's *A King and no King* (quarto 1625, as "Acted at the Blacke-Fryars, by his Majestie Servants"): "Enter Servant, Will. Adkinson" (*Works*, i. 430).

ADSON, F.

Apparently an actor or stage-attendant mentioned in Heywood's *The Late Lancashire Witches* ("lately Acted at the *Globe* on the Banke-side, by the Kings Majesties Actors"; printed 1634): "Enter an invisible spirit. F. Adson with a brace of greyhounds" (*Works*, iv. 196).

ALBERGHINI.

See Angelica Martinelli (?).

ALDERSON, WILLIAM.

A member of the Chapel Royal, 1509–13 (Brewer, *L. & P. Henry VIII*, i. 1. pp. 15, 41, 461, 482; ii. 2. pp. 1448, 1453, 1463; Chambers, *Eliz. Stage*, ii. 27*n*.).

ALKOK, JOHN.

A member of the Children of Paul's in 1554 (Hillebrand, *Child Actors*, p. 110).

ALLEN, JEREMY.

Jeremy Allen and Leonard Smith were at Coventry on August 19, 1640, as members of an unnamed company of players. They received a payment of 20*s*. under date of November 25, 1640 (Murray, ii. 254).

ALLEN, JOHN.

John Allen, a player, evidently distinct from John Alleyn (*q.v.*) or his son John, is recorded in the registers of St. Botolph's, Bishopsgate (*Eliz. Stage*, ii. 299). The parish registers note the baptism of a John Allen on October 17, 1570; the baptism of

A DICTIONARY OF ACTORS

Lowin, son of John, on December 15, 1588; the burial of Joan on May 13, 1593; and the burial of John on May 18, 1593. Under date of July 26, 1596, we find the curious baptismal record: "Bennett, reputed daughter of Jno Allen, which Jno went with Sr Fr. Drake to the Indians in which time the child was got by a stage-player." Lastly, on October 18, 1597, "Jone uxor Johis Allen player was buried with a still born child."

ALLEN, RICHARD.

Richard Allen appears in the actor-list of Jonson's *Epicoene*, which, according to the folio of 1616, was "Acted in the yeere 1609, by the Children of her Maiesties Revells." The 1679 folio of Beaumont and Fletcher names Allen as one of the "principal actors" in *The Coxcomb*, which may have been acted by the Lady Elizabeth's men about 1613 (*Eliz. Stage*, ii. 251).

ALLEN, WILLIAM.

William Allen was possibly with Queen Henrietta's men at the Cockpit in Drury Lane from their formation in 1625 to their dissolution in 1637. At the breaking up of the company in 1637 some of his fellows united with the Revels company at Salisbury Court and others joined Beeston's Boys at the Cockpit; but Allen is not known to have joined either of these troupes. By 1641 he was a King's man, his name appearing in a warrant of January 22 of that year (Stopes, *Jahrbuch*, xlvi. 103). His name is appended to the dedicatory epistle of the 1647 folio of Beaumont and Fletcher's plays, published by a group of the King's players (*Works*, i. p. x). From Wright's *Historia Histrionica* (1699) we learn that he was among the "eminent actors" listed as "of principal note at the Cockpit," and that he joined the King's army and became "a major and quartermaster-general at Oxford" (Hazlitt's *Dodsley*, xv. 406, 409). He is known to have acted the following parts in plays presented by Queen Henrietta's company (Murray, i. opp. 266): Captain Lanby in Shirley's *Wedding* (*c.* 1626); Pandolph in Davenport's *King John and Matilda* (*c.*

3

1629); Grimaldi, the Renegado, in Massinger's *Renegado* (pr. 1630); Mullisbeg, King of Fesse, in Heywood's *Fair Maid of the West*, Part I (c. 1630); and Hannibal, in Nabbes's *Hannibal and Scipio* (1635).

ALLEYN, EDWARD.

Edward Alleyn was born on September 1, 1566, the son of Edward Alleyn of Willen, Bucks, and Margaret Townley of Lancaster, and his baptism on the following day is recorded in the parish register of St. Botolph, Bishopsgate. His father, in 1555, is styled "of London, yeoman"; in 1566, when he purchased a house in Bishopsgate, he appears as "innholder," and he is so described in his will, dated September 10, 1570; in a document of 1567 he is named as "one of the Queens Maiesties porters." Edward Alleyn, the actor, is said to have been "bred a Stage-player" (Fuller, *Worthies*, edit. 1811, ii. 84), and we find him as a member of the Earl of Worcester's players in January, 1583, when he was sixteen years of age. The date at which he left Worcester's patronage and became a servant to the Lord Admiral is uncertain; but his elder brother, John, in 1589, is described as "servaunte to me the Lo. Admyrall," and with him during 1589–91 Edward was associated in the purchase of theatrical apparel. In the deeds relating to the property in Bishopsgate he is referred to as "yeoman" and "gentleman," and once, in 1595, as "musicion." For a time there was an amalgamation of the troupes under the patronage of Lord Strange and the Lord Admiral; and, on February 19, 1592, when Strange's men occupied the Rose under the management of Henslowe, Edward Alleyn was the leading actor, although he kept his personal status as the Lord Admiral's servant. The coming of Lord Strange's men to the Rose led to a close friendship between Henslowe and Alleyn, which was strengthened by Alleyn's marriage, on October 22, 1592, to Henslowe's stepdaughter, Joan Woodward. The common interests of the two men led to the formation of a business partnership

4

which soon became the most important single force in the theatrical life of the time. Joan Woodward may have been Alleyn's second wife, for in an undated letter to Alleyn from Richard Jones, which is generally assigned to February, 1592, there is mention of "mistris Allenes"; and this lends belief to the Dulwich tradition that Alleyn was thrice married. The playhouses were closed on account of the plague in February, 1593, and the company at the Rose was given permission to travel in the provinces. In the license granted by the Privy Council, May 6, 1593, Alleyn is specially designated as an Admiral's man, although the traveling company was under the patronage of Lord Strange. The letters that passed between Alleyn and his wife and his father-in-law during this tour give an intimate glimpse of their domestic affairs and bear pleasing testimony to Alleyn's amiable qualities and the affectionate terms upon which he lived with his "mouse" and her family. In one letter (Warner, p. 6) to his "good sweett mouse" Alleyn complains that she sends no news of her "domestycall matters," as how her "distilled watter proves of this or that or anything"; prays her to let his "orayng tawny stokins of wolen be dyed a very good blak" for the winter, and to remember to sow the bed which was parsley with "spinage" in September, since he will not be home till All Hallows. Alleyn, then twenty-six years of age, was at the height of his fame as an actor, and had been referred to in terms of highest eulogy by Nashe in *Pierce Penilesse* (1592): "Not *Roscius* nor *Aesop*, those admyred tragedians that haue liued euer since before Christ was borne, could euer performe more in action than famous *Ned Allen*" (*Works*, i. 215). The popularity he had won is shown in Nashe's *Strange Newes* (1592): "his very name (as the name of *Ned Allen* on the common stage) was able to make an ill matter good" (*Works*, i. 296). In 1594-97, as may be gathered from Henslowe's *Diary*, he was again acting at the Rose; but, towards the close of the latter year, he for some reason "leafte playinge," and for a time retired to the home of a friend in Sussex. In 1600 he built the

5

Fortune, and about the beginning of December of that year he returned to the stage as leader of the Admiral's company at this new playhouse. An undated letter (*H.P.*, p. 32) from W. P. to Alleyn refers to a theatrical wager that the great tragedian would equal Bentley or Knell in any of their own parts. The admirer writes: "If you excell them, you will then be famous; if equall them, you wynne both the wager and credit; yf short of them, we must and will saie Ned Allen still." About Christmas, 1603, the Admiral's men were taken into the service of Prince Henry; and on March 15, 1604, Alleyn appeared, as "seruant to the young Prince," in the magnificent entertainment presented to King James upon his triumphant passage through London (Dekker, *Works*, i. 280). Alleyn represented "Genius," and "his gratulatory speach was deliuered with excellent Action, and a well tun'de audible voyce." He probably soon retired from the stage, for his name does not appear in the patent issued to the Prince's troupe on April 30, 1606; but it is highly probable that he continued for a while to take part in the management of the Fortune. His business partnerships were varied, for, as early as 1594, he had been interested in the Bear Garden; and, in 1604, he and Henslowe received a joint-patent as Masters of the Royal Game of Bears, Bulls, and Mastiff Dogs. In 1613 the Bear Garden was displaced by the Hope playhouse; and upon Henslowe's death in January, 1616, his interest passed to his son-in-law. Alleyn's fame as an actor and his investments in theatrical affairs had brought him wealth, which was constantly growing; and his negotiations for the purchase of the manor of Dulwich probably began in 1605. He seems to have left Southwark and settled on his country estate in 1613, the same year in which he began the building of a school and hospital by the name of the College of God's Gift at Dulwich. The total cost of the property was about £10,000; the endowment of the college included real estate in London and the freehold of the Fortune; and Alleyn spent upon the college and his own household approximately £1,700 a year.

6

A DICTIONARY OF ACTORS

The corporate existence of the college dates from September 13, 1619, when Alleyn publicly read the Deed of Foundation in the chapel before a distinguished company, afterwards entertained at a dinner at which Francis Bacon was the guest of honor. Alleyn's diary for 1617-22 and his correspondence are preserved at Dulwich, and these give abundant evidence of his hospitality, patronage, and benevolence. He was host to distinguished literary friends; members of the Fortune troupe and other actors were often his guests; and on special occasions he entertained the poor people of the college. His trips to London were frequent; he visited the Red Bull, the Rose, and the Fortune; and a letter (Birch, *Court and Times of James I*, ii. 403) dated June 5, 1623, states that he rode "towards Winchester and Southampton, to take order for his majesty's entertainment with the prince and Lady Mary." His wife, Joan, died on June 28, 1623, and on December 3 he married Constance, daughter of John Donne, Dean of St. Paul's, settling on her £1,500. In a letter (Birch, ii. 441) from John Chamberlain to Sir Dudley Carleton we have a sample of contemporary gossip: "But the strangest match in mine opinion is, that Allen the player hath lately married a young daughter of the Dean of Paul's; which, I doubt, will diminish his charity and devotion towards his two hospitals." The marriage did not have the effect anticipated, and Alleyn's good work was interrupted only by his death on November 25, 1626. His will (Warner, p. xxxv) gives his wish, "without any vain funeral pomp or show, to be interred in the quire of that chapel which God of his goodness hath caused me to erect and dedicate to the honor of my Saviour by the name of Christs Chappell in Gods Gift College."

Something remains to be said about Alleyn's chief rôles and his histrionic fame as witnessed in the writings of his and later time. Of his excellence as an actor we have much testimony, but no detailed description of his method and no list of his parts. It is clear, however, that he was of fine physique, was best in

majestic characterizations, and that his impersonations gave a
new meaning to the art of tragic acting. Of his many parts, the
following are recorded: The title-rôle in *Tamburlaine the Great*
(Marlowe, *Works*, ii. 6); probably King Edgar, in *A Knack to
Know a Knave*, for the title-page carries the inscription: "as it
hath sundrie tymes bene played by Ed: Allen and his Companie"
(Hazlitt's *Dodsley*, vi. 504); according to Heywood's Prologue to
The Jew of Malta (1633), Barabas had been (originally?) played
by Alleyn:

> And he [Barabas], then by the best of actors [marginal
>   note, "Allin"] played;
> . . . . in Tamburlaine,
> This Jew, with others many, th' other wan
> The attribute of peerless, being a man
> Whom we may rank with (doing no one wrong)
> Proteus for shapes, and Roscius for a tongue,
> So could he speak, so vary;

and in his dedication of the play, Heywood writes: "the part of
the Jew presented by so unimitable an actor as Mr. Alleyn"
(Marlowe, *Works*, ii. 4, 6); probably the title-rôle of Orlando in
Robert Greene's *Orlando Furioso*, for a manuscript actor's-part of
this rôle, with corrections by Alleyn himself, is preserved at
Dulwich (*H.P.*, p. 155); Cutlack, in a non-extant play by that
title (E. Guilpin, *Works*, p. 18, *Skialetheia*, Epigram 43):

> *Clodus* me thinks lookes passing big of late,
> With *Dunstons* browes, and *Allens Cutlacks* gate;

Faustus, in Doctor Faustus (S. Rowlands, *Works*, ii. *Knave of
Clubs*, p. 29):

> The Gull gets on a surplis,
> With a crosse vpon his breast,
> Like *Allen* playing *Faustus*,
> In that manner he was drest;

Sebastian, in *Frederick and Basilea*; Muly Mahamet, in *The Battle
of Alcazar*; and Tamar Cam, in *1 Tamar Cam* (*H.P.*, pp. 153, 154).

Of his dramatic skill and his philanthropy we have testimonies as follow: An epigram by John Weever (*Epigrammes*, iv. 23):

In Ed: Allen

Rome had her *Roscius* and her Theater,
Her *Terence*, *Plautus*, *Ennius* and *Meander*,
The first to *Allen*, *Phoebus* did transfer
The next, *Thames* Swans receiu'd fore he coulde land her,
Of both more worthy we by *Phoebus* doome,
Then t' *Allen Roscius* yeeld, to *London Rome*.

An epigram by Ben Jonson (*Works*, viii. 191):

To Edward Allen

If Rome so great, and in her wisest age,
Fear'd not to boast the glories of her stage,
As skilful Roscius, and grave Æsop, men,
Yet crown'd with honours, as with riches, then:
Who had no less a trumpet of their name,
Than Cicero, whose every breath was fame:
How can so great example die in me,
That, Allen, I should pause to publish thee?
Who both their graces in thy self hast more
Out-stript, than they did all that went before:
And present worth in all dost so contract,
As others speak, but only thou dost act.
Wear this renown. 'Tis just, that who did give
So many poets life, by one should live.

Heywood (*Apology*, p. 43): "Among so many dead, let me not forget one yet alive, in his time the most worthy, famous Maister Edward Allen." An epigram by Thomas Campion (*Works*, edit. 1889, p. 279):

In Ligonem

Invideat quamvis sua verba Latina Britannis
Causidicis, docto nunc Ligo fertur equo.
Et medici partes agit undique notus; Alenum
Scenarum melius vix puto posse decus.

A DICTIONARY OF ACTORS

A poem by Sir William Alexander, Earl of Stirling (*Works*, ii.340):

To his deservedly honored friend, Mr. Edward Allane, the first
founder and master of the Colleige of Gods Gift

Some greate by bulk or chance, whom fortune blindes,
Where (if it were) trew virtue wold burst forth,
They sense not haveing, can afford no worth,
And by their meanes doe but condemne their myndes.
  To honour such I should disgrace my penne,
  Who might prove more, I count them lesse then men.

But thee to praise I dare be bould indeede,
By fortunes strictnesse whilst at first suppress'd,
Who at the height of that which thou profess'd
Both ancients, moderns, all didst far exceede:
  Thus vertue many ways may use hir pow'r—
  The bees draw honnie out of evrie flow'r.

And when thy state was to a better chang'd,
That thou enabled wast for doing goode,
To clothe the naked, give the hungrie foode,
As one that was for avarice estrang'd:
  Then what was fill thou scorn'd to seeke for more,
  Whilst bent to doe what was design'd before.

Then prosecute this noble course of thyne,
As prince or priest for state, in charge though none,
For acting this brave part, when thou art gone,
Thy fame more bright then somes' more high shall shyne,
  Since thou turn'd great, who this worlds stage doe trace,
  With whom it seems thou hast exchang'd thy place.

Baker, *Theatrum Redivivum* (1662), pp. 34, 48: "And what scurrility was ever heard to come from the best *Actours* of our Time, *Allen*, and *Bourbidge*? yet, what Plays were ever so pleasing, as where their Parts had the greatest part? . . . And lest he [Prynne] should say, that the Schoole of Plays is degenerated and grown worse, have we not seen in our time, a famous Scholer come out of this Schole: *Edward Allen* a Player himself: Famous as well for his Honesty as for his Acting: and who hath left behind him a worthy Testimony of his Christian Charity to all

Posterity" (*Notes and Queries*, 1880, i. 113). Fuller, *Worthies* (edit. 1811), ii. 84: "He was the Roscius of our age, so acting to the life, that he made any part (especially a majestick one) to become him." Baker, *Chronicle* (edit. 1674), p. 500: "*Richard Bourbidge* and *Edward Allen*, two such Actors as no age must ever look to see the like." Wright, *Historia Histrionica* (1699) (Hazlitt's *Dodsley*, xv. 407):

Lovewit. . . . I have read of one Edward Alleyn, a man so famed for excellent action, that among Ben Jonson's epigrams I find one directed to him, full of encomium, and concluding thus—

Wear this renown; 'tis just that who did give
So many poets life, by one should live.

Was he one of the Blackfriars?

Trueman. Never as I have heard (for he was dead before my time). He was master of a company of his own, for whom he built the Fortune Playhouse from the ground, a large round brick building. This is he that grew so rich, that he purchased a great estate in Surrey and elsewhere; and having no issue, he built and largely endowed Dulwich College in the year 1619, for a master, a warden, four fellows, twelve aged poor people, and twelve poor boys, &c. A noble charity!

For more detailed biographical sketches, see G. F. Warner, *Catalogue of the Manuscripts and Muniments of Alleyn's College of God's Gift at Dulwich* (1881); W. Young, *History of Dulwich College, with a Life of the Founder, Edward Alleyn, and an Accurate Transcript of his Diary, 1617–1622* (1889), vol. ii; and W. W. Greg, *Henslowe's Diary* (1908), vol. ii.

ALLEYN, JOHN.

John Alleyn, elder brother of the famous Edward, was born about 1556–57. He succeeded his father as innholder, and was, if not actually a performer, at least closely engaged in theatrical affairs. In 1580 he is styled "inholder" and servant to "the Lord Sheffeilde" (Warner, p. 123), and as "servaunte to me the Lo. Admyrall" in a letter on his behalf, dated July 14, 1589, from the

Privy Council to certain Aldermen (Warner, p. 85). In a deed of sale, of January 3, 1589, he is described with Edward Alleyn and Robert Browne as part-owner of "playinge apparelles, playe-Bookes, Instrumentes and other commodities," and from this time to May 6, 1591, we find him on several occasions associated with his brother in the purchase of similar properties (Warner, pp. 3, 4). During 1590 he was connected with the Admiral's men at the Theatre, and in November of that year went to the playhouse to have a settlement with Burbage for money due to him and his fellows (Wallace, *N.U.S.*, xiii. 101). When he testified, May 6, 1592, in the Brayne-Burbage controversy, he is referred to as "late of the parishe of St Buttollphes without Bishops gate London ffree of the company of the Inholders of london of the age of xxxv yeres or theraboutes" (Wallace, *ibid.*, p. 124), which is our authority for the approximate date of his birth. He died about the first of May, 1596, for on May 5 Letters of Administration were granted to Margaret Allen on the "goods of John Allen, her husband, late of the parish of St. Andrew, Holborn, deceased intestate" (Warner, p. 255). He had owned real estate in the parish of St. Saviour's, Southwark, for in June, 1618, "the Unicorn and other messuages, . . . late in the tenure of John Allen and others," were in dispute between the Attorney-General on the one part and William Henslowe and Jacob Meade on the other part (Warner, p. 269). Besides his widow, Alleyn left a son, John, who on May 19, 1613, witnessed an acquittance from Robert Daborne to Philip Henslowe (Warner, p. 41); and about 1618 he appears in connection with some bear-baiting transactions in which his uncle, Edward Alleyn, was concerned (Warner, p. 340). There is preserved among the manuscripts at Dulwich an undated letter from him asking a Mr. Burne for his "datter in marriage." His suit, however, was apparently unsuccessful, for an affidavit of Edward, son of Thomas Allen, June 6, 1642, declares him to have died "without issue and unmarried" (Warner, pp. 87, 149).

ALLEYN, RICHARD.

Richard Alleyn, apparently no kinsman of Edward, appears on May 8, 1594, as a witness to a loan by Philip Henslowe to his nephew, Francis Henslowe, "to laye downe for his share to the Quenes players," and may therefore have been a member of the same company (*H.D.*, i. 4; ii. 80). He was doubtless an Admiral's man from 1597 to his death in November, 1601. In 1597–98 he borrowed from Henslowe various small sums, including payments to the attorney Ceachen. On March 25, 1598, he bound himself to Henslowe for two years "as a hiered servante," and witnessed a similar agreement between Heywood and Henslowe (*H.D.*, i. 201, 204, 205). In the original performance of *Frederick and Basilea* by the Admiral's company on June 3, 1597, he appeared as the Prologue, as Frederick, and as the Epilogue. In the revival of *The Battle of Alcazar* by the same company, probably about 1600–01, he assumed the parts of the Presenter, a Portuguese, and Diego Lopis (*H.P.*, p. 153; *Eliz. Stage*, ii. 175). On April 7, 1599, Henslowe advanced 10s. to him and Towne "to go to the corte vpon ester euen" (*H.D.*, i. 104). Alleyn authorized payments on behalf of the Admiral's men on January 17 (?), 1599, and May 6, 1600 (*H.D.*, i. 101, 121). His daughters, Anna and Elizabeth, were baptized at St. Saviour's, Southwark, on May 13, 1599, and May 17, 1601, respectively. He is traceable in the token-books of St. Saviour's parish during 1538–1601, and was there buried on November 18, 1601, leaving a widow (*Eliz. Stage*, ii. 299).

ALLEYN'S BOY.

"Alleyn's boy" appeared as a page in *The Battle of Alcazar*, acted by the Admiral's men about 1600–01 (*H.P.*, p. 153; *Eliz. Stage*, ii. 175–76).

ALLINGHAM, JOHN.

John Allingham is named in a Ticket of Privilege granted on January 12, 1636, to the attendants "employed by his Majesty's servants the players of the Blackfriars, and of special use to them both on the Stage and otherwise for his Majesty's disport and service" (Stopes, *Jahrbuch*, xlvi. 99).

ANDREWE, HENRY.

A member of the Chapel Royal, 1509 and 1511 (Brewer, *L. & P. Henry VIII*, i. 1. pp. 15, 41; Hillebrand, *Mod. Phil.*, xviii. 244; Chambers, *Eliz. Stage*, ii. 27n.).

ANDREWES, RICHARD.

On March 6, 1584, the Earl of Worcester's players were engaged in a dispute with the authorities at Leicester. In the account of the quarrel there is an abstract of the license issued by the Earl of Worcester to his company, dated January 14, 1583, and listing Richard Andrewes as a member of the company (*Eliz. Stage*, ii. 222).

ANDROWES, GEORGE.

George Androwes owned one share in the syndicate that in 1608 leased the Whitefriars playhouse (Adams, *Playhouses*, pp. 313-15).

APILEUTTER, CHRISTOPHER.

In June and July, 1615, Christopher Apileutter visited Strassburg, Germany, with John Spencer (Herz, p. 50). He may have been the "Germanian" or the "Dutchman" mentioned with Spencer's troupe at Cologne in February, 1615. Since we hear no more of him, he may possibly be identified with the "Germanian," who "dies as a good Catholic" (Cohn, p. xci).

APPERLEY, JOHN.

The registers of St. Saviour's, Southwark, record the baptism of children of John Apperley (Atterley, Aperley), a musician: John, March 18, 1613; William, March 12, 1618; Margaret, March 9, 1620 (Bentley, *T.L.S.*, Nov. 15, 1928, p. 856).

ARCHER, RICHARD.

Richard Archer visited Hastings on March 25, 1603, as a member of a licensed troupe of four "common players of interludes" (cf. John Arkinstall).

ARCHER, ROBERT.

See Robert Arzschar.

ARKINSTALL, JOHN.

In a record of the town of Lewes, dated March 30, 1603, John Arkinstall is described as "of Ringy in the Parish of Bowden in the County of Chester, trumpeter." With Richard Archer, Barker, and Anthony Ward as his fellows, he formed a licensed troupe of "common players of interludes." On March 25, 1603, the company, while lodging at a tavern in Hastings, Sussex, heard that the Earl of Southampton had proclaimed Lord Beauchamp as king of England, and on March 30 Arkinstall reported this information to the constables at Lewes (*Hist. MSS. Comm.*, xiii. 4. p. 126).

ARMIGER, EDWARD.

Under license of November 10, 1629, Edward Armiger is named as a member of the Red Bull company that appeared at Reading on November 30 of the same year (Murray, ii. 386). His burial is recorded in the registers of St. Giles's, Cripplegate, on September 30, 1635 (Malcolm, *Londinium Redivivum*, iii. 304).

ARMIN, ROBERT.

Robert Armin, son of John Armin "of Lynn in the county of Norff. taylor," was apprenticed to John Lowyson, London goldsmith, on October 13, 1581 (Denkinger, *P.M.L.A.*, xli, 96). This confirms the tradition in *Tarlton's Jests*, "How Tarlton made Armin his adopted sonne to succeed him," that Armin began his career as apprentice to a goldsmith in Lombard Street (*Jest-Books*, ed. Hazlitt, ii. 216):

15

Tarlton keeping a taverne in Gracious street, hee let it to an-
óther, who was indebted to Armin's master, a goldsmith in
Lombard street, yet he himselfe had a chamber in the same house;
and this Armin, being then a wag, came often thither to demand
his masters money, which he sometimes had, and sometimes had
not. In the end the man, growing poore, told the boy hee had no
money for his master, and hee must beare with him. The man's
name being Charles, Armin made this verse, writing it with
chalke on a wainescot:

> O world, why wilt thou lye?
> Is this Charles the great? that I deny.
> Indeed Charles the great before,
> But now Charles the lesse, being poore.

Tarlton, coming into the roome, reading it, and partly acquainted
with the boyes humour, comming often thither for his master's
money, tooke a piece of chalk, and wrote this rhyme by it:

> A wagge thou art, none can prevent thee;
> And thy desert shall content thee.
> Let me divine. As I am,
> So in time thou'lt be the same,
> My adopted sonne therefore be,
> To enjoy my clownes sute after me.

And see how it fell out. The boy, reading this, so loved Tarlton
after that, regarding him with more respect, hee used to his
playes, and fell in a league with his humour: and private practise
brought him to present playing, and at this houre performes the
same where, at the Globe on the Banks side, men may see him.

The earliest extant edition of *Tarlton's Jests* is that of 1611, but
the Second Part, here quoted, was entered in the Stationers'
Registers on August 4, 1600 (Arber, iii. 168).

We do not know how long Armin received encouragement
from Tarlton, who died in September, 1588. Apparently Armin's
earliest reputation was made not as a comedian but as a writer.
When in 1590 he contributed a preface to *A Brief Resolution of the
Right Religion* he seems already to have gained some distinction
as an author. In Nashe's *Strange Newes* of 1592 (*Works*, i. 280) he
is referred to as a "son of Elderton," a popular ballad-writer of

the time; and in Harvey's *Pierces Supererogation* of 1593 (*Works*, ii. 280) he is introduced with Thomas Deloney and Philip Stubbes under the title, "the common Pamfletters of London." He may have been the R.A. who wrote verses to Robert Tofte's *Alba* (1598), but is not the R.A. (Robert Allot) who compiled *England's Parnassus* (1600). The first dramatic organization with which Armin was associated seems to have been Lord Chandos's men; it is impossible, however, to say when he joined this company. He writes in a dedicatory epistle to Mary, widow of William Brydges (Lord Chandos, 1594–1602), prefixed to his kinsman Gilbert Dugdale's *True Discourse of the Practises of Elizabeth Caldwell* (1604): "Your good honor knowes Pinck's poor heart, who, in all my services to your late deceased kind lord, never savoured of flatterie or fixion." That Armin's service to Lord Chandos had been as a player, there can be little doubt, for in his *Foole Vpon Foole or Sixe Sortes of Sottes* (1605), "Shewing their lives, humours, and behauiours, with their want of witte in their shew of wisedome" (*Works*, p. 27), he tells how Jack Miller of Esam (Evesham) crossed the Severn on thin ice to see again his favorite clown "Grumball" with "the Lord Shandoyes Players" at Partiar (Pershore in Worcestershire). Armin witnessed the incident, and not improbably played the part of "Grumball." *Foole Vpon Foole or Sixe Sortes of Sottes*, a collection of tales respecting persons of the Jack Miller type, was issued anonymously in 1600, the author describing himself as "Clonnico de Curtanio Snuffe," meaning that he was the clown at the Curtain (Halliwell-Phillipps, *Outlines*, i. 321). From this we gather that by 1599 Armin had probably joined the Chamberlain's men at the Curtain. A second edition appeared in 1605, as the work of "Clonnico del Mondo Snuffe," in other words, the clown at the Globe. A third and enlarged edition was published in 1608 as *A Nest of Ninnies*, with Armin's name on the title-page, dedicated to the "generous Gentlemen of Oxenford, Cambridge, and the Innes of Court,"

And praying euer that your Sunnie shine
May beautifie our GLOBE in euery line,

which gives a pun on the name of the playhouse at which Armin
was then an actor (*Works*, ed. Grosart, p. 45). "Clunnyco de
Curtaneo Snuffe" is also on the title-page of *Quips upon Questions*
(1600), which must therefore be by Armin, although attributed
to John Singer (Collier, *Bibl. Acc.*, iii. 255) because of "a MS.
note on the first leaf." In keeping with a theatrical custom of the
time, which allowed the spectators to fling upon the stage, or to
suggest verbally, various "themes" to which the clown would
reply in extempore verse, the author supposes diverse questions
propounded to him, followed by his replies, and closed by what
he terms a "Quip" or a satirical observation, a moral, or a re-
flection upon both question and answer (Collier, *Bibl. Acc.*, iii.
257). Armin is named as a King's man in the license of May 19,
1603, and in the procession list of March 15, 1604. In 1605 Augustine Phillips left him 20s. as his "fellowe." He is in the actor-
lists of Jonson's *Alchemist* (1610) and of Shakespeare's plays in
the folio of 1623. The registers of St. Bodolph Aldgate record
the baptism of Armin's daughter, Elizanna, May 11, 1603, and
the burial of two children, a daughter, who seems to have died
before she was christened, October 11, 1600, and a son, Robert,
April 4, 1606 (Denkinger, *P.M.L.A.*, xli. 95). On the title-page
of his *History of the Two Maids of More-clacke* (1609), played by
the Children of the King's Revels, he is described as a King's
man. The crude woodcut which adorns this title-page may be a
portrait of Armin in his fool's costume—a long coat, worn by
the natural whom he impersonated. In the preface "To the
friendly peruser," Armin writes: "I would haue againe inacted
Iohn my selfe, but *Tempora mutantur in illis*, & I cannot do as I
would," which has been taken to mean that in 1609 Armin was
"poor and infirm" (*Works*, ed. Grosart, p. viii), and from which
we learn that he had originally acted the part of John in the
play. He may have retired from the stage about this time, for

his name does not occur in the actor-list of Jonson's *Catiline* (1611). Armin's *Phantasma, the Italian Tailor and his Boy* was published in 1609. On the title-page, and also in the entry in the Stationers' Registers, February 6, 1609 (Arber, iii. 401), he is noted as a King's man. The *Phantasma* is an adaptation in verse from Straparola's *Piacevoli Notti*, Night viii, Fable 5. With an apology that "Fooles makes Bookes for Wise men to laugh at," Armin dedicated his versified story to Lord and Lady Haddington. The dedication is interesting for the author's claim to have been "writ downe for an Asse in his time," and for the reference to "his Constableship" (*Works*, p. 141), from which it is inferred that he had succeeded Kempe in the part of Dogberry in *Much Ado about Nothing*. He also asks the Lady to pardon "the boldness of a Begger," which may be merely a pun on his name, since "armin" means "a beggar" (Nares, i. 33). *The Valiant Welshman* was published in 1615 as "Written by R. A. Gent." The "R. A. Gent" has been associated with Robert Armin, "but without corroborative evidence supporting this reading of the initials" (J. S. Farmer's note in the *Tudor Facsimile* edition). Fleay (*Life of Shak.*, p. 300) finds a pun on "armine" (a beggar) in *London Prodigall* (*c.* 1603), V. i. 174, and suggests that Armin played Matthew Flowerdale:

> *Luce.* O here, God, so young an armine.
> *Flowerdale.* Armine, sweet-heart? I know not what you meane by that, but I am almost a beggar.

The clown in Wilkins's *Miseries of Enforced Marriage* (*c.* 1605) is addressed as Robin, possibly Armin (Hazlitt's *Dodsley*, ix. 498). In Dekker's *If It be not Good, the Devil is in It* (1610-12), acted by Queen Anne's men at the Red Bull, the clown Lurchall is sometimes addressed as Grumball (*Works*, iii. pp. 268, 270), and there is an allusion (*Ibid.*, p. 290) to *A Nest of Ninnies*, "If Ninies bring away the Nest"; but so far as known Armin never belonged to Queen Anne's men at the Red Bull. The register of St. Bodolph

Aldgàte records on November 30, 1615, the burial of Armin, describing him as "ffree of the Gouldsmithes, and a Player" (Denkinger, *P.M.L.A.*, xli. 95).

In the section headed "To Worthy Persons," John Davies of Hereford in his *Scourge of Folly* (Stationers' Registers, October 8, 1610; Arber, iii. 446) prints the following epigram (*Works*, ii. 60):

> *To honest-gamesome Robin Armin,*
> *That tickles the spleene like an harmeles vermin.*

Armine, what shall I say of thee, but this,
Thou art a foole and knaue? Both? fie, I misse;
And wrong thee much, sith thou in deede art neither,
Although in shew, thou playest both together.
Wee all (that's kings and all) but players are
Vpon this earthly stage; and should haue care
To play our parts so properly, that wee
May at the end gaine an applauditee.
But most men ouer-act, misse-act, or misse
The action which to them peculier is;
And the more high the part is which they play,
The more they misse in what they do or say.
So that when off the stage, by death, they wend,
Men rather hisse at them then them commend.
But (honest Robin) thou with harmelesse mirth
Dost please the world; and (so) amongst the earth
That others but possesse with care, that stings;
So makst thy life more happy farre then kings.
And so much more our loue should thee imbrace,
Sith still thou liu'st with some that dye to grace.
And yet art honest (in despight of lets),
Which earnes more praise then forced goodnesse gets.
So, play thy part, be honest still with mirth;
Then when th' art in the tyring-house of earth,
Thou being his seruant whome all kings do serue,
Maist for thy part well playd like praise deserue;
For in that tyring-house when either bee,
Y' are one mans men and equall in degree.
So thou, in sport, the happiest men dost schoole—
To do as thou dost,—wisely play the foole.

ARTHUR, THOMAS.

The only known record of Thomas Arthur is found in the proceedings of a lawsuit in 1528–29 between George Mayler, glazier
and trainer of players to Henry VIII, and Thomas Arthur, tailor,
whom Mayler took as an apprentice for a year, promising to
teach him to play and to obtain for him admission into the
King's company of interluders with the right to the privileges
thereof and "the Kinges bage." According to Mayler, he fur-
nished Arthur meat and drink and 4*d.* a day. Arthur served an
apprenticeship of seven weeks in the "science of playing," and
left without getting a license from Mayler. Nevertheless, Arthur,
beguiling away three of his master's covenant servants, went to
"sundry partiez of Englond in plainge of many interludes," from
which tour they gained a profit of £30. Mayler complains that,
according to the agreement, some of the income was his. He
testifies that Arthur was "right harde and dull too taike any
lernyng, wherby he was nothinge meate or apte too bee in service
with the Kinges grace too maike any plaiez or interludes before
his highness." Arthur, on the other hand, contended that Mayler
had broken the contract, and thus sued him before the sheriffs
of London for £26 to cover the losses that he had undergone.
Owing to the accident of Mayler's being in Ludgate prison and
unable to defend himself, the jury placed upon him a penalty of
£4, and he appealed to Chancery. The outcome is unknown.
(See Overend, *New Shak. Soc. Trans.*, 1877–79, p. 425.)

ARZSCHAR, ROBERT.

From 1608 to 1616 Robert Arzschar, whose correct name was
probably Archer, appears in German records as an English actor.
He was at Frankfort in the autumn of 1608 and 1610, and in September, 1613, at the Reichstag held by the Kaiser at Regensburg.
Early in 1614 he came into the service of John Sigismund, Elector
of Brandenburg, whose company appeared as the "Brandenburg
Comedians" at Wolffenbüttel in September, 1614, and at Danzig

in July, 1615. The Elector paid him a salary of 100 florins, besides board at the Court gratis and two suits. He was an Elector's man until May 16, 1616, when he was dismissed with a sum of 250 thalers as settlement of his claims (Cohn, p. lxxxviii; Herz, pp. 53, 56).

ASHBORNE, EDWARD.

Edward Ashborne is named in a Protection from Arrest issued by Herbert on December 27, 1624, to twenty-one men "imployed by the Kinges Maiesties servantes in theire quallity of Playinge as Musitions and other necessary attendantes" (Adams, *Dram. Rec.*, p. 74).

ASHTON.

Apparently an actor or stage-attendant mentioned in stage-directions of Beaumont and Fletcher's *Love's Pilgrimage* (a revival by the King's men about 1624–25?): "Enter two Servants, 1 Rowl: 2 Ashton," II. i; "Servant, Rowl: Ashton," IV. ii (*Works*, vi. 416, 417).

ASKEN, AARON.

Aaron Asken, "Aaron the Dancer," appears in Germany during 1627 and 1640 with Robert Reynolds's company of players. For some time between these dates he was in the service of the Polish king, Sigismund III (Herz, pp. 31, 55 ff.).

ATTERLEY, JOHN.

See John Apperley.

ATTEWELL, GEORGE.

On behalf of what appears to have been the combined Strange-Admiral's company, George Attewell received payment for performances at Court on December 27, 1590, and February 16, 1591. On June 1, 1595, he witnessed a loan from Philip to Francis Henslowe, and possibly belonged to the same company as the

A DICTIONARY OF ACTORS

latter, which may have been the Queen's men. A "Mr. Otwell" lived in St. Saviour's Close in 1599 (*Eliz. Stage*, ii. 120, 300; *H.D.*, ii. 240; Steele, pp. 100, 101).

ATTWELL, HUGH.

Hugh Attwell appears in the actor-list of Jonson's *Epicoene*, which, according to the folio of 1616, was "Acted in the yeere 1609, by the Children of her Maiesties Revells." The 1679 folio of Beaumont and Fletcher names Attwell as one of the "principal actors" in *The Coxcomb*, which may have been presented by the Lady Elizabeth's men about 1613 (*Eliz. Stage*, ii. 251). On April 25, 1613, he witnessed a loan from Philip Henslowe to Robert Daborne (Warner, p. 39). By March 20, 1616, he had joined Prince Charles's troupe, for on that date, with other members of the company, he signed an agreement with Alleyn and Meade (*H.P.*, p. 90). Early in 1619, as servant to the Prince, he appeared as New Year in Middleton's *Masque of Heroes* (*Works*, vii. 200). At the time of his death on September 25, 1621, he belonged to Prince Charles's men. William Rowley, a fellow-actor and member of the same company, wrote on him the following elegy and epitaph (Collier, i. 406):

> *For a Funerall Elegie on the Death of Hugh Atwell,*
> *Servant to Prince Charles, this fellow-feeling Farewell:*
> *who died the 25th of Sept. 1621.*

So, now Hee's downe, the other side may shout:
But did he not play faire? held he not out
With courage beyond his bone? full six yeares
To wrastle and tugge with Death? the strong'st feares
To meet at such a match. They that have seene
How doubtfull Victorie hath stood betweene,
Might wonder at it. Sometimes cunningly
Death gets advantage: by his cheeke and eye
We thought that ours had beene the weaker part,
And straight agen the little mans great heart
Would rouse fresh strength and shake him off awhile:
Death would retire, but never reconcile.

They too 't agen, agen; they pull, they tugge,
At last Death gets within, and with a hugge
The faint Soule crushes. This thou maist boast, Death,
Th' hast throwne him faire, but he was out of breath.
Refresh thee then (sweet Hugh); on the ground rest:
The worst is past, and now thou hast the best.
Rise with fresh breath, and be assur'd before,
That Death shall never wrastle with thee more.
Oh, hadst thou Death (as warres and battels may
Present thee so) a field of noble clay
To entertaine into thy rhewmie cell,
And thou wouldst have it be presented well,
Speake thy oration by this mans toung:
Mongst living Princes it hath sweetly sung,
(While they have sung his praise) but if thy Court
Be silence-tyde and there dwells no report,
Lend it to Life to store another flesh:
We misse it here; wee'l entertain 't afresh.

Epitaph

Here lyes the man (and let no lyars tell)
His heart a Saints, his toung a silver bell:
Friend to his friend he stood: by Death he fell:
He chang'd his *Hugh*, yet he remains At-well.

WILL. ROWLEY.

Hugh Attwell may perhaps be identified with the author or
singer or dancer of *Mr. Attowell's Jigge betweene Francis a Gentleman,
Richard a Farmer, and their wives* (A. Clark, *Shirburn Ballads*, p.
244). There are four parts to the dramatic sketch, with a different
tune for each scene. The first, "To the tune of Walsingham,"
represents the "iolly Palmer," Francis, making love to Besse,
Richard's wife; she pretends compliance and arranges for an
assignation. In the second, "Enter Richard, Bess'es husband, To
the tune of the Jewishe dance." In scene three, "Enter Mistris
Francis with Richard, To the tune of Buggle-boe"; and as a
climax, Francis enters "with his owne wife (having a maske
before her face) supposing her to be Besse, To the tune of Go
from my windo." The jig is a lively little piece, rough in work-

A DICTIONARY OF ACTORS

manship, and evidently depending for success on its rapid move-
ment and the variety of its tunes.

AUGUSTEN, WILLIAM.

A player, from whom Philip Henslowe bought his boy, James
Bristow, for £8, December 18, 1597 (H.D., i. 203). His daughter
Penelope, was baptized at St. Bodolph's Aldgate on November
19, 1595 (Denkinger, P.M.L.A., xli. 97).

AXEN, ROBERT.

Robert Axen was a member of Queen Henrietta's company
from 1631 to 1635. In Heywood's *Fair Maid of the West*, Parts I
and II (printed 1631, as "lately acted . . . by the Queen's
Majesties comedians"), he played the parts of an English merchant and the Duke of Mantua, respectively. In Nabbes's *Hannibal and Scipio* ("Acted in the year 1635 by the Queenes Majesties
Servants, at their Private house in Drurye Lane") he acted two
parts, Bomilcar and Gisgon (Murray, i. opp. 266). The registers
of St. James, Clerkenwell, record the following children of
Robert Axon, who may be identical with the player (Hovenden,
i. 116, 122, 126; iv. 202, 207): John, "kild with a cart," buried
June 5, 1631; Simon, baptized January 16 and buried January 21,
1633; Everelda, daughter "of Robert Axon and Mary his wife,"
baptized February 6, 1631; and William, baptized March 28, 1634.

AXON, ROBERT.

See Robert Axen.

AYNSWORTH, JOHN.

The registers of St. Leonard's, Shoreditch, record the burial of
"John Aynsworth, a player," on September 28, 1581 (Stopes,
Burbage, p. 139).

BABHAM, CHRISTOPHER.

Apparently Christopher Babham was in some way associated
with the King's men at Blackfriars, as suggested by an entry

dated November 12, 1632 (A. Nicoll, *Times Lit. Suppl.*, Nov. 22, 1923, p. 789): "A petition of William Blagrove & William Beeston that his Lo would restore vnto them a boy named Stephen Hamerton inveigled from them by one Christopher Babham & by him imployed at the Blackfryars playhouse."

BACKSTEAD, WILL.

See William Barksted.

BACKSTER, RICHARD.

See Richard Baxter.

BACON, JOB.

Apparently an actor or stage-attendant mentioned in a stage-direction of Beaumont and Fletcher's *Love's Pilgrimage* (a revival by the King's men about 1624–25?): "Job. Bacon ready to shoot off a Pistol," IV. ii (*Works*, vi. 417). Since he had a minor part in the play, perhaps he may be identified with the John Bacon named in a Ticket of Privilege granted on January 12, 1636, to the attendants of the King's players at Blackfriars (Stopes, *Jahrbuch*, xlvi. 99). The "Job" could quite possibly be "Joh," an abbreviation for John.

BACON, JOHN.

See Job. Bacon.

BADLOWE, RICHARD.

A member of the Children of Paul's in 1594 (Hillebrand, *Child Actors*, p. 111).

BAGSTARE, RICHARD.

Richard Bagstare is named in a Ticket of Privilege granted on January 12, 1636, to the attendants "employed by his Majesty's servants the players of the Blackfriars, and of special use to them both on the Stage and otherwise for his Majesty's disport and service" (Stopes, *Jahrbuch*, xlvi. 99). He may possibly be identified with Richard Baxter (*q.v.*), who seems to have assumed minor parts in Beaumont and Fletcher's *Mad Lover* (*c.* 1631) and Massinger's *Believe as You List* (*c.* 1631).

BAKER, HARRY.

Apparently the performer of Vertumnus in Nashe's *Summer's Last Will and Testament* (*Works*, iii. 282), acted in 1592 at Croydon, possibly by members of Archbishop Whitgift's household (*Eliz. Stage*, iii. 451–53):

Autumne. Now I beseech your honor it may be so.
Summer. With all my heart: *Vertumnus*, go for them.
                                                                [*Exit Vertumnus.*
Wil. Summer. This same *Harry Baker* is such a necessary fellow to go on arrants, as you shall not finde in a country. It is a pitty but he should haue another siluer arrow, if it be but for crossing the stage with his cap on. [Lines 1565–70.]

McKerrow (*Nashe*, iv. 440) suggests that possibly a jest on Harry Baker's name is intended in line 1716: "they must bring bread with them, I am no Baker."

BAKER, ROBERT.

A member of the Children of Paul's in 1574 (Hillebrand, *Child Actors*, p. 111).

BALLS.

Balls is apparently the actor or stage-attendant who assumed the part of the Queen in Massinger's *Believe as You List*, as suggested by marginal annotations in the manuscript (ed. Croker, p. 49). The play was licensed for the King's men on May 7, 1631 (Adams, *Dram. Rec.*, p. 33).

BANASTER, GILBERT.

Master of the Chapel Royal, 1478–84? (Wallace, *Evolution*, pp. 23 ff.; *Blackfriars*, p. 62).

BAND, THOMAS.

See Thomas Bond.

BANKES, WILLIAM.

William Bankes's name appears in a warrant of December 12, 1635, appointing certain members of Prince Charles's company as Grooms of the Chamber (Stopes, *Jahrbuch*, xlvi. 98).

BARFIELD, ROGER.

Of Roger Barfield's stage-career nothing more is known than the appearance of his name in a warrant to Queen Anne's men, March 7, 1606. His daughter Isabell was baptized at St. Giles's on January 2, 1611, and his daughter Susan was buried there on July 3, 1614 (*Eliz. Stage*, ii. 235, 301).

BARKER.

Barker is recorded at Hastings on March 25, 1603, as a member of a licensed troupe of four "common players of interludes" (cf. John Arkinstall).

BARKSTED, WILLIAM.

William Barksted appears in the actor-list of Jonson's *Epicoene*, which, according to the folio of 1616, was "Acted in the yeere 1609, by the Children of her Maiesties Revells." He belonged to the Lady Elizabeth's troupe by August 29, 1611, on which date he and his fellow-actors gave Philip Henslowe a bond of £500 to perform "certen articles" of agreement (*H.P.*, pp. 18, 111). The 1679 folio of Beaumont and Fletcher names him as one of the "principal actors" in *The Coxcomb*, which may have been acted by the Lady Elizabeth's men about 1613 (*Eliz. Stage*, ii. 251). He may be the "Baxter" named in the Articles of Grievance as a fellow of Lady Elizabeth's company with Joseph Taylor between March, 1613, and March, 1614. By March 20, 1616, he had joined the company under the patronage of Prince Charles, for on that date, with his fellow-actors, he signed an agreement with Alleyn and Meade. Since his signature does not appear with the undated letter (*c.* 1616–17) from his company to Alleyn, he had probably retired soon after joining Prince Charles's men

(*H.P.*, pp. 58, 87, 90, 93). In addition to being an actor he was also a poet and dramatist. His *Poems* (ed. Grosart, *Occasional Issues of Unique or Very Rare Books*, 1876, iii) are *Mirrha* (1607), 896 lines, with commendatory verses by his kinsman Robert Glover, I. W., Lewes Machin, and William Bagnall, and *Hiren* (1611), 912 lines, which has sonnets addressed to Henry Earl of Oxford and Elizabeth Countess of Derby. On the title-page of the latter Barksted is described as "one of the seruants of his Maiesties Revels," which led Fleay (*Drama*, i. 29) to suggest that the phrase was repeated from an earlier edition, not extant, of about 1607. This theory may receive some confirmation from the connection of Machin with the King's Revels, which presented his comedy of *The Dumb Knight*, (pr. 1608); but it must also be remembered that the Children of the Queen's Revels appear to have been sometimes referred to as the King's Revels in provincial records of about 1611 (*Eliz. Stage*, ii. 301). Barksted's name is found on the title-page of some copies of Marston's *Insatiate Countess* (quarto of 1631), and it has been suggested that Marston, "on entering the church, left this tragedy in a fragmentary state, and that it was completed by the actor Barksteed" (Bullen, *Marston*, i. p. li; iii. 125). John Taylor, the Water Poet, gives us two samples of seventeenth-century wit in which Barksted is the hero. In *Wit and Mirth* (1629), p. 11, he writes:

Will. Backstead the Plaier cast his Chamber-lye out of his window in the night, which chanced to light vpon the heads of the watch passing by; who angerly said, Who is it that offers vs this abuse? Why, quoth *Will*, who is there? Who is here, said one of the pickled watchmen, we are the Watch. The Watch, quoth *William*, why my friends, you know, *Harme watch, harme catch.*

And in his *Taylors Feast* (1638), p. 14 (*Works*, iii), he tells how "Will Baxted, a late well knowne fine Comedian, went in a Morning, on one of the Twelve dayes in *Christmas* time, upon occasion of businesse to speake with an old rich miserable House-keeper." When the business had been attended to, Barksted persuaded a servant that, as a matter of courtesy, he should go to the cellar and drink to the health of the master of the house. He ate "a goodly Coller of Brawne" and drank so much "strong Beere in a Horne-cup," that the "old Mizer in a rage gave his man warning to provide him another Master, for hee would keepe no such riotting knaves that would entertaine such bold Guests."

BARKSTEED.

See William Barksted.

BARNE, WILL.

From the extant plot of *1 Tamar Cam*, acted by the Admiral's men about October, 1602, it appears that "little Will Barne" was the boy-actor who assumed the parts of Tarmia in the play and a Pigmy in the procession (*H.P.*, p. 154). Fleay conjectures that he also acted Leonora in the Admiral's play of *Frederick and Basilea* in June, 1597 (*Stage*, p. 141).

BARNES, THOMAS.

Thomas Barnes's name appears in a warrant of July 2, 1629, appointing certain members of the Lady Elizabeth's (Queen of Bohemia's) company as Grooms of the Chamber (Stopes, *Jahrbuch*, xlvi. 95).

BARRET, JOHN.

John Barret is recorded at Norwich on March 10, 1635, when his troupe, presumably the King's Revels, applied for permission to act in that town. He played the title-rôle in Richard's *Messallina, the Roman Empress*, printed in 1640 as "acted with generall applause divers times by the Company of his Majesties Revells" (Murray, i. 279–81).

BARRETT, WALTER.

The name of Walter Barrett appears in a license granted to the Children of the Revels to the late Queen Anne on April 9, 1623 (Murray, i. 362; ii. 272–73).

BARRY, DAVID LORDING.

As a lessee of the Whitefriars playhouse in 1608 David Lording Barry owned one whole share in the syndicate. He died in 1610 (Adams, *Playhouses*, pp. 313–17; see also, Adams, "Lordinge (*alias* 'Lodowick') Barry," *Mod. Phil.*, ix. 567; Lawrence, "The Mystery of Lodowick Barry," *Stud. in Phil.*, xiv. 52). His play, *Ram Alley*, "A Comedy Divers times here-to-fore acted by the Children of the Kings Reuels," was printed in 1611.

BARTLE, ONYE (?).

Alexander Bartle, son of "Onye (?), a player," was baptized at St. Saviour's on February 27, 1603 (Bentley, *T. L. S.*, Nov. 15, 1928, p. 856). See the following entry.

BARTON, ONESIPHORUS.

A player, buried at St. Giles's on March 9, 1608 (*Eliz. Stage*, ii. 301).

BASSE, THOMAS.

On August 29, 1611, Thomas Basse and his fellow-actors of the Lady Elizabeth's troupe gave Philip Henslowe a bond of £500 to perform "certen articles" of agreement (*H.P.*, pp. 18, 111). The 1679 folio of Beaumont and Fletcher names him as one of the "principal actors" in *The Honest Man's Fortune*, played in 1613 by what is quite clearly the Lady Elizabeth's men. By 1617 he belonged to Queen Anne's men, for as a new member of the company on June 3, 1617, he refused to sign an agreement with Susan Baskervile. On May 13, 1619, he attended Queen Anne's funeral (*Eliz. Stage*, ii. 236, 238, 251). After the Queen's death her London company was known as the Players of the Revels at the Red Bull, of which Basse is noted in 1622 as one of the "chiefe players" (Adams, *Dram. Rec.*, p. 63).

BAXTER.

See William Barksted.

BAXTER, RICHARD.

In April, 1622, Richard Baxter (or Backster), a member of the Red Bull company, while acting, accidentally wounded John Gill, a feltmaker's apprentice, who was sitting on the stage during a play. Gill threatened "Mr. Baxter and the other Redbull players to ruyn theire house and persons," if they did not give him satisfaction. Nothing seems to have come of the threat except a noisy demonstration by the apprentices at Clerkenwell (Jeaffreson, *Middlesex*, ii. 166, 175). His name appears in a license granted on April 9, 1623, to the Children of the Revels to the late Queen Anne (Murray, i. 362; ii. 272–73). He is not mentioned in the patent of June 24, 1625, to the King's men, but later he acted minor parts in plays presented by the company. He is named in the list of actors prefixed to Ford's *Lover's Melancholy*, which was licensed on November 24, 1628 (Murray, i. opp. 172). He seems to have played in Beaumont and Fletcher's *Mad Lover* (possibly in a revival about 1630), as noted in the stage-direction, IV. i: "Enter a Servant and R. Bax" (*Works*, iii. 456). In Massinger's *Believe as You List* (licensed May 7, 1631) he is assigned three parts in marginal annotations to the play: Titus, Officer, Servant (Croker's edition, pp. 45, 79, 95; Adams, *Dram. Rec.*, p. 33). He is included in the "Players Pass" issued to the King's men on May 17, 1636 (Murray, *loc. cit.*). Since he appears to have assumed minor parts in both *The Mad Lover* and *Believe as You List*, he may possibly be identified with the "Richard Bagstare" named in a Ticket of Privilege granted on January 12, 1636, to the attendants of the King's men at Blackfriars (Stopes, *Jahrbuch*, xlvi. 99). Nothing is heard of him during the period of the Civil War and Commonwealth, but he is probably identical with the person of the same name who appears in the early Restoration company under the management of Thomas Killigrew. This troupe became His Majesty's Company of Comedians at the Theatre Royal, which was opened on May 7, 1663 (Pepys, *Diary*, iii. 107); but Baxter does not appear in any of the actor-lists as given by Downes (*Ros. Ang.*, pp. 2 ff.). He seems to have been dead or retired by February 8, 1667, when his name is deleted from the warrant for liveries (Nicoll, *Rest. Drama*, p. 283).

BAXTER, ROBERT.

In the 1616 folio of Jonson's plays Robert Baxter is named as one of the principal actors in *Cynthia's Revels*, presented by the Children of the Chapel Royal in 1600 (*Eliz. Stage*, iii. 363). He may have been a member of the Lady Elizabeth's troupe in 1613, for "one Baxter" is named in the Articles of Grievance as a fellow with Joseph Taylor between March, 1613, and March, 1614. However, there is a possibility that the "Baxter" of 1613, whose Christian name is not given, may be identified with William Barksted. There is no evidence that either was the author of the "Baxters tragedy" mentioned in Henslowe's *Diary* in 1602 (Greg, *H.P.*, pp. 58, 87).

BAYLYE.

A member of the Children of Paul's at some date before 1582. He appears as a legatee in the will of Sebastian Westcott, dated April 3, 1582, where he is named among the "sometimes children of the said almenerey," i.e. St. Paul's (*Eliz. Stage*, ii. 15*n.*). See Thomas Bayly.

BAYLY, EDWARD.

As a member of Ellis Guest's company under license of June 7, 1628, Edward Bayly was at Norwich on July 2 of the same year (Murray, ii. 103).

BAYLY, THOMAS.

Joseph Hunter (*Hallamshire*, p. 80) prints a Latin letter written by Thomas Bayly to Thomas Bawdewine, from Sheffield, on April 25, 1581. Bayly thanks Bawdewine for having supplied the tragedy presented at Sheffield, the seat of Lord Shrewsbury, on St. George's day. The tragedy had proved such a delightful diversion that Bayly requests Bawdewine to procure for him another play, "short, novel, pleasing, attractive, charming, witty, full of buffoonery, rascality, and wrangling, and replete with hangings, banditries, and panderings of every kind." He says that in matters of this kind, Wilson (doubtless Robert) of Leicester's troupe is "willing and able to do much." Chambers (*Eliz. Stage*, ii. 89, 301) suggests that Bayly belonged to a provincial company of players under the patronage of Lord Shrewsbury. However, the play referred to seems likely to have been a private performance rather than a production by a provincial troupe. This inference is supported by the facts that Bayly wrote good Latin, that the play was given in Latin, and that the audience was fashionable. Rather than a provincial player, perhaps Bayly was a member of Shrewsbury's household. Possibly he is to be identified with Baylye (*q.v.*) of Paul's boys, who would probably have had training in Latin. The letter follows:

Nos Domini nostri comediatores, gratulationes ad te nostras, summa cum gratiarum actione, presentamus; inter alia, in nos tua beneficia saepius illata, hoc imprimis in memoriam reducentes, quod traiediam hanc nostram (qua cum sancti Georgii festum hoc celebravimus) satis sane venustam et laudatam, necessariis implementis procuraveris: qua quidem actione, summa nobis (licet indignus) accidit commendatio. Audientes enim et non intelligentes, jestura et forma; intelligentes vero, res ipsa, tanta affecit oblectatione, ut quidam non inferioris conditionis homines, nos instanter aliquod simile quam breviter possumus, exercitare et ostendere postulant. Unde fit, ut tuam rursus opem petere cogimur, rogantes ut librum aliquem brevem, novum, iucundum, venestum, lepidum, hillarem, scurrosum, nebulosum, rabulosum, et omnimodis carnificiis, latrociniis, et lenociniis refertum, perscrutare et ad nos mittere digneris: qua in re dicunt quod Wilsonus quidam Leycestrii comitis servus (fidibus pollens) multum vult et potest facere, precipere si Morgani nostri nomine tantum postules. Valeas precor. Sheff. xxv. Aprill 1581.

tuus dum sit

Tho. Bayly.

Yf my brother Wm be at the court, I pray you commend me to him; and chyde him for that he will not take paines to write to me. And tell R. Rotherford that yf he want any money, he knoweth where I dwell. I have sent him tokens by this berar.

To my very lovinge frend Mr. Thomas Bawdewine, at Could-harbar, in London.

BEART, RUDOLF.

In the autumn of 1608 Rudolf Beart appeared as a player at Frankfort, Germany (Herz, p. 53). He was then in company with Robert Arzschar and Heinrich Greum.

BEDOWE, ELIS.

Elis Bedowe is recorded at Norwich on March 10, 1635, when his troupe, presumably the King's Revels, applied for permission to act in that town (Murray, i. 279–80).

BEE, WILLIAM.

Two references to "William Bee" are preserved. Kempe, on his famous dance from London to Norwich in 1599, was accompanied by "his servant" William Bee (*Nine Daies Wonder*, ed. Dyce, p. 3). This Bee is not known to have been an actor, but was not improbably associated with Kempe in the latter's stage clownery. Not until May 26, 1624, do we again find notice of a William Bee, who may or may not be identical with the Bee associated with Kemp in 1599. On this date Francis Wambus (*q.v.*), a member of the Lady Elizabeth's troupe, and William Bee, evidently a fellow-actor with Wambus, were discharged from the Norwich prison (Murray, ii. 350). The William Bee of the Norwich records, however, has been conjectured to be William Beeston (*q.v.*).

BEESTON.

The Beestons were an old theatrical family. In the Barnstaple records of 1560–61 there is a payment of 6s. to one "Beeston and his felowes for playinge an interlude" (Murray, ii. 198).

BEESTON, CHRISTOPHER.

The first appearance of Christopher Beeston in dramatic history rests upon the conjecture that he is the "Kit" who played a Soldier in "Envy" and a Captain in "Sloth" of *2 Seven Deadly Sins*, presented by Strange's company about 1590 (Greg, *H.P.*, 152; *R.E.S.*, i. 262). Possibly he remained with Strange's men until they became the Lord Chamberlain's, for he belonged to the latter company in 1598 when they played *Every Man in his Humor*, his name appearing in the list of the original "principall Comoedians" affixed to the text in the Jonson folio of 1616. But he is not named in the 1623 folio list of actors in Shakespeare's plays. Sometime during his stage-career he was apprenticed to Augustine Phillips, who in his will dated May 4, 1605, leaves "to my servaunte, Christopher Beeston, thirty shillings in gould" (Collier, *Actors*, p. 86). By 1602 he had become associated with the Earl of Worcester's men, to whom he sold properties in August and October of that year, and for whom he authorized payments in November, 1602, and January, 1603 (*H.D.*, i. 180, 184, 185, 186). Early in the reign of James I Worcester's men became Queen Anne's company, and Beeston, who bore the *alias* of Hutchinson, remained with this troupe until 1619. We find him in the list of players receiving red cloth for the procession of March 15, 1604, in the patent of April 15, 1609, in a warrant to appear before the Privy Council for playing during Lent, March 29, 1615, in arrears to contributions for the repair of highways near the Red Bull playhouse, October 4, 1616, and in Queen Anne's funeral procession, May 13, 1619. When Thomas Greene died in 1612 Beeston was chosen to take his place as general director and business manager of the company, at which time he was well-to-do, while the associate actors were men of small means. He was a witness to Greene's will dated July 25, 1612. The disposal of Greene's property led several years later to a lawsuit with Susan Baskervile, Greene's widow, in which Beeston took a prominent part. The 1623 account of the dispute shows quite clearly that Beeston's transactions in his managerial capacity were not always to his credit (the Baskervile documents are printed in Fleay, *Stage*, pp. 270–97). Another lawsuit also gives evidence as to how unsatisfactorily he managed the affairs of the company. Possibly from an earlier date, but certainly from 1612 to 1619, he purchased the apparel and other equipment used in staging plays. In 1612 he arranged with John Smith to supply the company with all "tinsell stuffes and other stuffe" that might be required. Between June 27 of that year and February 23, 1617, Smith delivered goods to the value of £46 5*s*. 8*d*., for which he claims he received no payment. This, together with Beeston's unsatisfactory manner of handling the company's money and rendering an account thereof, led to the Smith-Beeston dispute. Beeston apparently gave a false account for the expenditure of £400, and his associates accused him of having "much enritched himself" at their expense. In the proceedings of 1619 he is described as having been in 1612 "a thriving man, and one that was of ability and means." The result of the suit is unknown (the records of the dispute are printed by Wallace, *N.U.S.*, ix. 315–37). At the death of Queen Anne in 1619, Beeston went as manager to Prince Charles's company. He took with him, it is claimed, the apparel and furniture of the Red Bull stage, although these had been bought with the company's money (Wallace, *Ibid.*, p. 317). Charges against Beeston's honesty are not infrequent; but it is evident from his subsequent career that he was one of the most prominent theatrical managers of his time. In 1617 he erected the Cockpit in Drury Lane (Adams, *Playhouses*, pp. 350–58), where he seems to have successively managed Queen Anne's men (1617–19), Prince Charles's men (1619–22), Lady Elizabeth's men (1622–25), Queen Henrietta's men (1625–37), and the King and Queen's Young Company, popularly known as Beeston's Boys (1637–39). As a member of the Lady Elizabeth's company at the Cockpit in 1622, he is mentioned among "the chiefe of them at the Phoenix" (Adams,

Dram. Rec., p. 63). He seems to have died before August 10, 1639, for on that date his son, William, is referred to as the Governor of Beeston's Boys (Adams, *Playhouses*, p. 358*n*.). In 1639 the control of the lease of the Cockpit was in the hands of Mrs. Elizabeth Beeston, *alias* Hutchinson, seemingly Christopher's second wife, since the Middlesex records for 1615–17 give several true bills for recusancy against an earlier wife Jane. In these records Beeston is described as a gentleman or yeoman, and as "late of St. James-at-Clerkenwell," or, in one case, "of Turmil streete." In 1617 Henry Baldwin and Christopher Longe were held "for a riotous assalte and spoyle done upon the dwellinge house of Christopher Beeston" (Jeaffreson, *Middlesex*, ii. 107, 110, 114, 120, 128, 220). The registers of St. Leonard's, Shoreditch, record the baptism of the following children: Augustine, November 16, 1604; Christopher, December 1, 1605; and Robert, April 2, 1609; and the burial of Augustine, November 17, 1604; Jane, September 22, 1607; Christopher, July 15, 1610; and Robert, December 26, 1615, at which time Beeston's address is given as Clerkenwell (Stopes, *Burbage*, pp. 139, 140, 141). The registers of St. James, Clerkenwell, record the baptism of a daughter Anne on September 15, 1611, and the burial of a servant on July 1, 1615 (Hovenden, i. 62; iv. 131). He seems to have later returned to St. Leonard's, Shoreditch, for his name is traceable in the register up to 1637 (Collier, *Actors*, p. xxxii). He contributed verses to Heywood's *Apology* (1612), p. 11, where he addresses the author as his "good friend and fellow," and briefly vindicates the recreation that the playhouse offered to the public.

BEESTON, ROBERT.

Robert Beeston was probably a member of Queen Anne's company from its formation late in 1603 or early in 1604 (since his name appears in the undated draft license) till 1617, when the troupe visited Norwich. He took part in the coronation procession of March 15, 1604, wearing a cloak of red cloth. His name occurs in both the license of April 15, 1609, and the duplicate patent issued to the traveling company on January 7, 1612 (*M.S.C.*, i. 265, 270; Murray, i. 186, 191). He seems to have been with the Queen's men at Norwich on May 6, 1615, and May 31, 1617, for his name is given in the abstracts of the license in the Norwich records (Murray, ii. 340, 343); but this evidence is not conclusive, since Thomas Greene, who died in 1612, is also named in the Norwich records of 1615 and 1617.

BEESTON, WILLIAM.

If we may identify William Beeston with the "Willm Bee" of the Norwich records (but see William Bee), he was a member of the Lady Elizabeth's troupe when "Bee" and Francis Wambus were discharged from the Norwich prison on May 26, 1624 (Murray, ii. 350). The next two notices of him are also meagre, but show that he was concerned in theatrical matters (A. Nicoll, *Times Lit. Suppl.*, Nov. 22, 1923, p. 789). A brief entry, dated February 14, 1627, gives "A peticon of Wm: Beeston against Sr John Wentworth," and another records, November 12, 1632, "A petition of William Blagrove & William Beeston that his Lo would restore vnto them a boy named Stephen Hamerton inveigled from them by one Christopher Babham & by him imployed at the Blackfryars playhouse." At the latter date Beeston was probably one of the managers of the King's Revels company, which had been organized by Blagrove and Richard Gunnell when they built the Salisbury Court playhouse in 1629. We hear no more of Beeston until May 12, 1637, when he and his fellows of Beeston's Boys were summoned before the Privy Council for playing at the Cockpit during plague quarantine (*M.S.C.*, i. 392). In 1639 Christopher Beeston died, and William succeeded his father as Governor of Beeston's Boys at the Cockpit in Drury Lane. He is referred to as their Governor on August 10, 1639, when he obtained an order to prevent any other company from acting the plays belonging to his troupe. Nevertheless, his career as Governor was of short duration. Early in May, 1640, he allowed his Boys to act without license a play that gave great offense to King Charles I, because "it had relation to the passages of the Kings journey into the Northe, and was complaynd of by his Majestye, . . . with commande to punishe the offenders" (Adams, *Dram. Rec.*, p. 66). The company was ordered to stop playing, and on May 4 Beeston was committed to the Marshalsea prison. However, on May 7, the players having offered a "petition of submission," Sir Henry Herbert restored them to their liberty. But soon the players again abused their privileges, and as a result of the indiscretion, Beeston was deposed from his position as manager. On June 27, 1640, William Davenant succeeded him as Governor of the Cockpit players (Adams, *Playhouses*, pp. 358–61). Neither Beeston's misfortunes as manager nor the closing of the playhouses in 1642 quenched his theatrical interests. In 1649 he began negotiations for the purchase of the playhouse in Salisbury Court, which was dismantled by soldiers on March 24, 1649, before the deed of sale was signed. Three years later, however, he purchased the property, and in April, 1660, refitted the playhouse at a cost of about £329. Before he finished paying the carpenters, the building was destroyed by the Great Fire of 1666. The mortgage was apparently forfeited, and Beeston lost the property (Adams, *Playhouses*, pp. 380–83). The Middlesex documents cite him in a list of suspected recusants, April 22, 1680, at which time he is described as being of St. Leonard's, Shoreditch (Jeaffreson, iv. 145). Aubrey, who visited him on several occasions to glean information about the older poets and actors, records his death in 1682: "Old Mr. Beeston . . . died at his house in Bishopsgate street without, about Bartholomew-tyde, 1682" (*Lives*, i. 97). Beeston's son, George, continued the histrionic tradition of his family (Sidney Lee, *Nineteenth Century*, 1902, li. 210), and some of the following notices may refer to him rather than to his father. "Mr. Beeston" had a part in Shirley's *Sisters*, for his name is found in the prompter's copy which appears to have belonged to Davenant's company in Drury Lane about 1666 (*Works*, v. 354). Pepys records on February 2, 1668–69 (*Diary*, viii. 204) that he went to the—

King's playhouse, where the *Heyresse*, notwithstanding Kinaston's being beaten, is acted. . . . His part is done by Beeston, who is fain to read it out of a book all the while, and thereby spoils the part, and almost the play, it being one of the best parts in it. . . . But it was pleasant to see Beeston come in with the others, supposing it to be dark, and yet he is forced to read his part by the light of the candles: and this I observing to a gentleman that sat by me, he was mightily pleased therewith, and spread it up and down.

Downes records his parts as Roderigo in *The Moor of Vencie*, and Nigrinus in *Tyrannick Love* (*Ros. Ang.*, pp. 2, 7, 10). Beeston long retained the respect of the play-going and literature-loving public, and in the reign of Charles I the curious often resorted to his house in Hog Lane, Shoreditch, to listen to his reminiscences of Shakespeare and of the poets of Shakespeare's time. John Aubrey sought his personal acquaintance, in order to "take from him the lives of all the old English poets," and Dryden called him "the chronicle of the stage." To Aubrey goes the credit for having preserved the fragments of Beeston's conversation (*Lives*, i. 96 ff.; ii. 227, 233, 235). Richard Brome (*Works*, iii. 339) compliments him in a note appended to *The Antipodes* (1640):

Courteous Reader, You shal find in this Booke more then was presented upon the *Stage*, and left out of the *Presentation*, for superfluous length (as some of the *Players* pretended) I thoght good al should be inserted according to the allowed *Original*; and as it was, at first, intended for the *Cock-pit Stage*, in the right of my most deserving Friend Mr. *William Beeston*, unto whom it properly appertained; and so I leave it to thy perusal, as it was generally applauded, and well acted at *Salisbury Court*. Farewell.

RI. BROME.

A further testimony to Beeston's knowledge of stage-affairs is borne by Francis Kirkman, who, in dedicating to him *The Loves and Adventures of Clerico and Lozia* (1652), writes (Adams, *Playhouses*, p. 359):

Divers times in my hearing, to the admiration of the whole company, you have most judiciously discoursed of Poesie: which is the cause I preseume to choose you for my patron and protector, who are the happiest interpreter and judge of our English stage-plays this nation ever produced; which the poets and actors of these times cannot (without ingratitude) deny; for I have heard the chief and most ingenious acknowledge their fames and profits essentially sprung from your instruction, judgment, and fancy.

Thomas Nashe dedicated his *Strange Newes* (1592) to a "William Beeston," probably the theatrical manager's grandfather, whom he addresses as "Maister Apis lapis" and "Gentle M. William" (*Works*, i. 255). Nashe laughs at his patron's struggles with syntax in his efforts to write poetry, and at his indulgence in drink, which betrayed itself in his red nose. But, in spite of this characteristic frankness, Nashe greets the first William Beeston as a boon companion who was generous in his entertainment of threadbare scholars.

BEHEL, JACOB.

See Jacob Pedel.

BELT, T.

In 2 *Seven Deadly Sins*, presented by Lord Strange's company about 1590, T. Belt played a Servant in the Induction, and Panthea in "Lechery" (Greg, *H.P.*, p. 152; *R.E.S.*, i. 262).

BENFIELD, ROBERT.

The 1679 folio of Beaumont and Fletcher names Robert Benfield as one of the "principal actors" in *The Coxcomb* and *The Honest Man's Fortune*, both of which were probably acted by the Lady Elizabeth's company in 1613 (*Eliz. Stage*, ii. 251). Subsequently he became a King's man, but at what date is uncertain. William Ostler died on December 16, 1614, and Benfield may have

taken his place in the King's company, for in Webster's *Duchess
of Malfi* he assumed the part of Antonio which had been acted
by Ostler. As a King's man he appears in the patent of March 27,
1619; in the livery-allowance lists of May 19, 1619, and April 7,
1621; in the submission for playing *The Spanish Viceroy* without
license, December 20, 1624; in King James's funeral procession,
May 7, 1625; in the patent of June 24, 1625; in the cloak-allow-
ance list of May 6, 1629; and in the 1623 folio list of actors in
Shakespeare's plays. In 1635 he owned one share in the Globe
and one-third of a share in Blackfriars (Adams, *Mod. Phil.*, xvii.
8; Halliwell-Phillipps, *Outlines*, i. 313–14), which he doubtless
held until the closing of the playhouses in 1642. He seems to
have been a member of the company to the end, for he signed the
dedication of the Beaumont and Fletcher folio of 1647. The burial
of his son, Robert, October 15, 1617, is recorded at St. Bartholomew's the Great; and the registers of St. Giles's, Cripplegate,
give the burial of two more of his children, Bartholomew, July
21, 1631, and Elizabeth, August 1, 1631 (Collier, iii. 471, 472).
He had parts in many of the Beaumont and Fletcher plays (Murray, i. opp. 172): *The Knight of Malta* (*c.* 1618); *The Mad Lover* (*c.*
1618); *The Humorous Lieutenant* (*c.* 1619); *Women Pleased* (*c.* 1620);
The Custom of the Country (*c.* 1619–20); *The Double Marriage* (*c.* 1619–
20); *The Little French Lawyer* (*c.* 1620); *The False One* (*c.* 1620–21);
The Pilgrim (*c.* 1621); *The Prophetess* (1622); *The Spanish Curate*
(1622; *Works*, ii. 60); *The Lovers' Progress* (1623); *The Maid in the
Mill* (1623); *Wife for a Month* (1624); and De Gard, "a noble
stayd gentleman," in *The Wildgoose Chase* (a revival, 1631). He
also acted in the following plays: Boisise and a Captain in
Barnavelt (1619; ed. Frijlinck, p. clx); Antonio, formerly played
by Ostler, in Webster's *Duchess of Malfi* (*c.* 1619–23; Murray,
ii. 146ff.); Junius Rusticus in Massinger's *Roman Actor* (licensed
October 11, 1626); Ford's *Lover's Melancholy* (licensed November
24, 1628); Ladislaus, King of Hungary, in Massinger's *Picture*
(licensed June 8, 1629); the King in Carlell's *Deserving Favorite*

(published 1629); and Marcellus in Massinger's *Believe as You List* (licensed May 7, 1631). On January 28, 1648, he and other members of the King's company gave a bond to pay off an old Blackfriars debt to the heirs of Michael Bowyer. He was dead by the Easter term, 1655 (Hotson, pp. 31-34).

BENTLEY, JOHN.

John Bentley was born about 1553, for the record of his burial in 1585 gives his age as "yers 32" (Gower, *Reg. of St. Peter's, Cornhill*, i. 153). In 1583 he was a member of the Queen's troupe in London; for he is named in a City record that gives the personnel of the company at this time (*Eliz. Stage*, ii. 106). He was with the Queen's men at Norwich in June, 1583, when an affray occurred, concerning which depositions of witnesses remain. It seems that the company was performing at the Red Lion Inn, with Bentley playing "the Duke." After the play had started, one Wynsdon tried to gain admittance without paying, and in the ensuing scuffle overset the money. Three of the players, Tarlton, Bentley, and Singer, ran to see what the trouble was. Wynsdon then fled, and was pursued by Singer and Bentley, Tarlton in vain trying to restrain Bentley. During the pursuit, Wynsdon was joined by his servant, "a man in a blue coat," who threw a stone at Bentley and "broke his head." But Bentley, now joined by Henry Browne, Sir William Paston's man, continued the pursuit. When Bentley and Browne overtook the "man in the blue coat," they thrust at him with their swords, and one of them gave him the wound from which he died (Halliwell-Phillipps, *Illustrations*, p. 118). An undated letter from W. P. to Edward Alleyn refers to a theatrical wager that the great tragedian could equal Bentley and Knell in any of their own parts (*H.P.*, p. 32). Heywood mentions him with others as having flourished before his time, i.e. before about 1594 (*Apology*, p. 43). He is lauded by Nashe in *Pierce Penilesse* (1592), where he is noticed with Tarlton, Alleyn, and Knell (*Works*, i. 215). In *A*

Knight's Conjuring (1607), p. 75, Dekker places him in the company of the poets: "tho hee had bene a player, molded out of their pennes, yet because he had bene their louer, and a register to the Muses, inimitable Bentley." He may be the John Bentley whom Ritson records as "the authour of a few short poems in a manuscript collection belonging to Samuel Lysons esquire" (*Bibliographia Poetica*, p. 129). His burial is noted in the register of St. Peter's Cornhill, August 19, 1585: "Thursday John Bentley one of ye Queens players, pit in ye north ile. yers 32" (Gower, i. 133). His will was proved in 1585 in the Prerogative Court of Canterbury, and the *Index* describes him as "servaunt to the Queene, All Saints, Lombardstreet, London" (Smith-Fry, *Canterbury Wills*, iv. 39). The will, which might yield information on the Queen's men, has not been printed.

BIEL, JACOB.

See Jacob Pedel.

BIERDT, BURCHART.

Burchart Bierdt, "Englischer Musicant," was at Cologne, Germany, in November, 1612 (Cohn, *Jahrbuch*, xxi. 257).

BILLINGESLEY, JOHN.

For the performance of *Paris and Vienna* at Court by the Westminster boys on February 19, 1572, John Billingesley served as payee (Steele, p. 41).

BIRCH, GEORGE.

George Birch, carrier, aged 32, appears about 1530 as a witness in a lawsuit between John Rastell and Henry Walton concerning the use of certain playing garments for a royal banquet at Greenwich about 1527 (Pollard, *Fifteenth Century*, p. 316). He was doubtless a Court Interluder from 1538 to about 1559, for his name is traceable in the records, where his salary is given as £3 6s. 8d. a year. An annuity to a George Birch by a warrant on

January 7, 1560, is recorded in the Chamber Accounts of the early years of Elizabeth's reign (Collier, i. 116, 117, 136, 165; *Eliz. Stage*, ii. 83).

BIRCH, GEORGE.

George Birch was a member of the King's company. His name appears in the submission of the King's men for playing *The Spanish Viceroy* without license, December 20, 1624; in the list of players who took part in King James's funeral procession, May 7, 1625; and in the patent of June 24, 1625. He is not named in the patent of March 27, 1619, but apparently joined the company soon after this date, for he played Morier in *Barnavelt* (ed. Frijlinck, p. clx) about August, 1619. He also had parts in the following Beaumont and Fletcher plays acted by the King's men (Murray, i. opp. 172): *The Double Marriage* (c. 1619–20); *The False One* (c. 1620–21); *The Laws of Candy* (c. 1619; *Works*, iii. 236); *The Pilgrim* (c. 1621); *The Island Princess* (c. 1621); *The Prophetess* (1622); *The Lovers' Progress* (1623); and *Wife for a Month* (1624). The register of St. Saviour's, Southwark, records on November 18, 1623, the baptism of Bridgett Birch, daughter of George, "a player"; and the marriage on January 28, 1619, of George Birch and Elizabeth Cowley, "with license" (Bentley, *T.L.S.*, Nov. 15, 1928, p. 856).

BIRCH, JOHN.

From 1547 to 1556 John Birch seems to have been a Court Interluder, at a salary of £3 6s. 8d. a year (Collier, i. 136, 165).

BIRD, THEOPHILUS.

The date at which Theophilus Bird (or Bourne) joined Queen Henrietta's men is uncertain, for the dates of the plays in which he acted are conjectural. He is known to have had the following parts in plays given by the Queen's company at the Cockpit in Drury Lane (Murray, i. opp. 266): Paulina in Massinger's *Renegado* (pr. 1630); Toota, Queen of Fesse, in Heywood's *Fair Maid of the West*, Part II (*c.* 1630); and Massanissa, in Nabbes's *Hannibal and Scipio* (1635). His name, "Master Bird," appears at the close of the Prologue to *The Witch of Edmonton* (Ford, *Works*, iii. 173). This play, not printed until 1658, may have passed from Prince Charles's men to Queen Henrietta's company about 1625, when the latter troupe was organized (Murray, i. 236n.). When Queen Henrietta's company disbanded early in 1637, Bird doubtless joined Beeston's Boys, for on May 12, 1637, he and other members of Beeston's company were summoned before the Privy Council for playing at the Cockpit during plague quarantine (*M.S.C.*, i. 392). His name is found at the end of the Prologue to Ford's *Lady's Trial*, acted at the Cockpit in May, 1638 (*Works*, iii. 7). In Wright's *Historia Histrionica* (1699) we find Bird among the "eminent actors" listed as "of principal note at the Cockpit" (Hazlitt's *Dodsley*, xv. 406). By 1641 he was a King's man, his name appearing in a warrant of January 22 of that year (Stopes, *Jahrbuch*, xlvi. 103). His name is appended to the dedicatory epistle of the 1647 folio of Beaumont and Fletcher's plays, published by a group of the King's players (*Works*, i. p. x). In 1652 he served as William Beeston's agent in the purchase of the playhouse in Salisbury Court (Adams, *Playhouses*, p. 381). With Andrew Pennycuicke in 1657 he published Ford and Dekker's *Sun's Darling*, with a dedication to the Earl of Southampton (Hazlitt, *Coll. & Notes*, 1867–1876, p. 164). His name occurs in the list of actors constituting the company under the management of Thomas Killigrew, later known as His Majesty's Company of Comedians at the Theatre Royal, but in none of the actor-lists as given by Downes (*Ros. Ang.*, p. 2). He was dead by April 28, 1663, when Charles II took a hand in "the disposition of a share in the company fallen in by death of Theoph. Bird" (*S. P. D. Charles II*, lxxii. 45). On January 28, 1648, he joined certain other members of the King's company in signing a bond to pay off an old Blackfriars debt to Michael Bowyer's heirs. The debt was not paid by Easter term, 1655, at which time

Thomas Morrison, who had married Bowyer's widow, brought suit against Bird. He was Christopher Beeston's son-in-law (Hotson, pp. 31–34, 92).

BIRD, WILLIAM.

With several of his fellows of the Earl of Pembroke's company, William Bird, *alias* Bourne, is complainant in a lawsuit during 1597 against Francis Langley, builder and owner of the Swan playhouse (Wallace, *Eng. Studien*, xliii. 340; Adams, *Playhouses*, pp. 168–74). As a result of the dissolution of the Pembroke company, caused by the production of *The Isle of Dogs*, Bird on August 10, 1597, offered to bind himself to Henslowe to play with the Admiral's men at the Rose, and on October 11 his name is found in the company's accounts (*H.D.*, i. 82, 203). From this time to 1602 he appears in the *Diary* as repeatedly authorizing payments, borrowing from Henslowe, paying personal debts, selling properties, acknowledging company debts in the capacity of shareholder, and occasionally as a witness. On November 26, 1600, Henslowe lent Bird's wife £3 to free her husband from jail "for hurting of a felowe." Besides acting, Bird also turned his hand to writing. He and Rowley in collaboration completed Haughton's *Judas*, for which they received £6 in December, 1601. Again on November 22, 1602, he and Rowley were paid £4 for additions to *Doctor Faustus* (*H.D.*, i. 80, 151, 152, 172). As an Admiral's man he played Colmogra and Artabisus in *1 Tamar Cam* about October, 1602 (*H.P.*, p. 154). About Christmas, 1603, the Admiral's men were taken into the service of Prince Henry; and on March 15, 1604, Bird appeared as "one of the servants to the young Prince" in the magnificent entertainment presented to King James upon his triumphant passage through London. In this entertainment Bird represented "Zeal" (Middleton, *Works*, vii. 224). He is named in the patent to Prince Henry's men on April 30, 1606, and in the household list of 1610 (*Eliz. Stage*, ii. 187, 188). The Prince died in November, 1612, and his troupe

soon passed under the patronage of the Palsgrave. Bird is mentioned in the new patent of January 11, 1613 (*M.S.C.*, i. 275),
and in the lease of the Fortune by the Palsgrave's men on October
31, 1618 (*H.P.*, p. 27). On several occasions during 1618–21, in
company with his wife, his son, or his fellow-actors, he dined
with Edward Alleyn; and on February 23, 1621, he met Alleyn
at the Paul's Head (Young, ii. 81, 142, 185, 202, 204). Bird was
probably a member of the Palsgrave's company until 1622. He
is last heard of on May 20, 1622, when he was occupying a tene-
ment adjoining the Fortune playhouse. In his note on Richard
Bradshaw's bond, January 8, 1605, he had described himself as
"of Hogsdon" (Warner, pp. 16, 243). The register of St. Saviour's,
Southwark, records the baptism of two of his sons: William, May
18, 1600; Francis, January 26, 1602 (Bentley, *T.L.S.*, Nov. 15,
1928, p. 856).

"BLACK DICK."

In *Frederick and Basilea*, presented by the Admiral's men in
1597, "Black Dick" acted the part of a servant, a guard, a messenger, a confederate, and a jailor (*H.P.*, p. 153).

BLACKWAGE, WILLIAM.

Henslowe lent William Blackwage £5 before May 13, 1594.
He is described as "my lord chamberlenes man," but whether
he was an actor or a private servant is not known (*H.D.*, ii. 243).

BLACKWOOD, THOMAS.

The marriage of Thomas Blackwood, described as a player, and
Ann Clarke is recorded in the register of St. Bodolph Aldgate on
September 8, 1592 (Denkinger, *P.M.L.A.*, xli. 98). As a member
of the Earl of Leicester's troupe in 1602–03 he authorized payments on behalf of the company from August 19, 1602, to March
7, 1603. On March 12, 1603, he borrowed 10s. from Henslowe
"when he Ride into the contrey wth his company to playe"
(*H.D.*, ii. 244). When acting in London was suspended owing to

the illness of Queen Elizabeth, Blackwood must have promptly left for Germany, since he and John Thare visited Frankfort with Robert Browne's troupe at the Easter fair in 1603 (Herz, p. 42).

BLAGROVE, WILLIAM.

As Deputy to the Master of the Revels William Blagrove is mentioned several times from 1624 to 1635 in the records of the Office of the Revels in connection with the payments of various companies. In this capacity he licensed Glapthorne's *Lady Mother* on October 15, 1635; and during the same year he received a gratuity of £3 from the French players (Adams, *Dram. Rec.*, pp. 37, 62). In 1629 he and Richard Gunnell formed a theatrical partnership and built the Salisbury Court Playhouse, which was occupied by the Children of the King's Revels until December, 1631 (Adams, *Playhouses*, pp. 368–74). He and Gunnell probably served as managers. On November 12, 1632, he and William Beeston (*q.v.*) petitioned that one of their boy-actors, Stephen Hammerton (*q.v.*), should be returned to them. Blagrove is named in a warrant of January 24, 1635, for the payment of £30 to himself "and the rest of the company" for three plays acted by the Children of the Revels at Whitehall in 1631 (Steele, p. 239).

BLAK, JOHN.

John Blak was a joint-lessee of the new Fortune playhouse, in which he was granted a half-share on February 20, 1624 (Warner, p. 247).

BLANEY, JOHN.

John Blaney appears in the actor-list of Jonson's *Epicoene*, which, according to the folio of 1616, was "Acted in the yeere 1609, by the Children of her Maiesties Revells." By 1616 he had joined Queen Anne's men, for in June of that year he is mentioned in the Baskervile papers as a member of the company (*Eliz. Stage*, ii. 237). Again in June, 1617, he is named in an agreement with Susan Baskervile. On May 13, 1619, he attended Queen

Anne's funeral as a representative of her London company. After the Queen's death her London troupe was known as the Players of the Revels at the Red Bull; and Blaney is noted in 1622 as one of "the chiefe players" in this company (Adams, *Dram. Rec.*, p. 63). By May, 1623, the company seems to have disbanded, for on May 23 Blaney and two of his fellows pleaded to be excused from their payments to Susan Baskerville, in that the other players party to the original agreement were either dead or with another troupe; and in 1626 the court dismissed the plea of Blaney and Worth, the two surviving plaintiffs (Murray, i. 199). Subsequently he joined Queen Henrietta's men at the Cockpit, and is known to have played Asambeg, in Massinger's *Renegado* (pr. 1630), presented by this company (Murray, i. opp. 266). In 1623 he lived "neare the Red Bull in St Iohns Streete" (Wallace, *Jahrbuch*, xlvi. 347).

BLANK, WILLIAM ALEXANDER.

A Scottish dancer, who performed at Cologne, Germany, in April, 1605 (Cohn, *Jahrbuch*, xxi. 253).

BOND, THOMAS.

Thomas Bond (or Band) appeared as one of the Tritons in *The Two Noble Ladies*, as noted in margin of the Egerton MS. of the play (Boas, *Library*, 1917, viii. 232, 235). This play was "often tymes acted with approbation at the Red Bull in St. John's Streete by the company of the Revells" (Bullen, *Old Plays*, ii. 430), and is assigned by Fleay to 1619-22 (*Drama*, ii. 334). Bond is named in a license granted to the Children of the Revels to the late Queen Anne on April 9, 1623 (Murray, i. 362; ii. 272-73). We hear no more of him until December, 1631 (Adams, *Dram. Rec.*, p. 45), when he played Miscellanio, a tutor, in Marmion's *Holland's Leaguer*, presented by "the high and mighty Prince Charles his servants, at the private house in Salisbury Court" (Marmion, *Works*, pp. 2, 6). His name appears in a warrant of May 10, 1632, appointing several of Prince Charles's men as

Grooms of the Chamber (Stopes, *Jahrbuch*, xlvi. 96). There is a possibility that he played Bussy, in Chapman's *Bussy D'Ambois*, acted by the King's players on Easter-Monday, April 7, 1634, at the Cockpit-in-Court (Adams, *Dram. Rec.*, p. 55). This conjecture is set forth by Waldron, who notes that Kemble identified the "third man" in the Prologue to *Bussy D'Ambois* with Tom Bond (*Shak. Miscellany*, "English Stage," p. 25). Such an identification would give Bond some celebrity as an actor, which merit has not been otherwise accorded him. His picture is at Dulwich, and is described by Warner, p. 206: "Tom Bond's picture, an actor, in 'a band rought with imbrodery, bared neck,' on a board; in a black frame, very old." A reproduction of this portrait is given by Waldron (*op. cit.*, opp. p. 25).

BORNE, WILLIAM.

See William Bird.

BOSEGRAVE, GEORGE.

George Bosegrave is named in a license granted to the Children of the Revels to the late Queen Anne on April 9, 1623 (Murray, i. 362; ii. 272–73). He was a joint-lessee of the new Fortune playhouse, in which he obtained "half a twelfth part" on February 20, 1624 (Warner, pp. 244, 247).

BOSGRAVE.

See George Bosegrave.

BOURNE, THEOPHILUS.

See Theophilus Bird.

BOURNE, THOMAS.

Thomas Bourne is recorded at Norwich on March 10, 1635, when his troupe, presumably the King's Revels, applied for permission to act in that town (Murray, i. 279–80).

BOURNE, WILLIAM.

See William Bird.

BOUSET, JOHN.

See Thomas Sackville.

BOWER, RICHARD.

Master of the Chapel Royal, 1545–61. Because of the initials "R. B." on the title-page, Bower has been suggested as the author of *Apius and Virginia*, 1575 (Wallace, *Evolution*, pp. 69 ff., 77, 105 ff., 108 ff.).

BOWERS, RICHARD.

Richard Bowers is named in a Ticket of Privilege granted on January 12, 1636, to the attendants "employed by his Majesty's servants the players of the Blackfriars, and of special use to them both on the Stage and otherwise for his Majesty's disport and service" (Stopes, *Jahrbuch*, xlvi. 99). -

BOWRING, GEORGE.

A member of the Children of Paul's in 1574 (Hillebrand, *Child Actors*, p. 111). He may be identical with Gregory Bowringe, for "George" is possibly a clerical error for "Gregory," or *vice versa*.

BOWRINGE, GREGORY.

A member of the Children of Paul's at some date before 1582. He appears as a legatee in the will of Sebastian Westcott, dated April 3, 1582, where he is named among the "sometimes children of the said almenerey," i.e. St. Paul's (*Eliz. Stage*, ii. 15*n*.). Possibly he is to be identified with George Bowring (*q.v.*).

BOWYER, MICHAEL.

Michael Bowyer was probably with Queen Henrietta's men at the Cockpit in Drury Lane from their formation in 1625 to their breaking up in 1637. As a member of this company he had parts in the following plays (Murray, i. opp. 266): Beauford, a passionate lover of Gratiana, in Shirley's *Wedding* (*c.* 1626); King

John in Davenport's *King John and Matilda* (*c.* 1629); Mr. Spencer
in Heywood's *Fair Maid of the West*, Part I (*c.* 1630); Vitelli, a
gentleman of Venice disguised as a merchant, in Massinger's
Renegado (pr. 1630); and Scipio in Nabbes's *Hannibal and Scipio*
(1635). In Wright's *Historia Histrionica* (1699) Bowyer is listed
among the "eminent actors" described as "of principal note at
the Cockpit" (Hazlitt's *Dodsley*, xv. 406). When Queen Henrietta's company disbanded in 1637 some of the members united
with the Revels company at Salisbury Court, and others joined
Beeston's Boys at the Cockpit; but Bowyer is not known to have
joined either of these troupes. By 1641 he was a King's man, his
name appearing in a warrant of January 22 of that year (Stopes,
Jahrbuch, xlvi. 103). Davenport's poem "Too Late to Call Back
Yesterday" (1639) is dedicated "To my noble friends, Mr.
Richard Robinson, and Mr. Michael Bowyer" (Bullen, *Old
Plays*, New Series, iii. 311). The registers of St. Bodolph Aldgate
record two of Bowyer's sons: William, baptized and buried,
August 16, 1621; William, baptized September 1, buried September 11, 1622. His wife's name was Isabell or Elizabeth; both
forms are given (Denkinger, *P.M.L.A.*, xli. 98). Bowyer made his
will in September, 1645, and died shortly after. His widow,
Elizabeth, married one Thomas Morrison. In 1655 Morrison
brought suit against Theophilus Bird for the recovery of a debt
incurred some years earlier by members of the King's company
when Bowyer had advanced £200 for the company's use (Hotson,
pp. 31–34).

BRACKENBURY, RICHARD.

A member of the Children of Paul's in 1598 (Hillebrand, *Child
Actors*, p. 111).

BRADSHAW, RICHARD.

In a warrant of February 16, 1595, Richard Bradshaw and
Francis Coffin are named as members of Lord Edward Dudley's

provincial company of players; and with the license of this company they appeared at Chester on November 20, 1602 (Murray, ii. 234). On May 19, 1598, Bradshaw, described as Gabriel Spencer's man, fetched money for Spencer; and in October of the same year he received money on behalf of Dekker and Drayton (*H.D.*, i. 79, 97). On October 10, 1598, described as "yeoman . . . of St. Saviour's, Southwark," he and two others entered into a bond of £5 to repay 50s. to William Bird on March 2, 1599. This bond was forfeited, and on January 8, 1605, Bird made a note of a debt of 10s. to Edward Alleyn, with the privilege of recovering the amount from Bradshaw on the bond (Warner, p. 16). He borrowed 14s. and 5s. from Henslowe on December 15, 1600, and April 29, 1601, to be paid on his return to London (*H.D.*, i. 133). On the former date he bought from Henslowe one pound and two ounces of copper lace, which was probably for the use of Dudley's troupe. Coffin, his partner, is not again heard of; but Bradshaw seems to have become the leader of a company that acted at Reading in 1630 and at Banbury in 1633. At Banbury the town authorities, becoming suspicious of the validity of the company's license, arrested the players, and notified the Privy Council. The names of the six players as enclosed with the letter from the Banbury officials to the Privy Council are: Bartholomew Jones, Richard Whiting, *alias* Richard Johnson, Edward Damport, Drewe Turner, Robert Houghton, and Richard Collewell. From the examination of the six men we learn that Bradshaw as their manager had gone a few days before to London to renew the commission and would join them a few days later with more players. And from the records it appears that Edward Whiting (*q.v.*) either had been or was in some way connected with Bradshaw's troupe, and that he "let the commission in question to William Cooke and Fluellen Morgan, and they two went with it with a puppet-play until they had spent all, then they pawned the commission for 4s." Subsequently Bradshaw redeemed and bought the commission (Murray, ii. 106–09, 163–67).

BRADSTREET, JOHN.

John Bradstreet is named in a passport issued February 10, 1592, by the Lord Admiral, giving permission for a group of players under the leadership of Robert Browne to travel on the Continent (Cohn, p. xxix). He visited Arnhem, Netherlands, in 1592, with a license from Prince Maurice of Orange-Nassau (*Eliz. Stage*, ii. 274*n*.). In August, 1592, the company gave *Gammer Gurton's Needle* and some of Marlowe's plays at the Frankfort autumn fair. Again in 1593 and 1597 Bradstreet's name appears in the Frankfort records of English players at the fair (Herz, pp. 10, 11, 36). He seems to have remained for a long time in Germany, for his autograph, dated March 24, 1606, is found in an album of Johannes Cellarius of Nuremberg (Cohn, *Shak. in Germany*, Plate i, facsimile of autographs). He died in 1618 (*Eliz. Stage*, ii. 277).

BRAMPTON, JOHN.

A member of the Chapel Royal in 1423 (Hillebrand, *Mod. Phil.*, xviii. 235).

BRANDE, THOMAS.

A member of the Children of Paul's in 1574 (Hillebrand, *Child Actors*, p. 111).

BRAY, ANTONY.

Antony Bray is recorded at Norwich on March 10, 1635, when his troupe, presumably the King's Revels, applied for permission to act in that town (Murray, i. 279–80).

BRETTEN, WILLIAM.

A member of the Chapel Royal not later than 1546. Among the Documents Signed by Stamp in February, 1546, there is "A letter to the dean and chapter of Lichfelde to accept William Bretten, late one of the children of your Majesty's chapel, to be a singingman there" (Brewer, *L. & P. Henry VIII*, xxi. 1. p. 142).

BREW, ANTHONY.

Anthony Brew appeared as "a Lord of Babilon with his sword drawn," and as a soldier, in *The Two Noble Ladies*, as noted in margin of the Egerton MS. of the play (Boas, *Library*, 1917, viii. 232). The play was "often tymes acted with approbation at the Red Bull in St. John's Streete by the company of the Revells" (Bullen, *Old Plays*, ii. 430), and is assigned by Fleay to 1619–22 (*Drama*, ii. 334). Possibly he is to be identified with Anthony Brewer, author of *The Lovesick King* (ed. A. E. H. Swaen), a play that was published in 1655 but written probably about 1607 (cf. *Eliz. Stage*, iii. 237).

BREWER, ANTHONY.

See Anthony Brew.

BRISTOW, JAMES.

James Bristow was William Augusten's boy. On December 18, 1597, Philip Henslowe bought him for £8. His wages due from A. Jeffes to Henslowe were in arrears, August 8, 1600; and his wages from April 23, 1600, to February 15, 1601, were owing to Henslowe from the Admiral's men (*H.D.*, i. 131, 134, 203). He may be the "Jemes" who appears as a witness on March 27, 1599. He probably acted with the Admiral's men in minor parts from 1597 to 1602. A "James" is recorded in the plots of *The Battle of Alcazar* (*c.* 1600–01), as Ruben and a page, and of *1 Tamar Cam* (1602), as an Hermaphrodite in the procession (*H.P.*, pp. 153, 154); but Richard Jones also had a boy named James. He may fairly be identified with the "Jeames" mentioned together with Nicke in a letter from Joan Alleyn to her husband on October 21, 1603 (Warner, p. 25).

BROME, RICHARD.

Richard Brome's name appears in a warrant of June 30, 1628, appointing several members of the Lady Elizabeth's (Queen of Bohemia's) company as Grooms of the Chamber (Stopes, *Jahr-*

buch, xlvi. 94). He may perhaps be identified with the dramatist
(A. Thaler, "Was Richard Brome an Actor?" *M.L.N.*, xxxvi. 88).
That Brome the playwright was in some capacity apprenticed to
Ben Jonson we learn from Jonson's prefatory verses to *The North-
ern Lass*, published in 1632 (Brome, *Works*, iii. p. ix):

> *To my old Faithful Servant, and (by his continu'd Vertue) my
> loving Friend, the Author of this Work, Mr. Richard Brome.*
>
> I had you for a Servant, once, Dick Brome;
> And you perform'd a Servants faithful parts,
> Now, you are got into a nearer room,
> Of Fellowship, professing my old Arts.
> And you do doe them well, with good applause,
> Which you have justly gained from the Stage,
> By observation of those Comick Lawes
> Which I, your Master, first did teach the Age.
> You learn'd it well, and for it serv'd your time
> A Prentice-ship: which few do now adays.
> Now each Court-Hobby-horse will wince in rime;
> Both learned and unlearned, all write Playes.
> It was not so of old: Men took up trades
> That knew the Crafts they had bin bred in right:
> An honest Bilbo-Smith would make good blades,
> And the Physician teach men spue, or shite;
> The Cobler kept him to his nall, but now
> He'll be a Pilot, scarce can guide a Plough.
> —BEN. JOHNSON.

Brome's apprenticeship seems to have begun at least as early as
1614, when the Lady Elizabeth's men acted Jonson's *Bartholomew
Fair*, in which (Induction) the stage-keeper says: "I am looking,
lest the *Poet* heare me, or his man, *Master Broome*, behind the
Arras" (ed. C. S. Alden, p. 5).

BROMEFILD, RICHARD.

As a member of Ellis Guest's company under license of June 7,
1628, Richard Bromefild was at Norwich on July 2 of the same
year (Murray, ii. 103).

BROMEHAM.

A member of the Children of Paul's at some date before 1582. He appears as a legatee in the will of Sebastian Westcott, dated April 3, 1582, where he is named among the "sometimes children of the said almenerey," i.e. St. Paul's (*Eliz. Stage*, ii. 15*n*.).

BROMLEY, THOMAS.

Thomas Bromley appears as joint-legatee with Mary Clarke, *alias* Wood, in the will, dated July 22, 1603, of Thomas Pope, who left them his share in the Globe playhouse. Bromley was a minor. Basilius Nicoll, a scrivener, seems to have taken charge of Bromley's interest in the Globe (Adams, *Mod. Phil.*, xvii. 3 ff.).

BROWNE.

In October, 1596, Henslowe lent the Admiral's men 10*s*. "to feache browne" (*H.D.*, ii. 246). The meaning of this phrase and the identity of Browne are moot questions.

BROWNE, EDWARD.

In March, 1584, the Earl of Worcester's players were engaged in a dispute with the authorities at Leicester. The account of this quarrel gives an abstract of the license of Worcester's men, dated January 14, 1583, in which Edward Browne is mentioned (*Eliz. Stage*, ii. 222). On January 25, 1599 (?), he appears as a witness with Henslowe and Charles Massey, which seems to indicate that he was at this date with the Admiral's men (*H.D.*, i. 40). As an Admiral's man he played Crymm in the procession of *1 Tamar Cam* about October, 1602 (*H.P.*, p. 154). He may possibly have been the "Browne of the Boares head," alluded to in a letter from Joan to Edward Alleyn on October 21, 1603, as "dead, and dyed very poore" (Warner, p. 24). If so, his widow may have married Thomas Greene, whose will (Fleay, *Stage*, p. 192), dated July 25, 1612, mentions several stepchildren by the name of Browne. "William Brawne, son of Edward, player," was baptized at St. Saviour's on October 1, 1596 (Bentley, *T.L.S.*, Nov. 15, 1928, p. 856).

BROWNE, HENRY.

As Sir William Paston's man, Henry Browne joined John Bentley, of the Queen's men, in an affray at Norwich in 1583, and either he or Bentley fatally wounded the "man in the blue coat" (Halliwell-Phillipps, *Illustrations*, p. 118). He was possibly only a servant and not an actor.

BROWNE, JOHN.

John Browne seems to have been a Court Interluder from 1551 to 1563. He is traceable in the records as receiving a salary of £3 6s. 8d. and livery allowance of £1 3s. 4d. a year. He died in 1563 (*S.P.D. Edward VI*, xiv. 40; Feuillerat, *Edw. & Mary*, pp. 86, 280; Collier, i. 165; Murray, i. 3; *Eliz. Stage*, ii. 84).

BROWNE, JOHN.

On May 9, 1608, John Browne, "one of the playe boyes," was buried at St. Anne's (*Eliz. Stage*, ii. 55n.). He was probably one of the Children of the Revels.

BROWNE, OLD.

As an Admiral's man "old Browne" appeared as a Cannibal in the procession of *1 Tamar Cam* about October, 1602 (*H.P.*, p. 154).

BROWNE, ROBERT.

Robert Browne is named as a member of Worcester's troupe in the abstract of the license of January 14, 1583, in the Leicester records (*Eliz. Stage*, ii. 222). On January 3, 1589, he was concerned in a transfer to Edward Alleyn by Richard Jones of his share in a stock of theatrical goods held jointly with Edward and John Alleyn and Browne (*H.P.*, p. 31). This conveyance seems to mark either a break-up of Worcester's men or an internal change in the organization of the Admiral's men, and thus there is some uncertainty as to whether Browne was at this date with the Worcester or the Admiral troupe. He soon became one of the most prominent of the English actors on the Continent, where he spent considerable periods of time between 1590 and 1620. His career abroad began in October, 1590, with a visit to Leyden, Netherlands. Apparently his stay was only temporary, for he is named in a passport issued February 10, 1592, by the Lord Admiral, giving permission for a group of players to travel on the Continent (Cohn, pp. xxix, xxxi). He appeared at Arnhem, Netherlands, in 1592, with a license from Prince Maurice of Orange-Nassau (*Eliz. Stage*, ii. 274*n*.). In August, 1592, his company gave *Gammer Gurton's Needle* and some of Marlowe's plays at the Frankfort autumn fair; and in 1593 he is named in the Frankfort records of English players at the fair (Herz, pp. 10, 11). The company seems to have disbanded in 1593, and Browne is not traceable for a year or so either in Germany or in England. His wife, his children, and all his household died of the plague in Shoreditch about August, 1593 (*H.P.*, p. 37); but he married again, and a son, Robert, and a daughter, Elizabeth, were baptized at St. Saviour's on October 19, 1595, and December 2, 1599, respectively (*Eliz. Stage*, ii. 304). In the course of time Browne came to Cassel, one of the literary courts of Germany, the capital of Maurice the Learned, Landgrave of Hesse-Cassel. Certainly he was the Landgrave's man by April 16, 1595, when a warrant was issued allowing the export of a consignment of bows and arrows for which he had been sent over to England (*Cecil MSS.*, v. 174). Again in July, 1597, he was the agent in a similar transaction (*S.P.D. Elizabeth*, cclxiv. 24). He is named in an undated warrant, probably about 1594–95, appointing him and his company to serve the Landgrave as players and musicians. In August, 1596, he and one John Webster were at Cassel, during the visit of the Earl of Lincoln, who came from England to stand proxy for Queen Elizabeth as godmother at the christening of the Landgrave's daughter. In 1598 he and his company left Cassel for the court of Frederick IV at Heidelberg, and toward the end of 1599 proceeded to Frankfort and Strassburg (Herz, pp. 13, 14, 16).

The company on its arrival at Strassburg was under his leadership, but soon he seems to have left them and returned to England. During the winters of 1599–1600 and 1600–01 he appears as payee for the Earl of Derby's men when they performed at Court (Steele, pp. 119, 121). Subsequently he returned to Germany, for he was in Frankfort at Easter, 1601. From 1601 to 1607 he was in Germany (Herz, pp. 17–19). We find his appearance recorded at Frankfort in September, 1602; at Augsburg in the following November and December; at Nuremberg in February, 1603; at Frankfort for the Easter fair of 1603; at Frankfort in May, 1606; and at Strassburg in the following June. About this time he and his company seem to have come under the patronage of Maurice of Hesse, for they came to Frankfort in August, 1606, as the Hessian Comedians. During the following winter he settled at Cassel, but for only a short time. On March 1, 1607, one of the Landgrave's officers reported that the players found their salaries inadequate and declared they would leave. On March 17 he went to Frankfort for the last time as a member of the Hessian troupe (Herz, p. 20). His name now disappears from German records for a decade. William Sly in his will dated August 4, 1608, bequeathed "his part of the Globe" to Robert Browne, mentioned Browne's daughter, Jane, and his wife, Sisely, whom he appointed as executrix (Collier, *Actors*, p. 157). This may be the actor and his family. On January 4, 1610, Browne is named as one of the patentees of the Children of the Queen's Revels company at Whitefriars (Adams, *Playhouses*, p. 318). On April 11, 1612, he wrote to Edward Alleyn from Clerkenwell, requesting him to secure for the wife of one Rose, a member of Prince Henry's troupe, a position as gatherer (*H.P.*, p. 63). In 1618 he again went to Germany as the leader of a company of players. On May 28, 1618, he is noted at Nuremberg; in June and July, 1618, at Strassburg; for the autumn fair of the same year at Frankfort; and in October, 1619, at Cologne (Herz, pp. 21 ff.). He wintered at Prague, the court of the King and Queen of Bohemia. The last notices of him are his visits to Nuremberg in February and to Frankfort for the Easter fair of 1620 (Herz, p. 23). Possibly he is to be identified with a Robert Browne who was traveling as a puppet-showman in the English provinces during 1638–39 (Murray, ii. 253, 359).

BROWNE, WILLIAM.

William Browne is named in the will of Thomas Greene, July 25, 1612; at that date he was not twenty-one years of age. He was the son of Susan Baskervile, Greene's widow, formerly wife of one Browne. About 1616–17, when his wages were in arrears, he was playing with Queen Anne's company as a hired man. The occurrence of his name in the Baskervile documents sheds no further light on his theatrical career (Fleay, *Stage*, pp. 192 ff., 270 ff.); and we hear no more of him until December, 1631 (Adams, *Dram. Rec.*, p. 45), when he played Philautus, a lord enamored of himself, in Marmion's *Holland's Leaguer*, presented by "the high and mighty Prince Charles his servants, at the private house in Salisbury Court" (Marmion, *Works*, pp. 2, 6). His name appears in a warrant of May 10, 1632, appointing several of Prince Charles's men as Grooms of the Chamber (Stopes, *Jahrbuch*, xlvi. 96).

BRYAN, GEORGE.

During 1586–87 George Bryan was on the Continent. The Elsinore pay-roll shows that he was in the Danish service from June 17 to September 18, 1586. Soon he went to the Court of the Elector of Saxony at Dresden, Germany, where he held an appointment as actor-entertainer until July 17, 1587 (Cohn, *Shak. in Ger.*, pp. xxiii–xxvii; J. A. Riis, *Century Magazine*, lxi. 391; Herz, p. 3). In *2 Seven Deadly Sins*, presented by Strange's company about 1590, he played Warwick in the Induction and Damascus in "Envy" (Greg, *H.P.*, p. 152; *R.E.S.*, i. 262). He is named in the traveling license granted by the Privy Council to Strange's men on May 6, 1593 (*Eliz. Stage*, ii. 123). Subsequently he joined the Chamberlain's men, presumably when the troupe was organized in 1594, and on December 21, 1596, served as payee with Heminges for a performance at Court by this company (Steele, p. 110). His name occurs in the 1623 folio list of actors in Shakespeare's plays. He is mentioned in neither the 1598 list of players in *Every Man in his Humor* nor later records of the Chamberlain's or King's men. Possibly he left the stage to become an ordinary groom of the Chamber, which office he held in 1603 and 1611–13 (*Eliz. Stage*, ii. 304). His son, George, was baptized at St. Andrew's on February 17, 1600 (Collier, iii. 364).

BRYAN, MARY.

A joint-lessee of the Fortune playhouse, in which she obtained a whole share on March 24, 1624 (Warner, p. 247).

BUCKE, PAUL.

The registers of St. Anne's record the burial of two children of Paul Bucke, a player: a daughter, Sara, July 23, 1580, and a bastard son, Paul, July 23, 1599 (*Eliz. Stage*, ii. 304). Probably he may be identified with the Paul Bucke whose name appears for some unknown reason at the end of Wilson's *Three Ladies of London* (1584). "Paule Buckes praier for Sir Humfrey Gilberte" was entered in the Stationers' Registers on July 17, 1578 (Arber, ii. 333).

BUCKEREDGE, EDWARD.

A member of the Children of Paul's in 1594 (Hillebrand, *Child Actors*, p. 111).

BUGBY, JOHN.

Grammar Master of the Children of the Chapel Royal in 1401 (*Eliz. Stage*, ii. 24*n*.).

BUKLANK, ALEXANDER.

Alexander Buklank is named in a Protection from Arrest issued by Herbert on December 27, 1624, to twenty-one men "imployed by the Kinges Maiesties servantes in theire quallity of Playinge as Musitions and other necessary attendantes" (Adams, *Dram. Rec.*, p. 74).

BULL, JOHN.

A note by Anthony Wood suggests that John Bull joined the Chapel Royal about 1572 (*D.N.B.*, vii. 239). In January, 1586, he was sworn in as a Gentleman of the Chapel (Hillebrand, *Mod. Phil.*, xviii. 254). He later became famous as a musician.

BULL, THOMAS.

Thomas Bull was with a troupe of English players at the Danish court during 1579–80 (Bolte, *Jahrbuch*, xxiii. 99).

BURBAGE, CUTHBERT.

Cuthbert Burbage, the elder son of James Burbage, was proprietor of the Theatre and largely responsible for the erection of the Globe (Adams, *Playhouses*). He was not an actor, but during the greater part of his life was an active leader in theatrical affairs. In a deposition of February 16, 1591, he is described as servant to Walter Cope, who was gentleman usher to Lord Burghley, and as about twenty-four years of age (Wallace, *N.U.S.*, xiii. 59); hence 1566–67 may be taken as the approximate year of his birth. The subsidy rolls for 1597 give his address as Halliwell Street, where he was assessed at 10*s.* 8*d.* (Stopes, *Burbage*, p. 195). The registers of St. Leonard's, Shoreditch, record the following children: Walter, baptized June 22, 1595; James, buried July 15, 1597; and Elizabeth, baptized December 30, 1601 (*Eliz. Stage*, ii. 306). Cuthbert was buried at St. Leonard's on September 17, 1636, and his widow, Elizabeth, was buried on October 1 of the same year (Stopes, *Burbage*, p. 133). That he was in close friendship with members of the King's company is shown by the testimonies of esteem in the wills of William Sly (1608), Richard Cowley (1618), and Nicholas Tooley (1623), the last of whom died at Burbage's house.

BURBAGE, JAMES.

James Burbage, the father of Cuthbert and Richard, was the man who first realized that profit could be made from a playhouse, and had the courage to put his savings into the venture. He was about sixty years of age on February 16, 1591, and was therefore born in 1530–31 (Wallace, *N.U.S.*, xiii. 61). He was "a por man and but of small credit being by occupacion a joyner and reaping but a small lyving by the same gave it over and became a commen player in playes" (Wallace, *Ibid.*, p. 141). As an actor he was more successful, for as early as 1572 we find him at the head of Leicester's excellent troupe. As one of the Earl of Leicester's men in 1572 he signed a letter addressed to the Earl requesting his continued patronage, and he is named in the license granted to Leicester's players on May 10, 1574 (*M.S.C.*, i. 262, 348). The hostility of the authorities of London toward the drama, the unsatisfactory arrangements in the inn-yards, and the idea that "continual great profit" could be had from a building devoted solely to the drama, led Burbage in 1575 to resolve upon erecting a playhouse. He thus became a pioneer in a new field of business speculation. About this time he was not worth above a hundred marks, but fortunately had a wealthy brother-in-law, John Brayne, who was also interested in the novel undertaking as a money-making enterprise. His theatrical affairs are thereafter bound up with the history of the Theatre, which was doubtless used for dramatic performances in the autumn of 1576, and of the Second Blackfriars, which he planned during the last years of his life (Adams, *Playhouses*, pp. 27 ff., 48, 182). He seems to have settled in Shoreditch about 1576, for entries of his family then begin in the registers of St. Leonard's, where two daughters are recorded: Alice, baptized March 17, 1576, and Joane, buried August 18, 1582 (Stopes, *Burbage*, pp. 139, 140). Another daughter, Helen, was buried at St. Anne's, Blackfriars, on December 15, 1595 (*Eliz. Stage*, ii. 306). His two sons, Cuthbert and Richard, were born before 1576, and hence are not recorded in the registers of St. Leonard's. Burbage was buried at Shoreditch on February 2, 1597, and his widow, Helen, John Brayne's sister, was buried there on May 8, 1613 (Stopes, *Burbage*, p. 139). The registers generally give the family residence as Halliwell Street. At his death he left the Theatre to his elder son Cuthbert and the Blackfriars to his younger son Richard (Adams, *Playhouses*, p. 199). Cuthbert spoke of his father as "the first builder of play-howses, and was himselfe in his younger yeeres a player" (Halliwell-Phillipps, *Outlines*, i. 317). He was described as "joyner" in the lease of the Theatre site in 1576, but in later years usually as "yeoman" or "gentleman." The proceedings of the lawsuits represent him as a man of vehement temper and strong language. And in a letter of June 18, 1584, from William Fleetwood to Lord Burghley, he is referred to as "a stubburne fellow" (*Eliz. Stage*, iv. 298).

BURBAGE, RICHARD.

Richard Burbage, the younger son of James Burbage, enters theatrical annals in rather dramatic fashion in a brawl at the Theatre, which came as a result of the Chancery Order of November 13, 1590, restoring a moiety of the profits of the playhouse to John Brayne's widow. The widow, with her adjutant Robert Myles, his son Ralph, and his business partner, Nicholas Bishop, went "to the Theatre upon a play-day to stand at the door that goeth up to the galleries of the said Theatre to take and receive for the use of the said Margaret half of the money that should be given to come up into the said gallery." In the Theatre they were met by Richard Burbage, then about nineteen years old, and his mother, who "fell upon the said Robert Myles and beat him with a broom staff, calling him murdering knave." When Myles's partner, Bishop, ventured to protest at this contemptuous treatment of the order of the court, "the said Richard Burbage," so Bishop deposed, "scornfully and disdainfully playing with this deponent's nose, said that if he dealt in the matter, he would

beat him also, and did challenge the field of him at that time."
One of the actors then coming in, John Alleyn—brother of the
immortal Edward Alleyn—"found the foresaid Richard Burbage,
the youngest son of the said James Burbage, there with a broom
staff in his hand; of whom when this deponent Alleyn asked what
stir was there, he answered in laughing phrase how they came for
a moiety, 'But,' quod he (holding up the said broom staff) 'I
have, I think, delivered him a moiety with this, and sent them
packing.' " Alleyn thereupon warned the Burbages that Myles
could bring an action of assault and battery against them.
" 'Tush,' quod the father, 'no, I warrant you; but where my son
hath now beat him hence, my sons, if they will be ruled by me,
shall at their next coming provide charged pistols, with powder
and hempseed, to shoot them in the legs' " (Adams, *Playhouses*,
pp. 57ff.). Richard was probably playing with the Admiral's
men at the Theatre in November, 1590. His exact age is unknown,
but he was younger than Cuthbert, who was born about 1566–67.
Richard's histrionic career probably began as early as 1584, for
in 1619 Cuthbert spoke of his brother, "who for thirty-five yeeres
paines, cost and labour, made meanes to leave his wife and
children some estate" (Halliwell-Phillips, *Outlines*, i. 317). Because of conjectural dates and incomplete records, the early years
of his dramatic career are clouded by uncertainty. He appeared
as a messenger in *The Dead Man's Fortune*, possibly acted by the
Admiral's men at the Theatre about 1590 (*Eliz. Stage*, ii. 125,
136). In *2 Seven Deadly Sins*, presented by Lord Strange's company about 1590, he played Gorboduc in "Envy" and Tereus in
"Lechery" (Greg, *H.P.*, p. 152; *R.E.S.*, i. 262). For a time there
was an amalgamation of the troupes under the patronage of Lord
Strange and the Lord Admiral at the Rose. The playhouses were
closed on account of the plague in February, 1593, and the company at the Rose was given permission to travel in the provinces.
But Burbage's name does not appear in the traveling license.
However, when the companies separated in 1594, and the Cham-

berlain's company was formed, Burbage joined the new company and became its most prominent member. On March 15, 1595, he appears as joint-payee with William Kempe and William Shakespeare for plays given by the Chamberlain's men at Court in December, 1594 (Steele, pp. 107, 108). As a member of the Chamberlain's troupe he had parts in two of Jonson's plays: *Every Man in his Humor* (1598) and *Every Man out of his Humor* (1599). In 1603 the Chamberlain's company passed under royal patronage, and Burbage is named in the patent granted on May 19, 1603, to the King's men. He remained with this company until his death in 1619. His name appears in the 1623 folio list of actors in Shakespeare's plays; in the procession list of March 15, 1604; in the warrant of March 29, 1615, to appear before the Privy Council for playing during Lent; and in the patent of March 27, 1619, although he died on March 13. His relations with his fellows are reflected in the wills of Augustine Phillips (1605), by whom he is named as an executor; of William Shakespeare (1616), who bequeathed to him a memorial ring; and of Nicholas Tooley (1623), who left £29 13s. to Sara Burbage, daughter of his "late master." His father, who died in 1597, had left Blackfriars to him (Adams, *Playhouses*, p. 199). Of the eight shares in the Globe, after the retirement of Kempe in 1599, Richard and Cuthbert owned two shares each (Adams, *Ibid.*, pp. 240–41). The two brothers continued to live as close neighbors in Halliwell Street, Shoreditch, where their houses were robbed on the night of February 19, 1615 (Jeaffreson, *Middlesex*, ii. 108). The registers contain the following records relating to Richard's children (Stopes, *Burbage*, pp. 139–41): Julia or Juliet, baptized January 2, 1603, buried September 12, 1608; Frances, baptized September 16 and buried September 19, 1604; Anne, baptized August 8, 1607; Richard, buried August 16, 1607; Winifred, baptized October 10, 1613, buried October 14, 1616; a second Julia, baptized December 27, 1614, buried August 15, 1615; William, baptized November 6, 1616; and a posthumous Sara, baptized August 5, 1619, buried

April 29, 1625. Richard Burbage was himself buried on March 16, 1619. His nuncupative will, dated March 12, the day before his death, was witnessed by his brother, and by Nicholas Tooley and Richard Robinson of the King's men. He left his wife, Winifred, sole executrix (Collier, *Actors*, p. 45). She subsequently married Richard Robinson, and was still alive, as was Burbage's son, William, in 1635 (Adams, *Mod. Phil.*, xvii. 8; Halliwell-Phillipps, *Outlines*, i. 313, 317). According to contemporary gossip, he left "better than £300 land" to his heirs (Collier, *Actors*, p. 49). He is known from the actor-lists to have assumed parts in the following plays acted by the King's men (Murray, i. opp. 172): *Sejanus* (1603); *Volpone* (1605); *The Alchemist* (1610); *Catiline* (1611); *The Duchess of Malfi* (c. 1611), in which he acted Ferdinand; *The Captain* (c. 1612); *Valentinian* (c. 1611–14); *Bonduca* (c. 1613–14); *The Queen of Corinth* (c. 1617); *The Knight of Malta* (c. 1618); *The Mad Lover* (c. 1618); and *The Loyal Subject* (1618). On May 31, 1618, he and his fellow, John Rice, took part in a pageant on the Thames in honor of the creation of Prince Henry as Prince of Wales. He represented Amphion, "a graue and iudicious Prophet-like personage, attyred in his apte habits, euery way answerable to his state and profession, with his wreathe of Sea-shelles on his head, and his harpe hanging in fayre twine before him, personating the Genius of Wales" (Wallace, London *Times*, March 28, 1913, p. 6). In addition to the notices in the plots and actor-lists, we learn from the scattered allusions given below that Burbage played Jeronimo, Richard III, Malevole, Hamlet, Lear, and Othello. Collier (*Actors*, pp. 19 ff., 52 ff.) lists many other parts supposedly played by Burbage, but his authority is the third version of the epitaph (*vide infra*), which is now regarded as a forgery.

There have come down to us many testimonies to the histrionic skill of Burbage. His fame as an actor made him the natural rival of Edward Alleyn, and he was recognized as the most distinguished member of his company. By virtue of his wonderful power in the presentation of heroic character he won the esteem of his contemporaries and of later generations of playgoers. He and Kempe are introduced *in propria persona* into *2 Return from Parnasus* (1602), a Cambridge University play (ed. Arber, pp. 58–60):

> *Studioso.* Welcome M. *Kempe* from dancing the morrice ouer the Alpes.
>
> *Kempe.* Well you merry knaues you may come to the honor of it one day, is it not better to make a foole of the world as I haue done, then to be fooled of the world, as you schollers are? But be merry my lads, you haue happened vpon the most excellent vocation in the world for money: they come North and South to bring it to our playhouse, and for honours, who of more report, then *Dick Burbage* and *Will: Kempe*, he is not counted a Gentleman, that knowes not *Dick Burbage* and *Wil Kemp*, there's not a country wench than can dance Sellengers Round but can talke of *Dick Burbage* and *Will Kempe.* . . .
>
> *Burbage.* M. *Stud.* I pray you take some part in this booke and act it, that I may see what will fit you best, I thinke your voice would serue for *Hieronimo*, obserue how I act it and then Imitate mee.
>
> *Studioso.* Who calls *Hieronimo* from his naked bed?
>   And, etc. . . .
>
> *Burbage.* I like your face, and the proportion of your body for *Richard* the 3. I pray M. *Phil.* let me see you act a little of it.
>
> *Philomusus.* Now is the winter of our discontent,
>   Made glorious summer by the sonne of Yorke.
>
> *Burbage.* Very well I assure you, well M. *Phil.* and M. *Stud.* wee see what ability you are of: I pray walke with vs to our fellows, and weele agree presently.
>
> *Philomusus.* We will follow you straight M. *Burbage.*
>
> *Kempe.* Its good manners to follow vs, Maister *Phil.* and Maister *Otioso.*

Also in the Induction to Marston's *Malcontent* (1604), Burbage, who acted Malevole, appears with his fellows of the King's men: "*Enter D. Burbadge, H. Condell, and J. Lowin*" (Marston, *Works*, i. 201–05). A note of March 13, 1602, by John Manningham

(*Diary*, p. 39) records how Burbage's impersonation of Richard III touched the heart of a citizen's wife, and how Shakespeare anticipated him at a resultant assignation:

Vpon a tyme when Burbidge played Richard III there was a citizen grone soe farr in liking with him, that before shee went from the play shee appointed him to come that night vnto hir by the name of Richard the Third. Shakespeare ouerhearing their conclusion went before, was intertained and at his game ere Burbidge came. Then message being brought that Richard the Third was at the dore, Shakespeare caused returne to be made that William the Conqueror was before Richard the Third. Shakespeare's name William.

John Davies of Hereford mentions him with Shakespeare in *Microcosmos* (1603), among players whom he loved "for painting, poesie" (*Works*, i. 82). His acting of Hamlet is doubtless alluded to in *Ratseis Ghost* (1605) by Gamaliell Ratsey, who met a company of players at a provincial inn (Halliwell-Phillipps, *Outlines*, i. 326):

And for you, sirra, saies hee to the chiefest of them, thou hast a good presence upon a stage; methinks thou darkenest thy merite by playing in the country. Get thee to London, for, if one man were dead, they will have much neede of such a one as thou art. There would be none in my opinion fitter then thyselfe to play his parts. My conceipt is such of thee, that I durst venture all the money in my purse on thy head to play Hamlet with him for a wager.

John Davies of Hereford again couples him with Shakespeare in *Humours Heauen on Earth* (1609), among those whom Fortune "guerdond not, to their desarts" (*Works*, i. 37). Jonson compliments him in *Bartholomew Fair* (1614), V. iii. (*Works*, iv. 482):

Cokes. Which is your Burbage now?
Leatherhead. What mean you by that, sir?
Cokes. Your best actor, your Field?

The allusion to painting suggests that Burbage was the model for "An Excellent Actor" in the *Characters* (1614) by Thomas Overbury and others (Overbury, *Works*, ed. Rimbault, p. 148):

He is much affected to painting, and 'tis a question whether that make him an excellent player, or his playing an exquisite painter. . . . I observe, of all men living, a worthy actor in one kinde is the strongest motive of affection that can be: for when hee dyes, wee cannot be perswaded any man can doe his parts like him. But to conclude, I value a worthy actor by the corruption of some few of the quality, as I would doe gold in the oare; I should not mind the drosse, but the purity of the metall.

In Jonson's *Masque of Christmas* (1616), Venus, a deaf tire-woman, says (*Works*, vii. 263): "Master Burbage has been about and about with me, and so has old Master Hemings too." In a letter of July 17, 1617, John Chamberlain writes to Dudley Carleton: "The Lord Coke and his lady hath great wars at the council-table . . . she . . . declaimed bitterly against him, and so carried herself, that divers said Burbage could not have acted better" (Birch, *Court and Times of James I*, ii. 20). Shortly after Burbage's death the Earl of Pembroke wrote from Whitehall on May 20, 1619, to the Earl of Carlisle, ambassador to Germany: "My Lord Lenox made a great supper to the French Ambassador this night here and even now all the Company are at the play, which I being tender-harted could not endure to see so soone after the loss of my old acquaintance Burbadg" (Scott, *Athenæum*, January 21, 1882, p. 103). His death on March 13, 1619, called forth an outburst of eulogy and sorrow that surpassed the grief for Queen Anne, whose death had occurred on March 2. The city and the stage were shrouded in gloom. Several elegies and epitaphs upon Burbage are preserved. The shortest is merely "Exit Burbidge," printed 1674 in Camden's *Remains Concerning Britain* (edit. 1870, p. 433). Another is by Middleton (*Works*, vii. 413):

On the death of that great master in his art and quality,
painting and playing, R. Burbage

Astronomers and star-gazers this year
Write but of four eclipses; five appear,
Death interposing Burbage; and their staying
Hath made a visible eclipse of playing.

73

A third elegy (having eighty-two, eighty-six, or one hundred
and twenty-four lines, according to the particular version) has
been the subject of much controversy. Of the three versions, the
first two are generally taken to be genuine, the four extra lines
of the second having probably been omitted from the first only
by accident. The third version of one hundred and twenty-four
lines is now thought to be spurious, for the interpolation at-
tributes to Burbage parts in plays which belonged to other companies than the King's. I cite below the version of eighty-six
lines (Ingleby, "The Elegy on Burbadge," in *Shakespeare, the
Man and the Book*, ii. 180):

*A Funerall Elegye on ye Death of the famous Actor Richard Burbedg
who dyed on Saturday in Lent the 13 of March 1618*

> Some skilful Limner helpe me, if not soe
> Some sadd Tragedian helpe t'expres my woe
> But oh he's gone, that could both best; both Lime
> And Act my greife; and tis for only him
> That I inuoake this strange Assistance to itt
> And on the point inuoake himselfe to doe itt,
> For none butt Tully, Tullyes praise can tell,
> And as he could, no man could act soe well.
> This part of sorrow for him, no man drawe,
> Soe trewly to the life, this Mapp of woee
> That greifes trew picture, which his loss hath bred
> Hee's gone and with him what a world are dead.
> Which he reuiu'd, to be reuiued soe,
> No more young Hamlett, ould Heironymoe
> Kind Leer, the Greued Moore, and more beside,
> That liued in him; have now for ever dy'de,
> Oft haue I seene him, leap into the Graue
> Suiting the person, which he seem'd to haue
> Of a sadd Louer, with soe true an Eye
> That theer I would haue sworne, he meant to dye,
> Oft haue I seene him, play this part in ieast,
> Soe liuly, that Spectators, and the rest
> Of his sad Crew, whilst he but seem'd to bleed,
> Amazed, thought euen then hee dyed in deed,

A DICTIONARY OF ACTORS

O lett not me be checkt, and I shall sweare
Euen yett, it is a false report I heare,
And thinke that he, that did soe truly faine
Is still but Dead in ieast, to liue againe,
But now this part, he Acts, not playes, tis knowne
Other he plaide, but Acted hath his owne
Englands great Roscious, for what Roscious,
Was unto Roome, that Burbadg was to us.
How did his speech become him, and his pace,
Suite with his speech, and euery action grace
Them both alike, whilst not a woord did fall,
Without just weight, to ballast itt with all,
Hadst thou but spoake to death, and us'd thy power
Of thy Inchaunting toung, att that first hower
Of his assault, he had Lett fall his Dart
And quite been Charmed, by thy all Charming Art.
This he well knew, and to preuent this wronge
He therefore first made seisure on his tounge,
Then on the rest, 'twas easy by degrees
The slender Iuy tops the smallest trees,
Poets whose glory whilome twas to heare
Your lines so well exprest, henceforth forbeare,
And write no more, or if you doe let 't bee
In Commike sceans, since Tragick parts you see,
Dy all with him; nay rather sluce your eyes
And hence forth write nought els but Tragedyes,
Or Dirges, or sad Ellegies or those
Mournfull Laments that nott accord with prose,
Blurr all your Leaus with blotts, that all you writt
May be but one sadd black, and open it
Draw Marble lines that may outlast ye sunn
And stand like Trophyes, when the world is done
Turne all your inke to blood, your pens to speares
To pearce and wound the hearers harts and Eares,
Enrag'd, write stabbing Lines that euery woord
May be as apt for murther as a swoord
That no man may suruiue after this fact
Of ruthless death, eyther to heare or Act
And you his sad Compannions to whome Lent
Becomes more Lenton by this Accident,
Hence forth your wauing flagg, no more hang out

Play now no more att all, when round aboute
Wee looke and miss the Atlas of your spheare
What comfort haue wee (thinke you) to bee theer
And how can you delight in playing, when
Such mourning soe affecteth other men,
Or if you will still putt 't out lett it weere
No more light cullors, but death liuery there
Hang all your house with black, the Ewe it bears
With Iseckls of euer melting teares,
And if you euer chance to play agen
May nought but Tragedyes afflict your sceane
And thou deare Earth that must enshrine that dust
By Heauen now committed to thy trust
Keepe itt as pretious as ye richest Mine
That Lyes intomb'd, in that rich womb of thine,
That after times may know that much lou'd mould
From other dust, and cherrish it as gould,
On it be laide some soft but lasting stone
With this short Epitaph endorst thereon
 That euery Eye may reade, and reading weepe
 Tis Englands Roscious, Burbadg that I keepe.

In Sloane MS. 1786 appears the following epitaph (Stopes, *Burbage*, p. 118):

An epitaph upon Mr. Richard Burbage, the player

This Life's a play, sceaned out by Nature's Arte,
Where every man hath his allotted parte.
This man hath now (as many men can tell)
Ended his part, and he hath acted well
The Play now ended, think his grave to be
The retiring house of his sad Tragedie,
Where to give his fame this, be not afraid,
Here lies the best Tragedian ever played.

Burbage was famous not only as an actor but as a painter. Besides the above scattered allusions to his skill in painting, the accounts of the Earl of Rutland for the tilt of 1613 contain the entry: "31 Martii, to Mr. Shakespeare in gold about my Lorde's impreso, 44*s*.; to Richard Burbage for paynting and making yt, in gold 44*s*.''; and those for the tilt of 1616 record: "25 March. Paid given Richard Burbidg for my Lorde's shelde and for the embleance, £4 18*s*." (*Rutland MSS.*, iv. 494, 508). There is in the gallery at Dulwich a picture presented by William Cartwright, which is described as "A woman's head, on a board, done by 'Mr Burbige, ye actor'; in an old gilt frame" (Warner, p. 205). In the same collection there is also a portrait of Burbage; " 'Mr Burbig' his head; in a gilt frame; a small closet piece" (Warner, p. 205; reproduced in Adams, *Playhouses*, opp. p. 234). Evidence of his fame as Richard III is given in Richard Corbet's *Iter Boreale* (1647), where an old "host," described as "full of ale and history," is acting as a guide to visitors on the battlefield of Bosworth (Chalmers, *English Poets*, v. 580):

> Why, he could tell
> The inch where Richmond stood, where Richard fell:
> Besides what of his knowledge he could say,
> He had authenticke notice from the play;
> Which I might guesse, by 's mustring up the ghost,
> And policyes, not incident to hosts;
> But chiefly by that one perspicuous thing,
> Where he mistooke a player for a king.
> For when he would have sayd, "King Richard dyed,
> And call'd—A horse! a horse!"—he, "Burbidge" cry'de.

Richard Baker praises him in his *Theatrum Redivivum* (1622), p. 34: "And what scurrility was ever heard to come from the best *Actours* of our Time, *Allen*, and *Bourbidge*? yet, what Plays were ever so pleasing, as where their Parts had the greatest part?" (*Notes and Queries*, 1880, i. 113). Baker also mentions him in his *Chronicle* (edit. 1674, p. 500): "*Richard Bourbidge* and *Edward Allen*, two such Actors as no age must ever look to see the like." Richard Flecknoe in his *Discourse of the English Stage* (1664) writes (Spingarn, *Critical Essays of the Seventeenth Century*, ii. 94):

It was the happiness of the Actors of those Times to have such Poets as these to instruct them and write for them; and no less of those Poets, to have such docile and excellent Actors to Act their Playes, as a *Field* and *Burbidge*, of whom we may say that he was a delightful *Proteus*, so wholly transforming himself into his Part, and putting off himself with his Cloathes, as he never (not so much as in the Tyring-house) assum'd himself again until the Play was done; there being as much difference betwixt him and one of our common Actors, as between a Ballad-singer who onely mouths it, and an excellent singer, who knows all his Graces, and can artfully vary and modulate his Voice, even to know how much breath he is to give to every syllable. He had all the parts of an excellent Orator, animating his words with speaking, and Speech with Action; his Auditors being never more delighted then when he spake, nor more sorry then when he held his peace; yet even then he was an excellent Actor still, never falling in his Part when he had done speaking, but with his looks and gestures maintaining it still unto the heighth, he imagining *Age quod agis* onely spoke to him: so as those who call him a Player do him wrong, no man being less idle then he was whose whole life is nothing else but action; with only this difference from other mens, that as what is but a Play to them is his Business, so their business is but a play to him.

In Flecknoe's *Euterpe Restored* (1672) we find (Collier, iii. 279):

The Praises of Richard Burbage

Who did appear so gracefully on the stage,
He was the admir'd example of the age,
And so observed all your dramatic laws,
He ne'er went off the stage but with applause;
Who his spectators and his auditors
Led in such silent chains of eyes and ears,
As none, whilst he on the stage his part did play,
Had power to speak, or look another way.
Who a delightful Proteus was, and could
Transform himself into what shape he would;
And of an excellent orator had all,
In voice and gesture, we delightful call:
Who was the soul of the stage; and we may say
'Twas only he who gave life unto a play;
Which was but dead, as 'twas by the author writ,
Till he by action animated it:

And finally he did on the stage appear
Beauty to the eye, and music to the ear.
Such even the nicest critics must allow
Burbage was once; and such Charles Hart is now.

A more recent tribute, "When Burbadge Played," is given by
Austin Dobson in his *Collected Poems* (1898).

BURDE, JOHN.

A member of the Children of Paul's in 1554 (Hillebrand, *Child
Actors*, p. 110).

BURDE, SIMON.

A member of the Children of Paul's in 1554 (Hillebrand, *Child
Actors*, p. 110).

BURGES, ROBERT.

A player who was buried at St. Bennet's, Gracechurch, on
April 14, 1559 (*Eliz. Stage*, ii. 310).

BURNETT, HENRY.

A member of the Children of Paul's in 1607 (Hillebrand, *Child
Actors*, p. 112).

BURT, NICHOLAS.

From Wright's *Historia Histrionica* (1699) we learn that
Nicholas Burt "was a boy, first under Shank at the Blackfriars,
then under Beeston at the Cockpit," where he "used to play the
principal women's parts, in particular Clariana in *Love's Cruelty*"
(Hazlitt's *Dodsley*, xv. 404, 409-10). The date at which he joined
the King's men at Blackfriars is unknown, but John Shank died
in January, 1636. The King and Queen's company, popularly
known as Beeston's Boys, was organized early in 1637, and occupied the Cockpit. Burt possibly joined the new company in
1637. At the closing of the playhouses in 1642 and the beginning
of the Civil War, he enlisted in the King's army as cornet in
Prince Rupert's regiment. In the winter of 1648 a number of

players who survived the war formed a company and ventured to act cautiously at the Cockpit. During a presentation of *Rollo, or The Bloody Brother*, in which Burt assumed the part of Latorch, a group of soldiers plundered the playhouse and routed the players. Burt continued his theatrical career at the Cockpit after the Restoration. He signed the Submission of Players to Herbert's Authority on August 14, 1660, and the Petition of the Cockpit Players on October 13 of the same year; and he is named in the Articles of Agreement between Herbert and Killigrew on June 4, 1662 (Adams, *Dram. Rec.*, pp. 85, 94, 96, 113–14). Davies (*Dram. Misc.*, i. 124) writes: "After the Restoration, Hart represented Hotspur, Burt the Prince of Wales, and Wintershul the King [in *1 Henry IV*]. The excellency of Hart is universally acknowledged; of Burt we can only transcribe what Downes has recorded. He ranks him in the list of good actors, with Shotterel and Cartwright, but without any discriminating marks. That he was not a man of superior merit we may gather from his being obliged to resign the part of Othello to Hart, who had formerly acted Cassio when Burt played the principal character." Samuel Pepys gives several notices of Burt. On October 11, 1660, he saw him as Othello (*Diary*, i. 241): "To the Cockpit to see *The Moore of Venice*, which was well done. Burt acted the Moore." On September 24, 1662, Pepys went "to Mr. Wotton, the shoemaker's, and there bought a pair of boots, cost me 30s., and he told me how Bird ["Lord Braybrooke says that this was a mistake for Nicholas Burt" (*Diary*, ii. 323n.)] hath lately broke his leg, while he was fencing in Aglaura, upon the stage" (*Diary*, ii. 323). On December 11, 1667, Pepys was at Westminster Hall, where he "met Rolt and Sir John Chichly, and Harris, the player, and there we talked of many things, and particularly of *Catiline*, which is to be suddenly acted at the King's house; and they all agree that it cannot be well done at that house, there not being good actors enow: and Burt acts Cicero, which they all conclude he will not be able to do well" (*Diary*, vii. 221). Again on February 6, 1669, Pepys saw Burt in the part of Othello, this time without being so well pleased as formerly: "After dinner to the King's playhouse, and there . . . did see *The Moor of Venice:* but ill acted in most parts; Mohun, which did a little surprise me, not acting Iago's part by much so well as Clun used to do; nor another Hart's which was Cassio's; nor, indeed, Burt doing the Moor's so well as I once thought he did" (*Diary*, viii. 206-07). His Majesty's Company of Comedians opened their new playhouse, the Theatre Royal, on May 7, 1663 (Pepys, *Diary*, iii. 107), under the management of Thomas Killigrew. As a member of this organization Burt had the following parts (Downes, *Ros. Ang.*, 2 ff.): Seleucus in *The Humorous Lieutenant*; Don John Decastrio in *Rule a Wife, and have a Wife*; Corvino in *The Fox*; Cleremont in *The Silent Woman*; Surly in *The Alchemist*; Tygranes in *King and no King*; La Torch in *Rollo, Duke of Normandy*; Elder Loveless in *The Scornful Lady*; Charles in *The Elder Brother*; The Moor in *The Moor of Venice*; the Prince in *King Henry the Fourth*; Lysimantes in *The Maiden Queen*; Don Lopez in *The Mock Astrologer*; Vasquez in *The Indian Emperour*; Camillo in *The Assignation, or Love in a Nunnery*; Palamede in *Marriage Alamode*; Count Guesselin in *The Black Prince*; and Maherbal, in *Sophonisba, or Hannibal's Overthrow*.

BURTON, ANTHONY.

As a member of Ellis Guest's company under license of June 7, 1628, Anthony Burton is recorded at Norwich on July 2 of the same year (Murray, ii. 103).

BYLAND, AMBROSE.

Ambrose Byland is named in a Protection from Arrest issued by Herbert on December 27, 1624, to twenty-one men "imployed by the Kinges Maiesties servantes in theire quallity of Playinge as Musitions and other necessary attendantes" (Adams, *Dram. Rec.*, p. 74).

CANDLER, JAMES.

In 1569 James Candler was the leader of a company at Ipswich, as shown by an entry in the town records: "Paid to Jemes Candler and his company for playing in the Halle, 10s." (*Hist. MSS. Comm.*, ix. 1. p. 249).

CANE, ANDREW.

Andrew Cane is named in the 1622 Herbert lists of both the Palsgrave's and the Lady Elizabeth's players (Adams, *Dram. Rec.*, p. 63). In explanation of the apparently dual connection it is suggested that when the new Fortune was building in 1622, and the Palsgrave's men were preparing to open this playhouse, Cane joined them from the Lady Elizabeth's men (Murray, i. 215–16). Of Cane between 1622 and 1631 nothing is known. He may have remained with the Palsgrave's company until December, 1631, when this troupe seems to have passed under the patronage of the young Prince Charles. His name appears in the patent of December 7, 1631, granted to Prince Charles's company (Murray, ii. 358). During the same month (Adams, *Dram. Rec.*, p. 45) he played Trimalchio, a humorous gallant, in Marmion's *Holland's Leaguer*, presented by "the high and mighty Prince Charles his servants, at the private house in Salisbury Court" (Marmion, *Works*, pp. 2, 6). His name appears in a warrant of May 10, 1632, appointing several of Prince Charles's men as Grooms of the Chamber (Stopes, *Jahrbuch*, xlvi. 96). On December 10, 1635, and May 4, 1640, he served as joint-payee for performances at Court by Prince Charles's players (Steele, pp. 250, 275). On September 29, 1639, the Prince's men were summoned to appear for acting at the Red Bull a "scandalous and libellous play," *The Whore in Grain*, new vamped, in which Cane had spoken the words that libeled the alderman (Chalmers, *Apology*, p. 504). That Cane attained great popularity as a comedian is shown in contemporary and later writings. He is one of the speakers in *The Stage-Players Complaint, in a pleasant Dialogue be-*

tween Cane of the Fortune and Reed of the Friers, deploring their sad and solitary conditions for want of Imployment, in this heavie and Contagious time of the Plague in London (1641). In *The Complaint*, Cane and Reed are brought together in the street conversing about their misfortunes, and the dialogue commences thus:

Cane. Stay, Reed. Whither away so speedily? What, you goe as if you meant to leape over the Moon now! What's the matter?
Reede. The matter is plain enough. You incuse me of my nimble feet, but I thinke your tongue runnes a little faster and you contend as much to out-strip facetious Mercury in your tongue, as lame Vulcan in my feete.

In the next speeches, and for the rest of the dialogue, Cane is called *Quick* in the prefixes, and Reed, *Light*, which probably give the appellations by which they were then popularly known (Hazlitt, *Eng. Dr. & Stage*, p. 253). In *A Key to the Cabinet of the Parliament* (1648), Cane is mentioned with two other celebrated players: "We need not any more stage-players: we thank them [the Puritans] for suppressing them: they save us money; for I'll undertake we can laugh as heartily at Foxley, Peters, and others of their godly ministers, as ever we did at Cane at the Red Bull, Tom Pollard in *The Humorous Lieutenant*, Robins in *The Changling*, or any humourist of them all" (Collier, ii. 38). Edmund Gayton alludes to him in his *Pleasant Notes upon Don Quixot* (1654), p. 271: "It was not then the most mimicall nor fighting man, *Fowler*, nor *Andrew Cane* could pacifie; Prologues nor Epilogues would prevaile; the Devill and the fool were quite out of favour." His reputation long survived him, for he is mentioned as late as 1673, in a tract by Henry Chapman on the Bath waters: "Without which a pamphlet now a days finds as small acceptance, as a Comedy did formerly at the Fortune Play-house without a Jig of Andrew Keins into the bargain" (Collier, *Bibl. Acc.*, iv. 93). Fleay (*Drama*, i. 295-96) suggests that there is an allusion to Cane as "Andrew, our elder journeyman," in Heywood's *Fair*

Maid of the West, Part I, V. i. 112, acted by Queen Henrietta's men about 1630:

> It is not now as when Andrea liv'd,
> Or rather Andrew, our elder journeyman.

The identification is doubtful, for Cane was certainly not dead in 1630, as the above lines seem to imply. Besides, Andrew was a common name; and Andrew Pennycuicke was probably a member of the Queen's troupe about this time. The name Andrew Keyne occurs several times in the Clerkenwell burial registers of 1639 and 1640 (Hovenden, iv. 240, 241). The burials were of "a boy from Andrew Keyne's," on October 21, 1639; three servants "to Andrew Keyne," in November and December, 1639; and "Marye d. of Andrew Keyne," on January 4, 1640. A recent book by Leslie Hotson (*The Commonwealth and Restoration Stage*, 1928, pp. 7, 46, 51–53) gives additional information concerning the later life of Cane. After the wars he was a goldsmith, and was known as Decayne or De Caine. On December 12, 1642, "Cain the Clown at the Bull, and others came in great multitude, and filled the Hall and Yard," while the mayor and council were in meeting at the Guildhall. In June, 1644, he is referred to in *Mercurius Britanicus*, the Parliament newsbook, as engraver of the dies for the debased coinage of the Royalist Army: "I could wish that the Coine for his Majesties souldiers might not come too fast that way to this City, which is graved in the West, by the *quondam* foole of the Red Bull, now stampt for a knave in brasse, I mean farthing tokens, made now in the West." His company continued to give surreptitions performances at the Red Bull. In January, 1650, the players were surprised by soldiers, who took several of the principal actors to prison. *Mercurius Pragmaticus (for King Charles II)* refers to this encounter: "*Andr. Cane* is out of date and all other his complices; alas poor players they are acting their parts in prison, for their presumptions to break a Parliament Crack." On December 9, 1652, he signed a goldsmiths's petition to Parliament. In 1654 he was concerned in a Chancery suit against William Wintershall, the actor.

CAREY, GILES.

As a member of the Children of the Queen's Revels company, Giles Carey (or Gary) appears in the actor-list affixed to Jonson's *Epicoene*, which, according to the folio of 1616, was "Acted in the yeere 1609." He belonged to the Lady Elizabeth's troupe by August 29, 1611, on which date he and his fellow-actors gave Philip Henslowe a bond of £500 to perform "certen articles" of agreement (*H.P.*, pp. 18, 111). The 1679 folio of Beaumont and Fletcher names Carey as one of the "principal actors" in *The Coxcomb*, which may have been acted by the Lady Elizabeth's men about 1613 (*Eliz. Stage*, ii. 251).

CARLETON, NICHOLAS.

A member of the Children of Paul's at some date before 1582. He appears as a legatee in the will of Sebastian Westcott, dated April 3, 1582, where he is named among the "sometimes children of the said almenerey," i.e. St. Paul's (*Eliz. Stage*, ii. 15n.).

CARPENTER, WILLIAM.

As a member of the Lady Elizabeth's company, on August 29, 1611, William Carpenter with his fellow-actors gave Philip Henslowe a bond of £500 to perform "certen articles" of agreement (*H.P.*, pp. 18, 111). Subsequently he joined Prince Charles's troupe, for early in 1619, as servant to the Prince, he appeared as Time in Middleton's *Masque of Heroes* (*Works*, vii. 200). With Prince Charles's men he took part in King James's funeral procession on May 7, 1625 (Murray, i. 161, 237). In 1623 a William Carpenter, possibly the actor, was a porter at the Marshalsea (Wallace, *Jahrbuch*, xlvi. 347). His name is mentioned in the suit growing out of the performance at the Red Bull in 1624 of Dekker's *Keep the Widow Waking* (Sisson, *The Library*, N.S., 1927, viii, 235–36).

CARR, JOHN.

On September 23, 1631, John Carr is mentioned at Coventry with the Children of the King's Revels (Murray, ii. 13, 251).

CARTWRIGHT, WILLIAM, SENIOR.

On April 21, 1598, William Cartwright, senior, was associated with Richard Jones in borrowing 10s. from Philip Henslowe (*H.D.*, i. 38). At this time Jones was an Admiral's man, and Cartwright was probably a hired man of the same company. With the Admiral's troupe he appeared in *Fortune's Tennis*, *c.* 1597–98; as a Moor and as Pisano in *The Battle of Alcazar*, *c.* 1600–01; and as a nobleman, an attendant, a hostage, a captain, and a Bohar, in *1 Tamar Cam*, 1602 (Greg, *H.P.*, pp. 153, 154; *R.E.S.*, i. 270; Chambers, *Eliz. Stage*, ii. 175–76). In 1603 the Admiral's men were taken into the service of Prince Henry; but in their patent of 1606, Cartwright's name does not appear. On the death of Prince Henry the company came under the patronage of the Palsgrave, and Cartwright is named in the license of January 11, 1613, granted to the Palsgrave's men (*Eliz. Stage*, ii. 190). When the company leased the Fortune from Edward Alleyn on October 31, 1618, Cartwright appeared as one of the lessees (*H.P.*, p. 27). He is mentioned as dining with Alleyn on various occasions between March 22, 1617, and August 18, 1622. On the latter date he was still a member of the Palsgrave's company at the Fortune (Young, ii. 73, 148, 174, 204, 247). In 1623 he lived at the upper end of White Cross Street (Wallace, *Jahrbuch*, xlvi. 347). On April 30, 1624, he and others of the Palsgrave's men entered into a bond to Richard Gunnell, manager of the company (Hotson, pp. 52–53). There seems to be no further record of him until the Norwich list of March 10, 1635, when he visited the town as a member of, presumably, the King's Revels company (Murray, i. 279–80); he may have joined that troupe on its organization in 1629 at Salisbury Court (Adams, *Playhouses*, p. 374). With the King's Revels he played Claudius, the Emperor, in Richard's *Messallina*, *the*

Roman Empress, printed in 1640. On May 12, 1636, Herbert received £1 from "ould Cartwright for allowing the [Fortune] company to add scenes to an ould play, and to give it out for a new one" (Adams, *Dram. Rec.*, p. 37). There is in the Dulwich gallery a picture of "Old Mr. Cartwright, actor; in a gilt frame" (Warner, p. 207). The register of St. Giles's, Cripplegate, records the burial of a William Cartwright in 1650 (Malcolm, *Lond. Rediv.*, iii. 304).

CARTWRIGHT, WILLIAM, JUNIOR.

William Cartwright, junior, is generally thought to be the son of William Cartwright, senior. The Norwich list of March 10, 1635, shows that he and his father were associated in what was apparently the King's Revels company (Murray, i. 279–80). We have the authority of Wright in *Historia Histrionica* (1699) for the statement that the younger Cartwright acted at Salisbury Court (Hazlitt's *Dodsley*, xv. 404). He was probably a member of Queen Henrietta's troupe at Salisbury Court from 1637 to the closing of the playhouses in 1642, for the Queen's men and the King's Revels company were united at this playhouse about October, 1637 (cf. Adams, *Dram. Rec.*, p. 66). During the period of the Commonwealth he became a bookseller and publisher in Turnstile Alley, and among the works issued by him was a new edition of Heywood's *Apology for Actors*, under the title of *The Actor's Vindication* (c. 1658). After the Restoration he joined the company formed out of "the scattered remnants" of players belonging to several of the older houses during the reign of Charles I. He is named in the Petition of the Cockpit Players on October 13, 1660, and in the Articles of Agreement between Herbert and Killigrew on June 4, 1662 (Adams, *Dram. Rec.*, pp. 94, 113–14). His Majesty's Company of Comedians opened their new playhouse, the Theatre Royal, on May 7, 1663 (Pepys, *Diary*, iii. 107), under the management of Thomas Killigrew. As a member of this organization Cartwright played the following

parts (Downes, *Ros. Ang.*, pp. 2 ff.): Corbachio in *The Fox*;
Morose in *The Silent Woman*; Sir Epicure Mammon in *The Al-
chemist*; Lygones in *King and no King*; Brabantio in *The Moor of
Venice*; Falstaff in *King Henry the Fourth*; the Priest in *The Indian
Emperor*; Major Oldfox in *The Plain Dealer*; Apollonius in *Tyrannick Love*; Mario in *The Assignation, or Love in a Nunnery*; John in
The Destruction of Jerusalem; Hermogenes in *Marriage Alamode*;
Lord Latimer in *The Black Prince*; and Abenamar, in *The Conquest
of Granada*. On November 2, 1667, Pepys say him as Falstaff:
"After dinner my wife and Willett and I to the King's playhouse,
and there saw *Henry the Fourth*; and contrary to expectation, was
pleased in nothing more than in Cartwright's speaking of Falstaff's speech about 'What is Honour?' " (*Diary*, vii. 172).
Sometime during his career he seems to have played in Shirley's
Sisters, for "Mr. Cartrite" is named in the prompter's copy of this
play (Shirley, *Works*, v. 354). Downes ranks him in the list of
good actors with Nicholas Burt and Robert Shatterell, but with
no distinguishing comment (*Ros. Ang.*, p. 17). In 1682 there was
an amalgamation of the King's company and the Duke of York's
servants, at Drury Lane, under the leadership of Thomas Betterton. Cartwright is named in the list of the combined companies.
After the fusion he is known to have acted Cacafogo in *Rule a
Wife, and have a Wife* (Downes, *Ros. Ang.*, p. 39). He died in
December, 1687, and left his books, pictures, various household
articles, and a sum of money to Dulwich College (Warner, pp.
154, 204, 206, 207, 208). A catalogue of this collection of pictures,
apparently in Cartwright's own handwriting, is preserved, in
which there is listed a portrait of "Young Mr. Cartwright,
actor; in a gilt frame." This picture being lost, there is no way
of judging whether the portrait was that of the William Cartwright who owned the collection, and whose portrait is extant,
with the description: "My picture in a black dress, with a great
dog." Pictures of his wives are also in the Dulwich gallery: "My
first wife's picture like a shepherdess, on 3 quarters cloth; in a

gilt frame"; and "My last wife's picture, with a black veil on her head; in a gilt frame, 3 quarters cloth." It is likely that the British Museum Egerton MS. 1994 originally belonged to Cartwright, and was a part of his bequest to Dulwich College (Boas, *Library*, 1917, viii. 226, 237–38). The careers of the two Cartwrights cover almost a century of stage history, and form a link between Edward Alleyn of the Fortune and Thomas Betterton of Drury Lane.

CARVER, WILLIAM.

William Carver is named in a Protection from Arrest issued by Herbert on December 27, 1624, to twenty-one men "imployed by the Kinges Maiesties servantes in theire quallity of Playinge as Musitions and other necessary attendantes" (Adams, *Dram. Rec.*, p. 74).

CASTLE, THOMAS.

A player, whose son, Nicholas, and daughter, Hester, were baptized at St. Giles's on October 9, 1608, and April 15, 1610, respectively (*Eliz. Stage*, ii. 310).

CATTANES.

On January 24, 1602–03, Cattanes authorized a payment on behalf of Worcester's men (*H.D.*, i. 188).

CAVALLERIZZO, CLAUDIO.

Claudio Cavallerizzo is mentioned, in an undated letter from Petruccio Ubaldini to Queen Elizabeth, as concerned with Ferrabosco in the presentation of an Italian comedy (*M.S.C.*, ii. 147). He may have been a member of the Italian company of players ("Alfruso Ferrabolle and the rest of the Italian players") who received payment for a play presented at Court on February 27, 1576 (Steele, p. 59).

CHAMBERS, WILLIAM.

William Chambers is named in a Protection from Arrest issued by Herbert on December 27, 1624, to twenty-one men "imployed by the Kinges Maiesties servantes in theire quallity of Playinge as Musitions and other necessary attendantes" (Adams, *Dram. Rec.*, p. 74).

CHAPPELL, JOHN.

A member of the Chapel Royal about 1600–01. In Henry Clifton's complaint to the Star Chamber on December 15, 1601, as to how boys were pressed for the Chapel at Blackfriars, John Chappell is named as one so taken, and is described as "a gramer schole scholler of one Mr. Spykes schole neere Criplegate, London" (Wallace, *Blackfriars*, p. 80).

CHESSON, THOMAS.

Thomas Chesson may have been with the Earl of Oxford's plavers in 1580. On April 13, 1580, the Privy Council committed Robert Leveson and Lawrence Dutton, servants of the Earl of Oxford, to the Marshalsea for taking part in an affray with the gentlemen of the Inns of Court. On May 26 the matter was referred to three judges for examination. Thomas Chesson, "sometime servant to the Earl of Oxford," seems also to have been concerned, for on July 18 he was released on bond from the prison of the Gatehouse (Dasent, xi. 445; xii. 37, 112).

CHOFE, ROBERT.

A member of the Children of Paul's in 1554 (Hillebrand, *Child Actors*, p. 110).

CLARK, HUGH.

Hugh Clark was probably with Queen Henrietta's men at the Cockpit in Drury Lane from their formation in 1625 to their dissolution in 1637. As a member of this company he acted in the following plays (Murray, i. opp. 266): Gratiana, Sir Belfare's daughter, in Shirley's *Wedding* (c. 1626); Hubert in Davenport's *King John and Matilda* (c. 1629); Besse Bridges, the fair maid of the West, in Heywood's *Fair Maid of the West*, Part I (c. 1630; ed.

Bates, p. 145); and two parts, Nuntius and Syphax, in Nabbes's *Hannibal and Scipio* (1635). When Queen Henrietta's company disbanded in 1637 some of the members united with the Revels company at Salisbury Court, and others joined Beeston's Boys at the Cockpit; but Clark is not known to have joined either of these troupes. By 1641 he was a King's man, his name appearing in a warrant of January 22 of that year (Stopes, *Jahrbuch*, xlvi. 103). For a revival of Beaumont and Fletcher's *Custom of the Country* by the King's men, a special Prologue was written (which appears in only the 1647 folio), labeled "For my Sonne Clarke" (*Works*, i. 387, 456), meaning apparently that Clark was the "son" or poetic disciple of the unknown author of the Prologue. His name is appended to the dedicatory epistle of the 1647 folio edition of Beaumont and Fletcher's plays, published by a group of the King's players (*Works*, i. p. x). On January 28, 1648, he and other members of the King's company gave a bond to pay off an old Blackfriars debt to Michael Bowyer's heirs (Hotson, pp. 31–34). A Hugh Clark was buried at St. James, Clerkenwell, on October 7, 1653 (Hovenden, iv. 296).

CLARK, SILL.

Apparently an actor or stage-attendant mentioned in a stage-direction of *The Blind-Beggar of Bednal-Green*, written by John Day and Henry Chettle about 1600 and printed in 1659 as "divers times publickly acted by the Princes Servants." The stage-direction seemingly means that Sill Clark played Captain Westford: "Enter old Playnsey, old Strowd, and Captain Westford, Sill Clark" (Bullen's edit., p. 96). The Prince's men of the title-page are probably the later Prince Charles's servants (1631–41), and Clark may have been a minor actor in that troupe.

CLARKE, JOHN.

John Clarke, a former child of the Chapel Royal, was sworn in as a Gentleman of the Chapel on August 24, 1608 (Hillebrand, *Mod. Phil.*, xviii. 257).

CLARKE, MARY.

Mary Clarke, *alias* Wood, was joint-legatee with Thomas Bromley in the will, dated July 22, 1603, of Thomas Pope, who left to them his share in the Globe playhouse. Subsequently she appears to have married John Edmonds (or Edmans), a member of Queen Anne's company (Adams, *Mod. Phil.*, xvii. 3 ff.).

CLARKE, ROBERT.

A player, whose son, Ezekiel, was buried at St. Giles's on November 7, 1617 (*Eliz. Stage*, ii. 310). He is probably to be identified with the person of the same name mentioned in a Protection from Arrest issued by Herbert on December 27, 1624, to twenty-one men "imployed by the Kinges Maiesties servantes in theire quallity of Playinge as Musitions and other necessary attendantes" (Adams, *Dram. Rec.*, p. 74).

CLARKE, THOMAS.

As one of the Earl of Leicester's men in 1572 Thomas Clarke signed a letter addressed to the Earl requesting his continued patronage (*M.S.C.*, i. 348).

CLAY, HENRY.

Henry Clay is named in a Protection from Arrest issued by Herbert on December 27, 1624, to twenty-one men "imployed by the Kinges Maiesties servantes in theire quallity of Playinge as Musitions and other necessary attendantes" (Adams, *Dram. Rec.*, p. 74). The register of St. Giles's, Cripplegate, records the burial of a daughter of a Henry Cley in 1626 (Malcolm, *Lond. Rediv.*, iii. 304).

CLAY, NATHANIEL.

About April, 1618, Nathaniel Clay is named as a Queen Anne's man in a Letter of Assistance granting him, Martin Slater, and John Edmonds permission to play as "her Maiesties servants of her Royall Chamber of Bristol." Nothing further is heard of

Clay until December 30, 1629, when he is mentioned in a license issued to a group of players under the leadership of Robert Kimpton, presumably the Children of the King's Revels. They presented the license at Reading soon afterwards (Murray, ii. 5 ff., 13, 386).

CLAYTONE, RICHARD.

In 1623 Richard Claytone was an actor at the Fortune, and lived "in Goulding Lane." With Richard Grace, William Stratford, and Abraham Pedle, "all Actors at the fortune neere Golding lane," he was summoned to appear at court to answer a Bill of Complaint made by Gervase Markham (Wallace, *Jahrbuch*, xlvi. 348, 350). Since in 1623 the Fortune was occupied by the Palsgrave's men, Claytone doubtless belonged to that company.

CLEMENT, WILLIAM.

A London player in 1550, named in an order demanding that all plays be licensed by the King or his Council (Harrison, *England*, iv. 314-15).

CLEY, HENRY.

See Henry Clay.

CLIFTON, THOMAS.

On December 13, 1600, James Robinson, acting as deputy under the commission of Nathaniel Giles, impressed and carried off to the Blackfriars playhouse Thomas the only son and heir of Henry Clifton, a gentleman of some importance from Norfolk, who was temporarily residing in London for the purpose of educating the boy. Clifton says in his complaint that Giles, Evans, and their confederates, "well knowing that your subject's said son had no manner of sight in song, nor skill in music," on the above date, did "waylay the said Thomas Clifton" as he was "walking quietly from your subject's said house towards the said school," and "with great force and violence did seize and surprise, and him with like force and violence did, to the great terror and hurt of him, the said Thomas Clifton, haul, pull, drag, and carry away to the said playhouse." As soon as the father learned of this, he hurried to the playhouse and "made request to have his said son released." But Giles and Evans "utterly and scornfully refused to do" this. Whereupon Clifton threatened to complain to the Privy Council. But Evans and Giles "in very scornful manner willed your said subject to complain to whom he would." Clifton suggested that "it was not fit that a gentleman of his sort should have his son and heir (and that his only son) to be so basely used." Giles and Evans "most arrogantly then and there answered that they had authority sufficient so to take any nobleman's son in the land"; and further to irritate the father, they immediately put into young Clifton's hands "a scroll of paper, containing part of one of their said plays or interludes, and him, the said Thomas Clifton, commanded to learn the same by heart," with the admonition that "if he did not obey the said Evans, he should be surely whipped." Clifton at once appealed to his friend, Sir John Fortescue, a member of the Privy Council, at whose order young Clifton was released within twenty-four hours after seizure, and sent back to his studies (see Adams, *Playhouses*, p. 210; the complaint is given in full by Fleay, *Stage*, p. 127).

CLUN, WALTER.

Wright in his *Historia Histrionica* (1699) states that "Hart and Clun were bred up boys at the Blackfriars, and acted women's parts" (Hazlitt's *Dodsley*, xv. 404). There seems to be no record of Clun during the period of the Civil War and the Commonwealth. After the Restoration he continued his theatrical career at the Cockpit. He is named in the Petition of the Cockpit Players on October 13, 1660, and in the Articles of Agreement between Herbert and Killigrew on June 4, 1662 (Adams, *Dram. Rec.*, pp. 94, 113–14). As a member of His Majesty's Company of Comedians, under the management of Thomas Killigrew, he played the title-rôle in *The Humorous Lieutenant*, which opened the new playhouse, the Theatre Royal, on May 7, 1663 (Pepys,

Diary, iii. 107), and "was Acted Twelve Days Successively."
Shortly afterwards, he appeared as Cacafogo in *Rule a Wife, and
have a Wife*, which part was later taken by William Cartwright,
the younger (Downes, *Ros. Ang.*, pp. 2 ff., 39). Clun's stage-career
after the Restoration was brief, for he was murdered on the night
of August 2, 1664, near Kentish Town. On August 5 Pepys
visited the scene of the murder: "To my cozen, W. Joyce's,
. . . and he and I [rode] out of towne toward Highgate; in
the way, at Kentish-towne, showing me the place and manner of
Clun's being killed and laid in a ditch, and yet was not killed by
any wounds, having only one in his arm, but blead to death
through his struggling" (*Diary*, iv. 195). A poem upon his death
was published at the time, entitled: "An Elegy upon the most
execrable murder of Mr. Clun, one of the comedians of the
Theatre Royal, who was robbed and most inhumanly killed on
Tuesday night, being the 2nd of August, 1664, near Tatnam
Court, as he was riding to his country house at Kentish Town"
(Wheatley's note, Pepys, *Diary*, iv. 195). Clun was evidently a
great favorite with Pepys, who considered him one of the best
actors in the King's company, as shown by entries in the Diary
so late as 1669. On February 6, 1669, Pepys saw *Othello:* "After
dinner to the King's playhouse, and there . . . did see *The
Moor of Venice:* but ill acted in most parts; Mohun, which did a
little surprise me, not acting Iago's part by much so well as Clun
used to do." Again on April 17, 1669, Pepys remembers Clun:
"At noon home to dinner, and there find Mr. Pierce, the surgeon,
and he dined with us; and there hearing that *The Alchymist* was
acted, we did go, and took him with us to the King's house; and
it is still a good play, having not been acted for two or three
years before; but I do miss Clun, for the Doctor" (*Diary*, viii.
206–07, 279). Aubrey in one of his jottings notes in his characteristic gossipy way that "Ben Johnson had one eie lowre
than t'other, and bigger, like Clun, the player; perhaps he be-
gott Clun" (*Lives*, ii. 14).

COBORNE, EDWARD.

A player, whose son, John, was baptized at St. Giles's on November 23, 1616. He may be identical with Edward Colbrand (*Eliz. Stage*, ii. 310).

CODBOLT, LIGHTFOOT.

A member of the Children of Paul's in 1607 (Hillebrand, *Child Actors*, p. 112).

CODBOLT, THOMAS.

A member of the Children of Paul's in 1607 (Hillebrand, *Child Actors*, p. 112).

COFFIN, FRANCIS.

In a warrant of February 16, 1595, Richard Bradshaw and Francis Coffin are named as members of Lord Edward Dudley's provincial company of players; and with their license they appeared at Chester on November 20, 1602 (Murray, ii. 234).

COKE, RICHARD.

From 1547 to 1556 Richard Coke seems to have been a Court Interluder, at a salary of £3 6s. 8d. a year (Collier, i. 136, 165).

COLBRAND, EDWARD.

Edward Colbrand is named as one of Prince Henry's players in the household list of 1610. The Prince died in November, 1612, and his troupe soon passed under the patronage of the Palsgrave. Colbrand is mentioned in the new patent granted to the Palsgrave's company on January 11, 1613 (*Eliz. Stage*, ii. 188, 190).

COLES, ROBERT.

Robert Coles belonged to the Children of Paul's in 1598 (Hillebrand, *Child Actors*, p. 111). Apparently he was the performer of Andrugio mentioned in a stage-direction of Marston's *1 Antonio and Mellida*, IV. i. 29, presented by Paul's boys about 1599: "Enter Andrugio, Lucio, Cole, and Norwood" (Marston, *Works*, i. 63).

96

COLLEWELL, RICHARD.

Richard Collewell was a member of Richard Bradshaw's company, a troupe that got into trouble at Banbury in May, 1633. The town authorities, becoming suspicious of the validity of the company's license, arrested the players, and notified the Privy Council. The players appeared before the Privy Council in June, and were soon discharged "upon bond given to be forthcoming whensoever they should be called for." In the examination of the players by the Banbury officials, Collewell testified that he had been with the company about two years and was a servant to Edward Whiting (Murray, ii. 106 ff., 163 ff.).

COLLINS, EDWARD.

Edward Collins is named in a Ticket of Privilege granted on January 12, 1636, to the attendants "employed by his Majesty's servants the players of the Blackfriars, and of special use to them both on the Stage and otherwise for his Majesty's disport and service" (Stopes, *Jahrbuch*, xlvi. 99).

COLLINS, JEFFERY.

Jeffery Collins is named in a Protection from arrest, from impressment as soldiers, and from any other molestation whatsoever, issued by Herbert on December 27, 1624, to twenty-one men "imployed by the Kinges Maiesties servantes in theire quallity of Playinge as Musitions and other necessary attendantes" (Adams, *Dram. Rec.*, p. 74).

COLMAN, WILLIAM.

William Colman appears as a member of the Chapel Royal in 1509 and 1511. He may have subsequently been sworn in as a Gentleman of the Chapel, for a William Colman is found among the Gentleman of the Chapel in the lists of 1520, 1524, and 1526 (Brewer, *L. & P. Henry VIII*, i. 1. p. 15; Hillebrand, *Mod. Phil.*, xviii. 244-45; Chambers, *Eliz. Stage*, ii. 27n.).

COMBES, WILLIAM.

A lawsuit of 1594 names William Combes as one of the Children of Windsor. A Bill of Complaint, dated April 9, 1594, states that William Combes, senior, carpenter, father of William Combes, junior, had made an agreement with Nathaniel Giles, apparently at this date acting master of the chapel at Windsor, whereby the boy was to receive four years' instruction as chorister at the chapel of St. George's, Windsor. In return for the education of his son and a sum of money paid by Giles, Combes had agreed to buy and pasture a mare for the use of Giles. The lawsuit arose because Combes failed to observe the terms of the bargain (Hillebrand, *Child Actors*, pp. 158, 330-31).

CONDELL, HENRY.

The first appearance of Henry Condell in dramatic history rests upon the conjecture that he was the "Harry" who played Ferrex in "Envy" and a lord in "Lechery" of *2 Seven Deadly Sins*, presented by Lord Strange's company about 1590 (Greg, *H.P.*, p. 152; *R.E.S.*, i. 262). The first definite notice of him is in the list of the original "principal Comedians" who acted in Jonson's *Every Man in his Humor*, as played by the Chamberlain's men in 1598. With the same company he had a part in *Every Man out of his Humor*, presented in 1599. In 1603 the Chamberlain's company passed under royal patronage, and Condell is named in the patent granted on May 19, 1603, to the King's men. He was prominently associated with this troup until his death in 1627. His name appears in the 1623 folio list of actors in Shakespeare's plays; in the procession list of March 15, 1604; in the patent of March 27, 1619; in the livery-allowance lists of May 19, 1619, and April 7, 1621; in the list of players taking part in King James's funeral procession on May 7, 1625; and in the patent of June 24, 1625. He is introduced with his fellows of the King's men into the Induction to Marston's *Malcontent* (1604). The Globe was destroyed by fire in June, 1613, and Condell is mentioned in a contemporary ballad, entitled, *A Sonnett upon the pittiful burneing of the Globe playhouse in London* (Halliwell-Phillipps, *Outlines*, i. 310):

> The reprobates, thoughe druncke on munday,
> Prayd for the Foole and Henry Condye.

The esteem in which he was held by his fellows is shown by the wills of Augustine Phillips (1605), who left him 30*s.* in gold; of Alexander Cooke (1614), who named him as trustee; of William Shakespeare (1616), who bequeathed him a memorial ring; of Nicholas Tooley (1623), who appointed him executor and joint residuary legatee, and assigned sums of money to his wife and to his daughter, Elizabeth; and of John Underwood (1625), who designated him as executor. By 1599 he was married and apparently settled in St. Mary Aldermanbury, where he was a church-warden. The registers of the parish supply the following records of his children: Elizabeth (baptized February 27, 1599; buried April 11, 1599), Anne (baptized April 4, 1601; buried July 16, 1610), Richard (baptized April 18, 1602), Elizabeth (baptized April 14, 1603; buried April 22, 1603), Elizabeth (baptized October 26, 1606), Mary (baptized January 30, 1608; buried from Hoxton at St. Leonard's, Shoreditch, March 18, 1608), Henry (baptized May 6, 1610; buried March 4, 1630), William (baptized May 26, 1611), and Edward (baptized August 22, 1614; buried August 23, 1614): see Collier, *Actors*, pp. 134–39; *Variorum*, iii. 199, 476; Collier, iii. 367–72. Subsequently Condell had a "country-house" at Fulham, for on September 10, 1625, a pamphlet, written by certain players on their travels during the plague, entitled *The Run-awayes Answer to a Booke called A Rodde for Runne-awayes*, was addressed "To our much respected and very worthy friend, Mr. H. Condell, at his country-house at Fulham." The dedication shows the good terms in which Condell lived with his associates, and emphasizes the hospitality that he accorded the players, who express their gratitude for "a free and noble fare-

well" bestowed upon them as they went into the provinces
(Collier, *Actors*, p. 142). At his house in Fulham, on December 13,
1627, when "sick in body, but of perfect mind and memory," he
made his will, naming, with others, John Heminges and Cuthbert
Burbage as overseers. In 1619 he was described as "of greate
lyveinge, wealth, and power" (Wallace, *N.U.S.*, x. 311), and
the property assigned in his will lends emphasis to the statement.
He names his wife, Elizabeth, as sole executrix, and leaves to her,
to his sons Henry and William, and to his daughter Elizabeth,
wife of Herbert Finch, much property at Aldermanbury and elsewhere in London, including "rents and profits" by "leases and
terms of years" of "messuages, houses, and places" in Blackfriars and on the Bankside. He did not forget his old servant,
Elizabeth Wheaton, to whom he left 40*s*. and "that place or
priviledge which she now exerciseth and enjoyeth in the houses
of the Blackfryers, London, and the Globe on the Bankside"
(Collier, *Actors*, p. 148). Condell had not been an original sharer
of the Globe in 1599, but subsequently acquired an interest; he
was an original sharer of the Second Blackfriars in 1608. The
papers of 1635 show that his widow had controlled four-six-
teenths of the Globe and one-eighth of the Blackfriars, but had
transferred two-sixteenths of the Globe when Taylor and Lowin
were admitted as sharers (Adams, *Mod. Phil.*, xvii. 4 ff.; Halliwell-Phillipps, *Outlines*, i. 312, 313). Condell was buried on December 29, 1627, and his widow was buried on October 3, 1635,
both at St. Mary Aldermanbury (Collier, *Actors*, pp. 144, 150).
From the actor-lists Condell is known to have taken parts in the
following plays presented by the King's men (Murray, i. opp.
172): *Sejanus* (1603); *Volpone* (1605); *The Alchemist* (1610);
Catiline (1611); *The Duchess of Malfi* (*c.* 1611), the part of the
Cardinal, which by 1623 had probably passed to Richard Robinson
(Murray, ii. 146 ff.); *The Captain* (*c.* 1612); *Valentinian* (*c.* 1611–
14); *Bonduca* (*c.* 1613–14); *The Queen of Corinth* (*c.* 1617); *The
Knight of Malta* (*c.* 1618); *The Mad Lover* (*c.* 1618); *The Loyal*

Subject (1618); and *The Humorous Lieutenant* (*c.* 1619). This list seems to indicate that he left the stage about 1619. Thereafter he was with the King's men probably in some managerial capacity. John Roberts in his *Answer to Pope* (1729) asserts that Condell was a comic performer and a printer (*Variorum*, iii. 186, 199), but he adduced no authority for his improbable assertions beyond a vague stage-tradition, and neither statement can be verified. In only one of the actor lists mentioned above is Condell's specific part given; and that he played the Cardinal in *The Duchess of Malfi* entirely discredits Roberts's conjecture that he was a comedian. His greatest contribution to dramatic history is no doubt his work as joint-editor with Heminges on the First Folio of Shakespeare in 1623. In July, 1896, there was unveiled at St. Mary Aldermanbury a memorial to Heminges and Condell, with the inscription: "To the memory of John Heminge and Henry Condell, fellow actors and personal friends of Shakespeare. They lived many years in this parish, and are buried here. To their disinterested efforts the world owes all that it calls Shakespeare. They alone collected his dramatic writings, regardless of pecuniary loss, and, without the hope of any profit, gave them to the world. They thus merit the gratitude of mankind." They are mentioned in Scott's *Woodstock* (1826).

COOKE, ABELL.

Abell Cooke is recorded as a member of the Queen's Revels in a lawsuit of 1607. He was the son of Alice Cooke, who apprenticed him to Thomas Kendall on November 14, 1606, to remain three years as a player with the Queen's Revels. Trouble arose when the boy quit the troupe on May 31, 1607, before completing his apprenticeship. His mother deposed that he played at Blackfriars as often as he was required, and that he left the company by Kendall's written permission (Hillebrand, *Child Actors*, pp. 197-98).

COOKE, ALEXANDER.

A rather dubious conjecture assigns to Alexander Cooke the parts of Videna in "Envy" and Progne in "Lechery," assumed by "Sander" in *2 Seven Deadly Sins*, presented by Lord Strange's company about 1590 (Greg, *H.P.*, p. 152; *R.E.S.*, i. 262). He is named among the performers of Shakespeare's plays in the 1623 folio, and Malone ventures the guess that he "performed all the principal female characters" in the plays of the great dramatist (*Variorum*, iii. 211). As a King's man he appears in the actor-lists (Murray, i. opp. 172) of Jonson's *Sejanus* (1603), *Volpone* (1605), *The Alchemist* (1610), and *Catiline* (1611), and of Beaumont and Fletcher's *Captain* (c. 1612). From the fact that in the lists prefixed to *Sejanus* and *Volpone* his name occurs at the end, some critics have assumed that he played the female parts of Agrippina in the former and Fine-madam Would-be in the latter. In the postscript to a letter of October 21, 1603, from Joan Alleyn to her husband, "Mr. Cooke and his weife" commend themselves "in the kyndest sorte" to Edward Alleyn (Warner, p. 25). Augustine Phillips in his will dated May 4, 1605, bequeathed him as a fellow-actor 20s. in gold (Collier, *Actors*, p. 87). The token-books of St. Saviour's, Southwark, record an Alexander Cooke in Hill's Rents during 1604, 1607, 1609, and 1610. This is no doubt the actor, for the registers of the same parish in giving the baptism of his children specify his profession as that of a player: Francis, a son, October 27, 1605; Rebecca, October 11, 1607; Alice, November 3, 1611; and a posthumous son, Alexander, on March 20, 1614. The register records his burial on February 25, 1614. In his will dated January 3, 1614, he leaves £50 each to Francis, Rebecca, and the unborn child, and the residue of his estate to his wife. The portion left to the unborn child is stated to be "in the hand of my fellowes, as my share of the stock." Two brothers, Ellis and John, are also mentioned, and the latter is conjectured to be the author of *Greene's Tu Quoque*. He appoints "my Master Hemings," to whom he had probably been apprenticed, and

Condell as trustees for his children (Bentley, *T.L.S.*, Nov. 15, 1928, p. 856; Collier, *Actors*, pp. 183–85).

COOKE, EDWARD.

A member of the Chapel Royal in 1509 and 1511 (Brewer, *L. & P. Henry VIII*, i. 1. p. 15; Hillebrand, *Mod. Phil.*, xviii. 244; Chambers, *Eliz. Stage*, ii. 27*n.*).

COOKE, LIONEL.

In 1583 Lionel Cooke was with Queen Elizabeth's men in London, for he is named in a City record that gives the personnel of the company at this time (*Eliz. Stage*, ii. 106). Again in 1588 he is mentioned in a document concerning the Queen's players for the non-payment of 8*s.* 4*d.* subsidy (*M.S.C.*, i. 354).

COOKE, THOMAS.

On March 6, 1584, the Earl of Worcester's players were engaged in a dispute with the authorities at Leicester. In the account of the quarrel there is an abstract of the license, dated January 14, 1583, of Worcester's men, among whom Thomas Cooke is listed (*Eliz. Stage*, ii. 222).

COOKE, WILLIAM.

Three separate references to "William Cooke" have come down to us, which may concern one, two, or three men. The references are listed here in chronological order.

(1) William Cooke owned one-half of one share in the syndicate that in 1608 leased the Whitefriars playhouse (Adams, *Playhouses*, pp. 313–15).

(2) William Cooke is mentioned in the examination of Richard Bradshaw's players at Banbury in 1623, when the town authorities became suspicious of the validity of the company's license (Murray, ii. 106 ff., 163 ff.). From the records it appears that Edward Whiting (*q.v.*) either had been or was in some way connected with Bradshaw's troupe, and that he "let the commis-

sion in question to William Cooke and Fluellen Morgan, and they two went with it with a puppet-play until they had spent all, then they pawned the commission for 4*s*." Subsequently Bradshaw redeemed and bought the commission.

(3) William Cooke's name appears in a warrant of December 12, 1635, appointing several of Prince Charles's men as Grooms of the Chamber (Stopes, *Jahrbuch*, xlvi. 98).

COOLING, JOHN.

In *Wits Recreations* (1640) is printed the following epitaph (ii. 238):

On John Cooling a Player-foole

Death hath too soon remov'd from us *Jo. Cooling*,
That was so well belov'd, and liv'd by fooling.

CORDEN, GEORGE.

George Corden, described as servant to the Earl of Leicester, visited Coventry on January 9, 1640, with a company composed of players from various troupes. They received a payment of 48*s*. 2*d*. under date of November 25, 1640 (Murray, ii. 52, 254).

CORNISH, JOHN.

A Gentleman of the Chapel Royal, and pageant-master of the wedding of Prince Arthur and Katherine of Spain in 1501, in which two of the children of the Chapel were concealed in mermaids "singing right sweetly and with quaint hermony" (*Eliz. Stage*, ii. 28, 30*n*.).

CORNISH, KIT.

A "ghost-name," due to the juxtaposition of "kyte" (i.e. John Kite, later Archbishop of Armagh) and "Cornisshe" in a Chapel record of 1508: "mr kyte Cornisshe and other of the Chapell yt played affore ye king at Richemounte" (*Eliz. Stage*, ii. 29*n*., 30*n*.).

CORNISH, WILLIAM.

Master of the Song School at Westminster in 1479–80 (*Eliz. Stage*, ii. 30*n.*, 70).

CORNISH, WILLIAM.

Master of the Chapel Royal, 1509–23 (Wallace, *Evolution*, pp. 33–60).

COWLEY, RICHARD.

In the plot of *2 Seven Deadly Sins*, presented by Strange's company about 1590, Richard Cowley is cast for several minor parts: a lieutenant in the Induction, a soldier and a lord in "Envy," Giraldus and a musician in "Sloth," and a lord in "Lechery" (Greg, *H.P.*, p. 152; *R.E.S.*, i. 262). He was traveling in the provinces with Strange's men in 1593, as shown in the correspondence between Edward and Joan Alleyn. On August 1 Alleyn wrote to his wife from Bristol, whither a letter from her had been brought by Cowley (*H.P.*, p. 36). In March, 1601, he served as joint-payee for performances at Court by the Chamberlain's men (Steele, pp. 120, 121), which company he may have joined upon its formation in 1594. The stage-directions (IV. ii) of the Quarto (1600) and the Folio (1623) texts, where "Cowley" is substituted for "Verges," show that he played Verges to Kempe's Dogberry in *Much Ado about Nothing*, acted by the Chamberlain's men probably about 1598. In 1603 the Chamberlain's company passed under royal patronage, and Cowley is named in the patent granted on May 19, 1603, to the King's men; in the procession list of March 15, 1604; and in the 1623 folio list of actors in Shakespeare's plays. Augustine Phillipps, in his will dated May 4, 1605, bequeathed him as a fellow-actor 20*s.* in gold. He lived in Holywell Street, and for a short period in Alleyn's Rents, both in the parish of St. Leonard's, Shoreditch, where the registers supply the following records of his children (Collier, *Actors*, pp. 161–63): Robert (baptized March 8, 1596; buried ?March 20,

1597), Cuthbert (baptized May 8, 1597), Richard (baptized April 29, 1598; buried February 26, 1603), and Elizabeth (baptized February 2, 1602). His wife's burial is recorded on September 28, 1616, and his own on March 12, 1619. His nuncupative will, dated January 13, 1618, appoints his daughter, Elizabeth Birch, sole executrix. The will is witnessed by John Heminges, Cuthbert Burbage, John Shank, and Thomas Ravenscroft, the last of whom may be the madrigalist (Plomer, *Notes and Queries*, 1906, vi. 369).

CRANE, JOHN.

A London player in 1550, named in an order demanding that all plays be licensed by the King or his Council (Harrison, *England*, iv. 314–15).

CRANE, RALPH.

Ralph Crane has a place in dramatic history because he was scrivener to the King's men in 1619 and perhaps earlier, and was still making transcripts of their plays in 1625. He was also a writer. His one published book, *The Workes of Mercy* (1621), re-published about 1625 as *The Pilgrimes New-yeeres-Gift*, is a collection of tedious and pious reflections, less readable than the autobiographic induction. The chief sources of our knowledge of his life are this biographical preface in verse to *The Workes of Mercy*, the enlarged version of the preface in the latter edition, and the dedications of the manuscripts that he presented to his patrons. From these sources we learn that he was born in London, and that he was the son of a more or less prosperous member of the Merchant Taylors' Company. He was brought up to the law; served Sir Anthony Ashley seven years as clerk; afterwards wrote for the lawyers; escaped the ravages of the plague in the beginning of the seventeenth century; and began writing poetry late in life when he was suffering much from poverty and sickness. He employed himself in his later years in copying popular works and dedicating his transcripts to well-known persons, in the hope

of receiving pecuniary recompense. He is known to have been
the scribe of the following plays (F. P. Wilson, *Library*, 1926, vii.
195 ff.): Fletcher and Massinger's *Sir John van Olden Barnavelt* (*c.*
1619); Fletcher's *Humorous Lieutenant*, which Crane entitled
Demetrius and Enanthe (1625); Middleton's *The Witch* (*c.* 1620–27);
and two manuscripts of Middleton's *A Game at Chess* (1625).
From the preface to *The Workes of Mercy* we get the impression
that Crane was not a regular employee of the King's men, but
rather a scribe whose services were sought when occasion demanded:

> And some imployment hath my vsefull *Pen*
> Had 'mongst those ciuill, well-deseruing men,
> That grace the *Stage* with *honour* and *delight*,
> Of whose true honesties I much could write,
> But will comprise't (as in a Caske of Gold)
> Vnder the Kingly Seruice they doe hold.

More detailed accounts of Crane are as follow: F. P. Wilson,
Library (1926), vii. 194; T. S. Graves, *Stud. in Phil.*, (1924), xxi.
362; S. L. Lee, *D.N.B.*, xiii. 11.

CRANE, WILLIAM.

Master of the Chapel Royal, 1523–45 (Wallace, *Evolution*,
pp. 61 ff.).

CRANWIGGE, JAMES.

James Cranwigge played his challenge at the Rose on November 4, 1598, on which occasion Henslowe's share of the profits
amounted to £2. His name is found nowhere else in theatrical
records; he may have been only a dancer, a tumbler, or a fencer
(*H.D.*, i. 98; ii. 254). That the Elizabethan stage was not alto-
gether sacred to the sock and buskin is shown by Dekker's comment in his *Newes from Hell* (1606): "At sword and buckler,
little *Dauy* was no bodie to him, and as for Rapier and Dagger,
the *Germane* may be his iourneyman. Many the question is, in
which of the *Play-houses* he would haue performed his Prize, if it

had grown to blowes, and whether the money beeing gathered, he would haue cozende the Fencers, or the Fencers him, because *Hell* being vnder euerie one of their *Stages*, the Players (if they had owed him a spight) might with a false Trappe doore haue slipt him downe, and there kept him, as a laughing stocke to al their yawning Spectators" (Dekker, *Non-Dramatic Works*, ii. 92).

CROSSE, NICHOLAS.

A member of the Children of Paul's in 1607 (Hillebrand, *Child Actors*, p. 112).

CROSSE, SAMUEL.

The name of Samuel Crosse appears in the 1623 folio list of actors in Shakespeare's plays, but in no record of the Chamberlain's or the King's men. He may possibly be identified with the Crosse named by Heywood as having flourished before his time, i.e. before about 1594 (*Apology*, p. 43).

CUMBER, JOHN.

In 1616 John Cumber belonged to Queen Anne's men, for in June of that year he is mentioned in the Baskervile papers as a member of the company (*Eliz. Stage*, ii. 237). Again in June, 1617, he is named in an agreement with Susan Baskervile. On May 13, 1619, he attended Queen Anne's funeral as a representative of her London company. After the Queen's death her London troupe was known as the Players of the Revels at the Red Bull, and in 1622 Cumber is noted as one of "the chiefe players" in this company (Adams, *Dram. Rec.*, p. 63). By May, 1623, the company seems to have disbanded, for on May 23 of that year Cumber and two of his fellows pleaded to be excused from their payments to Susan Baskervile, on the ground that the other players bound by the original agreement were either dead or with another troupe (Murray, i. 199). In 1623 he was living in Aldermanbury (Wallace, *Jahrbuch*, xlvi. 347). He died before June 16, 1623, for the Baskervile papers of this date note him as "newly deceased"

(Fleay, *Stage*, p. 279). He has been conjectured (Fleay, *Drama*, i. 43) to be the I. C. who wrote *The Two Merry Milkmaids*, a play entered in the Stationers' Registers on May 22, 1620 (Arber, iii. 674), and printed shortly afterwards "As it was Acted before the King, with generall Approbation, by the Companie of the Reuels."

CURTEYS, JAMES.

A member of the Chapel Royal in 1509 and 1511 (Brewer, *L. & P. Henry VIII*, i. 1. p. 15; Hillebrand, *Mod. Phil.*, xviii. 244; Chambers, *Eliz. Stage*, ii. 27n.).

CUTLER, JAMES.

A member of the Chapel Royal not later than 1605, as shown by a record of October 7, 1605, when holland was provided for shirts for the twelve children of the Chapel, and "for James Cutler, a Chappell boy gone off" (*Eliz. Stage*, ii. 50n.).

DAB.

See Dob.

DABORNE, ROBERT.

Robert Daborne appears on January 4, 1610, with Philip Rosseter and others, as a patentee for the Children of the Queen's Revels at the Whitefriars playhouse (Adams, *Playhouses*, p. 318). He was the author of two extant plays, *A Christian Turned Turk*, printed in 1612, and *The Poor Man's Comfort*, printed in 1655; and he collaborated with Tourneur, Field, Massinger, and Fletcher. At some unknown date he took orders. In 1618 there was published a sermon preached by him at Waterford. He became Chancellor at Waterford in 1619, Prebendary of Lismore in 1620, and Dean of Lismore in 1621. On March 23, 1628, he "died amphibious by the ministry" (*Eliz. Stage*, iii. 270). For other details of his life see Greg's *Henslowe Papers*.

DAMPORT, EDWARD.

Edward Damport was a member of Richard Bradshaw's company, when that troupe got into trouble at Banbury in May, 1633. The town authorities, becoming suspicious of the validity of the company's license, arrested the players, and notified the Privy Council. The players appeared before the Privy Council in June, and were soon discharged "upon bond given to be forthcoming whensoever they should be called for." In the examination of the players by the Banbury officials, Damport testified that he had "gone with the company up and down the country playing stage plays these two years last past," and that Edward Whiting (*q.v.*) had been his "old master" (Murray, ii. 106 ff., 163 ff.).

DANIEL, JOHN.

On July 17, 1615, John Daniel, a musician in the service of Prince Charles, obtained through the influence of his brother, the poet, Samuel Daniel, a patent for the Children of the Queen's Chamber of Bristol. The company is not traceable in London; but in 1616–17 Daniel brought it to Norwich, where instead of being allowed to play he was given a gratuity. By April, 1618, he seems to have assigned his privilege to Martin Slater, John Edmonds, and Nathaniel Clay. Nevertheless, at a later date he apparently organized another troupe, for the Leicester accounts of 1624 record a payment of 5*s*. 4*d*. to "John Daniell who had a Pattent for the Children of Bristoll" (Murray, ii. 14 ff., 370, 5 ff., 316).

DANIEL, SAMUEL.

Samuel Daniel, poet, dramatist, and author of masks, became connected with the stage through his appointment as official censor for the Children of the Queen's Revels. Their patent of February 4, 1604, states that all their plays must receive his "approbacion and allowaunce." Evidently he took a more active part in the management of the troupe than merely licensing their plays, for he served as joint-payee with Evans for performances at Court on January 1 and 3, 1605 (Steele, pp. 141, 142). His connection with the troupe probably ceased later in the year, when Queen Anne's patronage was withdrawn from the Children as a result of their serious offense in acting *Eastward Hoe*. In 1615 he used his influence in obtaining for his brother, John, a patent for the Children of the Queen's Chamber of Bristol (*Eliz. Stage*, ii. 49, 50, 52, 272–74).

DANIEL, WILLIAM.

During 1621–22 a troupe called "the Kings Players" visited Canterbury under the leadership of William Daniel. Daniel is nowhere else mentioned as associated with the King's players; later, however, he appears as a King's Revels man, and thus the company referred to in the Canterbury records is doubtless the King's Revels. On November 28, 1634, the Master of the Revels granted a license to William Daniel, William Hart, John Townsend, Samuel Minion, Hugh Haughton, Thomas Doughton, and others; their company was known as the King's Revels. With Daniel as leader the troupe appeared at Coventry in June, 1635; at Norwich on September 3, 1635; at Coventry on April 22 and December 5, 1636; and at Gloucester in 1636–37 (Murray, ii. 8 ff., 11, 231, 252, 253, 285, 357).

DANNER, JOHN.

John Danner's name appears in a warrant of July 2, 1629, appointing several of the Lady Elizabeth's (Queen of Bohemia's) players as Grooms of the Chamber (Stopes, *Jahrbuch*, xlvi. 95).

DARBIE, RICHARD.

A player, whose son, Allstide, was baptized at St. Bodolph Aldgate on May 1, 1602. He may possibly be identical with Richard Darloe (Denkinger, *P.M.L.A.*, xli. 99).

DARLOE, RICHARD.

See Richard Darlowe.

DARLOWE, RICHARD.

Darlowe, who may be identical with Richard Darloe, appeared as an attendant in *The Dead Man's Fortune*, possibly acted by the Admiral's men at the Theatre about 1590 (*Eliz. Stage*, ii. 136; *H.P.*, p. 152). The registers of St. Bodolph Aldgate supply the following records of children of "Richard Darloe, a player" (Denkinger, *P.M.L.A.*, xli. 99): Margaret (baptized September 19, 1595; buried May 21, 1596), Jeane (baptized May 19, 1598; buried January 25, 1599), and John (baptized January 25, 1600; buried August 29, 1602).

D'AUNAY, JOSIAS (?).

Presumably D'Aunay was one of the French players in England during 1635 under the leadership of Josias de Soulas, better known by his stage-name of Josias Floridor (*q.v.*), as shown by a warrant of May 5, 1635, granted to "Josias D'Aunay, Hurfries de Lau, and others, for to act playes at a new house in Drury-lane, during pleasure" (Adams, *Dram. Rec.*, p. 61). Lawrence (*Eliz. Playhouse*, 1912, p. 133*n*.) suggests that "Floridor's real name was Josias d'Aunay." A more plausible explanation seems to be the suggestion of Adams (*Dram. Rec.*, p. 61*n*.) that a comma should be inserted after "Josias."

DAVENANT, WILLIAM.

William Davenant (1606–68) on June 27, 1640, succeeded William Beeston as Governor of the Cockpit Players, and under his direction the company continued to act at the Cockpit until the closing of the playhouses in 1642 (Adams, *Playhouses*, pp. 361–62). His subsequent career as theatrical manager and dramatist falls within the period of the Commonwealth and Restoration, and is here only briefly summarized. His foresight in a managerial capacity is notable for several outstanding innovations in stage-craft. In the later years of the Commonwealth he obtained permission to give a species of quasi-dramatic entertainments which would be tolerated by the authorities. His first performances were at Rutland House; but in 1658 he moved to the Cockpit, where *The Siege of Rhodes* was presented "*stylo recitativo*," and "did affect the eie and eare extremely" and "first brought scenes in fashion in England; before, at playes, was only a hanging" (Aubrey, *Lives*, i. 208). *The Siege of Rhodes* is in many respects an epoch-making play. The entertainment marks the re-establishment of the theatre after Puritan rule; scenery was for the first time employed in a play, as distinguished from the spectacular masks sponsored by the royalty; the first English professional actress appeared, for Mrs. Coleman assumed the part of Ianthe; and an opera was for the first time produced in England. The historical significance of the performance cannot easily be overrated. After the Restoration, Davenant continued his work as theatrical manager. In August, 1660, he secured a royal patent to organize a company of players, and opened at Salisbury Court in November of the same year. By the end of June, 1661, the new theatre of Lincoln's Inn Fields was completed, and the Duke of York's company moved there under the management of Davenant (Nicoll, *Rest. Drama*, p. 283). The star of this troupe was Thomas Betterton, whose splendid acting captivated London. *Hamlet* was one of the first plays given at the new playhouse: "Hamlet being perform'd by Mr. Betterton, Sir William (having seen Mr. Taylor of the Black-Fryars Company act it, who being instructed by the author Mr. Shaksepeur) taught Mr. Betterton in every particle of it; which by his exact performance of it, gain'd him esteem and reputation, superlative to all other plays. . . . No succeeding tragedy for several years got more reputation or money to the company than this" (Downes, *Ros. Ang.*, ed. J. Knight, pp. xviii-xxii, 19–21). Regardless of a strong prejudice against women appearing on the stage, Davenant obtained the insertion of the following clause in the patent granted to him: "That, whereas the women's parts in plays have hitherto been acted by men in the habits of women, of which some have taken offence, we permit and give leave for the time to come, that all women's parts be acted by women" (Davenant, *Works*, i. p. lxvii). Another innovation which seems to have been introduced by Davenant was the change in the position of the orchestra, which hitherto had been placed in an upper balcony. When the alteration of Shakespeare's *Tempest* by Dryden and Davenant was produced at the Duke's theatre in Lincoln's Inn Fields in 1667, the orchestra was doubtless "for the first time," as conjectured by Collier (*H.E.D. P.*, iii. 252), placed between the audience and the stage, as shown by the description prefixed to the play: "The front of the stage opened, and the band of twenty-four violins, with the harpsicals and theorbos, which accompany the voices, are placed between the pit and the stage" (Davenant, *Works*, v. 419). Davenant's importance in dramatic history is not to be measured by his own actual dramatic writings, but rather by the far-reaching and powerful forces that he set in motion. And, withal, he kept alive through the unauspicious years of the Civil War and Commonwealth some memory of a great national dramatic tradition.

DAVIS, HUGH.

Hugh Davis appears frequently in Henslowe's *Diary* as a witness between May 8, 1593, evidently an error for 1594 (*H.D.*, ii. 80), and November 26, 1603. On November 9, 1601, the Admiral's men paid 7*s*. 6*d*. for the mending of his tawny coat "which was eaten with the rattes." He was therefore in some way connected with the Admiral's troupe at the Fortune, and may have been a hired man (*H.D.*, ii. 255).

DAWES, ROBERT.

Robert Dawes is named in a patent granted on March 30, 1610, to the players under the patronage of Prince Charles, then Duke of York, and known as the Duke of York's men. After Prince

Henry's death in November, 1612, their title became Prince Charles's men. Dawes apparently remained with the company until about April 7, 1614, when he transferred to the Lady Elizabeth's men, at which time Articles of Agreement were drawn up between him and Henslowe and Meade (*Eliz. Stage*, ii. 242, 255).

DAWSON, JOHN.

A member of the Children of Paul's in 1607 (Hillebrand, *Child Actors*, p. 112).

DAY, JOHN.

A writer signing himself "Dramaticus," in *Shakespeare Society's Papers*, iv. 110, describes a copy of Dekker's *Shoemaker's Holiday* with alleged manuscript notes giving the cast of the play as produced by the Admiral's men about 1600. To Day is assigned the part of Lovell, an officer. Greg discredits the list as "an obvious forgery" (*H.D.*, ii. 203). John, son of John Day, a player, was baptized at St. Saviour's on June 3, 1604 (*Eliz. Stage*, ii. 313).

DAY, THOMAS.

As a member of the Chapel Royal, Thomas Day acted in Jonson's *Cynthia's Revels*, 1600, and *The Poetaster*, 1601 (*Eliz. Stage*, iii. 363, 365). Perhaps he is to be identified with the Thomas Day who appears as a musician in the establishment of Prince Henry in 1612, as a Gentleman of the Chapel in 1615, as organist of Westminster and master of the choristers from 1625 to 1632, and as master of the Children of the Chapel Royal in 1637 (Rimbault, *Old Cheque Book*, pp. 8, 205).

DECAYNE, ANDREW.
See Andrew Cane.

DENYGTEN, THOMAS.
See Thomas Downton.

DICK.
See "Black Dick."

A DICTIONARY OF ACTORS

DICK, E. DUTTON'S BOY.

Dick, E. Dutton's boy, assumed the part of Basilea in *Frederick and Basilea*, acted by the Admiral's men in June, 1597 (*H.P.*, p. 153).

DISHLEY.
See Distle.

DISTLE.

Distle (Distley, Dishley) seems to have been the leader of a company of players under the patronage of Lord Edward Dudley from 1610 to about ?1636. He is mentioned in the records as having visited Gawthorpe Hall, Lancashire, on March 13, 1610, October 7, 1612, and March 4, 1613; Leicester, in 1629; and Doncaster, on February 19, ?1636 (Murray, ii. 42 ff., 394, 395, 317, 257).

DISTLEY.
See Distle.

DOB.

Dob (or Dab) appeared as a ghost in *The Battle of Alcazar*, acted by the Admiral's men about 1600-01. He is probably identical with Dobe of the 1598 inventory of apparel belonging to the Admiral's company: "Dobes cotte of cloth and sylver" (*H.P.*, pp. 119, 138, 153; *Eliz. Stage*, ii. 176).

DOBE.
See Dob.

DOBSON, JOHN.

John Dobson played Camelion, Rowbone's man, in Shirley's *Wedding*, acted by Queen Henrietta's company about May, 1626 (Murray, i. opp. 266).

DONSTALL, JAMES.
See James Tunstall.

DONSTONE, JAMES.

See James Tunstall.

DOUBTON, THOMAS.

See Thomas Downton.

DOUGHTON, THOMAS.

As a member of Ellis Guest's company under license of June 7, 1628, Thomas Doughton is recorded at Norwich on July 2 of the same year. He is also named in a license of November 28, 1634, granted to a company under the leadership of William Daniel (*q.v.*) and known as the King's Revels (Murray, ii. 8 ff., 103). An identification of him with Thomas Downton would be somewhat hazardous.

DOVER, ANTONY.

Antony Dover is recorded at Norwich on March 10, 1635, when his troupe, presumably the King's Revels, applied for permission to act in that town (Murray, i. 279–80).

DOWGHTON, THOMAS.

See Thomas Downton.

DOWLAND, ROBERT.

See Robert Dulandt.

DOWLE, ROWLAND.

Rowland Dowle is named in a Ticket of Privilege granted on January 12, 1636, to the attendants "employed by his Majesty's servants the players of the Blackfriars, and of special use to them both on the Stage and otherwise for his Majesty's disport and service" (Stopes, *Jahrbuch*, xlvi. 99).

DOWNTON, THOMAS.

The variants of Thomas Downton's name are numerous: Doutone (?), Dowton, Dowghton, Dowten, Doubton, and

Denygten. There is a letter from John Pyk to Joan Alleyn, undated but evidently written while Strange's men were traveling in the provinces during 1593, which purports to have been written by "Mr. Doutone." Conjecture has assigned the letter to Thomas Downton, who may have been with Strange's men in 1593 (*H. P.*, p. 41; *Eliz. Stage*, ii. 124). By December 14, 1594, he had become a member of the Admiral's troupe, for his name occurs in a list of the company at this date (*H.D.*, i. 5). Subsequently he joined the Earl of Pembroke's men, for with several other members of the company he is complainant in a lawsuit during 1597 against Francis Langley, builder and owner of the Swan playhouse (Wallace, *Eng. Studien*, xliii. 340; Adams, *Playhouses*, pp. 168–74). As a result of the dissolution of Pembroke's company, caused by the production of *The Isle of Dogs*, Downton on October 6, 1597, bound himself to Henslowe to play with the Admiral's men at the Rose, and on October 11 his name is found in the accounts of the company (*H.D.*, i. 82, 203). From this time to 1603 he appears in the *Diary* as an Admiral's man. He authorized payments on behalf of the company, borrowed various sums from Henslowe, paid personal debts, bought a pair of crimson stockings from Henslowe, served as a witness to occasional transactions, and as a shareholder joined his fellows in acknowledging the company's debts. He received 5*s*. on December 28, 1597, to give to Anthony Munday for his play of *Mother Redcap* (*H.D.*, i. 70). During the Christmas seasons of 1597–98 and 1598–99 he served as joint-payee with Robert Shaw for performances at Court by the Earl of Nottingham's (Admiral's) men (Steele, pp. 113, 115, 116). As an Admiral's men he played Abdolmelec in *The Battle of Alcazar*, about 1600–01, and Mango Cham in *1 Tamar Cam*, 1602, and a Tartar in the Procession of the same play (*H.P.*, pp. 153, 154; *Eliz. Stage*, ii. 175). His boy performed in *Cupid and Psyche* (1600) and *1 Tamar Cam* (1602). About Christmas, 1603, the Admiral's men were taken into the service of Prince Henry; and on March 14, 1604, Downton and Edward Juby represented

the Prince's men in their reckoning with Henslowe (*H.D.*, i. 175).
His name occurs in the coronation list of March 15, 1604; in the
patent of April 30, 1606; and in the household list of 1610 (*Eliz.
Stage*, ii. 186, 187, 188). The Prince died in November, 1612, and
his troupe soon passed under the patronage of the Palsgrave.
Downton is named in the new patent of January 11, 1613, and in
the warrant of March 29, 1615, to appear before the Privy Council
for playing during Lent (*M.S.C.*, i. 275, 372). A lease to him of a
thirty-second part of the Fortune was drawn up in 1608, but not
executed. He was a witness to the joint-lease of the Fortune to
the Palsgrave's men on October 31, 1618 (Warner, pp. 237, 243).
Since he appeared as a witness, rather than as a lessee, he had
probably at this date retired from the stage. He apparently married a vintner's widow on February 15, 1618, and became a
vintner_(*Eliz. Stage*, ii. 313). On August 18, 1622, he dined with
Edward Alleyn (Warner, p. 193). The St. Saviour's registers
supply records of his family, including the baptism of Christopher, son of Thomas Dowton, "musycyon," on December 27,
1592; of Thomas Dowton "baseborne, the supposed son of
Thomas Dowton, a player," on May 25, 1600 (*Eliz. Stage*, ii.
313); "Francis Dowghton, son of Thomas, a player," April 18,
1597; and of Thomas Dowton, son of Thomas, a player, July 21,
1601 (Bentley, *T.L.S.*, Nov. 15, 1928, p. 856). He may have been
one of the Dutton family (*H.D.*, ii. 265). A copy of acrostic
verses on Downton's name by one John Day, whom J. F. Herbert
identifies with the dramatist, is given in *Shakespeare Society's
Papers*, i. 19:

> *Acrostic Verses upon the Name of his worthie
> friende, Maister Thomas Dowton*
> The wealthy treasure of America
> Hid in the vaines and artiers of the earthe,
> Or the riche pearle begotten in the sea,
> Made rounde and oriente in his naturall birthe,
> Are not all valewde, in the eye of arte,
> Soe much (by much) as a compassionate harte.

A DICTIONARY OF ACTORS

Determine, then, to keepe that wealthie mine,
Of all exchequers in the world the beste:
Wisdome the quoine, the stamp upon 't devine,
The man that owes it beares this motto, "Bleste,"
Of all my friendes ('twere shame to wrong desarte)
Not one of all beares a more passionate harte.

JOHN DAY.

DOWNTON'S BOY.

"Downton's boy" played in *Cupid and Psyche* in June, 1600, and assumed the parts of Tarmia's child and of Thia in *1 Tamar Cam*, acted by the Admiral's men in 1602 (*H.D.*, i. 122; *H.P.*, p. 154).

DOWTEN, THOMAS.

See Thomas Downton.

DOWTON, THOMAS.

See Thomas Downton.

DRAKE, ROBERT.

A London player in 1550, named in an order demanding that all plays be licensed by the King or his Council (Harrison, *England*, iv. 314–15).

DRAYTON, MICHAEL.

Michael Drayton, poet and dramatist, owned one whole share in the syndicate that in 1608 leased the Whitefriars playhouse. He seems to have been largely responsible for organizing the Children of His Majesty's Revels at Whitefriars. The closing of the playhouses by order of King James, followed by a violent outbreak of the plague, led to the dissolution of the company soon after its organization (Adams, *Playhouses*, pp. 311–17).

DREWE, BARTHOLOMEW.

A player, whose son, George, was baptized at St. Saviour's on November 12, 1614 (*Eliz. Stage*, ii. 313).

DREWE, THOMAS.

Thomas Drewe (or Drue) belonged to Queen Anne's men in 1616, for in June of that year he is mentioned in the Baskervile papers as a member of the company (*Eliz. Stage*, ii. 237). Again in June, 1617, he is named in an agreement with Susan Baskervile. On October 2, 1617, he with others of the Queen's company petitioned the Sessions of Peace against the various presentments that had been issued against them for not "repayringe the Highwayes neere the Red Bull" (Jeaffreson, *Middlesex*, ii. 170). He took part in Queen Anne's funeral on May 13, 1619, as a representative of her London company (Murray, i. 197). Subsequently he appears to have become a playwright (Lawrence, "Found: A Missing Jacobean Dramatist," *Times Literary Suppl.*, March 23, 1922, p. 191). He is presumably the author of *The Life of the Duchess of Suffolk*, licensed on January 2, 1624, as "Written by Mr. Drew," and published in 1631 as by Thomas Drue (Adams, *Dram. Rec.*, p. 27); the T. D. who wrote *The Bloody Banquet* (printed in 1639); and the Drew who appears as joint-author with Robert Davenport of *The Woman's Mistake*, entered in the Stationers' Registers on September 9, 1653 (Eyre, i. 428), but apparently never printed.

DROM, THOMAS.

Thomas Drom assumed the part of Nemesis in *The Battle of Alcazar*, presented by the Admiral's men about 1600–01 (*H.P.*, p. 153; *Eliz. Stage*, ii. 175–76).

DRUE, THOMAS.

See Thomas Drewe.

DRUSIANO.

See Martinelli.

DUKE, JOHN.

In *2 Seven Deadly Sins*, presented by Strange's men about 1590, John Duke played a pursuivant in the Induction, a soldier in

"Envy," Will Fool in "Sloth," and a lord in "Lechery" (Greg, *H.P.*, p. 152; *R.E.S.*, i. 262). Subsequently he joined the Chamberlain's men, for he is named in the list of "principal Comoedians" affixed to Jonson's *Every Man in his Humor*, acted by the Chamberlain's company in 1598. On September 21, 1600, he acknowledged a debt of £2 to Henslowe, but no mention is made of the company with which he was then associated. Nothing more is heard of him until August 18, 1602, when he authorized payments for Worcester's men from this date to May 9, 1603 (*H.D.*, i. 132, 179, 190). Early in the reign of James I Worcester's men became Queen Anne's company, and on February 19, 1604, Duke was paid for two plays performed by the Queen's men before Prince Henry on the previous January 2 and 13 (Steele, pp. 135, 137). He is named in a list of the Queen's men who took part in the coronation procession of March 15, 1604. On February 19, 1605, and April 30, 1606, he again served as payee for performances by the Queen's men at Court (Steele, pp. 141, 149). His name occurs in both the license of April 15, 1609, and the duplicate patent issued on January 7, 1612, to the traveling company under the patronage of Queen Anne. He seems to have been with the Queen's men at Norwich on May 6, 1615, and May 31, 1617, since his name is given in the abstracts of the license in the town records (Murray, i. 189; ii. 340, 343). He lived for a time in Holywell Street, a section of London where numerous actors resided, and had four children baptized at St. Leonard's, Shoreditch, at various dates between July, 1604, and January, 1609 (Collier, *Actors*, p. xxxi).

DULANDT, ROBERT.

Robert Dulandt (Dowland?) was a musician in Germany in the service of Philip Julius, Duke of Wolgast, during 1623. In a petition dated August 30, 1623, he asked permission, with his fellows, Richard Jones and Johan Kostressen, to leave Wolgast and return to England (Meyer, *Jahrbuch*, xxxviii. 209).

DUTTON, EDWARD.

In the performance of *Frederick and Basilea* by the Admiral's men in June, 1597, Edward Dutton appeared as Philippo (*H.P.*, p. 153). His boy, Dick, also had a part in the play. On July 18, 1597, he borrowed money from Henslowe (*H.D.*, i. 200). During 1600–02 children of his were baptized at St. Saviour's: Sara, January 16, 1600; Susan, October 2, 1600; Prudence, April 16, 1602 (Bentley, *T.L.S.*, Nov. 15, 1928, p. 856).

DUTTON, JOHN.

John Dutton in 1575–76 was a player in the Earl of Warwick's company, as shown by a payment to him, his brother Lawrence, and Jerome Savage, for plays presented at Court during the Christmas season of 1575–76 (Steele, pp. 57, 58). On Arpil 13, 1580, Lawrence Dutton (*q.v.*) is spoken of as servant to the Earl of Oxford, and before this date John had also doubtless transferred himself from the Warwick to the Oxford troupe, for some satirical lines (*Eliz. Stage*, ii. 98) describe how the "Duttons and theyr fellow-players, forsakyng the Erle of Warwycke theyr mayster, became followers of the Erle of Oxford," and as a result were called, instead of comedians, chameleons. John became associated with Queen Elizabeth's men when the troupe was first established in 1583, and is named in a London record that gives the personnel of the company at this time (*Eliz. Stage*, ii. 106). That he remained with the Queen's men is shown by the fact that he is mentioned in a document of June 30, 1588, concerning the non-payment of subsidy by certain members of the company (*M.S.C.*, i. 354). In 1588–89 he and his brother Lawrence were the leaders of the Queen's men on their visit to Nottingham (Murray, ii. 375). With John Laneham on March 15, 1590, and with Lawrence Dutton on March 7, 1591, he served as payee for performances at Court by the Queen's company (Steele, pp. 99, 100). Elizabeth, daughter of John Dutton, a player, was baptized at St. Botolph's on July 3, 1586. Lincoln's Inn paid him for musicians in 1567–68. As a Court Messenger, a John Dutton received payment on May 23, 1578, for carrying letters to Antwerp (*Eliz. Stage*, ii. 314).

DUTTON, LAWRENCE.

Lawrence Dutton was connected successively with companies under the patronage of Sir Robert Lane, 1571–72, the Earl of Lincoln (Lord Clinton), 1572–75, and the Earl of Warwick, 1575–76, as shown by warrants for payments for performances at Court during these years (Steele, pp. 39, 41, 45, 48, 57, 58, 59). By April 13, 1580, he had joined the Earl of Oxford's men, for on that date the Privy Council committed him and Robert Leveson, servants to the Earl of Oxford, to the Marshalsea for taking part in an affray with certain gentlemen of the Inns of Court (Dasent, xi. 445). Judging from their frequent shifting from one company to another, we may assume that the Duttons (John and Lawrence) were of an unstable temperament, an assumption that is further evidenced by some contemporary verses that emphasize their chameleon-like character (*Eliz. Stage*, ii. 98):

The Duttons and theyr fellow-players forsakyng the Erle of Warwycke theyr mayster, became followers of the Erle of Oxford, and wrot themselves his COMOEDIANS, which certayne Gentlemen altered and made CAMOELIONS. The Duttons, angry with that, compared themselves to any gentleman; therefore these armes were devysed for them:

> The fyeld, a fart durty, a gybbet crosse-corded,
> A dauncing Dame Flurty of all men abhorred;
> A lyther lad scampant, a roge in his ragges,
> A whore that is rampant, astryde wyth her legges,
> A woodcocke displayed, a calfe and a sheepe,
> A bitch that is splayed, a dormouse asleepe;
> A vyper in stynche, *la part de la drut*,
> Spell backwarde this Frenche and cracke me that nut.
>
> Parcy per pillery, perced with a rope,
> To slythe the more lytherly anoynted with sope;
> A coxcombe crospate in token of witte,

Two eares perforate, a nose wythe slytte.
Three nettles resplendent, three owles, three swallowes,
Three mynstrellmen pendent on three payre of gallowes,
Further sufficiently placed in them
A knaves head, for a difference from all honest men.

The wreathe is a chayne of chaungeable red,
To show they ar vayne and fickle of head;
The creste is a lastrylle whose feathers ar blew,
In signe that these fydlers will never be trew;
Whereon is placed the horne of a gote,
Because they ar chast, to this is theyr lotte,
For their bravery, indented and parted,
And for their knavery innebulated.

Mantled lowsy, wythe doubled drynke,
Their ancient house is called the Clynke;
Thys Posy they beare over the whole earthe,
Wylt please you to have a fyt of our mirthe?
But reason it is, and heraultes allowe welle,
That fidlers should beare their armes in a towelle.

John Dutton (*q.v.*) was a Queen's man in 1583 and 1588, and
we should expect to find the name of Lawrence in the lists with
that of his brother; but nothing further is known of Lawrence
until 1589, when he and John were associated in the leadership
of the Queen's company at Nottingham (Murray, ii. 375). On
March 7, 1591, the two brothers served as payees for performances
at Court by the Queen's men (Steele, p. 100). In October, 1588,
and June, 1590, when the Queen's players were also present, a
"Mr. Dutton" is recorded as having visited Latham House and
Knowsley Hall, Lancashire (Murray, ii. 296, 297); but his connection, if any, with the company is not apparent. In contemporary records are found other notices of a Lawrence Dutton,
which conjecture tends to identify with the player; but nothing
definite has been established. As a Court Messenger, a Lawrence
Dutton was paid for "sondry jorneys" in 1561–62 (*Eliz. Stage*, ii.
314); and he, or another of the same name, was from October,

1576, to July, 1581, a regular Messenger of the Chamber in the service of the Privy Council (Dasent, ix. 223; x. 223, 228; xi. 391, 423, 437; xii. 22, 23, 43; xiii. 135). On May 28, 1592, the Council recommended John, the son of Lawrence Dutton who had "of long tyme served her Majestie" as messenger, for admission as a Queen's Scholar at Westminster School (Dasent, xxii. 493). This Lawrence was apparently not the player, for he was serving as messenger on May 20, 1580 (Dasent, xii. 23), whereas the player had been committed to the Marshalsea on April 13 for participating in an affray with certain persons of the Inns of Court, and the matter was not referred to the judges for examination until May 26 (Dasent, xi. 445; xii. 37). In the reign of Edward VI (about 1552) a Thomas Dutton was employed as a government post between the Privy Council and Thomas Gresham, who was on official business in Antwerp; and the same Dutton appears about 1571 as Gresham's agent at Hamburg (Burgon, *Gresham*, i. 109; ii. 421). Also, the names John and Lawrence occur in the records of the house of Dutton of Dutton, which had an ancient and hereditary privilege for the licensing of minstrelsy in Cheshire (*Eliz. Stage*, i. 280, 299; iv. 271; *Med. Stage*, ii. 259).

EARLE, JOHN.

John Earle in 1640 was a hired man of Prince Charles's company. In an order of April 25, 1640, he is named as a Prince's man who is not "to be hindered or diverted in his service by being impressed, arrested, or otherwise molested, without leave first asked" (Stopes, *Jahrbuch*, xlvi. 103).

EATON, WILLIAM.

William Eaton appears as payee with Gilbert Reason for Prince Charles's provincial troupe at Coventry on December 23, 1622. He can not improbably be identified with the William Eyton of Ellis Guest's company, that was granted a license on June 7, 1628, and visited Norwich on July 2 of the same year (Murray, ii, 103, 249).

ECCLESTONE, WILLIAM.

As a King's man William Ecclestone assumed parts in *The Alchemist* (1610) and *Catiline* (1611). He belonged to the Lady Elizabeth's troupe by August 29, 1611, when he and his fellow-actors gave Henslowe a bond of £500 to perform "certen articles" of agreement (*H.P.*, pp. 18, 111), and with this company in 1613 he played in *The Honest Man's Fortune* (*Eliz. Stage*, ii. 251). Apparently later in the same year he again joined the King's men, for his name is in the actor-list of *Bonduca*, presented by that company in 1613-14. He is named as a King's man (*M.S.C.*, i. 280; Murray, i. opp. 172) in the patent of March 27, 1619; in the livery-allowance lists of May 19, 1619, and April 7, 1621; in the 1623 folio list of performers in Shakespeare's plays; and in the casts of the following Beaumont and Fletcher plays: *Bonduca* (1613-14), *The Loyal Subject* (1618), *The Mad Lover* (*c.* 1618), *The Humorous Lieutenant* (*c.* 1619), *The Custom of the Country* (*c.* 1619-20), *Women Pleased* (*c.* 1620), *The Little French Lawyer* (*c.* 1620), *The Island Princess* (*c.* 1620), *The Laws of Candy* (*c.* 1619-21), *The Sea Voyage* (1622), and *The Spamish Curate* (1622). Nicholas Tooley in his will dated June 3, 1623, forgave him a debt. He is conjectured to be the "William Eglestone" whose marriage to Anne Jacob is entered in the register of St. Saviour's, Southwark, on February 20, 1603 (Collier, *Actors*, pp. 241, 245). He is not named in the patent of June 24, 1625, by which date he had probably retired from the stage or was dead. It has been suggested that he may be the "W. E." who wrote the following commendatory verses to *The Wild-goose Chase*, published in 1652 by John Lowin and Joseph Taylor (Beaumont and Fletcher, *Works*, iv. 410):

An Epigram upon the long lost and fortunately recovered Wild-goose Chase, and as seasonably bestowed on Mr. John Lowen and Mr. Joseph Taylor, for their best advantage.

In this late dearth of wit, when *Jose* and *Jack*
Were hunger-bit for want of fowl and Sack;
His nobleness found out this happy meanes

To mend their dyet with these Wild-Goose scenes,
By which he hath revived in a day
Two Poets, and two Actors with one Play.

W. E.

EDMANS, JOHN.

See John Edmonds.

EDMONDS, JOHN.

About April, 1618, John Edmonds is named as a Queen Anne's man in a Letter of Assistance granting Martin Slater, Nathaniel Clay, and Edmonds permission to play as "her Majesties servants of her Royall Chamber of Bristol." On May 13, 1619, he attended the Queen's funeral with his fellow-actors (Murray, i. 196–97; ii. 5 f.). The marriage of a John Edmonds and Margaret Goodyere on February 22, 1600, and the baptism of children of John Edmonds, a player, between January 6, 1605, and July 17, 1615, are recorded in the registers of St. Saviour's (*Eliz. Stage*, ii. 315). But there was also a John Edmans (or Edmonds) as joint-legatee with Robert Goughe in the will, dated July 22, 1603, of Thomas Pope, who left them his wearing apparel and arms (Collier, *Actors*, p. 127). Another legatee in the will was Mary Clarke, who, with Thomas Bromley, received Pope's shares in the Curtain and the Globe playhouses. And subsequently, Edmans seems to have married his fellow-legatee, for an interest in the Globe, similar to that formerly held by Pope, was in the hands of John and Mary Edmonds and Basil Nicoll (Adams, *Mod. Phil.*, xvii. 3 ff.). A John Edmonds was buried at St. Saviour's, Southwark, on September 20, 1634 (Bentley, *T.L.S.*, Nov. 15, 1928, p. 856).

EDWARDS, RICHARD.

Master of the Chapel Royal, 1561–66, and author of various plays (Wallace, *Evolution*, pp. 106–16).

EGLESTONE, WILLIAM.

See William Ecclestone.

EICHELIN.

A company played at Nordlingen, Germany, in 1604, under the leadership of one Eichelin, apparently a German, whose repertory included a *Romeo and Juliet* and a *Pyramus and Thisbe*. This troupe has been conjectured to be the Blackwood-Thare combination that appeared at the Frankfort Easter fair in 1603; but the connection has not been established (Herz, pp. 43, 65).

ELDERTON, WILLIAM.

One Elderton, dressed as a fool, appeared as one of the Lord of Misrule's sons in the Christmas festivities of 1552–53 at the Court of Edward VI (Feuillerat, *Edw. & Mary*, p. 120). He may be identical with the Elderton who brought the Eton boys to Court on January 6, 1573, and the William Elderton who brought the Westminster boys to Court on January 1, 1574 (Steele, pp. 44, 47, 48). He has also been conjectured to be the bibulous ballad-writer who was frequently satirized by his contemporary pamphleteers. Little seems to be known of his life, for the references to him, though numerous, are chiefly concerned with his intemperate habits. Lyly (*Pappe with an Hatchet*, 1589) speaks of his "rimes lying a steepe in ale" (*Works*, iii. 398); Nashe (*Pierce Pennilesse*, 1592) says that he "consumd his ale-crammed nose to nothing" (*Works*, i. 197); and Harvey (*Foure Letters*, 1592) writes that "Rayling was the Ypocras of the drunken rimester" (*Works*, i. 163). He was a popular and voluminous composer of ballads, and some of his writing is valuable for the light it throws on the news-gathering activities of the ballad-mongers; but only a small proportion of his work has been preserved. Some of his ballads are reprinted in Collier, *Old Ballads*; H. Huth, *Ancient Ballads and Broadsides*; and H. L. Collman, *Ballads and Broadsides*. A "master Eldertun" was a justice at the Guildhall in the coining case of 1562 (Machyn, *Diary*, p. 290); and Stow speaks of a William Elderton as an attorney in the sheriff's court at the Guildhall about 1568 (*Survey*, i. 272). When *Foure Letters Con-*

futed was published in 1592, Elderton appears to have been dead, for Nashe refers to him as being "as dead as dead beere," and alludes to his ghost (*Works*, i. 280). A more detailed account of Elderton by H. E. Rollins may be found in *Studies in Philology* (1920), xvii. 199.

ENGLISH, JOHN.

John English was a Court Interluder in 1494, and his name is traceable in the accounts up to 1531. Henry VII had four players of interludes, who received each an annual fee of £3 6s. 8d., with special awards when they played before the King. When their services were not required at Court, they traveled in the provinces, as did the minstrels of the royal establishment. In 1494 English appears to have been the leader of the company of interluders, which included Edward May, Richard Gibson, and John Hammond. In 1503 the interlude players of Henry VII, with English as leader, accompanied the Princess Margaret to Scotland for her wedding with James IV at Edinburgh, where they "did their devoir" before the Scottish Court. After the death of Henry VII in 1509 the royal troupe was continued under the patronage of Henry VIII; and English, as a performer of experience and eminence, remained at the head of the company, apparently with a salary of £6 13s. 4d. He is often individually mentioned in the documents, and appears as leader of the interluders until 1531 (Collier, i. 44, 45, 49, 79, 96, 113; Chambers, *Med. Stage*, ii. 187).

ERRINGTON, RICHARD.

In 1622 Richard Errington appears at Norwich as manager of a company under the patronage of King James. This company was doubtless a provincial one, for Errington is not mentioned in the lists of the King's troupe in London (Murray, ii. 6 ff., 371). Shortly after the accession of Charles I in 1625, some members of the company united with the players at the Red Bull (cf. Adams, *Playhouses*, pp. 301 f.). In November, 1627, the troupe visited Ludlow, and while the players were performing at an inn, at about ten or eleven o'clock on the night of November 21, five or six drunken men caused a disturbance. Errington, who was serving as gatherer at the door, fearing an attack, "took his money out the boxe and putt ytt in his hand." Another player appeared at the door and demanded the cause of the noise. Whereupon one Powell drew his rapier and attempted to stab Errington. William Baker, the town sergeant, then sought to restore peace, and was seized by the drunken men, dragged through the streets, and given a severe beating. The next day Errington was called before the town authorities to report the trouble. In his deposition he is described as "of the Citty of London, pewterer, aged 50 yeares or thereaboute" (Murray, ii. 326). Subsequently, he left the Red Bull company, for on July 15, 1631, a license was granted to him and Ellis Guest; and their troupe visited Reading on July 18. This troupe seems to have been later taken under the patronage of Queen Henrietta as her traveling company, for when the men visited Norwich on June 22, 1633, they were designated as "the Quenes players" (Murray, ii. 104, 354, 386–87). The company probably disbanded in 1635, since it is not mentioned after that year; and on April 22, 1636, Errington is recorded at Coventry as joint-payee for William Daniel's King's Revels players (Murray, ii. 9, 252).

ESTOTEVILLE, GEORGE.

George Estoteville in 1640 belonged to Beeston's Boys at the Cockpit in Drury Lane. Early in May, 1640, Beeston allowed his boys to act without license a play that gave great offense to King Charles I. As a result, on May 3, Beeston, Estoteville, "and the rest of the Company of Players at the Cockpit in Drury Lane" were ordered to stop playing until further notice from the Master of the Revels (Murray, i. 369). Estoteville contributed commendatory verses to Thomas Heywood's *Nine Worthy Women* (1640), in which he expressed astonishment at the poet's continued productivity:

Will neither rugged time or vast expence
Of thy unfathom'd fancy and cleare sence
Perswade thee to leave off, but thou wilt still
Make all 'twixt heaven and hell flow from thy Quill?

EVANS, GOULDWAIS.

The register of St. Saviour's, Southwark, records on August 13, 1629, the baptism of William, son of Gouldwais Evans, "a musitoan" (Bentley, *T.L.S.*, Nov. 15, 1928, p. 856).

EVANS, HENRY.

Henry Evans, a Welsh scrivener, was lessee of the First Blackfriars playhouse in 1583 and of the Second Blackfriars from 1600 to 1608 (Adams, *Playhouses*, pp. 107, 201–23). He served as payee for *Agamemnon and Ulysses*, presented at Court by Oxford's troupe on December 27, 1584 (Steele, p. 91). In 1600 he "set up" the Children of the Chapel Royal at Blackfriars, and was associated in their management until about 1603, when the company became known as the Children of the Queen's Revels, for which he served as joint-payee with Samuel Daniel for performances at Court on January 1 and 3, 1605 (*Eliz. Stage*, ii. 41–50; Steele, pp. 141, 142). In 1582 he had been overseer to the will of Sebastian Westcott, Master of the Children of St. Paul's (*Eliz. Stage*, ii. 15n.).

EVESEED, HENRY.

Henry Eveseed belonged to the Children of the Chapel Royal for some time before November 30, 1585, on which date he was sworn in as a Gentleman of the Chapel. He appears to have died on November 18, 1614 (Hillebrand, *Mod. Phil.*, xviii. 254, 258).

EYDTWARTT, JOHN.

A player with Robert Reynolds's company at Torgau, Germany, in 1627 (Herz, p. 31).

EYTON, WILLIAM.

See William Eaton.

FARMER, JOHN.

A member of the Children of Paul's in 1554 (Hillebrand, *Child Actors*, p. 110).

FARNABY, RICHARD.

Richard Farnaby, son of the composer Giles Farnaby, was a musician in Germany about 1623–24, at the Court of Philip Julius, Duke of Wolgast (Meyer, *Jahrbuch*, xxxviii. 209; Fellowes, *Eng. Madg. Composers*, p. 233).

FARRANT, RICHARD.

Master of the Children of Windsor, 1564–80; Acting Master of the Children of the Chapel Royal, and lessee of the First Black-friars playhouse, 1576–80 (Chambers, *Eliz. Stage*, ii. 36; Adams, *Playhouses*, pp. 91–110).

FENN, EZEKIEL.

Ezekiel Fenn (Fen or Phen) played Sophonisba in Nabbes's *Hannibal and Scipio*, acted in 1635 by Queen Henrietta's men at the Cockpit in Drury Lane (Murray, i. opp. 266). His name appears at the close of the Epilogue to *The Witch of Edmonton* (Dekker, *Works*, iv. 428). Since the Epilogue is spoken by Winnifrede, Sir Arthur Clarington's maid, we may infer that the part was acted by Fenn. The play, not printed until 1658, may have passed from Prince Charles's men to Queen Henrietta's company about 1625, when the latter troupe was organized (Murray, i. 236n.). When the Queen's men disbanded early in 1637, Fenn doubtless joined Beeston's Boys, for on May 12, 1637, he and other members of Beeston's company were summoned before the Privy Council for playing at the Cockpit during plague quarantine (*M.S.C.*, i. 392). Henry Glapthorne in his *Poems* (1639) gives a "Prologue" entitled, *For Ezekiel Fen at his first Acting a Mans Part*, in which he compares Fenn's trepidation at his début in a masculine rôle to a merchant's fear on launching an untried vessel (*Plays and Poems*, ii. 196).

, The verses imply that Fenn was accustomed to the impersonation of female characters, an implication supported by his playing Sophonisba and Winnifrede in the above plays; and although he seems to have subsequently changed to male characterizations we have no record of his later appearances on the stage.

FERRABOSCO, ALFONSO.

"Alfruse Ferrabolle and the rest of the Italian players" received payment for a performance at Court on February 27, 1576 (Steele, p. 59). The entry no doubt refers to Alfonso Ferrabosco, the eminent Italian musician who lived in England during the sixteenth century. He appears to have already won the favor of the English Court by 1562, when he was granted an annuity of 100 marks. With various interruptions he remained in the service of Elizabeth until 1578, when he came under the patronage of the Duke of Saxony. His son and grandson in turn contributed to the gaiety of the Jacobean and Caroline courts (Grove's *Dict. Music*, ii. 21 ff.).

FERRET, JAMES.

James Ferret is recorded at Norwich on March 10, 1635, when his troupe, presumably the King's Revels, applied for permission to act in that town (Murray, i. 279–80).

FERRIS, DAVID.

Under a license dated November 10, 1629, David Ferris is named as a member of the Red Bull company that appeared at Reading on November 30 of the same year (Murray, ii. 386).

FETHERSON, WILLIAM.

An unlicensed player of Danby, Yorkshire, in 1612 (*Eliz. Stage*, i. 305*n*.).

FIDGE, WILLIAM.

William Fidge may have been a player, as suggested by a record of 1571, when with one Whetstone he owed Robert Betts, a deceased Canterbury painter, 35*s*. 4*d*. "for their portions in buy-inge of certen playe-bookes" (Plomer, *Library*, 1918, ix. 252).

FIELD, HENRY.

Henry Field is recorded at Norwich on March 10, 1635, when his troupe, presumably the King's Revels, applied for permission to act in that town (Murray, i. 279–80).

FIELD, NATHAN.

Nathan Field was baptized at St. Giles's, Cripplegate, on October 7, 1587 (Collier, iii, 425). He was the son of John Field, a Puritan preacher who was an ardent opponent of the stage. John, in 1583, saw a judgment of God in the collapse of the Bear Garden on a Sunday, and published a vehement attack upon all theatrical performances, entitled, *A Godly Exhortation by Occasion of the Late Judgment of God, Shewed at Parris-Garden the Thirteenth Day of Januarie*. If John Field, who died in 1588, had lived to mold the life of his son, dramatic history would no doubt have been deprived of one of its most interesting figures. Nathan has been the subject of much controversy. Collier, finding that another son of John Field had been baptized "Nathaniel" on June 13, 1581, and not allowing for the idiosyncrasies of the puritanical theologian who might well call his sons by the easily-confused names of "Nathan" and "Nathaniel" (Field already had sons named "John" and "Jonathan"), assumed that Nathaniel must have died before the birth of Nathan. This assumption led to the error that accredits to Nathan Field the double life of actor and bookseller. Contemporary pros and cons of the argument are detailed by Greg (*Times Lit. Suppl.*, April 15, 1926, p. 283, and June 3, 1926, p. 374) and Baldwin (*Mod. Lang. Notes*, 1926, xli. 32, and *Times Lit. Suppl.*, May 27, 1926, p. 355); a more recent article by Miss Brinkley (*Mod. Lang. Notes*, 1927, xlii. 10) corroborates Greg's view that Nathan the player is distinct from Nathaniel the stationer. Nathaniel did not die in infancy, as Collier supposed, but was apprenticed to Ralph Jackson, stationer, at Michaelmas, 1596, took up his freedom on June 3, 1611, and became a publisher. He issued some books during 1624–27, and seems to have dealt chiefly in theological literature, including sermons by a third brother, Theophilus Field, Bishop of Llandaff (McKerrow, *Dictionary*, p. 101). When his brother registered as an apprentice in 1596 Nathan was not yet nine years old, whereas fifteen or sixteen was the customary age of apprenticeship in the Stationers' Company. Until some one produces evidence either that Nathaniel, whom Collier unreasonably murdered in infancy, died before 1587, or that Nathan was ever a printer or publisher, we must regard the two brothers as distinct persons in their respective professions of publishing and acting. About 1600, at the age of thirteen, Nathan was impressed to join the Children of the Chapel Royal at Blackfriars. At this time, as shown by Clifton's complaint in 1601, he was a "scholler of a gramer schole in London, kepte by one Mr. Monkaster" (Wallace, *Blackfriars*, p. 80), i.e. St. Paul's Grammar School under the mastership of Richard Mulcaster. He also received instruction from Ben Jonson, who in 1619 told William Drummond of Hawthornden that "Nid Field was his schollar, and he had read to him the Satyres of Horace, and some Epigrames of Martiall" (*Conversations*, ed. Patterson, p. 15). From 1600 to 1613 he was a member of the Chapel Royal, after 1603 designated as the Queen's Revels, or Children of the Revels. His name appears in the casts of *Cynthia's Revels* (1600), *The Poetaster* (1601), and *Epicoene*, which, according to the folio of 1616, was acted in 1609. He possibly acted Humphrey in *The Knight of the Burning Pestle* (c. 1610), for the Citizen's Wife asks (I. ii. 25): "Were you never one of Master Moncaster's scholars?" In March, 1613, there was an amalgamation of the Queen's Revels, under the management of Philip Rosseter, and the Lady Elizabeth's men, under Philip Henslowe; and Field, as leader of the combined troupe under the patronage of the Lady Elizabeth, repre-

A DICTIONARY OF ACTORS

sented the company in an agreement with Henslowe and Meade (*H.P.*, pp. 23 ff.). The 1679 folio of Beaumont and Fletcher names Field as one of the "principal actors" in *The Coxcomb* and *The Honest Man's Fortune*, both of which were probably acted by the Lady Elizabeth's company in 1613 (*Eliz. Stage*, ii. 251). In *Bartholomew Fair* (V. iii), presented by the Lady Elizabeth's company in 1614, Jonson pays him a high compliment by coupling him with Burbage and introducing his name as synonymous with "best actor" (*Works*, iv. 482):

> *Cokes.* Which is your Burbage now?
> *Leatherhead.* What mean you by that, sir?
> *Cokes.* Your best actor, your Field?
> *Littlewit.* Good, i'faith! you are even with me, sir.

The part of Littlewit was presumably taken by Field himself. The Articles of Grievance against Henslowe in 1615 seem to imply that Field was suspected of accepting bribes from Henslowe to promote the interest of the manager rather than that of the players (*H.P.*, p. 88). The suspicion may have been unwarranted; but certainly his financial difficulties necessitated his appealing to Henslowe on more than one occasion (*H.P.*, pp. 66, 67, 84). On June 11, 1615, he served as payee for *Bartholomew Fair*, which had been presented at Court by the Lady Elizabeth's men (Steele, p. 189). During 1615 there seems to have been some kind of fusion of Prince Charles's company and the Lady Elizabeth's men, but Field does not appear in the combined troupes. The friction noted in the Articles of Grievance may account for his withdrawal. Subsequently, possibly in 1615, he joined the King's men. He appears as a King's man in the actor-lists of the following Beaumont and Fletcher plays (Murray, i. opp. 172): *The Queen of Corinth* (*c.* 1617), *The Knight of Malta* (*c.* 1618), *The Mad Lover* (*c.* 1618), and *The Loyal Subject* (1618). His name is also given in the 1623 folio list of performers in Shakespeare's plays; in the patent of March 27, 1619; and in the livery-allowance list of May 19, 1619. His connection with the King's company apparently lasted only about four years, for he is neither among the players named in the stage-directions to *Sir John van Olden Barnavelt*, of August, 1619, nor in the livery allowance of April 7, 1621. And recent evidence shows that he died between May 19, 1619, when his name is given in the livery allowance, and August 2, 1620, when Letters of Administration were issued to his sister; that he was a bachelor; and that he was a resident of the parish of St. Giles, Cripplegate (Brinkley *Mod. Lang. Notes*, 1927, xlii. 13):

> The second day (of August 1620) a commission was granted to Dorcas Rise otherwise Feild natural and lawful sister of Nathan Feild late of the parish of Saint Giles in the county of Middlesex bachelor deceased having etc. to administer the good rights and credits of the deceased etc. sworn.

Moreover, the same article clarifies the distinction between the two brothers with similar names but entirely different professions, for on March 26, 1633, Anne Field received a commission for the administration of the goods of her husband, Nathaniel, whose burial is recorded in the register of St. Anne, Blackfriars, on February 20, 1633, and whose children (Collier, iii. 436–38) are recorded in the same parish (Brinkley, *Mod. Lang. Notes*, 1927, xlii. 14):

> On the 26th of March 1632 [1633] Letters of Administration were granted to Anne Feild relict of Nathaniel Feild late of the parish of Saint Anne Blackfryers London intestate deceased to administer the goods credits chattels etc. of the said deceased, etc.

Field was the author of two excellent plays, *A Woman is a Weathercock* (1612) and *Amends for Ladies* (1616). In the address "To the reader" of the former play, he writes: "If thou hast anything to say to me, thou know'st where to hear of me for a yeer or two, and no more, I assure you" (Hazlitt's *Dodsley*, xi. 7, 8), which has been taken to mean that he had no intention of spending his life on the stage. Besides the two plays published under his name alone, he collaborated with Massinger in *The*

Fatal Dowry (1632), a King's men's play that probably dates from 1616–19. The Henslowe papers (*H.P.*, pp. 65 ff., 84) show him also as a collaborator with Daborne, Fletcher, and Massinger in plays for the Lady Elizabeth's troupe, which has led to the conjecture that he possibly had a share in the authorship of several of the plays belonging to the Beaumont and Fletcher series. He also, about 1609–10, contributed a commendatory poem (Beaumont and Fletcher, *Works*, ii. 519) of thirty-six lines to *The Faithful Shepherdess*, with the address, "To my lov'd friend M. John Fletcher, on his Pastorall," in which he expresses the hope that his own "muse in swathing clowtes" may rise "to perfect such a work as" Fletcher's,—

> Clad in such elegant proprietie
> Of words, including a mortallitie.

And in 1616, about the time that he joined the King's men, he entered the controversial field of writing with a defense of the stage, which took the form of a remonstrance to the Reverend Mr. Sutton for his disloyalty in denouncing the players who are patronized by the King. The tractate is entitled *Feild the Players Letter to Mr. Sutton, Preacher att St. Mary Overs* (Halliwell-Phillipps, *Illustrations*, p. 115). Field was obviously susceptible to the charms of Aphrodite, as evidenced by a punning epigram preserved in various Jacobean and Caroline commonplace books, apparently referring to his "too much familiarity" with "the Lady May" (Collier, iii. 434):

> *Field, the Player, on his Mistress, the Lady May*
> It is the fair and merry month of May,
> That clothes the Field in all his rich array,
> Adorning him with colours better dyed
> Than any king can wear, or any bride.
> But May is almost spent, the Field grows dun
> With too much gazing on that May's hot sun;
> And if mild Zephirus, with gentle wind,
> Vouchsafe not his calm breath, and the clouds kind
> Distil their honey-drops, his heat to 'lay,
> Poor Field will burn e'en in the midst of May.

And on June 5, 1619, Sir William Trumbull, ambassador to Holland, wrote from Brussels to Lord Hay that he was told that the Earl of Argyll had paid "for the nourseing of a childe which the worlde says is a daughter to my lady and N. Feild the Player" (Scott, *Athenæum*, January 21, 1882, p. 103). Lady Argyll was Anne, daughter of Sir William Cornwallis of Brome (*Eliz. Stage*, ii. 317). Field is alluded to in a letter of May 24, 1619, from the Reverend Thomas Lorkin to Sir Thomas Puckering: "The Bishop of LLandaff shall be advanced higher . . . and Dr. [Theophilus] Field (Field, the player's brother), shall succeed Llandaff" (Birch, *Court and Times of James I*, ii. 167). John Taylor, the Water Poet, in *Wit and Mirth* ((1629), p. 30, gives a jest about him (*Works*, p. 345):

A Quiblet

Master *Field* the Player riding vp *Fleetstreet* a great pace, a Gentleman called him, and asked him what Play was played that day: hee (being angry to be stayd vpon so friuolous a demand) answered, that he might see what Play was to be playd vpon euery *Poste*. I cry you mercy (said the Gentleman) I tooke you for a *Poste*. you road so fast.

Field and Underwood of the Children of the Chapel Royal are mentioned by Wright in *Historia Histrionica* (1699): "Some of these chapel-boys, when they grew men, became actors at the Blackfriars; such were Nathan Field and John Underwood" (Hazlitt's *Dodsley*, xv. 416). Although we have no detailed list of the characters in which Field won fame, we do know that his histrionic ability placed him beside Edward Alleyn and Richard Burbage. Richard Flecknoe in *A Discourse of the English Stage* (1664) mentions him with the most eminent artists of his time: "In this time were Poets and Actors in their greatest flourish, *Johnson*, *Shakespear*, with *Beaumont* and *Fletcher* their Poets and *Field* and *Burbidge* their Actors. . . . It was the happiness of the Actors of those Times to have such Poets as these to instruct them and write for them; and no less of those Poets, to have such docile and excellent Actors to Act their Playes, as a *Field* and *Burbidge*" (Spingarn, *Crit. Essays of Seventeenth Cent.*, ii. 92, 94 f.). As witnessed by the complimentary allusion to him in *Bartholo-mew Fair* (1614), Field was the chief actor of the Lady Elizabeth's troupe, corresponding to Burbage of the King's men. Early in his career he seems to have undertaken female parts (*Variorum*, iii. 213), which he later abandoned and attained much celebrity as the hero of Chapman's *Bussy D'Ambois*, originally published in 1607. In the Prologue to the edition of 1641, he is praised as Bussy (Parrott, *Trag. of Chapman*, p. 3):

Field is gone,
Whose action did first give it name.

The performances by Field referred to in the Prologue were presumably by the King's men not earlier than 1616, by which date he seems to have joined the company. His portrait is at Dulwich, with the description: " ' Master Feild's ' picture in his shirt; on a board, in a black frame, 'filited' with gold; an actor" (Warner, p. 207). For further details see Roberta F. Brinkley, *Nathan Field, the Actor-Playwright*, Yale University Press, 1928.

FISHER, JOHN.

A joint-lessee of the new Fortune playhouse, in which he obtained a half-share on May 20, 1622 (Warner, pp. 246-47).

FLETCHER, LAWRENCE.

Lawrence Fletcher appears to have been the leader of a company of players in Scotland during 1595, 1599, and 1601. On March 22, 1595, George Nicolson, the English agent at Edinburgh, wrote to Robert Bowes, treasurer of Berwick, that, "The King heard that Fletcher, the player, was hanged, and told him and Roger Aston so, in merry words, not believing it, saying very pleasantly that if it were true he would hang them also" (*S.P. Scottish*, ii. 676). On November 12, 1599, Nicolson wrote to Sir Robert Cecil concerning "Performances of English players,

Fletcher, Martin, and their company, by the King's permission; enactment of the Town Sessions, and preaching of the ministers against them. The bellows blowers say that they are sent by England to sow dissension between the King and the Kirk" (*S. P. Scottish*, ii. 777). The players were in high favor with King James, and this led to rather critical relations between him and the Kirk, which passed an act that "none should resort to these profane comedeis" (Calderwood, *History*, v. 765.) Whereupon the Sovereign ordered the Kirk to rescind the act, "and to give a special ordinance to the ministers, that, in their sermons on Sunday next, they publickly admonish their said flocks, that they will not restrain nor censure any of them that shall repair to the said comedies and plays" (*S.P. Scottish*, ii. 778). By 1601 the trouble seems to have subsided, as suggested by an entry of October 22 in the Aberdeen register. The players came in the company of "Sir Francis Hospitall of Haulszie, Knycht, Frechman," and were given the freedom of the city. Among those "admittit burgesses" was Lawrence Fletcher, "comediane to his Majestie" (Stuart, *Extracts*, ii. p. xxii). Conjecture has identified this Scottish troupe with the Chamberlain's men, on the supposition that the latter company was inhibited in London for acting *Richard II* in 1601 (Fleay, *Stage*, p. 136), but there is no evidence to support the theory. Little is known of Fletcher outside of Scotland. He may be the person referred to in the Admiral's accounts of October, 1596, where Henslowe records certain sums "lent vnto Martyne to feache Fleacher," and "lent the company to geue Fleatcher" (*H.D.* i. 45). His name stands first in the patent of May 19, 1603, granted to the King's men, and third in the coronation list of March 15, 1604. He does not appear to have joined the company acting at the Globe, for he is not named in the cast of *Sejanus* (1603) or in the 1623 folio list of performers in Shakespeare's plays. The explanation seems to be that since he was a favorite with the King in Scotland, he retained his status as a King's servant when James succeeded to

he English throne. On May 4, 1605, he is described in the will
of Augustine Phillips as his "fellow," but the meaning of the
term is somewhat vague and does not necessarily mean that he
was actively associated with the King's players (*Eliz. Stage*, ii.
109, 270). He lived in St. Saviour's, Southwark, where he had a
homonym, a victualler, who survived him. The token-books record a Lawrence Fletcher as living in Hunt's Rents, Maid Lane,
during 1605, 1606, and 1607. This may have been the actor,
who was buried on September 12, 1608. The entry, "Lawrence
Fletcher, a man: in the church," of the register is expanded in
the monthly accounts of deaths in the parish to "Lawrence
Fletcher, a player, the King's servant, buried in the church, with
an afternoon's knell of the great bell, 20s." (Collier, *Actors*, pp.
x–xi; Rendle, *Bankside*, p. xxvii).

FLORIDOR, JOSIAS.

On May 10, 1635, a warrant was issued for the payment of £30
to "Mons. Josias Floridor, for himself and the rest of the French
players for three plays" presented at the Cockpit. Again on January 8, 1636, there was a payment of £10 to "Josias Floridor for
himself and the rest of the French players for a tragedy by them
played before His Majesty Dec. last." The French players, under
the leadership of Josias de Soulas, generally known by his stage-
name of Floridor, had come to London in February, 1633. They
won the favor of the Court, played at the Cockpit in Drury Lane,
and were later permitted to equip a temporary playhouse in the
riding-school of one M. Le Febure (or Fevure) in Drury Lane
(Adams, *Playhouses*, pp. 401, 420–24; *Dram. Rec.*, pp. 60 ff.).
Floridor's career on the French stage is recorded in Hawkins's
Annals of the French Stage (1884), i. 148 ff. "Every gift required by
the actor," says Hawkins, "was possessed by Floridor." Henry
Glapthorne in his comedy entitled *The Ladies Privilege* (1640)
gives a good-natured burlesque on the vivacious characteristics
of the French players (*Plays and Poems*, ii. 106):

> *Lactantio.*   But *Adorni*,
> What thinke you of the *French*?
>   *Adorni.* Very ayry people, who participate
> More fire than earth; yet generally good,
> And nobly disposition'd, something inclining
>   [*Enter Corimba.*
> To over-weening fancy—This Lady
> Tells my remembrance of a Comick scene,
> I once saw in their Theatre.
>   *Bonivet.* Adde it to
> Your former courtesies, and expresse it.

And the stage-direction notes that "*Adorni Acts furiously.*"

FLOWER.

A writer signing himself "Dramaticus," in *Shakespeare Society's Papers*, iv. 110, describes a copy of Dekker's *Shoemaker's Holiday* with alleged manuscript notes giving the cast of the play as produced by the Admiral's men about 1600. To Flower is assigned the part of Warner, a citizen. Greg discredits the list as "an obvious forgery" (*H.D.* ii. 203).

FOSTER, ALEXANDER.

Alexander Foster belonged to the Lady Elizabeth's troupe on August 29, 1611, when he and his fellow-actors gave Philip Henslowe a bond of £500 to perform "certen articles" of agreement (*H.P.*, pp. 18, 111). On April 1, 1612, he received payment on behalf of the Lady Elizabeth's men for plays presented at Court during the Christmas season of 1611-12. In 1615-16 there seems to have been some kind of amalgamation of Prince Charles's company and the Lady Elizabeth's men, and Foster appears as payee for the Court performances by the Prince's men at Christmas, 1615-16 (Steele, pp. 171, 174, 195). He was again a member of the Lady Elizabeth's troupe on March 20, 1618, when a license was granted to him, John Townsend, Joseph Moore, and Francis Wambus; and with this company he seems to have remained until 1629. He is named in a license of March 20, 1622; in a bill of March 13, 1622, signed by the Lord Chamberlain; in a warrant of June 30, 1628, appointing as Grooms of the Chamber several of the Lady Elizabeth's (Queen of Bohemia's) players; and in a license of December 9, 1628. He also appears in provincial records of the visits of the company: at Norwich, May 23, 1618, April 22, 1620, May 10, 1623; and at Reading, December 24, 1629 (Murray, i. 252, 255, 259; ii. 344, 345, 346–47, 386; Stopes, *Jahrbuch*, xlvi. 94).

FOUCH, RICHARD.

In December, 1631 (Adams, *Dram. Rec.*, p. 45), Richard Fouch played Margery, maid to Millescent, in Marmion's *Holland's Leaguer*, presented by "the high and mighty Prince Charles his servants, at the private house in Salisbury Court" (Marmion, *Works*, pp. 2, 6).

FOWLER, RICHARD.

Richard Fowler is mentioned in the lease of the Fortune by Edward Alleyn to the Palsgrave's men on October 31, 1618 (*H. P.*, p. 27), and in the 1622 Herbert list of the Palsgrave's company (Adams, *Dram. Rec.*, p. 63). In 1623 he was living "in Redcrosse Streete" (Wallace, *Jahrbuch*, xlvi. 348.) On April 30, 1624, he and others of the Palsgrave's men entered into a bond to Richard Gunnell, manager of the company (Hotson, pp. 52–53). He may have remained with the Palsgrave's company until December, 1631, when the troupe seems to have passed under the patronage of the young Prince Charles, for during the same month (Adams, *Dram. Rec.*, p. 45) he played Snarl in Marmion's *Holland's Leaguer*, presented by "the high and mighty Prince Charles his servants, at the private house in Salisbury Court" (Marmion, *Works*, pp. 2, 6). He is named in a warrant of May 10, 1632, appointing as Grooms of the Chamber several of Prince Charles's men (Stopes, *Jahrbuch*, xlvi. 96). Edmund Gayton makes an allusion to him in his *Pleasant Notes upon Don Quixot* (1654), p. 271: "It was not then the most mimicall nor fighting man, *Fowler*, nor *Andrew*

Cane could pacifie; Prologues nor Epilogues would prevaile; the Devill and the fool were quite out of favour." The register of St. Giles, Cripplegate, records the burial of Thomas, son of Richard Fowler, in 1624, and the burial of a Richard Fowler in September, 1643 (Malcolm, *Lond. Rediv.*, iii. 304).

FREYERBOTT, BARTHOLOMEUS.

Bartholomeus Freyerbott was in the service of the Elector of Brandenburg in 1615, when he and Johann Friedrich Virnius visited Danzig as the Brandenburg comedians (Bolte, p. 41).

FRITH, MARY.

Chambers (*Eliz. Stage*, iii. 296–97) suggests that the lines in the Epilogue to Middleton and Dekker's comedy of *The Roaring Girl* (Dekker, *Works*, iii. 234),

> The *Roring Girle* her selfe some few dayes hence,
> Shall on this Stage, giue larger recompence,

"refer to a contemplated personal appearance of Mary Frith," the heroine of the play, on the Fortune stage about 1610. The play was printed in 1611 "As it hath lately beene Acted on the Fortune-stage by the Prince his Players."

FROST, JOHN.

As a member of the Children of the Chapel Royal, John Frost appears in the cast of Jonson's *Cynthia's Revels*, acted in 1600 (*Eliz. Stage*, iii. 363).

GARLAND, JOHN.

John Garland became associated with Queen Elizabeth's men when the troupe was first established in 1583, and is named in a London record that gives the personnel of the company at this time (*Eliz. Stage*, ii. 106). He no doubt remained with the Queen's men, for he is mentioned in a document of June 30, 1588, concerning the non-payment of subsidy by certain members of the company (*M.S.C.*, i. 354). By March, 1605, he belonged to the company under the patronage of the Duke of Lennox, who may have taken over some members of the Queen's troupe at her death in 1603. On March 1, 1605, Abraham Saverey gave Francis Henslowe a Power of Attorney to recover £40 from John Garland of "the ould forde," forfeited on a bond "for the deliuere of a warrant, which was mayd vnto me frome the gratious the duke of Linox"; and on March 16, 1605, Francis Henslowe gave his uncle Philip a bond of £60 to observe articles of an agreement that he had made with Garland and Saverey "his ffellowes, servantes to the most noble Prince the duke of Lennox" (*H.P.*, pp. 62 ff.). There was also an undated loan, probably of 1604, of £7 by Philip Henslowe to his nephew Francis "to goyne with owld Garlland and Symcöckes and Saverey when they played in the duckes nam at their laste goinge owt" (*H.D.*, i. 160). Garland is named in a patent granted on March 30, 1610, to the company under the patronage of Prince Charles, then Duke of York, and known as the Duke of York's men. After Prince Henry's death in November, 1612, they became entitled to the designation of Prince Charles's players; and this troupe is perhaps a continuation of the company formerly patronized by the Duke of Lennox (*Eliz. Stage*, ii. 243). On May 18, 1615, the Prince's men visited Norwich, where they were allowed to play eight days; the records give the names of Garland, William Rowley, and Thomas Hobbes (Murray, ii. 340). By March 20, 1616, he had doubtless retired from the stage, for his name does not appear in the agreement between the Prince's company and Alleyn and Meade, although both Rowley and Hobbes are mentioned. As noted in the transaction of March 1, 1605, with Saverey and Henslowe, Garland apparently lived at "the ould forde," which was on the River Lea, near Hackney Marsh (*H.P.*, p. 62*n.*).

GARLICK.

A comic player named Garlick seems to have appeared in jigs on the Fortune stage, as recorded by I. H. in *This World's Folly*

(1615): "I will not particularize those . . . *Fortune*-fatted fooles, . . . who are faine to produce blinde *Impudence* ["Garlicke" printed in margin], to personate himselfe vpon their stage, behung with chaynes of Garlicke, as an Antidote against their owne infectious breaths, lest it should kill their Oyster-crying Audience" (*Eliz. Stage*, iv. 254). Other apparent allusions to him are made by Dekker, *If It be not Good, the Devil is in It*, 1610–12 (*Works*, iii. 325):

> *Scumbroth.* No, no, if Fortune fauourd me, I should be full, but Fortune fauours no body but Garlicke, nor Garlicke neither now, yet she has strong reason to loue it; for tho Garlicke made her smell abhominably in the nostrils of the gallants, yet she had smelt and stuncke worse but for garlicke;

by Henry Parrott, *Laquei Ridiculosi*, 1613 (Collier, *Bibl. Acc.*, iv. 282): "Greene's Tu Quoque and those Garlick Jigs"; by Robert Tailor, *The Hog Hath Lost His Pearl*, 1614 (Hazlitt's *Dodsley*, xi. 434):

> *Haddit.* A small matter! you'll find it worth Meg of Westminster, although it be but a bare jig.
> *Player.* O Lord, sir, I would it had but half the taste of garlic.
> *Haddit.* Garlic stinks to this; if it prove that you have not more whores than e'er garlic had;

and by John Taylor, the Water Poet, *A Cast over the Water*, about 1615 (*Works*, 1630, p. 321):

> And for his action he eclipseth quite
> The Iigge of Garlick, or the Punks delight.

GARRETT, JOHN.

John Garrett appears among the representatives of Queen Anne's London and provincial companies of players who attended her funeral on May 13, 1619 (Murray, i. 196–97). Perhaps he is to be identified with the John Garrett, player-fool and jester, celebrated by John Taylor, the Water Poet, in *Wit and Mirth* (1629), described on the title-page as "Apothegmatically

148

bundled vp and garbled at the request of old John Garrett's
Ghost," and having an introduction of 102 verses entitled "John
Garrets Ghost," in which the ghost of the jester speaks to the
poet. That Garrett was a favorite at the Elizabethan, Jacobean,
and Caroline Courts is evidenced by the introductory verses:

> And to the Court I often made resort
> When *Englands* mighty *Queene Elizabeth*
> Allow'd me entertainment for disport;
> Then by the foretop did I take old time:
> Then were not halfe so many fooles as now;
> Then was my haruest, and my onely prime,
> My purse receiuing what my wit did plow.
> Then in such compasse I my jests would hold,
> That though I gaue a man a gird or twaine,
> All his reuenge would be to giue me gold,
> With commendations of my nimble braine.
> Thus liu'd I, till that gracious Queene deceast,
> Who was succeeded by a famous King,
> In whose blest Sons reigne (I with yeeres opprest)
> Me to my graue sicknesse and death did bring.

And in the dedicatory epistle addressed to "Master Archibold
Rankin," Taylor alludes to Garrett as "that old honest mirrour
of mirth, deceased," and informs the dedicatee that he might
have inscribed the "bundle of mirth" to that "peerelesse Princesse . . . to whose seruice, and for whose happiness, his [Gar-
rett's] life and best endeauours, with his prayers and implora-
tions at his death, were vnfainedly consecrated" (Hazlitt, *Jest-
Books*, iii). There is an allusion to him in *Verses uppon C[hrist]
C[hurch] play, made by Mr. Holliday, acted before the King at Wood-
stocke*, 1638 (Halliwell-Phillipps, *Marriage of Wit and Wisdom*,
p. 86):

> Why, all the guard, that never knew a letter
> But that uppon ther coates, whose witt consists
> In Archyes bobs and Garretts sawcy jeasts.

In *Wits Recreations* (1640) is printed the following epitaph (ii.
239):

A DICTIONARY OF ACTORS

On John Garret

Gone is John Garret, who to all men's thinking,
For love to Claret kill'd himselfe with drinking.

GARY, GILES.

See Giles Garey.

GASCOIGNE, WILLIAM.

On February 29, 1589, William Gascoigne served as joint-payee with William Spencer for a performance at Court by the Admiral's men (Steele, p. 98). Possibly he is to be identified with the William Gascoyne (*q.v.*) employed by the King's men in 1624.

GASCOINE.

See Willaim Gascoyne.

GASCOYNE, WILLIAM.

William Gascoyne is named in a Protection from Arrest issued by Herbert on December 27, 1624, to twenty-one men "imployed by the Kinges Maiesties servantes in theire quallity of Playinge as Musitions and other necessary attendantes" (Adams, *Dram. Rec.*, p. 74). He may fairly be identified with the Gascoine mentioned in the marginal notes with one Hubert as a minor actor or stage-attendant to open the trap-door for Antiochus played by Joseph Taylor in Massinger's *Believe as You List* (ed. Croker, p. 66), licensed for the King's men on May 7, 1631 (Adams, *Dram. Rec.*, p. 33). See William Gascoigne.

GERDLER, ADAM.

The accounts of the Clifford family record a payment of 5*s.* in 1635 "To Adam Gerdler, whom my Lord sent for from York to act a part in *The Knight of the Burning Pestell*," which was played at Skipton Castle, the seat of Lord Clifford (Whitaker, *Hist. of Craven*, p. 394).

GERRY.

Presumably Gerry was a member of the Children of the King's Revels in 1607. The register of St. Dunstan's, Whitefriars, records his burial on September 29, 1607. "Gerry out of the playhouse in the Friars buried" (Jonas, *Shak. and the Stage*, p. 132).

GEW.

Gew (or Gue), although often referred to as "an actor who had gone blind," seems more likely to have been "a blind performing baboon" (see W. Strunk, jr., "The Elizabethan Showman's Ape," *Mod. Lang. Notes*, 1917, xxxii. 220–21). Numerous allusions to him in Elizabethan literature give evidence of his popularity with the amusement-loving public. Guilpin, *Skialetheia* (1598), Epigram xi and Satire v (*Works*, ed. Grosart, pp. 7, 57):

To Gue

Gue, hang thy selfe for woe, since gentlemen
Are now growne cunning in thy apishnes:
Nay, for they labour with their foolishnes
Thee to vndoe, procure to hang them then:
It is a strange seeld seene vncharitie
To make fooles of themselues to hinder thee.
But who's in yonder coach? my lord and foole,
One that for ape-tricks can put Gue to schoole.

Marston, *1 Antonio and Mellida* (acted 1599; printed 1602), Induction (*Works*, i. 13):

'T had been a right part for Proteus or Gew.
Ho! blind Gew would ha' done 't rarely, rarely.

Meeting of Gallants (1604; ed. Halliwell-Phillipps, p. 14):

For blinde Gue you know has six-pence at the
least for groping in the Darke.

Jonson, *Epigrams* (1616), cxxix, *To Mime* (*Works*, viii. 228):

Yet take thy due,
Thou dost out-zany Cokely, Pod; nay Gue.

Cokely and Pod were managers of puppet-shows and exhibitors at Bartholomew Fair.

GIBBES, GEORGE.

George Gibbes's name appears in a warrant of June 30, 1628, appointing several of the Lady Elizabeth's (Queen of Bohemia's) players as Grooms of the Chamber (Stopes, *Jahrbuch*, xlvi. 94).

GIBBORNE, THOMAS.

A joint-lessee of the Fortune playhouse, in which he obtained a whole share on April 21, 1624 (Warner, p. 247).

GIBBS.

Gibbs appeared as a Gete in the Procession of *1 Tamar Cam*, acted by the Admiral's men in 1602 (*H.P.*, p. 154).

GIBES, ANTONY.

As a member of Ellis Guest's company under license of June 7, 1628, Antony Gibes is recorded at Norwich on July 2 of the same year (Murray, ii. 103).

GIBSON, H.

Gibson is named in several marginal notes to the prompt-books in the British Museum Egerton MS. 1994. In *The Captives* he appears as a factor; in *The Two Noble Ladies*, as a soldier; and in *Edmond Ironside*, as a messenger. His Christian name seems to have begun with "H" (Boas, *Library*, 1917, viii. 231–33). On September 3, 1624, *The Captives* was licensed for the Cockpit company (Adams, *Dram. Rec.*, p. 29), i.e. the Lady Elizabeth's men. *The Two Noble Ladies* was "Often tymes acted with appro-bation at the Red Bull in St. John's Streete by the company of the Revells" (Bullen, *Old Plays*, ii. 430), and is assigned by Fleay to 1619–22 (*Dram.*, ii. 334).

GIBSON, RICHARD.

From 1494 to about 1508 Richard Gibson belonged to Henry VII's Court Interluders under the leadership of John English.

Early in the reign of Henry VIII he was appointed Yeoman of the Revels, which position he held for many years and performed its duties with distinction (Collier, i. 44, 68, 70, 106, 109; *Eliz. Stage*, i. 72; ii. 78, 80).

GIDEON.

Gideon appeared as a Gete in the Procession of *1 Tamar Cam*, presented by the Admiral's men in 1602 (*H.P.*, p. 154).

GILBOURNE, THOMAS.

See Thomas Gibborne.

GILBURNE, SAMUEL.

Samuel Gilburne is named in the 1623 folio list of actors in Shakespeare's plays, but is not otherwise known except in the will of Augustine Phillips, May 4, 1605: "I geve to Samuell Gilborne, my late apprentice, the some of fortye shillings, and my mouse colloured velvit hose, and a white taffety dublet, a blacke taffety sute, my purple cloke, sword, and dagger, and my base viall" (Collier, *Actors*, p. 87). He may have played, as Collier infers, "upon the instrument thus left to him by his master and instructor in the business of the stage." He has been conjectured to be the "b[oy?] Sam" of the plot of *The Dead Man's Fortune* (*H.P.*, pp. 133, 152), a play possibly acted by the Admiral's men at the Theatre about 1590 (*Eliz. Stage*, ii. 136).

GILES, NATHANIEL.

Master of the Children of Windsor, 1595–1634; and Master of the Children of the Chapel Royal, 1597–1634 (Rimbault, *Old Cheque Book*, pp. 198–99; Adams, *Playhouses*, pp. 201–13.)

GILES, THOMAS.

Master of the Children of Paul's, from 1585 to about 1590; and presumably Instructor in Music to Prince Henry, 1606, and Prince Charles, 1613 (*Eliz. Stage*, ii. 17 ff., 19*n*.).

GILES'S BOY.

Giles's boy appeared as a Pigmy in the Procession of *1 Tamar Cam*, played by the Admiral's men in 1602 (*H.P.*, p. 154).

GOAD, CHRISTOPHER.

As a member of Queen Henrietta's company at the Cockpit in Drury Lane, Christopher Goad played Oxford in Davenport's *King John and Matilda* (c. 1629), and Forset and a Spanish captain in the first part of Heywood's *Fair Maid of the West*, and the Duke of Ferrara in the second part, acted about Christmas, 1630. There seems to be no further record of him until the Norwich list of March 10, 1635, when he was a member of, presumably, the King's Revels company; with this troupe he acted Silius, the chief favorite to the Empress, in Richards's *Messallina, the Roman Empress*, printed in 1640 (Murray, i. pp. 266, 279–81). The registers of St. James, Clerkenwell, record the children of a Christopher Goad, and in one entry give his wife's name as Ruth (Hovenden, i. 112, 118, 121; iv. 204, 207, 251): Constance (baptized July 23, 1629), Christopher (baptized October 19, 1631; buried January 2, 1632), John (baptized November 28, 1632; buried January 18, 1633), and Mary (buried January 16, 1642). He may be the C. G. who contributed commendatory verses to Thomas Rawlins's *The Rebellion* (1640; Hazlitt's *Dodsley*, xvi. 6), and to Thomas Nabbes's *The Unfortunate Mother* (1640; Bullen, *Old Plays*, N. S., ii. 88). "Among the *Lacrymae Cantabrigienses* for Queen Anne, 1619, is a brief Latin lament signed *Christ. Goade Bac. Art. of Coll. Royal Soc.*" (*Heywood*, ed. Bates, p. 254).

GODWIN, RICHARD.

In December, 1631 (Adams, *Dram. Rec.*, p. 45), Richard Godwin played Faustina, sister to Philautus, in Marmion's *Holland's Leaguer*, presented by "the high and mighty Prince Charles his servants, at the private house in Salisbury Court" (Marmion, *Works*, pp. 2, 6).

GOFFE, ALEXANDER.

See Alexander Goughe.

GOFFE, ROBERT.

See Robert Goughe.

GOLDING.

One Golding, supposedly a player, is alluded to by Thomas Rawlins in his tragedy of *The Rebellion* (1640): "Why forty-pound Golding of the beggars' theatre speaks better, yet has a mark for the sage audience to exercise their dexterity, in throwing of rotton apples, whilst my stout actor pockets, and then ' eats up, the injury" (Hazlitt's *Dodsley*, xiv. 81).

GOODALE, BAPTISTE.

A Baptiste Goodale is included in a forged list of "her Maiesties poore Playeres . . . sharers in the blacke Fryers playhouse" in November, 1589, printed by Collier (*New Facts*, p. 11). The certificate has been discredited as "a recent fabrication," and is not known to rest on any genuine information (Ingleby, *Complete View*, p. 249).

GOODALE, THOMAS.

On July 11, 1581, Arthur King and Thomas Goodale, members of a troupe of players under the patronage of Lord Berkeley, were committed to the Counter for having taken part in an affray with certain gentlemen of Gray's Inn (Harrison, *England*, iv. 320). In the plot of *2 Seven Deadly Sins*, played by Stange's company about 1590, Goodale is cast for the parts of Lucias in "Envy," Phronesias and a messenger in "Sloth," and a lord in "Lechery" (Greg, *H. P.*, p. 152; *R. E. S.*, i. 262). His name appears in a marginal notation as a messenger in *Sir Thomas More*, III. iii. 1, thought to have been written between 1594 and 1602 (*Shak. Apoc.*, pp. 402, 437; *Eliz. Stage*, iv. 33); Tannenbaum, however, contends that this marginal note is a forgery by Collier.

The registers of St. Bodolph Aldgate record the baptism and burial of two sons of the player (Denkinger, *P. M. L. A.*, xli. 100): Symon (May 12, 1594; April 30, 1595), and Richard (August 19, 1599; November 23, 1599). He has been doubtfully identified with the Thomas Goodale, mercer, who, together with John Alleyn and Robert Lee, entered into a bond to Edward Alleyn on May 18, 1593 (Warner, p. 127).

GOSSON, STEPHEN.

Lodge, in his *Defence of Plays* of about 1579 (*Works*, i. 8), refers to Stephen Gosson as "a player." Gosson had left the stage by 1579, when he published *The School of Abuse*, "conteining a plesaunt inuective against Poets, Pipers, Plaiers, Iesters, and such like Caterpillers of a Commonwealth."

GOST, ELIAS.

See Ellis Guest.

GOUGHE, ALEXANDER.

Alexander Goughe (or Goffe), son of Robert Goughe (*q.v.*), a player, was baptized at St. Saviour's, Southwark, on August 7, 1614 (Collier, iii. 474). At an early age he became associated with the King's men at Blackfriars, and apparently won some distinction as an actor of female parts. With the King's company he played (Murray, i. opp. 172) Caenis, Vespasian's concubine, in Massinger's *Roman Actor*, licensed October 11, 1626, at which date he was twelve years old; an unassigned part in Ford's *Lover's Melancholy*, licensed November 24, 1628; Acanthe, a maid of honor, in Massinger's *Picture*, licensed June 8, 1629; and Lillia-Bianca in *The Wildgoose Chase*, a revival, 1631. He is also named in the "Players Pass" issued to the King's men on May 17, 1636. After the closing of the playhouses in 1642 he helped to organize surreptitious performances at noblemen's houses, particularly Holland House at Kensington. Wright in *Historia Histrionica* (1699) says that "Alexander Goffe, the woman-actor at Blackfriars (who had made himself known to persons of quality), used to be the jackal, and give notice of time and place" of the privately-acted plays (Hazlitt's *Dodsley*, xv. 410). During the Commonwealth he became a publisher, and is known to have issued three plays: the Jonson-Fletcher-Middleton comedy of *The Widow* (1652), with an address to the reader (Bullen, *Middleton*, v. 121); *The Queen, or the Excellency of her Sex* (1653), ascribed to Ford, with a dedication to the Lady Catherine Mohun; and Carlell's *Passionate Lovers* (1655), dedicated "To the Illustrious Princess, Mary Dutchess of Richmond and Lennox" (*The Queen*, ed. Bang, p. vii, *note*).

GOUGHE, ROBERT.

Robert Goughe (or Goffe) is probably the "R. Go" cast for Aspasia in "Sloth" in the plot of *2 Seven Deadly Sins*, presented by Strange's company about 1590 (Greg, *H. P.*, p. 152; *R. E. S.*, i. 262). Nothing is known of him between 1592 and 1603. He may have joined the King's men soon after the royal patent was granted on May 19, 1603, for he is next found with them. He is a joint-legatee with John Edmans (or Edmonds) in the will, dated July 22, 1603, of Thomas Pope, who left them his wearing apparel and arms. He witnessed the will of Augustine Phillips on May 4, 1605. Phillips names as legatee a sister, Elizabeth Goughe, who is no doubt the Elizabeth recorded in the register of St. Saviour's, Southwark, as marrying Robert Goughe on February 13, 1603. His name is found in the 1623 folio list of Shakespearean players; in the King's men's patent of March 27, 1619; and in the livery-allowance lists of May 19, 1619, and April 7, 1621 (*M. S. C.*, i. 280; Murray, i. opp. 172). A stage-direction (line 1723) of *The Second Maiden's Tragedy* (1611) shows that he played Memphonius: "Enter Mr. Goughe" (ed. Greg, p. 54). In 1619 he acted Leidenberch in *Sir John van Olden Barnavelt* (ed. Frijlinck, p. clx). The token-books of St. Saviour's give his residence in Hill's Rents during 1604, Samson's Rents in

A DICTIONARY OF ACTORS

1605 and 1606, and Austin's Rents in 1612-22; and the registers record his children: Anne (baptized December 11, 1603), Elizabeth (baptized May 30, 1605), Nicholas (baptized November 24, 1608), Dorothy (baptized February 10, 1611; buried January 12, 1613), and Alexander (baptized August 7, 1614), the last of whom became a member of the King's company. His burial is recorded in the same parish on February 19, 1625 (Collier, iii. 472–74; Bentley, *T.L.S.*, Nov. 15, 1928, p. 856; Rendle, *Bankside*, p. xxvii). A Robert Goughe (or Goffe) is also noted as living "on the Banckesyde" in 1623 (Wallace, *Jahrbuch*, xlvi. 347), and as "one of the Messengers of his Majesties Chamber" on August 30, 1624 (*M. S. C.*, i. 381).

GOUGHE, THOMAS.

Thomas Goughe and John Greaves are named as payees for a performance at Court by Sir Robert Lane's men on February 17, 1572 (Steele, p. 41).

GRACE, FRANCIS.

Francis Grace is named as one of Prince Henry's players in the household list of 1610 (*Eliz. Stage*, ii. 188). The Prince died in November, 1612, and his troupe soon passed under the patronage of the Palsgrave. Grace is mentioned in the new patent granted to the Palsgrave's company on January 11, 1613 (*M. S. C.*, i. 275); in the lease of the Fortune by the Palsgrave's men on October 31, 1618 (*H. P.*, p. 27); and in the 1622 Herbert list of the troupe (Adams, *Dram. Rec.*, p. 63). In 1623 he lived "att the George Alley in Gouldings lane" (Wallace, *Jahrbuch*, xlvi. 347).

GRACE, RICHARD.

In 1623 Richard Grace was an actor at the Fortune, and lived "in Goulding Lane." With Richard Claytone, William Stratford, and Abraham Pedle, "all Actors at the fortune neere Golding lane," he was summoned to appear at court to answer a bill of complaint made by Gervase Markham (Wallace, *Jahrbuch*,

158

xlvi. 348, 350). In 1623 the Fortune was occupied by the Pals-grave's men, and Grace doubtless belonged to this company. The register of St. Giles, Cripplegate, records the burial of a Richard Grace in 1627 (Malcolm, *Lond. Rediv.*, iii. 304).

GRADWELL, HENRY.

In December, 1631 (Adams, *Dram. Rec.*, p. 45), Henry Gradwell played Capritio, a young novice, in Marmion's *Holland's Leaguer*, presented by "the high and mighty Prince Charles his servants, at the private house in Salisbury Court" (Marmion, *Works*, pp. 2, 6). His name also appears in a warrant of May 10, 1632, appointing as Grooms of the Chamber several of Prince Charles's men (Stopes, *Jahrbuch*, xlvi. 96). The marginal notes to the Egerton MS. of *Edmond Ironside* assign to him the parts of a nobleman's son and a herald in that play (Boas, *Library*, 1917, viii. 233, 235).

GRAUNGER, JOHN.

A member of the Chapel Royal in 1509 and 1511 (Brewer, *L. & P. Henry VIII*, i. 1. p. 15; Hillebrand, *Mod. Phil.*, xviii. 244; Chambers, *Eliz. Stage*, ii. 27*n*.).

GRAY, MARGARET.

A joint-lessee of the Fortune playhouse, in which she obtained a half-share on August 1, 1623, and a whole share on January 29, 1624 (Warner, p. 247).

GREAVES, JOHN.

John Greaves and Thomas Goughe are named as payees for a performance at Court by Sir Robert Lane's men on February 17, 1572 (Steele, p. 41).

GREEN, JOHN.

John Green is heard of only on the Continent, where he was for a time associated with Robert Browne in the troupe known as the Hessian Comedians, under the patronage of Maurice of

Hesse. He was at Strassburg in June, 1606; at Frankfort in August, 1606, and March, 1607; and at Elbing and Danzig during 1607. He then seems to have entered the service of Archduke Ferdinand, for an English troupe attended the Archduke at Graz in November, 1607, later at Passau, and again at Graz in February, 1608. This company has been plausibly identified upon the following evidence with the one under the leadership of Green. The repertory of the company included *Nobody and Somebody*, of which play there is extant at Rein a German manuscript with a dedication by Green to Ferdinand's brother the Archduke Maximilian, who was no doubt present at the Graz performances. The visit to Graz was apparently terminated by a duel in which a Frenchman was killed by one of the English actors, "the man with long red hair, who always played a little fiddle," who may have been Green himself, for a portrait of a red-haired actor, in the traditional costume of Nobody, accompanies the manuscript in the Rein library. Before 1608 Green may have acted in France, for in the dedication of *Nobody and Somebody* he says that he had been in that country (*Eliz. Stage*, ii. 282, 294). Green, like Robert Browne, now disappears for some years from German annals. A record at Utrecht in November, 1613, suggests that he probably spent some time in the Netherlands. Subsequently he returned to Germany. In July, 1615 and 1616, he visited Danzig. On this last visit Robert Reynolds, late of Queen Anne's company, was with him. In 1617 he appears at Prague on the occasion of the coronation of the Archduke Ferdinand as King of Bohemia, and in July of the same year at Vienna (Meissner, *Jahrbuch*, xix. 139). Although his name is not found in the records for about two years, he may now have joined his old leader, Robert Browne, for Reynolds, who had accompanied Green to Danzig in 1616, was with Browne at Strassburg in 1618. In April, 1620, Green came to Cologne and Utrecht. Following the outbreak of the Thirty Years' War, he probably, about 1620, withdrew from Germany. But in 1626-27 he again appears in that country. During 1626 he was at Frankfort and Dresden, and during 1627, at Torgau, Dresden, Nuremberg, and Frankfort. Reynolds, who won some notoriety as a clown under the name of Pickleherring, accompanied him on this last tour and apparently succeeded him as leader of the troupe. We hear no more of Green (Herz, pp. 19 ff., 24 ff.). He may have been a brother of Thomas Greene (*q. v.*).

GREENE, ROBERT.

Harvey, in his *Four Letters* of 1592 (*Works*, i. 190), seems to speak of Greene as "a Player." Nothing is known of his stage-career. Chambers (*Eliz. Stage*. iii. 327) is of the opinion "that the theory that Greene himself was actor as well as playwright rests on a misinterpretation of a phrase of Harvey's, and is inconsistent with the invariable tone of his references to the profession."

GREENE, THOMAS.

Early in the reign of James I the Earl of Worcester's men were taken into the patronage of Queen Anne, and Thomas Greene was a member of Queen Anne's company at its formation late in 1603 or early in 1604, since his name appears in the undated draft license; he continued with this company till his death in 1612. He took part in the coronation procession of March 15, 1604, wearing a cloak of red cloth; and his name occurs in both the license of April 15, 1609, and the duplicate patent issued to the traveling company on January 7, 1612 (*M. S. C.*, i. 265, 270; *Eliz. Stage*, ii. 229; Murray, ii. 343). From 1609 to 1612 he was payee for the Court performances of the troupe (Steele, pp. 159, 162, 164, 169, 171). In his will (Fleay, *Stage*, p. 192), dated July 25, 1612, he mentions his wife Susan, formerly wife of one Browne, his daughter Honor, his sons-in-law (i.e. stepsons) Robert and William Browne, his daughters-in-law Susanna, Elizabeth, and Anne Browne, his brothers John and Jeffery Greene, his sister Elizabeth Barrett, and John Cumber, who belonged to Queen Anne's company by 1616. He leaves 40*s.* to "my fellowes of the house of the redd Bull . . . to buy gloves for them," and names Christopher Beeston and Richard Perkins as overseers. Beeston, Perkins, and Thomas Heywood were among the witnesses of the will, which was probated by his widow on October 10, 1612. The register of St. James, Clerkenwell, records on August 7, 1612, the burial of "Thomas Greene, householder, in the Chancell" (Hovenden, iv. 120), and his will describes him as of this parish. The disposal of Greene's property led several years later to a lawsuit between Queen Anne's company and Susan Baskervile, Greene's widow. (The Baskervile documents are printed in Fleay, *Stage*, pp. 270-97.) Thus his death not only deprived the Red Bull of its chief attraction but involved his fellows in a hampering net of financial difficulties that prepared the way for the final dissolution of the Queen's troupe upon her death in 1619. Greene was one of the chief actors of Shakespeare's time, and was to Queen Anne's company what Burbage was to the King's men. His excellence as a clown made him known to all Londoners as the best comedian since Tarlton and Kempe. For a possible allusion to him as "the lean fool" see under John Shank, p. 319. He is now chiefly remembered for the amusing comedy named after him—Cooke's *City Gallant* (*c.* 1611), a play to which Greene's comic success in the part of Bubble had given the new and lasting title, *Greene's Tu Quoque*, in which Greene is spoken of by name (Hazlitt's *Dodsley*, xi. 240):

Scattergood. Yes, faith, brother, if it please you: let's go to see a play at the Globe.
Bubble. I care not; any whither, so the clown have a part; for, i' faith, I am nobody without a fool.
Geraldine. Why then we'll go to the Red Bull: they say Green's a good clown.
Bubble. Green! Green's an ass.
Scattergood. Wherefore do you say so?
Bubble. Indeed, I ha' no reason; for they say he is as like me as ever he can look.

The play was published in 1614 with an epistle to the reader by Thomas Heywood, who writes:

> As for Master Green, all that I will speak of him (and that without flattery) is this (if I were worthy to censure), there was not an actor of his nature, in his time, of better ability in performance of what he undertook, more applauded by the audience, of greater grace at the court, or of more general love in the city: and so with this brief character of his memory I commit him to his rest.

A couplet signed "W. R." (probably William Rowley), was also prefixed to the play (Hazlitt's *Dodsley*, xi. 179):

Upon the Death of Thomas Greene

How fast bleak Autumn changeth Flora's dye!
What yesterday was Green, now's sear and dry.
W. R.

In Richard Braithwaite's *Remains after Death* (1618) are printed four epigrams on him (Hazlitt's *Dodsley*, xi. 177):

Upon an actor now of late deceased: and upon his action Tu Quoque: and first upon his travel

Hee whom this mouldered clod of earth doth hide,
New come from sea, made but one face and dide.

Upon his creditors

His debtors now no fault with him can finde,
Sith he has paid to nature all's behinde.

Upon his fellow actors

What can you crave of your poore fellow more?
He does but what *Tu quoque* did before:
Then give him dying, actions second wreath,
That second'd him in action and in death.

A DICTIONARY OF ACTORS

In actorem Mimicum cui vix parem cernimus superstitem Quaecunque orta sunt occidunt. Sallust.

Ver vireat quod te peperit (viridissima proles)
Quaeque tegit cineres, ipsa virescat humus.
Transis ab exiguis nunquam periture theatris
Ut repetas sacri pulchra theatra Jovis.

The line in the first epigram, "New come from sea, made but one face and dide," seems to imply that Greene had died suddenly on his return from a voyage, which leads to the conjecture that he may have been on the Continent with John Green (*q.v.*), who has been suggested as his brother. I. H., in *This World's Folly* (1615), mentions his performance of a baboon (*Eliz. Stage*, iv. 254): "*Vos quoque* [in margin, "Or *Tu quoque*"], and you also, who with *Scylla*-barking, *Stentor*-throated bellowings, flash choaking squibbes of absurd vanities into the nosthrils of your spectators, barbarously diuerting *Nature*, and defacing Gods owne image, by metamorphising humane [in margin, "*Greenes* Baboone"] shape into bestiall forme." Greene is generally taken to be the author of *A Poets Vision and a Princes Glorie*, "Dedicated to the high and mightie Prince James, King of England, Scotland, France, and Ireland," and printed in 1603 as "Written by Thomas Greene, Gentleman" (Hazlitt, *Hand-Book*, 1867, p. 243); and of some commendatory verses prefixed to the 1605 edition of Drayton's *Barons' Wars* (*Works*, i. 87):

To Mr. Michael Drayton

What ornament might I devise, to fit
Th' aspiring height of thy admired spirit?
Or what fair garland worthy is to sit
On thy blest brows, that compass in all merit?
Thou shalt not crowned be with common bays,
Because for thee it is a crown too low;
Apollo's tree can yield thee simple praise,
It is too dull a vesture for thy brow:
But with a wreath of stars shalt thou be crown'd,

Which when thy working temples do sustain,
Will, like the spheres, be ever moving round
After the royal musick of thy brain.
Thy skill doth equal Phoebus, not thy birth;
He to Heaven gives musick, Thou to Earth.
                                        THOMAS GREENE.

GREGORY, JACK.

Jack Gregory appeared as Tarmia's child and as Heron in
1 Tamar Cam, and as an Amazon in the Procession of the same
play, presented by the Admiral's men in 1602 (*H.P.*, p. 154).

GREUM, HEINRICH.

In the autumn of 1608 Heinrich Greum appeared as a player
at Frankfort, Germany. He was then in company with Robert
Arzschar and Rudolf Beart (Herz, p. 53).

GREVILLE, CURTIS.

Curtis Greville is named in the 1622 Herbert lists of both the
Palsgrave's and the Lady Elizabeth's players (Adams, *Dram.
Rec.*, p. 63). In explanation of this apparently dual connection
it is suggested that when the new Fortune was building in 1622,
and the Palsgrave's men were preparing to open the playhouse,
Greville joined them from the Lady Elizabeth's men (Murray,
i. 215–16). Subsequently he passed to the King's men, for his
name appears in the casts or stage-directions of the following
plays acted by that company (Murray, i. opp. 172): Latinus, a
player, in Massinger's *Roman Actor* (licensed October 11, 1626);
Ford's *Lover's Melancholy* (licensed November 24, 1628); and a
merchant, in Massinger's *Believe as You List* (licensed May 7,
1631). He is also generally taken to be the "Curtis" of the stage-
directions to *The Two Noble Kinsmen*, printed in 1634 as "Presented at the Blackfriars by the Kings Maiesties servants, with
great applause." He appears as a messenger, IV. ii. 75, and with
"T. Tucke" (?Thomas Tuckfeild) as an attendant, V. iii (Brooke,
Shak. Apoc., pp. 337, 344).

GREY, MARGARET.

See Margaret Gray.

GRIFFIN.

Griffin acted the part of Athanasia in *Frederick and Basilea*, presented by the Admiral's men in June, 1597 (*H.P.*, p. 153).

GRIMES, ARTHUR.

On March 16, 1625, Herbert issued a license to a company of players under the leadership of Ellis Guest, Thomas Swinnerton, and Arthur Grimes. These men visited Leicester on March 6, 1626, and were given a reward of £1 (Murray, ii. 101, 102). Arthur Grimes may be identical with Anthony Grymes, for both were associated with Guest, and "Arthur" may be a clerical error for "Anthony," or *vice versa*.

GRYMES, ANTHONY.

As a member of Ellis Guest's company under license of June 7, 1628, Anthony Grymes is recorded at Norwich on July 2 of the same year (Murray, ii. 103). Possibly he is to be identified with Arthur Grimes (*q.v.*).

GRYMES, THOMAS.

A member of the Chapel Royal about 1600–01. In Henry Clifton's complaint to the Star Chamber on December 15, 1601, as to how boys were pressed for the Chapel at Blackfriars, Thomas Grymes is named as one so taken, and is described with Philip Pykman as "apprentices to Richard and Georg Chambers" (Wallace, *Blackfriars*, p. 80).

GRYMMESBY, JOHN.

A member of the Chapel Royal in 1423 (Hillebrand, *Mod. Phil.*, xviii. 235).

GRYNES.

The Coventry accounts record a payment of 5*s.* to one "Grynes & other players who came by warrant" during December, 1633 (Murray, ii. 252).

GUE.

See Gew.

GUEST, ELLIS.

From 1625 to 1634 Ellis Guest was engaged in the leadership of a company of players known only in provincial records. On March 16, 1625, Herbert issued a license to Ellis Guest, Thomas Swinnerton, and Arthur Grimes. The company visited Norwich on May 28, 1625, and Leicester on March 6, 1626. On June 7, 1628, a new license was granted to Guest and his company, which is recorded at Norwich on July 2 of the same year. He again visited Norwich on June 27, 1629, describing himself as one of the company of Joseph Moore, Alexander Foster, Robert Guilman, and John Townsend, i.e. the Lady Elizabeth's company, presenting a warrant dated June 8, 1629, and affirming that his fellows were at Thetford. The town clerk doubtless made a mistake in the entry, or else the license was spurious, for Guest is not otherwise connected with the Lady Elizabeth's men and there is no further clue to such a license of this date. He did not play, but the Norwich authorities gave him a gratuity of 40*s.*, which he "thankfully accepted." During 1629 he also visited Leicester, and on (?) November 12, 1630, Reading. On July 15, 1631, a license was issued to him and Richard Errington, and these two players are named in the Reading accounts on July 18 of the same year. Up to this date the troupe seems to have been an unpatronized organization; but subsequently Queen Henrietta apparently took it under her patronage, for on June 22, 1633, the Norwich annals record a visit of "Elias Gost and his Company of the Quenes players." On June 25, 1634, he obtained another license, which he

A DICTIONARY OF ACTORS

presented at Norwich on September 13, of the same year (Murray, ii. 101–05, 316, 317, 352, 353, 354, 355–56, 386–87). That is the last we hear of Guest.

GUILMAN, ROBERT.

Robert Guilman's name appears in a warrant of June 30, 1628, appointing as Grooms of the Chamber several of the Lady Elizabeth's (Queen of Bohemia's) players; in a license granted to the Lady Elizabeth's men on December 9, 1628; and in the Reading accounts of a visit by the company on December 24, 1629 (Stopes, *Jahrbuch*, xlvi. 94; Murray, i. 259; ii. 386).

GUNNELL, RICHARD.

Richard Gunnell appears as a Palsgrave's man in the patent of January 11, 1613 (*M.S.C.*, i. 275); in the lease of the Fortune on October 31, 1618; and in the lease of the new Fortune on May 20, 1622 (*H.P.*, pp. 27, 29). By 1622 he had become manager of the company (Adams, *Dram. Rec.*, p. 63). In addition to managing the troupe, he also wrote several plays that were licensed for the Palsgrave's men at the Fortune, but which are now lost (Adams, *Dram. Rec.*, pp. 26, 28, 30n.): *The Hungarian Lion* (December 4, 1623), *The Way to Content All Women, or How a Man may Please his Wife* (April 17, 1624), and possibly *The Masque* (November 3, 1624). To complete his versatility in the theatrical field, in 1629 he and William Blagrove, Herbert's deputy, formed a partnership and built the Salisbury Court Playhouse, which was occupied by the Children of the King's Revels until about December, 1631 (Adams, *Playhouses*, pp. 368–74). Gunnell and Blagrove probably served as managers. In the *Middlesex County Records* under the date of December 30, 1622, a recognizance was entered "For the appearance of Richard Peagott bodymaker at the next Session of the Peace, to aunswer the complaint of Mr. Gunnell the Player" (Jeaffreson, ii. 173). Gunnell contributed commendatory verses to Captain John Smith's *A Description of New England* (1616; *Works*, p. 182):

168

A DICTIONARY OF ACTORS

To that worthy and generous Gentleman, my verie good friend,
Captaine Smith

May Fate thy Proiect prosper, that thy name
May be eternised with liuing fame:
Though foule Detraction Honour would peruert,
And Enuie euer waits vpon desert:
In spight of *Pelias*, when his hate lies colde,
Returne as *Iason* with a fleece of Golde.
Then after-ages shall record thy praise,
That a *New England* to this Ile didst raise:
And when thou dy'st (as all that liue must die)
Thy fame liue heere; thou, with Eternitie.

R: GUNNELL.

Notices of Gunnell's family appear in the register of St. Giles, Cripplegate, 1614–30 (*Eliz. Stage*, ii. 320), among which are the records of the baptism of a daughter in 1623 and of his own burial on January 22, 1630 (Malcolm, *Londinium Redivivum*, iii. 304). Leslie Hotson in his recent work, *The Commonwealth and Restoration Stage* (1928), pp. 52–53, gives an account of a lawsuit of 1654, in which the heirs of Gunnell are concerned (cf. William Wintershall). According to the testimony submitted, Gunnell "died intestate in 1633 or 1634." These dates are not in agreement with the burial entry, given above, in Malcolm's *Londinium Redivivum*. Perhaps the Richard Gunnell buried on January 22, 1630, was the son of the actor. Thomas Jordan published an elegy on him in his *Poeticall Varieties* (1637):

An Elegie on his Inestimable friend, Mr. Richard Gunnell, Gent.

Goe sell your smiles for weeping, change your mirth
For mourning dirges, lave the pretious earth
Of my inestimable friend with teares
(Fertill as them the cheeke of Aprill weares,
When Flora propagates her blessing on
Th' approaching Daffadills) under this stone
Lyes his neglected ashes, Oh that they
Who knew his vertues best should let his Clay
Lye unregarded so, and not appeare

With a full sorrow, in each eye a teare
Once, daily ore his urne, how can they thinke
A pleasing thought, sit and securely drinke
In satiate carrowses; these are they
Can lose both friends and sorrowes in one day
(Not worth my observation) let me turne
Againe to my sad duty, where ile mourne
Till my corporeall essence doe become
A glyding rivolet; and pay the summe
To thy deare memory; my streame shall lend
A drop to none les he hath lost a friend:
The melancholly mad-man that will prove
His passion for his Mistresse is but love,
Were best be thrifty in his teares, for I
Will not supply him though his mistresse dye;
My ford is thine deare Gunnell and for thee
My Christall Channell flowes so currently,
Tagus and great Pactolus may be proud
Of their red sands, let me my Rivers shrowd
In course Meanders, where the waters shall
In a griev'd murmure, Gunnell, Gunnell, call,
It is for thee I flow, for thee I glide,
I had retain'd my floods hadst thou not dyed.
And little water birds shall chaunt this theame,
Thy Iordan mourner is a Iordan streame.

GWALTER, WILLIAM.

William Gwalter, innholder, acquired on May 20, 1622, a lease of one-sixth part of the Fortune playhouse. This lease was surrendered to Edward Alleyn on June 19, 1623. On the following day, June 20, a new lease was granted to him of a moiety of the same sixth part. The other half of the sixth part was leased to Robert Leigh (Greg, *H.P.*, p. 30).

GYLLOME, FOKE.

Possibly Foke Gyllome was in 1581 a player in the service of Alexander Houghton of Lea in Lancashire. On August 3, 1581, Houghton wrote (*Eliz. Stage*, i. 280*n.*): "Yt ys my wyll that Thomas Houghton of Brynescoules my brother shall have all my instrumentes belonginge to mewsyckes and all maner of playe clothes yf he be mynded to keppe and doe keppe players. And yf he wyll not keepe and maynteyne playeres then yt ys my wyll that Sir Thomas Heskethe Knyghte shall haue the same instrumentes and playe clothes. And I moste hertelye requyre the said Syr Thomas to be ffrendlye unto Foke Gyllome and William Shakshafte now dwellynge with me and ether to take theym unto his servyce or els to helpe theym to some good master."

GYRDLER, RUSSELL.

A member of the Children of Paul's in 1598 (Hillebrand, *Child Actors*, p. 111).

GYRKE, RICHARD.

A London player in 1550, named in an order demanding that all plays be licensed by the King or his Council (Harrison, *England*, iv. 314–15).

HALL, WILLIAM.

William Hall's name appears in a warrant of May 10, 1632, appointing as Grooms of the Chamber several of Prince Charles's men (Stopes, *Jahrbuch*, xlvi. 96). Subsequently he joined the King's Revels company, and played Mela, Seneca's brother, in Richards's *Messallina*, printed in 1640 as "acted with generall applause divers times by the Company of his Majesties Revells."

HALLAWAIE, "THE YOUNGER."

A member of the Children of Paul's, as shown by a record of Christ's Hospital on March 5, 1580: "Mr. Sebastian Westcott, of Paulls, is appointed to have Hallawaie the younger out of this House to be one of the singing children of the Cathedral Church of Paulls in this citie" (*Eliz. Stage*, ii. 16n.).

HALLEY, RICHARD.

Richard Halley is named in a Ticket of Privilege granted on January 12, 1636, to the attendants "employed by his Majesty's servants the players of the Blackfriars, and of special use to them both on the Stage and otherwise for his Majesty's disport and service" (Stopes, *Jahrbuch*, xlvi. 99).

HAMERTON, HENRY.

Henry Hamerton's name appears in a warrant of December 12, 1635, appointing several of Prince Charles's men as Grooms of the Chamber (Stopes, *Jahrbuch*, xlvi. 98).

HAMERTON, STEPHEN.

See Stephen Hammerton.

HAMLEN, ROBERT.

See Robert Hamlett.

HAMLETT, ROBERT.

As a member of the Lady Elizabeth's company on August 29, 1611, Robert Hamlett (or Hamlen) with his fellow-actors gave Philip Henslowe a bond of £500 to perform "certen articles" of agreement. By March 20, 1616, he had joined Prince Charles's troupe, for on that date, with other members of the company, he signed a contract with Alleyn and Meade. He also signed an undated letter (*c.* 1616–17) from certain members of his company to Alleyn. With Prince Charles's men he took part in King James's funeral procession on May 7, 1625 (*H.P.*, pp. 18, 91, 93, 111; Murray, i. 161, 237).

HAMLUC, W.

W. Hamluc and W. Mago, appearing in the *dramatis personæ* prefixed to Ford's *Witch of Edmonton*, were probably two of the minor actors in the tragedy (Ford, *Works*, iii. 175, 236). Hamluc appears in a stage-direction, V. i: "Enter W. Hamluc with thatch and a lighted link." His name is also prefixed to speeches. The play, not printed until 1658, may have passed from Prince Charles's men to Queen Henrietta's men about 1625, when the latter troupe was organized (Murray, i. 236*n*.). The notice on the title-page assigns the play to the Prince's men, but Ezekiel Fenn and Theophilus Bird, both of whom are mentioned in the quarto, were members of the Queen's troupe, and are not traceable in the Prince's company.

HAMMERTON, STEPHEN.

Stephen Hammerton seems to have begun his theatrical career with the King's Revels company before November 12, 1632, when William Blagrove, who had organized the troupe at Salisbury Court in 1629, and William Beeston (*q.v.*) petitioned for the return of "a boy named Stephen Hamerton inveigled from them" and "imployed at the Blackfryars playhouse" as a member of the King's company. Evidently he did not return to his former managers, for the actor-list of Fletcher's *Wildgoose Chase* (1652) assigns to him the part of Oriana (*Works*, iv. 314, 411); and this is thought to refer to a revival of the play by the King's men in 1631 (Fleay, *Drama*, i. 215–16). He is named as a King's man in a warrant of January 22, 1641 (Stopes, *Jahrbuch*, xlvi. 103). His name is appended to the dedicatory epistle of the 1647 folio of Beaumont and Fletcher's plays, published by a group of the King's players (*Works*, i. p. x). Wright in *Historia Histrionica* (1699) says of him: "Amyntor ["a young gentleman of the Court" in Beaumont and Fletcher's *Maid's Tragedy*] was played by Stephen Hammerton (who was at first a most noted and beautiful woman-actor, but afterwards he acted with equal grace and applause a young lover's part)" (Hazlitt's *Dodsley*, xv. 405). The following allusion in the Epilogue to Suckling's *Goblins* (1646; *Works*, p. 215) presumably is to him:

> O, if Stephen should be kill'd,
> Or miss the lady, how the plot is spill'd!

He seems also to be referred to as the actor of Ferdinand, King of Murcia, in the Epilogue to Shirley's *Doubtful Heir* (1653): "How did king Stephen do, and t'other prince?" (*Works*, iv. 361); and as the actor of Master Wild in the quasi-Epilogue to Killigrew's *Parson's Wedding* (1663): "Think on 't: Stephen is as handsome, when the play is done, as Master Wild was in the scene. . . . If you refuse, Stephen misses the wench, and then you cannot justly blame the poet; for, you know, they say that alone is enough to spoil the play" (Hazlitt's *Dodsley*, xiv. 534, 535). On January 28, 1648, Hammerton and other members of the King's company gave a bond to pay off an old Blackfriars debt to Michael Bowyer's heirs (Hotson, pp. 31–34).

HAMMOND, JOHN.

In 1494 John Hammond belonged to Henry VII's Court Interluders under the leadership of John English (Collier, i. 44).

HAMOND.

On January 13 and 14, 1565, the Earl of Worcester's company visited Haddon Hall, Derbyshire, under the leadership of one Hamond (*Eliz. Stage*, ii. 220).

HANLY, RICHARD.

As a member of Ellis Guest's company under license of June 7, 1628, Richard Hanly is recorded at Norwich on July 2 of the same year (Murray, ii. 103).

HANSON, NICHOLAS.

On June 14, 1623, Nicholas Hanson presented at Norwich a license dated May 28, 1622, on behalf of an unnamed company of players. He appears as a King's Revels man at Coventry in April, 1628, and received payment on November 28 of the same year (Murray, ii. 250, 347–48). At the time of the 1623 visit to Norwich he was probably a member of the Revels company.

HARRIS, JOHN.

John Harris is recorded at Norwich on March 10, 1635, when his troupe, presumably the King's Revels, applied for permission to act in that town (Murray, i. 279–80).

A DICTIONARY OF ACTORS

HARRISON, JOHN.

A player, whose daughter, Suzanna, by his wife Anne, was baptized at St. Helen's on January 10, 1602 (*Eliz. Stage*, ii. 320).

HARRISON, RICHARD.

On October 2, 1617, Richard Harrison and others of Queen Anne's company petitioned the Sessions of Peace against the various presentments that had been issued against them for not "repayringe the Highwayes neere the Red Bull" (Jeaffreson, *Middlesex County Records*, ii. 170).

HARRISON, WILLIAM.

On March 6, 1584, the Earl of Worcester's players were engaged in a dispute with the authorities at Leicester. In the account of the quarrel there is an abstract of the patent granted to Worcester's men, dated January 14, 1583, naming William Harrison as one of the licensees (*Eliz. Stage*, ii. 222).

HART, CHARLES.

Charles Hart, Shakespeare's grand-nephew, and presumably the son of William Hart (*q.v.*), was called the Burbage of his day. From Wright's *Historia Histronica*, 1699 (Hazlitt's *Dodsley*, xv. 404, 409–10), we learn that he and Clun "were bred up boys at the Blackfriars, and acted women's parts. Hart was Robinson's boy or apprentice; he acted the Duchess in the tragedy of *The Cardinal*, which was the first part that gave him reputation." The date at which he joined the King's men at Blackfriars is not known. At the closing of the theatres in 1642 and the beginning of the Civil War, he enlisted in the King's army as a lieutenant under Sir Thomas Dallison in Prince Rupert's regiment. In the winter of 1648 a number of players who survived the war formed a company and ventured to act cautiously at the Cockpit. During a presentation of *Rollo, or the Bloody Brother*, in which Hart is supposed to have played Otto, a group of soldiers plundered the playhouse and routed the players. Hart continued his theatrical çareer at the Cockpit after the Restoration. He signed the Petition of the Cockpit Players on October 13, 1660; and he is named in the Articles of Agreement between Herbert and Killigrew on June 4, 1662 (Adams, *Dram. Rec.*, pp. 94, 96, 113–14). His Majesty's Company of Comedians opened their new playhouse, the Theatre Royal, on May 7, 1663 (Pepys, *Diary*, iii. 107), under the management of Thomas Killigrew. As a member of the organization Hart acted the following parts (Downes, *Ros. Ang.*, pp. xxxiv, 2 ff.): Demetrius in *The Humorous Lieutenant*; Michael Perez in *Rule a Wife and have a Wife*; Mosca in *The Fox* (*Volpone*); Amintor in *The Maid's Tragedy*; Arbaces in *King and no King*; Rollo in *Rollo, Duke of Normandy*; Welford in *The Scornful Lady*; Cassio in *The Moor of Venice*; Hotspur in *King Henry the Fourth*; Celadon in *The Maiden Queen*; Wildblood in *The Mock Astrologer*; Brutus in *Julius Caesar*; Cortez in *The Indian Emperor*; Manly in *The Plain Dealer*; Porphyrius in *Tyrannick Love*; Aureng Zeb in *Aureng Zeb*; Alexander in *Alexander the Great*; Marc Anthony in *All for Love, or the World Well Lost*; Aurelian in *The Assignation, or Love in a Nunnery*; Zipares in *Mythridates, King of Pontus*; Phraartes in *The Destruction of Jerusalem*; Lord Delaware in *The Black Prince*; Almanzer in *The Conquest of Granada*; Massinissa in *Sophonisba, or Hannibal's Overthrow*; and Othello, in *Othello*. Of his excellence in several characters, Downes writes (*Ros. Ang.* p. 16): "Mr. Hart, in the Part of Arbaces, in *King and no King*; Amintor, in *The Maids Tragedy*; Othello; Rollo; Brutus, in *Julius Caesar*; Alexander, towards the latter End of his Acting; if he Acted in any of these but once in a Fortnight, the House was fill'd as at a New Play, especially Alexander, he Acting that with such Grandeur and Agreeable Majesty, That one of the Court was pleas'd to Honour him with this Commendation; That Hart might Teach any King of Earth how to Comport himself; He was no less Inferior in Comedy; as Mosca in *The Fox*; Don John in *The Chances*; Wildblood in *The Mock Astrologer*; with sundry other Parts. In all the Comedies and Tragedies, as he was concern'd he Perform'd with that Exactness and Perfection, that not any of his Successors have Equall'd him." Not only an actor on the stage but also in the society scandals of his time, he became a star in amorous intrigue. He is accredited with being the first successful lover of the famous Nell Gwyn, whom he brought from an inconspicuous seller of oranges to an eminent actress, ultimately the mistress of Charles II. Samuel Pepys has preserved some of the gossip in which Hart was concerned. Pepys writes, on August 26, 1667: "Nell is already left by my Lord Buckhurst; . . . and Hart, her great admirer, now hates her" (*Diary*, vii. 77); on December 28, 1667: "to the King's house and there saw *The Mad Couple*, which is but an ordinary play; but only Nell's and Hart's mad parts are most excellently done, but especially her's" (*Diary*, vii. 236); and, on April 7, 1668: "She [Mrs. Knepp, an actress] tells me mighty news, that my Lady Castlemayne is mightily in love with Hart of their house [King's playhouse]: and he is much with her in private, and she goes to him, and do give him many presents" (*Diary*, vii. 370). At the union of the Duke's and the King's companies in 1682, Hart was given a pension of 40s. a week by the united companies, and "never Acted more, by reason of his Malady; being Afflicted with the Stone and Gravel, of which he Dy'd some time after" (Downes, *Ros. Ang.*, p. 39). He was buried on August 20, 1683, at Stanmore Magna, Middlesex, where he had a country house (Genest, i. 375; Pepys, *Diary*, vii. 77*n*.). In *Euterpe Restored* (1672), Flecknoe writes "The Praises of Richard Burbage," and closes (Collier, iii. 279):

> Such even the nicest critics must allow
> Burbage was once; and such Charles Hart is now.

HART, WILLIAM.

William Hart is named in a license of November 28, 1634, granted to a company under the leadership of William Daniel, and known as the King's Revels (Murray, ii. 8 f.). By January

12, 1636, he was associated with the King's men at Blackfriars, as shown by a Ticket of Privilege issued to the attendants "employed by his Majesty's servants the players of the Blackfriars, and of special use to them both on the Stage and otherwise for his Majesty's disport and service" (Stopes, *Jahrbuch*, xlvi. 99). As a King's man he also appears in the "Players Pass" of May 17, 1636 (Murray, i. opp. 172). Some critics have identified him with the Hart mentioned by Wright as Robinson's apprentice, but the latter is quite clearly Charles Hart (*q.v.*), the famous Restoration actor. Charles was no doubt the son of William Hart, Shakespeare's nephew (son of Joan Hart, Shakespeare's sister), who was buried at Stratford on March 28, 1639 (*Variorum*, iii. 167).

HARVEY.

Apparently an actor or stage-attendant mentioned in *1 Henry IV*, acted by the Chamberlain's men at the Theatre in 1597. Poins says in the course of a speech to the Prince, I. ii. 181: "Falstaff, Harvey, Rossill, and Gadshill shall rob those men that we have already waylaid." But in the scene of the robbery, II. ii, the characters here called Harvey and Rossill are discovered to be Bardolph and Peto, which led to Theobald's suggestion that Harvey and Rossill were the actors who took the parts of Bardolph and Peto. A. Gaw (*P.M.L.A.*, xl. 531) regards Harvey and Rossill, not as actors, but, as "ghost-names."

HARVYE, WILLIAM.

As a member of Ellis Guest's company under license of June 7, 1628, William Harvye is recorded at Norwich on July 2 of the same year (Murray, ii. 103).

HAUGHTON, HUGH.

Hugh Haughton is named in a license of November 28, 1634, granted to a company under the leadership of William Daniel, and known as the King's Revels (Murray, ii. 8 ff.).

HAWKINS, ALEXANDER.

Alexander Hawkins appears as a lessee of the Second Black-friars in October, 1601, when Henry Evans deeded his property to him, and as a patentee for the Children of the Queen's Revels on February 4, 1604 (Adams, *Playhouses*, pp. 211, 215).

HAWLEY, RICHARD.

Richard Hawley is named as a King's man in the "Players Pass" issued on May 17, 1636 (Murray, i. opp. 172).

HAYSELL, GEORGE.

Apparently as an Earl of Worcester's man, under license of February 6, 1583, George Haysell, "of Wisbiche in the Ile of Elye in the Countie of Cambridge," was concerned in the dispute with the Leicester authorities in March, 1584, at which date he was said to be "the chefe playor" (*Eliz. Stage*, ii. 221-24). Possibly he is to be identified with the "Geo. Haysyll, of Cambridge," who, with others in December, 1575, made a complaint against the Bishop of Ely for "divers enormities and wrongs" committed by him and his officers (*S.P.D. Eliz.*, cv. 88).

HEARNE, THOMAS.

On July 27, 1597, Thomas Hearne bound himself to Henslowe to play with the Admiral's men for two years (*H.D.*, i. 201).

HELLE, JOHN.

On August 3, 1597, John Helle, a clown, borrowed 10s. from Henslowe, and bound himself to play with the Admiral's men till Shrovetide (*H.D.*, i. 201).

HEMINGES, JOHN.

On March 2, 1629, a confirmation of arms was issued to "John Hemings of London Gent. of long tyme Servant to Queen Eliza-beth of happie Memory, also to King James hir Royal Successor and to King Charles his Sonne now raigning which John was Sonne and Heire of George Hemings of Draytwiche in the Countye of Worcester Gent" (*Variorum*, iii. 188). This is quite probably John Heminges the player, although Malone found records that led him to believe that Heminges was of Stratford origin (*Variorum*, iii. 187). The date and place of his birth are unknown. He had a wife Rebecca, and is plausibly identified with the John Heminges who was married on March 10, 1588, to Rebecca Knell, widow of William Knell, late of St. Mary's, Aldermanbury. The register of the same parish records the marriage of William Knell and Rebecca Edwards on January 30, 1586, and the burial of an older Willam Knell on September 24, 1578 (*Variorum*, iii. 471–72, 473*n*.). One of these is doubtless the Knell mentioned in Heywood's *An Apology for Actors* (1612), where his Christian name is not given. Knell had belonged to Queen Elizabeth's troupe, and Heminges possibly began his theatrical career with the same company. By May 6, 1593, however, he had joined Strange's men, for his name occurs on this date in the traveling license granted to the company by the Privy Council (*Eliz. Stage*, ii. 123). Subsequently he became associated with the Chamberlain's men, probably when the troupe was organized in 1594, for on December 21, 1596, he and George Bryan served as payees for Court performances of the company. From this date to April 20, 1603, he regularly appears, alone or with Pope or Cowley, as payee for the plays acted at Court by his troupe (Steele, pp. 110, 111, 113, 116, 117, 120, 122, 125). With the same organization he had parts in two of Jonson's plays: *Every Man in his Humor* (1598) and *Every Man out of his Humor* (1599). In 1603 the Chamberlain's company passed under royal patronage, and Heminges is named in the patent granted on May 19, 1603, to the King's men. He was actively engaged in the affairs of this company until his death in 1630. His name appears in the 1623 folio list of Shakespearean players; in the procession list of March 15, 1604; in the warrant of March 29, 1615, to appear before the Privy Council for playing during Lent; in the patent of March 27, 1619; in the livery-allowance lists of May 19, 1619, and April 7,

1621; in the list of players taking part in King James's funeral procession on May 7, 1625; in the patent of June 24, 1625; and in the cloak allowance of May 6, 1629. He was doubtless chief director and business manager of the company, for he served as payee for the Court performances from December 3, 1603, to April 3, 1630 (Steele, pp. 133, 134, 137, 139, 143, 148, 150, 152, 156, 160, 161, 164, 167, 168, 172, 175, 176, 182, 189, 195, 196, 199, 202, 203, 205, 210, 213, 216, 220, 231, 235, 237, 238). He is introduced with his fellows of the King's men into the Induction to Marston's *Malcontent* (1604); and he is known from the actor-lists to have acted in the following plays presented by the company (Murray, i. opp. 172): *Sejanus* (1603), *Volpone* (1605), *The Alchemist* (1610), and *Catiline* (1611). This list seems to indicate that he ceased acting about 1611. Thereafter he not improbably gave his full time to the management of the business affairs of the troupe. John Roberts in his *Answer to Pope* (1729) says that he was a tragedian, and was in partnership with Condell as a printer (*Variorum*, iii. 186), but neither assertion can be verified. Malone (*Variorum*, iii. 187) writes that "In some tract, of which I have forgot to preserve the title, he is said to have been the original performer of Falstaff." His "boy" John Rice (*q.v.*) took part in the entertainment given by the Merchant Taylors in honor of King James on July 16, 1607; and "Heminge's boy" appeared in Chapman's *Middle Temple and Lincoln's Inn Mask* on February 15, 1613 (*Eliz. Stage*, ii. 321; iii. 262). The Globe was destroyed by fire in June, 1613, and Heminges is mentioned in a contemporary ballad, entitled, *A Sonnett upon the pittiful burneing of the Globe playhowse in London* (Halliwell-Phillipps, *Outlines*, i. 311):

> Then with swolne eyes, like druncken Flemminges,
> Distressed stood old stuttering Heminges.

In Jonson's *Masque of Christmas* (1616), Venus, a deaf tire-woman, says: "Master Burbage has been about and about with me, and so has old master Hemings too" (*Works*, vii. 263). His personal relations with his fellows are reflected in the wills of Augustine Phillips (1605), who named him as legatee and overseer, and executor if "my wyfe do at any tyme marrye after my decease"; of Alexander Cooke (1614), who appointed him trustee and called him his "master"; of William Shakespeare (1616), who bequeathed him a memorial ring; of Richard Cowley (1618), to which he was a witness; of John Underwood (1624) and Henry Condell (1627), both of whom designate him as legatee and overseer; and in his appointment as trustee for Shakespeare's Blackfriars property in 1613 (Halliwell-Phillipps, *Outlines*, ii. 31). His business ability seems to have been recognized by other companies than the King's, for in an entry preserved from the officebook of Sir George Buc he appears as agent for the "four companys" in transactions with the Master of the Revels (Adams, *Dram. Rec.*, p. 48): "[Received] Of John Hemminges, in the name of the four companys, for toleration in the holy-dayes, 44*s*. January 29, 1618." That there was a union of four companies after Shakespeare's death in 1616, we learn from Malone (*Variorum*, iii. 224): "Soon after his death, four of the principal companies then subsisting, made a union, and were afterwards called The United Companies; but I know not precisely in what this union consisted." Heminge's character undoubtedly fitted him to discharge with ability and credit his duties as agent for the allied theatrical organizations. Another suggestive record of his relations with the actors of the day is an entry in Edward Alleyn's diary under the date of June 4, 1622: "I dind wt Mr. Hemings" (Warner, p. 192). This probably records only one of many such dinners, at which the affairs of the various companies were discussed. Heminges for some years lived in the parish of St. Mary's, Aldermanbury, where he held the office of sidesman (*Notes and Queries*, 1896, x. 110), and where the registers record his children: Alice (baptized November 1, 1590; married John Atkins February 11, 1612), Mary (baptized May 26, 1592; buried August 9, 1592), Judith (baptized August 29, 1593), Thomasine (baptized January 15, 1595), Joan (baptized May 2, 1596), John (baptized April 2, 1598; buried June 17, 1598), John (baptized August 12, 1599), Beavis (baptized May 24, 1601), William (baptized October 3, 1602), George (baptized February 12, 1604), Rebecca (baptized February 4, 1605), Elizabeth (baptized March 6, 1608), Mary (baptized June 21, 1611; buried July 23, 1611), and Swynnerton (buried June 8, 1613). His wife's burial is recorded on September 2, 1619, and his own, on October 12, 1630 (Collier, iii. 308–10, 315). By 1619 he had apparently moved from the parish of St. Mary's, Aldermanbury, to the vicinity of the Globe, as shown by the documents of the Witter-Heminges lawsuit, that refer to Heminges's house near the Globe (Wallace, *N.U.S.*, x. 332): "And the said deft Hemmynges hath adioyninge therevnto vpon the same ground and soile [i.e. of the Globe] soe therewth demised and letten as is aforesaid a faire howse newe builded to his owne vse for wch he payeth but twentie shillinges yearely in all at the most." As Heminges grew older he probably found his residence at St. Mary's too far from the playhouse for his convenience as business manager of the King's men, and so built himself a house upon land that had been leased for the Globe (J. W. Hebel, *The Plays of William Heminges*, MS. thesis in the Cornell University Library, p. 5). The language of his will, dated October 9, 1630, seems to indicate that he was not living in St. Mary's at the time it was made, for he refers to the parish as "where I long lived, and whither I have bequeathed my body for burial." In his will (Collier, iii. 317–20) he describes himself as "citizen and grocer of London." There is no evidence, however, that he was ever a tradesman, and how he obtained the freedom of the Grocers' Company we cannot tell. He names his son William sole executor and trustee for his younger and unmarried children, appoints Cuthbert Burbage and "Mr. Rice," probably John Rice the player, overseers, and mentions as legatees his daughters Rebecca, wife of Captain William Smith, Margaret, wife of Thomas Sheppard, who is not named in the register, Elizabeth, and Mrs. Merefield, who was probably a widow, and his son-in-law John Atkins "and his now wife," and his grandson Richard Atkins; and he leaves 10*s.* each for memorial rings "unto every of my fellowes and sharers, his majesty's servants." Heminges fails to mention in his will his daughter, Thomasine, who may have died before 1630. She may, however, have become estranged from her father as a result of the Ostler-Heminges lawsuit of 1615–16 (Wallace, London *Times*, October 2 and 4, 1909). In 1611 the sixteen-year-old Thomasine had married William Ostler, a King's man, who was shortly afterwards admitted as a sharer in the Globe property. They evidently lived in Heminges's neighborhood, for on May 18, 1612, their son Beaumont was baptized at St. Mary's, Aldermanbury. On December 16, 1614, Ostler died intestate, and six days after his death Thomasine procured Letters of Administration from the Archbishop of Canterbury. For safe keeping she delivered to her father, to be held in trust for her, the leases for shares in the Globe and Blackfriars that had been acquired by her late husband. She lost no time in taking advantage of her freedom as a young widow, and, in spite of her father's remonstrances, was soon involved in a romantic episode with the rakish young Walter Raleigh, son of Sir Walter, not long returned from Paris, where he had amused himself with playing knavish pranks on his tutor Ben Jonson (Jonson, *Conversations*, ed. Patterson, p. 27). Thomasine fared badly in the romance, for in 1615–16 she sued young Raleigh for insult and slander, and was awarded damages of £250 in default of his appearance in the Court of Barons. Evidently Heminges wished to restrain his daughter by withholding from her the income from her shares in the playhouses, for she is pictured as making unsuccessful appeals for funds. In 1615, she brought suit in Chancery against her father, but the affair was settled out of court before the serving of the subpoena. Soon differences again arose, and Thomasine had a bill drawn up, suing her father for £600 damages for the detention of the shares and the profits. Again the case was apparently settled out of court, and the conclusion is not known. William Heminges (see J. W. Hebel, *The Plays of William Heminges*, MS. thesis, pp. 23 ff.), who inherited his father's interest in the Globe and Black-friars, had been well educated, first at Westminster School, and later at Christ Church, Oxford, where he received his Master's degree in 1628 (Wood, *Ath. Oxon.*, iii. 277). William was not, it would seem, an actor; but he took enough "hours of recess" to compose several plays: *The Coursing of a Hare, or the Mad Cap* (licensed for the Fortune playhouse, March, 1632–33) is not extant, and was doubtless destroyed by Warburton's cook; *The Fatal Contract*, published in 1653 by A. P. and A. T., probably Andrew Pennycuicke (*q.v.*) and Anthony Turner (*q.v.*), both former members of Queen Henrietta's troupe. He is also the author of an *Elegy on Randolph's Finger* (written about 1630–32), which contains the well-known lines "On the Time-Poets." The playhouse shares that passed to William in 1630 were the result of many investments made by his father over an extended period. John Heminges was an original sharer in both the leases of the Globe in 1599 and of the Blackfriars in 1608. During the following years the business of the two playhouses prospered, and as the old "housekeepers" died or left the company, Heminges was financially able to increase his holdings, until at his death in 1630 he appears to have controlled three-sixteenths of the Globe and two-eights of the Blackfriars. And some of these shares he had "injoyed . . . thirty yeeres without any molestacion, beeing the most of the sayd yeeres both player and housekeeper, and after hee gave over playing diverse yeeres" (Adams, *Mod. Phil.*, xvii. 2 ff.; Halliwell-Phillipps, *Outlines*, i. 312, 316). In 1619 he was described as of "great lyveinge wealth and power" (Wallace, *N.U.S.*, x. 311). Although William came into possession of these theatrical interests he apparently had nothing to do with the management of the playhouses with which his father had been so prominently connected. This is shown by one of the petitions in the lawsuit of 1635, which says (*Outlines*, i. 316): "and his sonne, William Heminges, fower yeers after, though hee never had anything to doe with the sayd stage, injoyed the same [i.e. the profits from the shares] without any trouble." During 1633 and 1634 he sold his shares in both houses to John Shank, a King's man, for £506; and these transactions led to a petition by some of the other members of the King's company for the compulsory sale to them of shares from the larger shareholders (*Outlines*, i. 312–17). From Shank's counter-petition we learn that William Heminges was in pecuniary straits, and that he had been imprisoned, possibly for debt. Shank says (*Outlines*, i. 314): "Your suppliant hath besides disbursed to the sayd William Hemings diverse other small summes of money since hee was in prison." John Heminges's greatest claim to fame and to our regard is his connection with Condell in the publication of the First Folio of Shakespeare's plays in 1623. By their own statement these two men collected the plays of their friend and fellow-actor, and gave them to the press, with no desire for monetary profit. In July, 1896, an appropriate memorial to their memory was unveiled at St. Mary's, Aldermanbury, with the inscription: "To the memory of John Heminge and Henry Condell, fellow actors and personal friends of Shakespeare. They lived many years in this parish, and are buried here. To their disinterested efforts the world owes all that it calls Shakespeare. They alone collected his dramatic writings, regardless of pecuniary loss, and, without the hope of any profit, gave them to the world. They thus merit the gratitude of mankind." Heminges is alluded to in Scott's *Woodstock* (1826).

HENSLOWE, FRANCIS.

Francis Henslowe, son of Richard and nephew of Philip Henslowe, first appears in an undated letter, about 1590, begging his uncle to obtain his release from "ye counter in Woodstret." Many entries in Henslowe's *Diary* and other accounts record his imprisonment on various charges of stealing and liability for debt, with the resultant requests for loans from his uncle. From January, 1593, to May, 1594, he was employed in Philip's business of pawnbroking. His earliest connection with a theatrical oraganization is recorded under date of May 8, 1593, conceivably an error for 1594, when he borrowed £15 "to laye downe for his share to the Quenes players" when he went with them into the country to play. On June 1, 1595, he again had a loan of £9 "to laye downe for his halfe share wth the company wch he dothe playe wth all," which is thought by Greg to refer to a troupe other than the Queen's. By March, 1605, he belonged to the company under the patronage of the Duke of Lennox, who may have taken over some members of the Queen's company at her death in 1603. On March 1, 1605, Abraham Savery gave him a power of attorney to recover £40 from John Garland, forfeited on a bond "for the deliuere of a warrnt, which was mayd vnto me frome the gratious the duke of Linox"; and on March 16, 1605, he gave his uncle a bond of £60 to observe articles of an agreement which he had made with Garland and Saverey, "his ffellowes, servantes to the most noble Prince the duke of Lennox." There was also an undated loan, made probably in 1604, of £7 by Philip Henslowe to his nephew "to goyne with owld Garlland and Symcockes and Saverey when they played in the duckes nam at ther laste goinge owt." He lived in the liberty of the Clink on the Bankside in 1594, in a house also on the Bankside called the Upper Ground in 1597, and in the parish of St. George's, Southwark, in 1606. On March 30, 1606, he acknowledged a debt of £2 to one Benjamin Harrys of Newington. Both he and his wife died between this date and October 6, 1606, as shown by an entry of charges for their funerals, and an acquittance from John Filter to Philip Henslowe as administrator of Francis Henslowe, deceased (Greg, H.D., ii. 277–78; H.P., pp. 62 ff.; Warner, pp. 27, 28, 131, 132).

HENSLOWE, PHILIP.

Philip Henslowe, no doubt the greatest theatrical proprietor and manager of the Tudor-Stuart period, was the son of Edmond Henslowe of Sussex, Master of the Game in Ashdown and Brill Park. By 1577 he was lving in the Liberty of the Clink, Southwark, where he continued to reside until his death in 1616. At first, he appears as a poor man and "servant" of one Woodward. Upon the death of his employer he married the widow, Agnes Woodward, and thus came into the possession of considerable property. Agnes Woodward had a daughter Joan, who in 1592 married Edward Alleyn, which union cemented the friendship between the families and led to the closest business and personal relations between Henslowe and Alleyn. In documents of 1584–87 Henslowe is described as "citizen and dyer of London," but he is not known to have been actively engaged as a dyer. He had a marked talent for gaining profit from investments, and soon amassed considerable wealth through various business transactions. He was also an important figure in other than purely mercenary matters. By 1592 he was a Groom of the Chamber to Queen Elizabeth; in 1603, Gentleman Sewer of the Chamber to James I; in 1607, vestryman of St. Saviour's, Southwark; in 1608, churchwarden; in 1612, one of the governors of the free grammar school. His source of greatest profit was his position as owner and manager of playhouses; but he was also engaged in the manufacture of starch, in pawnbroking, in bear-bating, and in other commercial speculations of lesser importance. From at least 1587 onwards he was interested in theatrical property. In 1587 he and John Cholmley entered into a partnership and built the Rose, about which playhouse little is known until February, 1592, when it was occupied by Strange's men under the leadership of Alleyn, an Admiral's man; in 1600 he and Alleyn erected the Fortune; in 1613 he and Jacob Meade singed a contract with a carpenter named Gilbert Katherens for the erection of the Hope, which was used for both the performance of plays and the baiting

A DICTIONARY OF ACTORS

of animals; and for a time he was probably manager of White-friars. Henslowe died on January 6, 1616, and was buried on January 10 in St. Saviour's church. His private and theatrical records remain as a most valuable collection for both dramatic and social history. (This sketch is abridged from Greg's detailed biography in his edition of *Henslowe's Diary*, 1908, ii. pp. 1–147).

HERIOT, HENRY.

From 1547 to 1552 Henry Heriot seems to have been a Court Interluder, at a salary of £3 6s. 8d. a year (Collier, i. 136; *Eliz. Stage*, ii. 83).

HETON, ROBERT.

Robert Heton, who describes himself as "one of the Sewers of Her Majesty's Chamber Extraordinary," became manager of Salisbury Court about 1635, at which time the playhouse was occupied by the King's Revels. On February 8, 1637, he received payment for Court performances by the "Salisbury Court players" in October, 1635 (Steele, p. 254). On May 12, 1636, the play-houses were closed on account of the plague. When acting was resumed on October 2, 1637, Queen Henrietta's men seem to have united with the Revels company as the Queen's players at Salis-bury Court, which was still under the management of Heton (Adams, *Playhouses*, pp. 379–80).

HEWSE, RICHARD.

A member of the Children of Paul's in 1554 (Hillebrand, *Child Actors*, p. 110). He is obviously identical with the Richard Huse mentioned in the will of Sebastian Westcott, Master of Paul's, April 3, 1582 (*Eliz. Stage*, ii. 15n.).

HEYWOOD, JOHN.

Aside from his work as the author of several delightful farces, John Heywood probably took some part in the training or man-agement of the Children of Paul's. In March, 1538, there is reçorded a payment to one Heywood, who is generally identified with the dramatist: "Item geuen to Heywood playeng an enterlude with his children bifore my lades grace"; in February, 1551–52, he seems to have been at Hatfield with Sebastian Westcott when the latter brought children to play before the Princess Elizabeth; and in 1553 is mentioned a play "of childerne sett owte by Mr. Haywood" at Court. These entries are thought to refer to the Paul's boys, for whom Heywood in all probability wrote plays, although he is not known to have been their master (*Eliz. Stage*, ii. 12 ff., *notes*).

HEYWOOD, THOMAS.

Thomas Heywood was not only a dramatist of note and a writer of non-dramatic works both in prose and verse, but also a player. His earliest appearance as an actor is on March 25, 1598, when he bound himself to Henslowe for two years to play at the Rose, which was then occupied by the Admiral's men (*H. D.*, i. 204). He wrote two plays for this company between December, 1598, and Febraury, 1599, after which date he disappears from the *Diary* until September, 1602. During this interval he may have become associated with Derby's men, who in 1599 acted *Edward IV*, thought to be a play by Heywood. He reappears as a sharer in Worcester's company in the autumn of 1602, and on September 1 borrowed 2s. 6d. from Henslowe to buy silk garters (*H.D.*, i. 781). From October 21, 1602, to May 9, 1603, he appears as authorizing payments on behalf of Worcester's men. He and William Kempe served as payees for a Court performance by Worcester's troupe on January 3, 1602 (Steele, p. 123). Early in the reign of James I the Earl of Worcester's men were taken into the patronage of Queen Anne; Heywood became a member of the Queen's troupe at its formation late in 1603 or early in 1604, for his name appears in the undated draft license. In the dedication of his *Gunaikeion* (1624) to the Earl of Worcester he refers to the transfer of the company by

Worcester to the Queen; "I was (my Lord) your creature, and (amongst other of your servants) you bestowed me vpon the excellent Princesse Q. *Anne* (to whose memorie I haue celebrated in these Papers the zeale of a subiect and a seruant) but by her lamented death your Gift (my Lord) is returned againe into your hands, being stil yours, either to keepe vnto your selfe, or to conferre where your noble disposition shall best please." With the Queen's company he continued till its dissolution at her death in 1619. We find him in the list of players receiving red cloth for the coronation procession of March 15, 1604; in both the patent of April 15, 1609, and the duplicate license issued on January 7, 1612, to the traveling company under the patronage of the Queen; in the Baskerville documents of June, 1616, and June, 1617 (*Eliz. Stage*, ii. 229, 231, 237, 238); in the petition of October 2, 1617, to the sessions of Peace against the various presentments that had been issued against the Queen's players for not "repayringe the Highwayes neere the Red Bull" (Jeaffreson, *Middlesex*. ii. 170); and at Queen Anne's funeral on May 13, 1619. He seems to have been with the Queen's men at Norwich on May 6, 1615, and May 31, 1617, for his name is given in the abstracts of the license in the Norwich records (Murray, i. 196; ii. 340, 343). After 1619 he is not traceable as an actor in the records of any of the companies. Nevertheless, there is a possibility that he continued on the stage for some years, as suggested by an epigram in the *Musarum Deliciae* (1640), in which he is told that "groveling on the stage" did not become his years (*Heywood*, ed. Bates, pp. xxxiii, lxxi):

To Mr. Thomas Heywood

Thou hast writ much and art admir'd by those
Who love the easie ambling of thy prose;
But yet thy pleasingest flight was somewhat high,
When thou didst touch the angels Hyerarchie;
Fly that way still, it will become thy age
And better please then groveling on the stage.

The register of St. Saviour's, Southwark, records the baptism of the following children of Thomas Hayward, "a player": Mary, October 5, 1600; Joseph, June 5, 1603; Alice, September 16, 1604; Richard, September 5, 1605 (Bentley, *T.L.S.*, Nov. 15, 1928, p. 856). In 1623 a Thomas Haywarde lived "neare Clarkenwell Hill" (Wallace, *Jahrbuch*, xlvi. 347), who was no doubt the actor-dramatist. "Tho. Heywood, Poet," was buried at St. James, Clerkenwell, on August 16, 1641 (Hovenden, iv. 248). His most important non-dramatic work is the *Apology for Actors*, published in 1612 but written some years earlier, in which he defends players under three heads: Their Antiquity, Their Ancient Dignitie, and The True Use of their Quality. The quarto is dedicated to the Earl of Worcester, the patron of the company of which Heywood was formerly a member. His mention of the older actors is praiseworthy, and his views on the art of acting are sane and cheerful. The volume appeared with commendatory verses by three of his fellow-actors: Richard Perkins, Christopher Beeston, and Robert Pallant. For a detailed biographical sketch of Heywood, see the Introduction to K. L. Bates's edition of his plays in the *Belles-Lettres Series*, and Otelia Cromwell, *Thomas Heywood*, in *Yale Studies in English*, 1928.

HILL, JOHN.

See John Hull.

HINSTOCK, ROBERT.

As a Court Interluder Robert Hinstock is traceable in the records from 1538 to 1551 (Collier, i. 116, 117, 136; *Eliz. Stage*, ii. 82).

HINT, ROBERT.

Under a license dated November 10, 1629, Robert Hint is named as a member of the Red Bull company that appeared at Reading on November 30 of the same year (Murray, ii. 386).

HOBBES, THOMAS.

Thomas Hobbes is named in a patent granted on March 30, 1610, to the company under the patronage of Prince Charles, then Duke of York, and known as the Duke of York's men (*M. S. C.*, i. 272). After Prince Henry's death in November, 1612, they became entitled to the designation of Prince Charles's players. On May 18, 1615, the Prince's men visited Norwich, where they were allowed to play eight days; the records give the names of John Garland, William Rowley, and Hobbes (Murray, ii. 340). He joined his fellows in signing an agreement with Alleyn and Meade on March 20, 1616, and took part in King James's funeral procession on May 7, 1625 (*H. P.*, p. 91; Murray, i. 161, 237). Soon after the accession of Charles I, James's players came under his patronage, and several members of the old Prince Charles's company were no doubt transferred to the King's men. William Rowley is the only one of the Prince's troupe mentioned in the King's men's license of June 24, 1625; but Anthony Smith and William Penn, both former Prince's men, appear in the cast of Ford's *Lover's Melancholy*, licensed for the King's troupe on November 24, 1628, and Hobbes is found with the King's men in 1629. The omission of their names from the 1625 patent is not explained, but conceivably their transfer occurred about this time. As a King's man Hobbes appears in the livery allowance of May 6, 1629; in a stage-direction to Massinger's *Believe as You List* (ed. Croker, p. 43), licensed May 7, 1631 (Adams, *Dram. Rec.*, p. 33), where he is assigned the part of Calistus; and in the "Players Pass" of May 17, 1636 (Murray, i. opp. 172). He was living "att the upper end of Shoreditch" in 1623 (Wallace, *Jahrbuch*, xlvi. 348). Rowley dedicated his *Search for Money* (1609) "To his entire and deare-esteemed friend, Maister Thomas Hobbs," who is doubtless the actor, although Thomas Hobbes (1588-1679), the philosopher, remembered chiefly for his treatise on the theory of politics under the title of *Leviathan* (1651), has also been suggested as the dedicatee.

HOLCOMBE, THOMAS.

Thomas Holcombe began his theatrical career with the King's men as a boy, as shown by the testimony of John Shank in the *Sharers' Papers* of 1635 (Halliwell-Phillipps, *Outlines*, i. 316). With this company he had parts in the following plays (Murray, i. opp. 172): *The Queen of Corinth* (*c.* 1617); *The Knight of Malta* (*c.* 1618); *Sir John van Olden Barnavelt* (1619), in which he acted the Provost's wife; *The Custom of the Country* (*c.* 1619-20); *The Little French Lawyer* (*c.* 1620); *Women Pleased* (*c.* 1620); and *The Prophetess* (1622). The register of St. Giles's, Cripplegate, records the burial of a Thomas Holcome in September, 1625 (Malcolm, *Lond. Rediv.*, iii. 304).

HOLE, RICHARD.

Richard Hole appears as a Court Interluder in 1526 and 1530 (Collier, i. 97, 115).

HOLLAND, AARON.

Aaron Holland was the builder of the Red Bull playhouse, about 1605 (Adams, *Playhouses*, p. 294). His sale of a seventh part of the Red Bull to Thomas Swinnerton (*q. v.*) about 1605, and Swinnerton's subsequent transfer of the share to Philip Stone, who sold it to Thomas Woodford about 1612-13, led to disputes before the Court of Requests in 1613 and 1619 between Woodford and Holland (Wallace, *N. U. S.*, ix. 291 ff.). Sisson writes ("*Keep the Widow Waking*," in *The Library*, N. S., 1927, viii. p. 235): "I have found a later record of a case in the Court of Chancery in 1623-4 which concludes the story of his relations with the Red Bull, and recapitulates the incidents of his long struggle with Thomas Woodford, which he finally won. . . . In the chancery suit, however, I find that Holland in his answer declares that he had sold not only all his share in the profits, but also his lease, before 6 November, 1623, the date of his answer, though he reserved a small annuity to be derived from the theatre during his life."

HOLLAND, JOHN.

In 2 *Seven Deadly Sins*, acted by Strange's men about 1590, Holland played a warder in Induction, an attendant in "Envy," and a captain in "Sloth" (Greg, *H. P.*, p. 152; *R. E. S.*, i. 262).

HOLMAN, THOMAS.

Thomas Holman is named in a license of December 30, 1629, granted to a group of players, presumably the King's Revels, under the leadership of Robert Kimpton. They presented this license at Reading soon afterwards (Murray, ii. 13, 386).

HOLT, JAMES.

James Holt is known as a member of Queen Anne's company from its formation in 1603–04 to its dissolution in 1619. His name appears in the list of players receiving red cloth for the coronation procession of March 15, 1604; in both the patent of April 15, 1609, and the duplicate license issued on January 7, 1612, to the traveling company; in the Norwich records of May 6, 1615, and May 31, 1617; and at the Queen's funeral on May 13, 1619 (*Eliz. Stage*, ii. 229; *M. S. C.*, i. 270; Murray, i. 196; ii. 340, 343).

HOLT, JOHN.

A "momer" who helped the Westminster boys with a pageant in 1561, as shown by the payment "to John Holt momer in reward for attendance given of the children in the pageant." He may have been an actor, as suggested by the term "momer" (mummer). He is perhaps identical with the Yeoman of the Revels of that name, who helped the boys in 1564–65: "Geuen to Mr. Holte yeoman of the reuells." Holt's tenure of the Yeomanship extended from 1547 to 1571. He had a house to the north of the churchyard in the Blackfriars (*Eliz. Stage*, i. 73, 79; ii. 72, 492).

HOLZHEW, BEHRENDT.

During 1614–15 Behrendt Holzhew was in Germany with a group of English players in the service of John Sigismund, Elector of Brandenburg (Cohn, p. lxxxviii).

HONEYMAN, JOHN.

See John Honyman.

HONIMAN, JOHN.

See John Honyman.

HONNAN, RICHARD.

Richard Honnan was a hired man of Prince Charles's company in 1640. In an order of April 25 he is named as a Prince's man who is not "to be hindered or diverted in his service by being impressed arrested, or otherwise molested, without leave first asked" (Stopes, *Jahrbuch*, xlvi, 103).

HONTE, THOMAS.

See Thomas Hunt.

HONYMAN, JOHN.

John Honyman (the name is variously spelled Honeyman, Honiman, Hunnyman, Hunnieman) began his theatrical career with the King's company as a boy, as shown by the testimony of John Shank in the *Sharers' Papers* of 1635 (Halliwell-Phillipps, *Outlines*, i. 316). He played the following parts with the King's men (Murray, i. opp. 172): Domitilla, cousin-germane to Caesar, in Massinger's *Roman Actor* (licensed October 11, 1626); an unassigned part in Ford's *Lover's Melancholy* (licensed November 24, 1628; *Works*, i. 6); Sophia, wife to Mathias, in Massinger's *Picture* (licensed June 8, 1629); Clarinda, daughter to Utrante, in Carlell's *Deserving Favorite* (1629); a merchant in Massinger's *Believe as You List* (licensed May 7, 1631); and a young factor, in Fletcher's *Wildgoose Chase* (a revival, 1631). The register of St. Giles's, Cripplegate, records his burial in 1636 (Malcolm, *Lond. Rediv.*, iii. 304). Thomas Jordan, a member of the Company of his Majestie's Revels, published an epitaph on him in his *Poeticall Varieties* (1637):

An Epitaph on his kind friend, Mr. Iohn Honiman, Gent.

Thou that couldst never weepe, and know'st not why
Teares should be spent but in mans infancy,
Come and repent thy error for here lyes
A Theame for Angels to write Elegies,
Had they the losse as we have; such a one
As nature kild for his perfection,
And when shee sends those vertues backe agen
His stocke shall serve f.)r twenty vertuous men.
In Aprill dyed this Aprill to finde May.
In Paradise, or celebrate a day
With some celestiall creature, had he beene
Design'd for other then a Cherubin;
Earth would have gave him choice; he was a man
So sweetly good, that he who wisely can
Describe at large, must such another be,
Or court no Muses but Divinitie.
   Here will I rest, for feare the Readers eyes
   Vpon his urne become a Sacrifice.

According to Thomas Davies (*Dramatic Miscellanies*, i. 183),
Honyman was also a playwright (cf. Lawrence, *R. E. S.*, iii.
220). Davies writes:

John Hunnieman . . . was the author of a play, with the
name of which I should be glad to enrich the dramatic catalogue,
but I cannot learn whether it was a tragedy, a comedy, or a
mixture of both. From a copy of verses to the author, by Sir
Aston Cockaine, we are informed that this dramatic piece was
much approved by the public: as Sir Aston's epistle contains the
only information of Hunnieman's authorship, I shall transcribe
it as a theatrical curiosity:

To Mr. John Hunnieman

On, hopeful youth, and let thy happy strain
Redeem the glory of the stage again;
Lessen the loss of Shakespeare's death, by thy
Successful pen and fortunate phantasy.
He did not only write but act, and so
Thou dost not only act, but writest too.

Between you there no difference appears,
But what may be made up with equal years.
This is my suffrage, and I scorn my pen
Should crown the heads of undeserving men.

HOOPE, RICHARD.

Richard Hoope borrowed £3 from Henslowe on January 14, 1595(?). He is described as a "Lord chamberlenes man," but whether he was an actor or a private servant is not known (*H. D.*, ii. 285).

HORN, JAMES.

James Horn is known as a King's man (Murray, i. 161, opp. 172) in the actor-list of Beaumont and Fletcher's *Pilgrim* (c. 1621); in King James's funeral procession on May 7, 1625; in Massinger's *Roman Actor* (licensed October 11, 1626), where he seems to have played Entellus, a lictor; in Ford's *Lover's Melancholy* (licensed November 24, 1628); and in the livery allowance of May 6, 1629 (Stopes, *Jahrbuch*, xlvi. 95).

HORTON, EDWARD.

As a King's man Edward Horton acted Mariana, sister to Lysander, in Carlell's *Deserving Favorite* (1629; ed. Gray, p. 75). He seems also to have played in Beaumont and Fletcher's *Mad Lover* (possibly in a revival about 1630), as noted in a stage-direction, II. i: "Enter Stremon and his Boy Ed. Hor." (*Works*, iii. 456).

HOUGHTON, ROBERT.

Robert Houghton was a member of Richard Bradshaw's company, a troupe that got into trouble at Banbury in May, 1633. The town authorities becoming suspicious of the validity of the company's license, arrested the players, and notified the Privy Council. The players appeared before the Privy Council in June, and were soon discharged "upon bond given to be forthcoming whensoever they should be called for." In the examination of the players by the Banbury officials, Houghton testified on May 2,

1633, that he "came to this company the Thursday before Easter last, and played his part in stage plays at Sir William Spencer's [and] at Keinton two or three days this week"; and that he "received nothing but meat and drink" (Murray, ii. 106 ff., 163 ff.).

HOVELL, WILLIAM.

On February 27, 1615, a license was granted to William Hovell, William Perry, and Nathan May, as representatives of, presumably, the King's Revels company. Nothing is heard of these players in London, and their only recorded provincial appearance is at Norwich on June 17, 1615. Their license was apparently condemned and withdrawn by an order of the Earl of Pembroke on July 16, 1616 (Murray, ii. 10, 340, 343).

HOWARD, THOMAS.

The registers of St. Saviour's record on March 4, 1598, the baptism of "Francis Howard, daughter of Thomas, a player" (Bentley, *T.L.S.*, Nov. 15, 1928. p. 856).

HOWELL, STEPHANUS.

A member of the Chapel Royal in 1423 (Hillebrand, *Mod. Phil.*, xviii. 235).

HOWES, OLIVER.

Oliver Howes's name appears in a warrant of June 30, 1628, appointing several of the Lady Elizabeth's (Queen of Boehmia's) players as Grooms of the Chamber (Stopes, *Jahrbuch*, xlvi. 94).

HUBERT.

Hubert and Gascoine appear as minor actors or stage-attendants who open the trap-door for Antiochus in Massinger's *Believe as You List* (ed. Croker, p. 66), licensed for the King's men on May 7, 1631 (Adams, *Dram. Rec.*, p. 33).

HUDSON, RICHARD.

Richard Hudson, weaver, is mentioned as an unlicensed player of Hutton Bushell, Yorkshire, in 1612 (*Eliz. Stage*, i. 305*n*.).

HULL, JOHN.

John Hull (or Hill) visited Frankfort in March, Nuremberg in April, 1600, and Frankfort at Easter, 1601, with a group of English players under the patronage of Maurice of Hesse (Herz, p. 38). "Alyce Hill, daughter of John, a player," was baptized at St. Saviour's, Southwark, on August 13, 1601 (Bentley, *T. L. S.*, Nov. 15, 1928, p. 856).

HUNNIEMAN, JOHN.

See John Honyman.

HUNNIS, JOHN.

A "ghost-name" in the Chapel records of payment on January 12, 1572, for a performance at Court (Steele, p. 41). This is obviously a clerical error for William Hunnis, which led Chalmers to infer the existence of two Masters of the Chapel Royal by the name of Hunnis (*Variorum*, iii. 439).

HUNNIS, WILLIAM.

Master of the Chapel Royal, 1566–97 (Stopes, *Hunnis*, 1910, *Materialien*, xxix).

HUNNYMAN, JOHN.

See John Honyman.

HUNT, ROBERT.

In December, 1631 (Adams, *Dram. Rec.*, p. 45), Robert Hunt played Jeffry in Marmion's *Holland's Leaguer*, presented by "the high and mighty Prince Charles his servants, at the private house in Salisbury Court" (Marmion, *Works*, pp. 2, 6). Murray, i. 219, gives the name as "Robert Huyt [White]."

HUNT, THOMAS.

As an Admiral's man Thomas Hunt appears in the plots of *Frederick and Basilea* (1597), as servant, guard, lord, messenger, jailor; of *Troilus and Cressida* (*c.* 1599); and of *The Battle of Alcazar* (*c.* 1600–01), as a Moor, attendant, and ambassador (*H. P.*, pp. 153, 154; *Eliz. Stage*, ii. 175). Nothing further is known of him until August 29, 1611, when he joined his fellow-actors of the Lady Elizabeth's troupe in giving Henslowe a bond of £500 to perform "certen articles" of agreement (*H. P.*, pp. 18, 111). By April 15, 1621, he seems to have belonged to the Palsgrave's men, when his name appears in a list of players of the Fortune company who dined with Alleyn (Warner, p. 188). Since he is not mentioned in the leases of 1618 or 1622, he was evidently not a shareholder in the Palsgrave's company that occupied the Fortune. He is probably identical with the Thomas Honte who received payment from the Admiral's men through Alleyn in October, 1596 (*H. D.*, ii. 285).

HUNTLEY, DICK.

Apparently the book-holder (prompter) or an actor in Nashe's *Summer's Last Will and Testament* (*Works*, iii. 233), acted in 1592 at Croydon, possibly by members of Archbishop Whitgift's household (*Eliz. Stage*, iii. 451–53). As Will Summers enters "in his fooles coate but halfe on," he says (line 14): "*Dick Huntley* cryes, 'Begin, begin': and all the whole house, 'For shame, come away'; when I had my things but now brought me out of the *Lawndry*."

HUSE, RICHARD.

See Richard Hewse.

HUTCHINSON, CHRISTOPHER.

See Christopher Beeston.

HUYT, ROBERT.

See Robert Hunt.

HYLL, NICHOLAS.

A member of the Chapel Royal in 1423 (Hillebrand, *Mod. Phil.*, xviii. 235).

IOY, NICHOLAS.

See Nicholas Joe.

ISLIPP, ADAM.

On May 20, 1622, Adam Islipp, stationer, obtained a lease of one whole share in the Fortune playhouse (Greg, *H. P.*, p. 112).

IVY, NICHOLAS.

See Nicholas Joe.

JACKSON.

Jackson played Chester in Davenport's *King John and Matilda*, acted by Queen Henrietta's company at the Cockpit in Drury Lane, probably about 1629 (Murray, i. opp. 266).

JACKSON, EDWARD.

A joint-lessee of the new Fortune playhouse, in which he obtained a whole share on May 20, 1622 (Warner, p. 246).

JAMES, RICHARD JONES'S BOY.

James, Richard Jones's boy, fetched a loan from Henslowe on November 17, 1599 (*H. D.*, ii. 286). He is perhaps identical with "Jones's boy" who played a waiting-maid and a beggar with the Admiral's men in *Troilus and Cressida*, about 1599 (*H. P.*, p. 154). The James who acted in *The Battle of Alcazar* (c. 1600–01) and in *1 Tamar Cam* (1602) may be either he or James Bristow (*q. v.*).

JARMAN, ANTHONY.

Anthony Jarman, carpenter, was a joint-lessee of the new Fortune playhouse, in which he obtained a whole share on May 20, 1622 (Warner, p. 244).

A DICTIONARY OF ACTORS

JARVICE.

Apparently a musician at Salisbury Court when Glapthorne's *Lady Mother* was produced there in 1635: "*Sucket*. Ever, ever, whilst you live, *Jarvice*; the dauncers alwayes payes the musike" (Bullen, *Old Plays*, ii. 132).

JEFFES, ANTHONY.

Anthony Jeffes may have been a Chamberlain's or a Pembroke's man before he became associated with the Admiral's company in 1597 (*Eliz. Stage*, ii. 133, 200). He is first known as an Admiral's man in the accounts dated October 11, 1597, following the merger of the Admiral and Pembroke companies. He appears in Henslowe's records from October, 1597, to February, 1602, as borrowing and repaying various amounts, as acknowledging company debts, and once as authorizing a payment n behalf of the Admiral's men (*H. D.*, ii. 286-87). With the Admiral's troupe he played (*H. P.*, pp. 153, 154; *Eliz. Stage*, ii. 175) Young Mahamet in *The Battle of Alcazar* (*c.* 1600-01), and Linus and a Moor in *1 Tamar Cam* (1602). About Christmas, 1603, the Admiral's men were taken into the service of Prince Henry. As a member of the Prince's company, he appears in the coronation list of March 15, 1604; in the patent of April 30, 1606; and in the household list of 1610 (*Eliz. Stage*, ii. 186, 187, 188). Subsequently he seems to have retired, receiving £70 for his interest in the company, as shown by a letter from Charles Massey to Edward Alleyn, not dated, but from internal evidence written not long after the death of Prince Henry on November 6, 1612 (Warner, p. 36). Anthony, son of Richard Jeffes, baptized at St. Saviour's, Southwark, on December 14, 1578, may be the same whose marriage to Faith Jones is recorded on February 19, 1601. Children of Anthony Jeffes, called "player," are entered in the registers of St. Giles's, Cripplegate, from June 11, 1602, to May 1, 1609; in later entries from May 30, 1610, to October 30, 1619, Anthony is described as "brewer" (*Eliz. Stage*, ii. 324).

JEFFES, HUMPHREY.

The relation, if any, between Anthony and Humphrey Jeffes is unknown, but the same early theatrical connection has been suggested for both—that they were Chamberlain's or Pembroke's men before they joined the Admiral's company in 1597 (*Eliz. Stage*, ii. 133, 200). Humphrey's earliest appearance as an Admiral's man is in the list of October 11, 1597, following the union of the Admiral's and the Pembroke's troupes. From this date to September 9, 1602, he is named in the accounts as borrowing and repaying various sums, as acknowledging company debts, and as authorizing a payment in one transaction for the troupe. On July 6, 1601, the tailor was paid for making Humphrey's suit for a part in *The Six Yeomen of the West*, a play that is now lost (*H. D.*, ii. 287). As an Admiral's man he acted (*H. P.*, pp. 153, 154; *Eliz. Stage*, ii. 175) Muly Mahamet Xeque in *The Battle of Alcazar* (*c.* 1600–01); Otanes in *1 Tamar Cam* (1602); and presumably a serving-man, addressed as "Humphery" (lines 1767–68), in *Look About You*, published in 1600 as "lately played" by the Admiral's company (ed. Greg, p. viii). He has been conjectured to be the "Humfrey" mentioned in the Folio *3 Henry VI*, III. i. 1: "Enter Sinklo, and Humfrey, with Crosse-bowes in their hands," which possibly refers to a production by Pembroke's men in 1592–93, or to a revival by the Chamberlain's men (*Eliz. Stage*, ii. 129–30, 200). About Christmas, 1603, the Admiral's men came under the patronage of Prince Henry. With the Prince's men he is named in the coronation list of March 15, 1604; in the patent of April 30, 1606; and in the household list of 1610 (*Eliz. Stage*, ii. 186, 187, 188). The Prince died in November, 1612, and his players were taken into the service of the Palsgrave. Jeffes is mentioned in the new patent of January 11, 1613, and in a warrant of March 29, 1615, ordering certain players to appear before the Privy Council for playing during Lent (*M.S.C.*, i. 275, 372). During 1615–16 Charles Marshall, Humphrey Jeffes, and William Parr secured a duplicate of the 1613 patent to the Palsgrave's men, organized a troupe, and traveled in the provinces. This duplicate warrant was condemned and withdrawn by order of the Earl of Pembroke on July 16, 1616 (Murray, ii. 4 ff.). The register of St. Giles's, Cripplegate, records his burial on August 21, 1618. His daughter, Mary, was baptized at St. Saviour's, Southwark, on January 25, 1601. The register of St. Saviour's records also, on October 22, 1599, the baptism of "Susan Jeffes the supposed daughter of Humphrey Jeffes" (Collier, *Actors*, p. xxx; Bentley, *T.L.S.*, Nov. 15, 1928, p. 856). The last entry may not refer to the player.

JENNYNGES, GILES.

A member of the Children of Paul's in 1594 (Hillebrand, *Child Actors*, p. 111).

JOE, NICHOLAS.

Nicholas Joe (or Ioy) was a member of the Chapel Royal in 1509 and 1511 (Hillebrand, *Mod. Phil.*, xviii. 244). Chambers (*Eliz. Stage*, ii. 27n., 324) gives the name as Ivy, which may be the correct reading.

JOHNSON, HENRY.

A gatherer at the Theatre. When he testified in the lawsuit between Cuthbert Burbage and Gyles Alleyn on April 26, 1600, he is described as a silk-weaver, fifty years old, of the parish of St. Leonard's, Shoreditch. In his deposition he says that "he was A gatherer of the proffyttes therof vnder James Burbage and John Braynes" (Wallace, *N.U.S.*, xiii. 218, 222), that is at some period between the opening of the Theatre in 1576 and the death of Brayne in August, 1586.

JOHNSON, RICHARD.

Richard Johnson played Montanus, a knight, in Richards's *Messallina, the Roman Empress*, printed in 1640 as "acted with generall applause divers times by the Company of his Majesties Revells." Fleay (*Stage*, pp. 330–31) identifies him with Richard

Whiting, of the Bradshaw company that got into trouble at Banbury in 1633, whose name is given in the second examination as "Richard Johnson, alias Bea . . ." The identification seems unlikely (cf. Murray, ii. 109*n.*).

JOHNSON, THOMAS.

A member of the Children of Paul's in 1574 (Hillebrand, *Child Actors*, p. 111).

JOHNSON, WILLIAM.

As one of the Earl of Leicester's men in 1572 William Johnson signed a letter addressed to the Earl requesting his continued patronage; and he is named in the license granted to Leicester's players on May 10, 1574 (*M.S.C.*, i. 262, 348). He became associated with Queen Elizabeth's men when the troupe was first established in 1583; he is named in a London record that gives the personnel of the company at this time (*Eliz. Stage*, ii. 106). Apparently he remained with the Queen's men, for he is mentioned in a document of June 30, 1588, concerning the non-payment of subsidy by certain members of the company (*M.S.C.*, i. 354), and is referred to as a Queen's man in 1587. The registers of St. Giles's, Cripplegate, record the baptism on February 10, 1587, of "Comedia, base-borne daughter of Alice Bowker, and, as she saithe the father's name is William Johnson, one of the Queen's plaiers"; and the burial on March 3, 1593, of "Comedia, daughter of William Johnson, player" (*Eliz. Stage*, ii. 324). He is a legatee in Tarlton's will dated September 3, 1588. He may be the William Johnson, vintner, who served as trustee for Shakespeare's Blackfriars property from 1613 to 1618 (Lee, *Shakespeare*, pp. 459, 493).

JOHNSON, WILLIAM.

William Johnson, described as servant to Lord Clifford, is recorded at Coventry on January 9, 1640, with a company composed of players from various troupes. They received a payment of 48*s.* 2*d.* under date of November 25, 1640 (Murray, ii. 52, 254).

JONES, BARTHOLOMEW.

Bartholomew Jones was a member of Richard Bradshaw's company, a troupe that was in trouble at Banbury in May, 1633. The town authorities, becoming suspicious of the validity of the company's license, arrested the players, and notified the Privy Council. The players appeared before the Privy Council in June, and were soon discharged "upon bond given to be forthcoming whensoever they should be called for." In the examination of the players by the Banbury officials, Jones testified on May 2, 1633, that he "has gone with this company up and down the country these two years, and has acted his part in divers places" (Murray, ii. 106 ff., 163 ff.).

JONES, JACK.

Apparently the actor or stage-attendant who assumed the part of Palmeda in *1 Tamar Cam*, presented by the Admiral's men in 1602 (*H.P.*, pp. 15, 154). See John Jones.

JONES, JAMES.

James Jones appears in a license granted to the Children of the Revels to the late Queen Anne on April 9, 1623 (Murray, i. 362; ii. 272–73).

JONES, JOHN.

The register of St. Bodolph Aldgate records the baptism of "John Jones soone to John Jones a Player in Houndsditch" on June 14, 1615. This actor is conjectured to be identical with Jack Jones (Denkinger, *P.M.L.A.*, xli. 101).

JONES, RICHARD.

Richard Jones is named as a member of Worcester's troupe in the abstract of the license of January 14, 1583, in the Leicester records (*Eliz. Stage*, ii. 222). On January 3, 1589, he transferred to Edward Alleyn his share in a stock of theatrical goods which he held jointly with Edward and John Alleyn and Robert Browne

(*H.P.*, p. 21). This conveyance seems to mark either a break-up of Worcester's men or an internal change in the organization of the Admiral's men, and thus there is some uncertainty as to whether Jones was at this date with the Worcester or the Admiral troupe. In 1592 he joined Robert Browne's traveling company, for he is named in a passport issued on February 10, 1592, by the Lord Admiral, giving permission for that company to travel on the Continent (Cohn, p. xxix). During 1592–93 the company, under the leadership of Browne, traveled in the Netherlands and in Germany, visiting Arnhem and Frankfort. In the autumn of 1593 it was apparently disbanded. Jones certainly went back to England before September 2, 1594, when he bought from Henslowe "a manes gowne of pechecoler Jn grayne" (*H.D.*, i. 29). At this date he had no doubt already become associated with the Admiral's men at the Rose, with which troupe he seems to have continued during 1594–96. He appears as joint-payee with Alleyn and Singer for the Court performances by the Admiral's company in December and January, 1594–95 (Steele, p. 108). Subsequently he joined the Earl of Pembroke's men, for with several other members of this company he is complainant in a lawsuit during 1597 against Francis Langley, builder and owner of the Swan playhouse (Wallace, *Eng. Studien*, xliii. 340; Adams, *Playhouses*, pp. 168–74). As a result of the dissolution of Pembroke's company, caused by the production of *The Isle of Dogs*, Jones, on August 6, 1597, bound himself to play with the Admiral's company at the Rose; on October 11 his name is found in the accounts of that troupe (*H.D.*, i. 82, 202), and from this time until 1602 he appears in the *Diary* as an Admiral's man. He borrowed various sums from Henslowe, paid personal debts, served as a witness to occasional transactions, and joined his fellows in acknowledging the company's debts. As an Admiral's man (*H.P.*, pp. 153, 154; *Eliz. Stage*, ii. 175) he played Priam in *Troilus and Cressida* (*c.* 1599) and Silva in *The Battle of Alcazar* (*c.* 1600–01). By February 7–13, 1602, he and Robert Shaw had left the Admiral's company, and

the two had received £50 at their departure (*H.D.*, i. 164).
Nothing further is heard of him until January 4, 1610, when he
appears with his old leader Robert Browne, as patentees for the
Children of the Queen's Revels company at Whitefriars (Adams,
Playhouses, p. 318). A letter from Jones to Edward Alleyn (*H.P.*,
p. 33), conjecturally dated about 1615 (*Eliz. Stage*, ii. 287), implies that Jones was again going to Germany, probably with a
company under John Green. About 1616, his wife, Harris, inherited a lease of the Leopard's Head in Shoreditch from her
father, as shown by a letter to Alleyn, undated, but from internal
evidence written before Henslowe's death on January 6, 1616, or
at least before Jones had heard of Henslowe's death (*H.P.*, p. 94).
Jones and his wife were then away from England, and they apparently remained on the Continent for an extended period. On
April 1, 1620, Harris Jones wrote to Alleyn from Danzig. She was
then expecting to join her husband, who was "with the prince,"
probably George William, Elector of Brandenburg (Warner, p.
53). By 1622 Jones was a "musician" in the service of Philip
Julius, Duke of Wolgast. Two petitions from him are preserved
(Meyer, *Jahrbuch*, xxxviii. 209-10). On August 30, 1623, he asked
permission, with his fellows Johan Kostressen and Robert
Dulandt, to leave Wolgast and return to England. On July 10,
1624, he wrote to the Duke that he had failed to get profitable
employment in England, and asked to be taken again under his
patronage. A Richard Jones is traceable in the Southwark token-
books from 1588 to 1607, and is perhaps the same whose
marriage to Anne Jube is recorded on February 14, 1602 (*Eliz.
Stage*, ii. 324). If this last record refers to the player, Harris was
probably his second wife. A Richard Jones is recorded as a puppet-
showman at Coventry on January 12, 1638 (Murray, ii. 253).

JONES, ROBERT.

Robert Jones appears with Robert Browne at Frankfort in
September, 1602 (Herz, p. 18). This, however, may be an error for

Richard Jones, who traveled extensively with Browne, whereas Robert Jones is not otherwise known in the Continental records. On June 3, 1615, Robert Jones, Philip Rosseter, and others are named as patentees for the erection of Porter's Hall playhouse in Blackfriars (Adams, *Playhouses*, p. 343). He was one of the most eminent lutenist-composers of his time (Fellowes, *Eng. Mad. Comp.*, pp. 266–68).

JONNS, DANIEL.

Daniel Jonns was Kempe's boy in Denmark during 1586. The Elsinore pay-roll for September, 1586, records that "Wilhelm Kempe, instrumentist, got two months' board money for himself and a boy named Daniel Jonns." He had entered the Danish service on June 17, and an extra month's pay was given him as a parting gift (Riis, *Century Magazine*, 1901, lxi. 391).

JONSON, BEN.

Ben Jonson's career on the stage is obscure. John Aubrey (*Lives*, ii. 12, 226) tells us that Jonson, following his military service in the Netherlands, "came over into England, and acted and wrote, but both ill, at the Green Curtaine, a kind of nursery or obscure playhouse, somewhere in the suburbes (I thinke towards Shoreditch or Clarkenwell)," and further that he "was never a good actor, but an excellent instructor." We have no evidence for Jonson's acting in Shoreditch or in Clerkenwell, and the earliest records associate him with Henslowe on the Bankside. On July 20, 1597, Henslowe entered a loan of £4 to "Bengemen Johnson player," and on the same day opened an account under the heading, "Received of Bengemenes Johnsones Share," with an initial payment of 3*s*. 9*d*., to which nothing more was added (*H.D.*, ii. 289). This entry would seem to mean that Jonson had contemplated the acquisition of a share in the Admiral's troupe at the Rose, but proof is lacking. As a result of the production of *The Isle of Dogs* by Pembroke's men at the Swan about July, 1597, Jonson, who had a part in the writing of the play, was committed to the Marshalsea. His participation in this episode has led to the conjecture that he was a member of Pembroke's company in 1597 (*Eliz. Stage*, ii. 132, 133). He is satirized as Horace in Dekker's *Satiromastix* (1602), which contains several allusions to his acting (Dekker, *Works*, i. 202, 229). Tucca taunts Horace with: "I ha seene thy shoulders lapt in a Plaiers old cast Cloake, like a Slie knaue as thou art: and when thou ranst mad for the death of Horatio: thou borrowedst a gowne of Roscius the Stager." Later, Tucca makes Horace admit that he had played at Paris Garden, i.e. the Swan:

Tucca. . . . Thou hast been at Parris garden hast not?
Horace. Yes Captaine, I ha plaide Zulziman there.
Sir Vaughan. Then M. Horace you plaide the part of an honest man.
  Tucca. Death of Hercules, he could neuer play that part well in's life, no Fulkes you could not: thou call'st Demetrius Iorneyman Poet, but thou putst vp a Supplication to be a poore Iorneyman Player, and hadst beene still so, but that thou couldst not set a good face vpon't: thou hast forgot how thou amblest (in leather pilch) by a play-wagon, in the high way, and took'st mad Ieronimoes part, to get seruice among the Mimickes: and when the Stagerites banisht thee into the Ile of Dogs, thou turn'dst Ban-dog (villanous Guy) & euer since bitest; therefore a aske if th'ast been at Parris-garden, because thou hast such I good mouth; thou baitst well, read, *lege*, saue thy selfe and read.

The writer indicates that Jonson for a time had belonged to a traveling troupe, and had acted the part of Hieronimo in Kyd's ever-popular *Spanish Tragedy*, had later got service at the Swan, and had been wrecked through the performance of *The Isle of Dogs*. Since then, he had turned a bitter satirist, like the dogs at the bear and bull baiting houses at Paris Garden, and was biting other authors—namely Marston and Dekker. Perhaps this is a fairly accurate account of Jonson's career as an actor. In 1598 he achieved a great success with his play, *Every Man in his Humor*, and apparently he supported himself thereafter by writing. His most recent biographers are Herford and Simpson, *Ben Jonson: the Man and his Work* (1925).

JORDAN, THOMAS.

Thomas Jordan is primarily a writer of the Commonwealth and Restoration periods, but did some acting before the closing of the playhouses in 1642. He was at Norwich on March 10, 1635, when his troupe, presumably the King's Revels, applied for permission to act in that town; and he played Lepida, mother to Messallina, in Richards's *Messallina, the Roman Empress*, printed in 1640 as "acted with generall applause divers times by the Company of his Majesties Revells" (Murray, i. 279–81). He also contributed commendatory verses to Richards's play (ed. Skemp, p. 15), and to Rawlins's *Rebellion* (1640; Hazlitt's *Dodsley*, xiv. 9). Subsequently he appeared as an actor in his own comedy, *Money is an Ass* (published in 1668, but probably acted much earlier), assuming the part of Captain Penniless (Genest, x. 118). Besides plays he also wrote masks and non-dramatic works both in verse and prose. His *Poeticall Varieties* (1637) contains epitaphs on the actors John Honyman and Richard Gunnell. Perhaps Jordan is to be chiefly remembered for his Prologue introducing the first English woman to appear in a regular drama on a public stage. The first professional English actress played the part of Desdemona, probably on December 8, 1660. (Mrs. Coleman took the part of Ianthe in *The Siege of Rhodes*, acted at the Cockpit in 1658, but this was an operatic or quasi-dramatic performance. See William Davenant.) The half-apologetic tone of the composition shows that the experiment was approached with misgivings. Malone reprints the verses from a rare miscellany (*Variorum*, iii. 128):

> *A Prologue to introduce the first woman that came to*
> *act on the stage, in the tragedy called*
> The Moor of Venice.

> I come, unknown to any of the rest,
> To tell you news; I saw the lady drest:
> The woman plays to-day: mistake me not,
> No man in gown, or page in petticoat:

A woman to my knowledge; yet I can't,
If I should die, make affidavit on't.
Do you not twitter, gentlemen? I know
You will be censuring: do it fairly though.
'Tis *possible* a virtuous woman may
Abhor all sorts of looseness, and yet play;
Play on the stage,—where all eyes are upon her:—
Shall we count that a crime, France counts an honour?
In other kingdoms husbands safely trust 'em;
The difference lies only in the custom.
And let it be our custom, I advise;
I'm sure this custom's better than th' excise,
And may procure *us* custom: hearts of flint
Will melt in passion, when a woman's in't.

But gentlemen, you that as judges sit
In the star-chamber of the house, the pit,
Have modest thoughts of her; pray, do not run
To give her visits when the play is done,
With "damn me, your most humble servant, lady";
She knows these things as well as you, it may be:
Not a bit there, dear gallants, she doth know
Her own deserts,—and your temptations too.—
But to the point:—In this reforming age
We have intents to civilize the stage.
Our women are defective, and so siz'd,
You'd think they were some of the guard disguis'd:
For, to speak truth, men act, that are between
Forty and fifty, wenches of fifteen;
With bone so large, and nerve so incompliant,
When you call Desdemona, enter Giant.—
We shall purge every thing that is unclean,
Lascivious, scurrilous, impious, or obscene;
And when we've put all things in this fair way,
Barebones himself may come to see a play.

JUBY, EDWARD.

Edward Juby is named as an Admiral's man on December 14, 1594, in the first list of the company in Henslowe's accounts. Thereafter until March 7, 1603, he appears in various records of the Admiral's men as witnessing occasional transactions, as authorizing payments on behalf of the troupe, and as acknowledging company debts (*H.D.*, ii. 290). With the Admiral's men (*H.P.*, pp. 153, 154; *Eliz. Stage*, ii. 175) he played the King in *Frederick and Basilea* (1597), Calcipius Bassa and Avero in *The Battle of Alcazar* (*c.* 1600–01), and Pitho and a Moor, in *1 Tamar Cam* (1602). About Christmas, 1603, the Admiral's men were taken into the service of Prince Henry; and on March 14, 1604, Juby and Thomas Downton represented the Prince's men in their reckoning with Henslowe (*H.D.*, i. 175). His name occurs in the coronation list of March 15, 1604; in the patent of April 30, 1606; and in the household list of 1610 (*Eliz. Stage*, ii. 186, 187, 188). He appears regularly as payee for the Court performances by the Prince's men from February 19, 1604, to June 18, 1612, alone at all dates except the first, when he was joint-payee with Edward Alleyn (Steele, pp. 136, 138, 139, 140, 148, 152, 156, 159, 162, 164, 169, 172). The Prince died in November, 1612, and his company soon passed under the patronage of the Palsgrave. Juby is named in the new patent of January 11, 1613 (*M.S.C.*, i. 275). He was payee for the Palsgrave's men's Court performances during the seasons of 1612–13 and 1614–15 (Steele, pp. 175, 189). About 1613 he is mentioned, apparently as manager of the company, in Charles Massey's letter to Alleyn (*H.P.*, p. 64). He and his wife dined, "vnlookt for," with Alleyn on September 13, 1618 (Young, ii. 103). His name heads the list of the Palsgrave's men who leased the Fortune from Alleyn on October 31, 1618 (Warner, p. 242). The register of St. Saviour's, Southwark, records the baptism of the following children of Edward Juby, "player": Elizabeth, June 3, 1599; Thomas, September 27, 1600; Francis, June 30, 1603; William, May 25, 1606; Edmund, November 8, 1610; Marie, January 26, 1612; Tabitha, September 15, 1614, buried August 11, 1617. On November 20, 1618, is recorded, "Edward Jubye a man buried in the church." This entry corresponds with the date of his disappearance from other records

(Bentley, *T.L.S.*, Nov. 15, 1928, p. 856). Frances Juby, presumably his widow, was a shareholder in the lease of the Fortune, on May 20, 1622 (Warner, p. 246).

JUBY, RICHARD.

With the Admiral's men Richard (Dick) Juby acted in *The Battle of Alcazar* (*c.* 1600–01) as Abdula Rais and Tavora, and in *1 Tamar Cam* (1602) as Chorus, Trebassus, Diaphines, trumpet, attendant, messenger, nobleman, and Cathayan in the Procession (*H.P.*, pp. 153, 154; *Eliz. Stage*, ii. 175–76). His son, Richard, was baptized at St. Saviour's, Southwark, on May 1, 1602 (*Eliz. Stage*, ii. 325).

JUBY, WILLIAM (?).

At various dates from January 20, 1599, to October 21, 1602, a William Juby appears as authorizing payments on behalf of the Admiral's men, and must therefore have been a sharer in the company. There is no other evidence for him as an actor or sharer, and the name may be a clerical error for Edward (*H.D.*, ii. 290; *Eliz. Stage*, ii. 158*n*.).

JUGLER, RICHARD.

A London player in 1550, named in an order demanding that all plays be licensed by the King or his Council (Harrison, *England*, iv. 314).

KAYNE, ANDREW.

See Andrew Cane.

KEMP, JOHN.

On November 26, 1601, a company of English players, under the leadership of John Kemp, reached Münster, following a tour on the Continent that had brought them to Cologne, Amsterdam, Redberg, and Steinfürt. They presented five different comedies in English, and had a clown who performed in German between the acts (Herz, p. 11).

KEMPE, WILLIAM.

Apparently the earliest notice of William Kempe, one of the most famous of Elizabethan clowns, occurs in a letter from Thomas Doyley to the Earl of Leicester, dated at Calais on November 12, 1585, in which he states: "There remayneth in Dunkerk . . . also Mr Kemp, called Don Gulihelmo" (T. Wright, *Elizabeth*, ii. 268). He is generally identified with Leicester's comedian mentioned in Sir Philip Sidney's letter to Sir Francis Walsingham, dated at Utrecht on March 24, 1586, as carrying despatches from the Low Countries to London: "I wrote to yow a letter by Will, my lord of Lester's jesting plaier" (Bruce, *Shak. Soc. Papers*, i. 89). From the Netherlands he seems to have gone to Denmark, as shown by the Elsinore pay-roll for September, 1586, which records that "Wilhelm Kempe, instrumentist, got two months' board money for himself and a boy named Daniel Jonns." He had entered the Danish service on June 17, and received an extra month's pay as a parting gift (Riis, *Century Magazine*, 1901, lxi. 391). His reputation as a clown was obviously already established in London by 1590, when *An Almond for a Parrat* was addressed (Nashe, *Works*, iii. 341) "To that Most Comicall and conceited Caualeire Monsieur du Kempe, Iestmonger and Vice-gerent generall to the Ghost of Dicke Tarlton." The anonymous author, presumably Nashe, writes in the dedicatory epistle:

For coming from Venice the last Summer, and taking Bergamo in my waye homeward to England, it was my happe, soiourning there some foure or fiue dayes, to light in felowship with that famous Francatrip' Harlicken, who, perceiuing me to bee an English man by my habit and speech, asked me many particulars of the order and maner of our playes, which he termed by the name of representations: amongst other talke he enquired of me if I knew any such Parabolano here in London as Signior Chiarlatano Kempino. Very well, (quoth I), and haue beene oft in his company. He, hearing me say so, began to embrace me a new, and offered me all the courtesie he colde for his sake, saying, although he knew him not, yet for the report he had hard of his pleasance, hee colde not but bee in loue with his perfections being absent.

In *Strange Newes* (1592) Nashe refers to one of Gabriel Harvey's comical actions, and concludes (*Works*, i. 287): "for what can bee made of a Ropemaker more than a Clowne? *Will Kempe*, I mistrust it will fall to thy lot for a merriment, one of these dayes." By May 6, 1593, he belonged to Strange's men, as shown by the license giving permission for this company to travel in the provinces because of the closing of the London playhouses on account of the plague (*Eliz. Stage*, ii. 123). In 1594 *A Knack to Know a Knave*, played by Strange's company, was printed "With Kemps applauded Merrimentes of the men of Goteham, in receiuing the King into Goteham." These merriments appear quite jejune in print, but Kempe's personal appearance in the scene was no doubt taken as a guarantee of amusing clownage (see Hazlitt's *Dodsley*, vi. 565). In 1594 Strange's men passed under the patronage of the Lord Chamberlain. On March 15, 1595, Kempe served as joint-payee with Burbage and Shakespeare for plays given by the Chamberlain's men at Court in December, 1594 (Steele, pp. 107, 108). As a Chamberlain's man he appears in the cast of *Every Man in his Humor* (1598), as given in the Jonson folio of 1616. He is alluded to by Carlo, in Jonson's *Every Man out of his Humor*, IV. vi: "Would I had one of Kemp's shoes to throw after you" (*Works*, ii. 157). He acted Peter in *Romeo and Juliet* (IV. v) and Dogberry in *Much Ado about Nothing* (IV. ii), as evidenced by the substitution of the name Kempe for the name of the character in the text of the two plays. His name appears in the 1623 folio list of Shakespearean actors. A reference to him and the clown's tricks is found in *The Pilgrimage to Parnassus* (1597), V. 674 (ed. Macray, p. 22), a Cambridge University play, where Dromo, "drawing in a clowne with a rope," says:

Why, what an ass art thou! dost thou not knowe a playe cannot be without a clowne? Clownes have bene thrust into playes by head and shoulders ever since Kempe could make a scurvey face. . . . Why, if thou canst but drawe thy mouth awrye, laye thy legg over thy staffe, sawe a peece of cheese asunder with thy dagger, lape up drinke on the earth, I warrant thee theile laughe mightilie.

There are frequent allusions to Kempe's jigs, and four, now lost, were entered in the Stationers' Registers during 1591–95 (Arber, ii. 297, 600, 669; iii. 50): "the thirde and last parte of Kempes Jigge"; "a pleasant newe Jigge of the broomeman," ascribed in the margin to Kempe; "Master Kempes Newe Jigge of the kitchen stuffe woman"; and, "Kemps newe Jygge betwixt a Souldiour and a Miser and Sym the clown." That he was also famous for his performance of jigs is shown by Marston, *Scourge of Villainy* (1598), Satire xi. 31 (*Works*, iii. 372):

> A hall, a hall!
> Room for the spheres, the orbs celestial
> Will dance Kempe's jig.

E. Guilpin, *Skialetheia* (1598), Satire v (ed. Grosart, p. 55), writes:

> But oh purgation! you rotten-throated slaues
> Engarlanded with coney-catching knaues,
> Whores, Bedles, bawdes, and Sergeants filthily
> Chaunt *Kemps* Iigge, or the *Burgonians* tragedy.

Apparently he left the Chamberlain's company about 1599, for his name does not occur in the actor-list of *Every Man out of his Humor* (1599); and soon after the lease of the Globe on February 21, 1599, he sold his share to Shakespeare, Heminges, Phillips, and Pope (Adams, *Playhouses*, p. 240). Perhaps his most famous escapade was his dance from London to Norwich, an account of which was published by himself in 1600, with the title: *Kemps nine daies wonder. Performed in a daunce from London to Norwich. Containing the pleasure, paines and kinde entertainment of William Kemp betweene London and that Citty in his late Morrice. Wherein is somewhat set downe worth note; to reprooue the slaunders spred of him:*

many things merry, nothing hurtfull. Written by himselfe to satisfie his friends. The title-page depicts him as dancing the morris on the way to Norwich, "attended on by Thomas Slye my Taberer." The pamphlet is dedicated to Anne Fitton, whom he describes, not improbably by confusion with her sister Mary, as "Mayde of Honour to the most sacred Mayde Royall, Queene Elizabeth." In the dedicatory epistle he alludes to several (now unknown) ballads on his morris, deprecates their publication, and takes their spurious accounts as an excuse to publish his own authoritative story. He also says: "I haue without good help daunct my selfe out of the world," which is possibly a punning allusion to his withdrawal from the company at the Globe. He describes himself as "Caualiero Kemp, head-master of Morrice-dauncers, high Head-borough of heighs, and onely tricker of your Trill-lilles and best bel-shangles betweene Sion and mount Surrey." At the completion of the trip he hung in the Guildhall at Norwich the buskins in which he had danced from London. As an Epilogue to his description he appended "Kemps humble request to the impudent generation of Ballad-makers and their coherents; that it would please their rascalities to pitty his paines in the great iourney he pretends, and not fill the country with lyes of his neuer done actes, as they did in his late Morrice to Norwich," and implies his proposed crossing of the English Channel from Dover to Calais (ed. Dyce, pp. 20, 22). Apparently he took the contemplated "great iourney," visiting both Germany and Italy; but he had returned to England by September 2, 1601, as shown by an entry in the diary of one William Smith of Abingdon (Halliwell-Phillipps, *Ludus Coventriae*, p. 410):

1601, Sept. 2. Kemp, mimus quidam, qui peregrinationem quandam in Germaniam et Italiam instituerat, post multos errores et infortunia sua reversus: multa refert de Anthonio Sherly equite aurato, quem Romae (legatum Persicum agentem) convenerat.

On returning from his Continental tour, he seems to have joined Worcester's men. He borrowed 20s. from Henslowe "for his necessarye vsses" on March 10, 1602; authorized payment for the troupe on August 22, 1602; and had a suit purchased for him by the company early in September of the same year (*H.D.*, ii. 291). He and Thomas Heywood served as payees for a Court performance by Worcester's men on January 3, 1602 (Steele, p. 123). He is not traceable after the close of Elizabeth's reign. A William Kempe is recorded in the token-books of St. Saviour's, Southwark, as a resident of Samson's Rents in 1595, 1596, 1598, and 1599, of Langley's New Rents in 1602, and later near the old playhouse (Collier, *Actors*, p. 116; Rendle, *Bankside*, p. xxvi). Collier contends that he was alive and playing at Blackfriars in 1605, but the statement cannot be verified, and Collier's proof is presumably a fabrication. The burial entry of "Kempe a man" at St. Saviour's on November 2, 1603 (Rendle, *Bankside*, p. xxvii), agrees with the approximate date of Kempe's disappearance from theatrical records; but without further evidence the notice can hardly be accepted as conclusive proof of his death in 1603, for the name was a common one in other parishes, as shown by extracts from the registers (Collier, *Actors*, p. xxxvi). Kempe's popularity as a comedian is shown by numerous references to him and to his famous morris-dance. At Englefield, Dudley Carleton wrote to John Chamberlain on October 13, 1600: "In our way from Witham hither, we met a company of mad wenches, whereof Mrs. Mary Wroughton and young Stafford were ringleaders, who travelled from house to house, and to some places where they were little known, attended with a concert of musicians, as if they had undertaken the like adventure as Kemp did from London to Norwich" (*S.P.D. Eliz.*, cclxxv. 93). In *Jack Drum's Entertainment* (1601), I. 45, a character remarks (Simpson, *Sch. of Shak.*, ii. 136):

> I had rather that *Kemps* Morice were their chat;
> For of foolish actions, may be theyle talke wisely, but of
> Wise intendments, most part talke like fooles.

He and Burbage are introduced *in propria persona* into *2 Return from*

Parnassus (1602), a Cambridge University play, where he is greeted with an allusion to his "dancing the morrice ouer the Alpes" (see R. Burbage). In *Westward Hoe* (1607), V. i, Linstock says: " 'S foot, we'll dance to Norwich" (Webster, *Works*, i. 147). His visit to Italy and his meeting with Sir Anthony Sherley are dramatized in *The Travels of Three English Brothers* (1607), where he enters the play as one of the characters:

Enter Kempe

Sir Ant. Kemp! bid him come in. Welcome, honest *Will*; And how doth all thy fellowes in England?

Kemp. Why, like good fellowes, when they haue no money liue vpon credit.

Sir Ant. And what good new Plays haue you?

Kemp. Many idle toyes, but the old play that *Adam and Eue* acted in bare action vnder the figge tree drawes most of the Gentlemen.

Sir Ant. Iesting *Will*.

Kemp. In good earnest it doth, sir.

Sir Ant. I partly credit thee, but what Playe of note haue you?

Kemp. Many of name, some of note, especially one; the name was called *Englands Ioy*. Marry he was no Poet that wrote it! he drew more Connies in a purse-nette then euer were taken at any draught about London.

For the entire scene, see John Day, *Works*, ed. Bullen, pp. 55 ff. In T. Weelkes, *Ayres or Fantasticke Spirites* (1608), appears the following song (Halliwell-Phillipps, *Lud. Cov.*, p. 410):

> Since Robin Hood, Maid Marian,
> And little John are gone-a,
> The hobby-horse was quite forgot,
> When Kempe did dance alone-a.
> He did labour after the tabor
> For to dance: then into France
> He tooke paines
> To skip it;
> In hope of gaines
> He will trip it,
> On the toe,
> Diddle, diddle, doe.

William Rowley in the address prefixed to his *Search for Money* (1609), speaks of "the wild morrise to Norrige" (ed. Collier, p. iv). Dekker, *Gull's Horn-Book* (1609), p. 11, writes: "*Tarleton, Kemp*, nor *Singer*, nor all the litter of Fooles that now come drawling behinde them, never played the clownes more naturally then the arrantest Sot of you all shall." Heywood, *Apology* (1612), p. 43, says: "Here I must needs remember Tarleton, in his time gratious with the queene, his soveraigne, and in the people's generall applause, whom succeeded Wil. Kemp, as wel in the favour of her majesty, as in the opinion and good thoughts of the generall audience." Jonson, *Epigrams* (1616), cxxxiii, remarks: "Did dance the famous morris unto Norwich" (*Works*, viii. 234). R. Braithwaite, *Remains after Death* (1618), prints the following epitaph (Collier, iii. 355):

> *Upon Kempe and his Morice,*
> *with his Epitaph*
> Welcome from Norwich, Kempe: all joy, to see
> Thy safe returne moriscoed lustily!
> But out, alasse! how soone's thy morice done!
> When pipe and taber, all thy friends be gone,
> And leave thee now to dance the second part
> With feeble nature, not with nimble art:
> Then all thy triumphs, fraught with strains of mirth,
> Shall be cag'd up within a chest of earth.
> Shall be? they are. Thou'st danc'd thee out of breath,
> And now must take thy parting dance with Death.

In R. Brome, *Antipodes* (1638), II. ii (*Works*, iii. 260), we find:

> *Letoy.* Yes in the dayes of *Tarlton* and [of] *Kempe*,
> Before the stage was purg'd from barbarisme,
> And brought to the perfection it now shines with,
> Then fooles and jesters spent their wits, because
> The Poets were wise enough to save their owne
> For profitabler uses.

KEMPSTON, ROBERT.
See Robert Kimpton.

KENDALL, RICHARD.

Richard Kendall is recorded at Norwich on March 10, 1635, when his troupe, presumably the King's Revels, applied for permission to act in that town (Murray, i. 279–80).

KENDALL, THOMAS.

Thomas Kendall was a partner with Edward Kirkham and William Rastell in the management of Blackfriars, as shown by Articles of Agreement signed on April 20, 1602. On February 4, 1604, he was a patentee for the Children of the Queen's Revels at Blackfriars (Adams, *Playhouses*, pp. 213, 215). He died in 1608 (*Eliz. Stage*, ii. 327).

KENDALL, WILLIAM.

On December 8, 1597, William Kendall bound himself to Henslowe to play for two years with the Admiral's men at the Rose, with wages of 10s. a week when playing in London and 5s. a week in the country (*H.D.*, ii. 291). With this company he played Abdelmenen, an attendant, a ghost, and Hercules in *The Battle of Alcazar*, about 1600–01 (*Eliz. Stage*, ii. 175–76; *H.P.*, p. 153). Although his name appears in no other records of the Admiral's men, or after they passed successively under the patronage of Prince Henry (1603) and the Palsgrave (1613), there is a possibility that he advanced from a hired man in 1597 to an actor of some notoriety in 1614. During 1614, in the course of a wit-combat between William Fennor, a shifty rhymer and pamphleteer, and John Taylor the Water Poet, Fennor boasts of his histrionic talent and mentions one Kendall, apparently a player (*Fennor's Defence*, in Taylor, *Works*, 1630, p. 314):

> And let me tell thee this, to calme thy rage,
> I chaleng'd *Kendall* on the Fortune Stage;
> And he did promise 'fore an Audience,
> For to oppose me, note the accidence:
> I set vp Bills, the people throng'd apace,
> With full intention to disgrace, or grace;
> The house was full, the trumpets twice had sounded:

And though he came not, I was not confounded,
But stept vpon the Stage, and told them this;
My aduerse would not come: not one did hisse:
But flung me Theames: I then *extempore*
Did blot his name from out their memorie,
And pleased them all, in spight of one to braue me,
Witnesse the ringing Plaudits that they gaue me.

The register of St. Saviour's, Southwark, records the baptism on January 5, 1615, of John Kendall, son of William, "a player." A "Wm. Kendall" was living in Maid-lane in 1620, and one was married to Bettris Seele on August 1, 1619 (Bentley, *T.L.S.*, Nov. 15, 1928, p. 856).

KENEDE, RICHARD.

A member of the Children of Paul's in 1607 (Hillebrand, *Child Actors*, p. 112).

KERKE, JOHN.

See John Kirke.

KEYNE, ANDREW.

See Andrew Cane.

KEYSAR, ROBERT.

Robert Keysar, a London goldsmith was a lessee of the second Blackfriars from about 1605 to 1608, during which period he was manager of the Children of the Revels. After the surrender of the lease of Blackfriars to Richard Burbage for the King's men in 1608, he appears as payee for Court performances by the "Children of Blackfriars" during the Christmas season of 1608–09. In the autumn of 1609 he and Philip Rosseter and others reorganized the Children, placing them at Whitefriars. During the winter of 1609–10 he was payee for five plays given at Court by the "Children of Whitefriars." He is not named in the new patent granted to Rosseter and others on January 4, 1610, when the troupe again became known by its old name of the Children of the Queen's

Revels; but he nevertheless appears as one of the sharers (Adams, *Playhouses*, pp. 218–19, 222–24, 317–20). Walter Burre, the publisher, in 1613 dedicated Beaumont and Fletcher's *Knight of the Burning Pestle* "To his many waies endeered friend Maister Robert Keysar" (Beaumont and Fletcher, *Works*, vi. 412).

KIMPTON, ROBERT.

On December 30, 1629, a license was granted to a group of players under the leadership of Robert Kimpton (or Kempston), presumably the Children of the King's Revels. They presented the license at Reading soon afterwards. On September 23, 1631, he and John Carr were leaders of the "players of the Revells" at Coventry; and on September 8, 1632, Kimpton and his company visited Norwich (Murray, ii. 13, 251, 354, 386).

KING, ARTHUR.

On July 11, 1581, Arthur King and Thomas Goodale, members of a company of players under the patronage of Lord Berkeley, were committed to the Counter for having taken part in an affray with certain gentlemen of Gray's Inn (Harrison, *England*, iv. 320).

KING, THOMAS.

During 1586–87 Thomas King was on the Continent. The Elsinore pay-roll records that he was in the Danish service from June 17 to September 18, 1586. Soon he went to the Court of the Elector of Saxony, at Dresden, Germany, where he held an appointment as actor-entertainer until July 17, 1587 (Cohn, pp. xxiii–xxvi; Riis, *Century Magazine*, lxi. 391; Herz, p. 5).

KINGMAN, PHILIP.
See Philip Kingsman.

KINGSMAN, PHILIP.

Philip Kingsman (Kingman) was the leader of a company of players at Strassburg in August, 1596 (Cruger, *Archiv*, xv. 114). On June 3, 1615, he and Philip Rosseter and others are named as

patentees for the erection of Porter's Hall playhouse in Blackfriars (Adams, *Playhouses*, p. 343). "Mr Kyngman the elder"
served as a witness for Henslowe on April 16, 1599 (*H.D.*, ii. 292).

KINGSMAN, ROBERT.

Robert Kingsman was a member of Robert Browne's troupe at
Heidelberg, Frankfort, and Strassburg in 1599, and at Frankfort
for Easter, 1601 (Herz, pp. 16, 17). Subsequently he gave up the
life of a strolling player and became a tradesman in Strassburg,
where Coryat saw him in 1603 and wrote that it was "a place
of . . . passing fatnesse and fertility (as a certaine English
Merchant told me called Robert Kingman an Herefordshire man
borne, but then commorant in Strasbourg with his whole family
when I was there)" (*Coryat's Crudities*, ii. 183). Kingsman became
a freeman of Strassburg, and was able to befriend his old leader
Browne in 1618, and other players, when they visited the city
(Herz, pp. 15, 22, 31, 37).

KIRCK, JOHN.

John Kirck (Kirckmann) was a member of a troupe of English
players at the Danish Court during 1579–80 (Bolte, *Jahrbuch*,
xxiii. 99 ff.).

KIRCKMANN, JOHN.

See John Kirck.

KIRKE, JOHN.

John Kirke (or Kerke) is named in a license of November 10,
1629, as a member of the Red Bull company that visited Reading
on November 30 of the same year (Murray, ii. 386), and in a
warrant of December 12, 1635, appointing several of Prince
Charles's men as Grooms of the Chamber (Stopes, *Jahrbuch*, xlvi.
98). He was also a playwright (W. J. Lawrence, "John Kirke,
the Caroline Actor-Dramatist," *Stud. in Phil.*, xxi. 586). The only
extant play that may be assigned to him with certainty is *The*

Seven Champions of Christendom, published in 1638 as "Acted at the
Cocke-pit, and at the Red-Bull in St. Johns Streete, with a generall liking." The title-page gives only Kirke's initials, "Written
by J. K.," but his full name is found at the close of the dedicatory
epistle addressed to "Master John Waite," and also in the entry
in the Stationers' Registers on July 13, 1638 (Arber, iv. 424).
In the same year he dedicated Henry Shirley's *Martyred Soldier* to
Sir Kenelme Digby (Bullen, *Old Plays*, i. 171). Under date of June
8, 1642, Herbert records that he received from "Mr. Kirke" £2
each "for a new play which I burnte for the ribaldry and offense
that was in it," and "for another new play called *The Irishe
Rebellion*" (Adams, *Dram. Rec.*, p. 39). Kirke's official position
in the two transactions has not been determined, but he was not
necessarily the author of either of the plays. At the closing of the
playhouses he possibly became a merchant, as suggested by an
epitaph in Thomas Jordan's *A Nursery of Novelties*, published
without date:

> *Epitaph on my worthy friend; Mr. John Kirk, Merchant*
>
> Reader, within this Dormitory lies
> The wet memento of a Widdow's Eys;
> A Kirk, though not of Scotland, one in whom
> Loyalty liv'd and Faction found no room:
> No Conventicle Christian, but he died
> A Kirk of England by the Mother's side.
> In brief, to let you know what you have lost,
> Kirk was a Temple of the Holy Ghost.

KIRKHAM, EDWARD.

Edward Kirkham, presumably Yeoman of the Revels, was
associated with Thomas Kendall and William Rastell in the
management of the Children of the Chapel at Blackfriars, as
shown by Articles of Agreement signed on April 20, 1602. He was
a patentee for the Children of the Queen's Revels at Blackfriars
on February 4, 1604, and payee for a Court performance by the
Children later in the same month. In 1605 his company acted

Eastward Hoe without permission of the Lord Chamberlain, which led to the suppression of the troupe. Soon he became an assistant to Edward Pearce in the management of Paul's boys, for whom he served as payee on March 31, 1606, for two plays given at Court. About July 26, 1608, he formally withdrew from the Blackfriars syndicate (Adams, *Playhouses*, pp. 213–22; Steele, pp. 138, 148).

KITE.
See Knight.

KITE, JOHN.
John Kite was a Gentleman of the Chapel Royal, as shown by a payment to "mr kyte Cornisshe and other of the Chapell yt played affore ye king at Richemounte," dated December 25, 1508. The juxtaposition of "kyte" and "Cornisshe" has led some critics to assume there was a person named Kit (Christopher) Cornish. He was later Archbishop of Armagh (*Eliz. Stage*, ii. 29*n*., 30*n*.).

KNAGGES, RICHARD.
An unlicensed player of Moorsham, Yorkshire, in 1612 (*Eliz. Stage*, i. 305*n*.).

KNELL, WILLIAM (?).
Knell was a Queen's man, presumably at some date not later than 1588. He acted with Tarlton in *The Famous Victories of Henry V*, as told in *Tarlton's Jests* (1611): "Knel, then playing Henry the fift, hit Tarlton a sound boxe indeed, which made the people laugh the more" (Hazlitt, *Jest-Books*, ii. 218). By 1588, it is thought, he was dead; the belief rests on the assumption that he is the William Knell whose widow married John Heminges (*q.v.*) on March 10, 1588. Heywood mentions him with others as having flourished before his time, i.e. before about 1594 (*Apology*, p. 43). He is lauded by Nashe in his *Pierce Penilesse* (1592), where he is noticed with Tarlton, Alleyn, and Bentley (*Works*, i. 215). An

undated letter from W. P. to Edward Alleyn refers to a theatrical wager that Alleyn could equal Knell or Bentley in any of their own parts (*H.P.*, p. 32).

KNELLER, JAMES.

James Kneller (or Sneller) is named in a license granted to the Children of the Revels to the late Queen Anne on April 9, 1623 (Murray, i. 362; ii. 272–73). We hear no more of him until December, 1631 (Adams, *Dram. Rec.*, p. 45), when he played Autolicus, an impostor's disciple, in Marmion's *Holland's Leaguer*, presented by "the high and mighty Prince Charles his servants, at the private house in Salisbury Court" (Marmion, *Works*, pp. 2, 6). His name appears in a warrant of May 10, 1632, appointing several of Prince Charles's men as Grooms of the Chamber (Stopes, *Jahrbuch*, xlvi. 96).

KNIGHT.

A company under the leadership of one Knight visited Leicester in 1628, and received a reward of 10s. Apparently the same troupe again appeared at Leicester shortly afterwards, as evidenced by the payment of 10s. to "Mr. Kite a playe[r] and his Companie" (Murray, ii. 106, 317).

KNIGHT.

Knight appears as book-keeper of the King's men on October 12, 1632, and October 21, 1633 (Adams, *Dram. Rec.*, pp. 21, 34).

KNIGHT, ANTHONY.

Anthony Knight is named in a Protection from Arrest issued by Herbert on December 27, 1624, to twenty-one men "imployed by the Kinges Maiesties servantes in theire quallity of Playinge as Musitions and other necessary attendantes" (Adams, *Dram. Rec.*, p. 74).

KNIGHT, EDWARD.

Edward Knight is mentioned in a Protection from Arrest granted by Herbert on December 27, 1624, to twenty-one men

"imployed by the Kinges Maiesties servantes in theire quallity
of Playinge as Musitions and other necessary attendantes"
(Adams, *Dram. Rec.*, p. 74). In 1623 he seems to have lived "att
the George Alley in Gouldinge Lane" (Wallace, *Jahrbuch*, xlvi.
347). A person of the same name witnessed an agreement between
Alleyn and certain of Prince Charles's men on March 20, 1616
(*H.P.*, p. 91).

KNIGHT, ROBERT.

A member of the Children of Paul's in 1574 (Hillebrand, *Child
Actors*, p. 111). He is a legatee in the will of Sebastian Westcott,
dated April 3, 1582, where he is mentioned among the "sometimes
children of the said almenerey," i.e. St. Paul's (*Eliz. Stage*, ii.
15*n.*).

KOSTRESSEN, JOHAN.

Johan Kostressen was a musician in Germany in the service of
Philip Julius, Duke of Wolgast, during 1623. In a petition dated
August 30, 1623, he asked permission, with his fellows, Richard
Jones and Robert Dulandt, to leave Wolgast and return to Eng-
land (Meyer, *Jahrbuch*, xxxviii. 209).

KRAFFT, JOHN.

John Krafft was a member of a troupe of English players at the
Danish Court during 1579–80 (Bolte, *Jahrbuch*, xxiii. 99 ff.).

KYTE, JOHN.

See John Kite.

LACY, JOHN.

John Lacy, who won considerable popularity as a comedian
after the reopening of the theatres in 1660, was born near Doncaster, in Yorkshire. In 1631, Aubrey tells us, he had come to
London "to the playhouse," the name of which is not specified,
and was apprenticed to John Ogilby, a dancing-master (*Lives*, ii.
28, 101). Presumably his training as a dancer was in connection

with his theatrical pursuits; he is not known to have been a teacher of dancing, although this is sometimes inferred. During the Civil War he was a lieutenant and quartermaster under Lord Gerard. After the Restoration he joined the company formed out of "the scattered remnants" of players belonging to several of the older houses during the reign of Charles I. His Majesty's Company of Comedians opened their new playhouse, the Theatre Royal, on May 7, 1663 (Pepys, *Diary*, iii. 107), under the management of Thomas Killigrew. As a member of this organization Lacy had the following parts (Downes, *Ros. Ang.*, pp. xxxiv, 2 ff.): Sir Politique Would-be in *The Fox* [*Volpone*]; Captain Otter in *The Silent Woman*; Ananias in *The Alchemist*; Sir Roger in *The Scornful Lady*; and Bessus, in *King and no King*. To this list other parts may be added from the frequent notices by Lacy's great admirer, Samuel Pepys, whose criticisms afford the most original commentary on the art of the popular comedian, both before and after the opening of the Theatre Royal. Pepys records on May 21, 1662: "We went to the Theatre to *The French Dancing Master*. . . . The play pleased us very well; but Lacy's part, the Dancing Master, the best in the world" (*Diary*, ii. 225); and on May 8, 1663: "To the Theatre Royal, being the second day of its being opened. . . . The play was *The Humerous Lieutenant*, a play that hath little good in it, nor much in the very part which, by the King's command, Lacy now acts instead of Clun" (*Diary*, iii. 108). On four occasions Pepys praises Lacy as Johnny Thump, Sir Gervase's man, in Shirley's *Changes, or Love in a Maze*, one of his most celebrated parts: May 22, 1662: "The play hath little in it but Lacy's part of a country fellow, which he did to admiration"; June 10, 1663: "The play is pretty good, but the life of the play is Lacy's part, the clown, which is most admirable"; May 1, 1667: "But a sorry play: only Lacy's clowne's part, which he did most admirably indeed; and I am glad to find the rogue at liberty again"; and April 28, 1668: "wherein very good mirth of Lacy, the clown, and Wintersell, the country-knight, his master"

(*Diary*, ii. 226; iii. 154; vi. 282; vii. 384). On June 12, 1663, he saw Robert Howard's *The Committee*, "a merry but indifferent play, only Lacey's part, an Irish footman [Teague or Teg], is beyond imagination"; and again on August 13, 1667, "Lacy's part is so well performed that it would set off anything" (*Diary*, iii. 155; vii. 62). Another of Lacy's most successful parts was Sauny in *Sauny the Scot, or the Taming of the Shrew*, which Pepys witnessed on April 9, 1667 (*Diary*, vi. 249 ff.). The play, altered from Shakespeare's *Taming of the Shrew*, is generally attributed to Lacy himself. On April 15, 1667, Pepys pronounced Edward Howard's *Change of Crowns* "the best that ever I saw at that house, being a great play and serious; only Lacy did act the country-gentleman come up to Court, who do abuse the Court with all the imaginable wit and plainness about selling of places, and doing everything for money." Charles II was angered by the effrontery of Lacy's characterization, and committed him to the porter's lodge. Upon his release Lacy insulted the author of the play, which resulted in a temporary closing of the playhouse by royal command (*Diary*, vi. 258, 262). On July 13, 1667, Pepys heard that Lacy was dying (*Diary*, vii. 19); but the veteran comedian recovered and continued acting for several years. Perhaps he was not now so active as formerly. Pepys, on January 11, 1669, when he saw Richard Brome's *Jovial Crew*, complained that it was "ill acted to what it was heretofore, in Clun's time, and when Lacy could dance"; and again, on January 19, 1669, he expressed disappointment in Lacy's dancing between the acts of Corneille's *Horace*, and for his "invention not extraordinary" (*Diary*, viii. 185, 192 ff.). John Evelyn also commends Lacy's acting of Teague in *The Committee*, as shown by an entry in his *Diary* under the date November 27, 1662, "where the mimic, Lacy, acted the Irish footman to admiration" (*Diary*, i. 371). Genest, i. 302, gives Lacy's later characters: Drench in *The Dumb Lady* (1669); Bayes in the Duke of Buckingham's *Rehearsal* (1671); Alderman Gripe in *Love in a Wood* (1672);

and Intrigo, in *Love in the Dark* (1675). Downes (*Ros. Ang.*, p. 16) chronicles his successes thus:

> For his Just Acting, all gave him due Praise,
> His part in *The Cheats*, Jony Thump, Teg, and Bayes,
> In these Four Excelling; the Court gave him the Bays.

He was a great favorite with Charles II, who had Michael Wright to paint him in three of his more famous parts; Evelyn, on October 3, 1662, notes: "Visited Mr. Wright, a Scotsman, who had lived long at Rome, and was esteemed a good painter; . . . his best, in my opinion, is Lacy, the famous Roscius or comedian, whom he has painted in three dresses, as a gallant, a Presbyterian minister, and a Scotch highlander in his plaid" (*Diary*, i. 369). The three parts are either Galliard or Lord Vaux in the Duke of Newcastle's *Variety* (the identification is a moot question), Scruple in John Wilson's *Cheats*, and Sauny, in *Sauny the Scot*. Langbaine, Aubrey, and others following their error, have made the mistake of ascribing the third part to Teague (or Teg) in *The Committee* (cf. Planché, *Cyclop. of Costume*, ii. 243). Besides *Sauny the Scot*, Lacy is the author of three comedies, stage-successes in his day and subsequently favorably noticed by some dramatic critics, although his genius appears rather flimsy (cf. Nicoll, *Rest. Drama*, pp. 200 ff.): *The Old Troop, or Monsieur Raggou*; *The Dumb Lady, or the Farrier made Physician*; and *Sir Hercules Buffoon, or the Poetical Squire*. He is mentioned by Scott in *Woodstock* (1826), and in an appended note entitled *Cannibalism imputed to the Cavaliers*. He died on September 17, 1681, and was buried "in the farther churchyard of St. Martyn's in the fields" (Aubrey, *Lives*, ii. 28).

LANCASTER, SYLVESTER.

Sylvester Lancaster seems to have been a hired man of Prince Charles's company. In an order of April 25, 1640, he is named as a Prince's man who is not "to be hindered or diverted in his service by being impressed, arrested, or otherwise molested, without leave first asked" (Stopes, *Jahrbuch*, xlvi. 103).

LANEHAM, JOHN.

As one of the Earl of Leicester's men in 1572 John Laneham signed a letter addressed to the Earl requesting continued patronage; he is named in the license granted to Leicester's players on May 10, 1574 (*M.S.C.*, i. 262, 348). He became associated with Queen Elizabeth's men when that troupe was first established in 1583; his name is found in a London record that gives the personnel of the company at this time (*Eliz. Stage*, ii. 106). Apparently he remained with the Queen's men, for he is mentioned in a document of June 30, 1588, concerning the non-payment of subsidy by certain members of the company (*M.S.C.*, i. 354), and was payee for a Court performance by the Queen's players on January 1, 1591 (Steele, p. 100). Heywood mentions him with others as having flourished before his time, i.e. before about 1594 (*Apology*, p. 43). The entry "Laneham" in *Sir Thomas Moore* is probably, as Tannenbaum suggests, a forgery.

LANGLEY, FRANCIS.

Francis Langley, goldsmith of London, was the builder in 1595 of the Swan playhouse. He died in 1601 (Adams, *Playhouses*, pp. 161, 162, 176).

LANMAN, HENRY.

Proprietor of the Curtain playhouse from about 1582 to 1592, and probably from as early as 1577, when it was built (Adams, *Playhouses*, pp. 76, 78 f., 83 ff.).

LAU, HURFRIES DE.

A member of the company of French players in England during 1635, under the leadership of Josias de Soulas, better known by his stage-name of Josias Floridor (*q.v.*), as shown by a warrant of May 5, 1635, granted to "Josias D'Aunay, Hurfries de Lau, and others, for to act playes at a new house in Drury-lane, during pleasure" (Adams, *Dram. Rec.*, p. 61).

A DICTIONARY OF ACTORS

LEBERWURST, HANS.

The leader of a company of players at Leipzig, Germany, in April, 1613 (Grabau, *Jahrbuch*, xlv. 311).

LEDBETTER, ROBERT.

Robert Ledbetter was an Admiral's man in 1597, when he played Pedro in *Frederick and Basilea* (*H.P.*, p. 153). He is not otherwise known except on the Continent, where he is recorded as a member of Robert Browne's company at Frankfort in 1599, 1601, and 1606 (Herz, p. 16; Meissner, *Jahrbuch*, xix. 125).

LEE, ROBERT.

Robert Lee (or Leigh) is first heard of as an attendant in *The Dead Man's Fortune*, possibly acted by the Admiral's men at the Theatre about 1590 (*Eliz. Stage*, ii. 136; *H.P.*, p. 152). He is presumably the Robert Lee who, together with John Alleyn and Thomas Goodale, signed a bond to Edward Alleyn on May 18, 1593 (Warner, p. 127), and who sold "a boock called the myller" to the Admiral's men for 20s. on February 22, 1598 (*H.D.*, ii. 294). Subsequently he probably joined Worcester's men; the non-appearance of his name in Henslowe's records may be explained by the fact that he was not a sharer (Greg, *H.D.*, ii. 294). That he was a Worcester's man, however, seems quite likely, for he is found in Queen Anne's company, which was a continuation of the Worcester troupe after the change of patronage late in 1603. As a Queen's man he appears in the procession list of March 15, 1604; in a warrant of March 7, 1606; in both the license of April 15, 1609, and the duplicate patent issued on January 7, 1612, to the traveling company; in a warrant of March 29, 1615, to appear before the Privy Council for playing during Lent; and at Queen Anne's funeral on May 13, 1619 (*Eliz. Stage*, ii. 229, 235; *M.S.C.*, i. 270, 372; Murray, ii. 343). For the Court performances of 1613–16 he served as payee (Steele, pp. 184, 189, 195). He was possibly with the Queen's provincial company at Norwich on May 6, 1615, and was certainly there on March 30, 1616, and May 31,

1617 (Murray, ii. 340, 341, 343). By October 31, 1617, he had left the Queen's men and joined Philip Rosseter, William Perry, and Nicholas Long as patentees for the Queen's Revels company; he visited Norwich on August 29, 1618 (Murray, i. 192, 361; ii. 345). Before May 13, 1619, when he appeared in the Queen's funeral procession, he had returned to the Queen's men. After the Queen's death her London troupe was known as the Players of the Revels at the Red Bull. Lee is noted in 1622 as one of "the chiefe players" of this company (Adams, *Dram. Rec.*, p. 63), and is named with Richard Perkins in a warrant of November, 1622 (*M.S.C.*, i. 284). The registers of St. Bodolph Aldgate record three of his children: Rachel (baptized November 21, 1596); Robert (baptized October 22, 1598); and Mary (buried April 3, 1608). The last entry describes Lee as "a Stage player in Houndsditch." He is perhaps the Robert Lee of the same parish who married Constance Balderstone on February 8, 1595 (Denkinger, *P.M.L.A.*, xli. 102). In 1623 he was living "in Clarkenwell Close" (Wallace, *Jahrbuch*, xlvi. 347). On June 20 of the same year he appears as a joint-lessee of the Fortune playhouse (Greg, *H.P.*, p. 30).

LEEKE, DAVID.

In 1571 David Leeke, Richard Winter, and John Singer were in arrears for board due Robert Betts, a deceased Canterbury painter. Plomer (*Library*, 1918, ix. 253) has suggested that these men may have been players, because another entry in the same inventory records that William Fidge and one Whetstone, presumably actors, owed Betts "for their portions in buyinge of certen playe-bookes."

LEIGH, ROBERT.
See Robert Lee.

LEVESON, ROBERT.
On April 13, 1580, the Privy Council committed Robert Leveson and Lawrence Dutton, players under the patronage of the

Earl of Oxford, to the Marshalsea for taking part in an affray with certain gentlemen of the Inns of Court (Dasent, xi. 445).

LILLIE, GEORGE.

George Lillie's name appears in a warrant of June 30, 1628, appointing several of the Lady Elizabeth's (Queen of Bohemia's) players as Grooms of the Chamber (Stopes, *Jahrbuch*, xlvi. 94). Possibly he was a brother of John Lillie.

LILLIE, JOHN.

John Lillie's name appears in a warrant of June 30, 1628, appointing several of the Lady Elizabeth's (Queen of Bohemia's) players as Grooms of the Chamber (Stopes, *Jahrbuch*, xlvi. 94). Possibly he was a brother of George Lillie.

LISTER, EDWARD.

Edward Lister, weaver, is mentioned as an unlicensed player of Allerston, Yorkshire, in 1612 (*Eliz. Stage*, i. 305*n*.).

LOFFDAY, THOMAS.

See Thomas Loveday.

LONG, NICHOLAS.

On May 20, 1612, Nicholas Long was the leader of the Queen's Revels at Norwich. By March 2, 1614, he was manager of the Lady Elizabeth's players, appearing at Norwich on that date. He was again with the Queen's Revels on October 31, 1617, when a new troupe was organized under his leadership, associated with Robert Lee, Philip Rosseter, and William Perry. The troupe visited Norwich on August 29, 1618. In February, 1620, he had left the Queen's Revels to take the management of an unnamed company, the only recorded appearance of which is at Norwich on May 20, of the same year (Murray, i. 360, 361; ii. 3, 101, 339, 345). The register of St. Giles's, Cripplegate, records his burial on January 21, 1622 (*Eliz. Stage*, ii. 328).

LOVEDAY, THOMAS.

Thomas Loveday is recorded at Norwich on March 10, 1635, when his troupe, presumably the King's Revels, applied for permission to act in that town (Murray, i. 279–80). Perhaps he is to be identified with the Restoration actor of the same name who appears in the warrants for liveries to the King's company as early as July 29, 1661, and as late as February 8, 1667, probably 1668 (Nicoll, *Rest. Drama*, pp. 325, 326). He is probably the Thomas Loffday recorded as a member of the company of English actors present at The Hague during 1644-45 (Hotson, p. 21).

LOVEKYN, ARTHUR.

A member of the Chapel Royal, 1509–13 (Brewer, *L. & P. Henry VIII*, i. 1. pp. 15, 41, 461, 482; ii. 2. pp. 1448, 1453, 1463; *Eliz. Stage*, ii. 27n.).

LOVELL, THOMAS.

Thomas Lovell is recorded at Norwich on March 10, 1635, when his troupe, presumably the King's Revels, applied for permission to act in that town (Murray, i. 279–80).

LOWE, NICHOLAS.

As a member of Ellis Guest's company under license of June 7, 1628, Nicholas Lowe was at Norwich on July 2 of the same year (Murray, ii. 103).

LOWIN, G.

G. Lowin played Barnavelt's daughter in *Sir John van Olden Barnavelt* (ed. Frijlinck, pp. clx, 86), presented by the King's men in 1619. Perhaps he was John Lowin's son.

LOWIN, JOHN.

A portrait of John Lowin, in the Ashmolean Museum at Oxford, bears the inscription: "1640, Aetat. 64." He may therefore be identified with the John, son of Richard Lowen, whose baptism is recorded in the register of St. Giles's, Cripplegate, on

December 9, 1576 (Collier, iii. 391). Like his fellow, Robert Armin, he apparently began his career as an apprentice to a London goldsmith, as shown by the entry: "I, John Lowen, the sonne of Richard Lowen of London . . . have put my self prentise to Nicholas Rudyard for the terme of eight years beginninge at Cirstmas in Anno 1593" (Denkinger, *P.M.L.A.*, xli. 97). He first appears as an actor during 1602–03 in Worcester's company with Henslowe at the Rose. From November 12, 1602, to March 12, 1603, he authorized payments on behalf of Worcester's men, and on the latter date borrowed 5s. from Henslowe when he accompanied the troupe on a provincial tour (*H.D.*, ii. 295). During the course of the year he must have left Worcester's for the King's men, for he is named in the cast of *Sejanus* (1603), and is introduced into the Induction to *The Malcontent* (1604). Evidently he joined the King's company as a hired man, for his name is not given in the patent of May 19, 1603, or in the procession list of March 15, 1604. Through a long life he continued with the King's men, ultimately becoming one of the most prominent members of the company. The register of St. Botolph, Bishopsgate, records the marriage of a John Lowen and Joan Hall, widow, on October 29, 1607, "*p. licent. ex officio facultatum*" (Collier, iii. 396). He is presumably the John Lowen who lived in the liberty of the Clink, Southwark, and who, shortly after the marriage noted above, was paying a poor-rate of 2d. a week. The register of St. Saviour's, Southwark, records, also, the marriage of a "John Lewin and Katheren Woodden, with license," on February 1, 1620. John, son of John Lowin, "one of ye kings players," was baptized at St. Saviour's on January 29, 1639 (Bentley, *T.L.S.*, Nov. 15, 1928, p. 856). At various dates from 1601 to 1642 the Southwark token books record his residence "near the playhouse" or in other parts of the parish; in 1617–18 he was overseer of Paris Garden; and in 1623 he lived in Lambeth (Collier, iii. 397 ff.; Rendle, *Bankside*, p. xxvi; Wallace, *Jahrbuch*, xlvi. 348; Chambers, *Eliz. Stage*, ii. 329). On August

13, 1620, he and his wife dined with Edward Alleyn (Warner,
p. 185). He seems to have written one pamphlet, *Conclusions
upon Dances, both of this Age and of the Olde* (1607), which is
dedicated to Lord Dennie, November 23, 1606, and signed "I. L.
Roscio"; Collier claimed to have found a copy with the note on
the title-page: "By Jhon Lowin. Witnesseth Tho. D. 1610"
(Collier, iii. 394-96). He is named in the will of John Underwood,
dated October 4, 1624, as legatee and overseer. He appears as a
King's man in the 1623 folio list of Shakespearean players; in the
patent of March 27, 1619; in the livery allowances of May 19,
1619, and April 7, 1621; in the submission of December 20, 1624,
for playing *The Spanish Viceroy*; at King James's funeral on May
7, 1625; in the patent of June 24, 1625; in the cloak allowance of
May 6, 1629 (*M.S.C.*, i. 280, 282; Murray, i. opp. 172). On October 24, 1633, he and Swanston craved the pardon of Herbert
"for their ill manners" in acting an unpurged version of Fletcher's
Woman's Prize, or the Tamer Tamed (Adams, *Dram. Rec.*, pp. 20 ff.).
His name appears in the warrants for liveries on April 22, 1637,
March 12, 1639, and March 20, 1641 (Stopes, *Jahrbuch*, xlvi. 99,
101, 104). He had parts in the following plays (Murray, i. opp.
172): *Volpone* (1605); *The Alchemist* (1610); *Catiline* (1611);
Valentinian (c. 1611-14); *Bonduca* (c. 1613-14); *The Queen of
Corinth* (c. 1617); *The Loyal Subject* (1618); *The Knight of Malta*
(c. 1618); *The Mad Lover* (c. 1618); possibly Barnavelt in *Sir John
van Olden Barnavelt* (1619; cf. Frijlinck, p. 86); *The Humorous
Lieutenant* (c. 1619); *The Custom of the Country* (c. 1619-20); *The
Double Marriage* (c. 1619-20); Bosola in *The Duchess of Malfi* (c.
1619-23); *Women Pleased* (c. 1620); *The Little French Lawyer* (c.
1620); *The False One* (c. 1620-21); *The Laws of Candy* (c. 1621);
The Island Princess (c. 1621); *The Pilgrim* (c. 1621); *The Spanish
Curate* (1622); *The Sea Voyage* (1622); *The Prophetess* (1622);
Lovers' Progress (1623); *The Maid in the Mill* (1623); Domitianus
Caesar in *The Roman Actor* (licensed October 11, 1626); *Lover's
Melancholy* (licensed November 24, 1628); Jacomo in *The Deserving*

Favorite (published 1629); Eubulus in *The Picture* (licensed June 8, 1629); Flaminius in *Believe as You List* (licensed May 7, 1631); and Belleur, "most naturally acted," in *The Wildgoose Chase* (a revival, 1631). He also appeared as Lepston in the Lord Mayor's Pageant produced by the goldsmiths in 1611 (Denkinger, *P.M. L.A.*, xli. 96). That he was a versatile player is evidenced by the numerous actor-lists citing his name. He and Joseph Taylor are mentioned in Alexander Gill's satirical verses on Jonson's *Magnetic Lady* in 1632 (Jonson, *Works*, vi. 116):

> Lett Lownie cease, and Taylore feare to touch
> The loathed stage; for thou hast made ytt such.

Besides playing he was concerned in the business management of the troupe. In 1635 he controlled two-sixteenths of the Globe and one-eighth of the Blackfriars, which shares he seems to have acquired after the death of Condell in 1627 (Adams, *Mod. Phil.*, xvii. 7 ff.; Halliwell-Phillipps, *Outlines*, i. 312–13). From this time to the closing of the playhouses in 1642, he, Taylor, and Swanston were the mainstays of the King's men. They served as payees for the performances at Court from April 27, 1634, to March 20, 1641 (Steele, pp. 244, 249, 262, 267, 274, 276). On several occasions during 1630–38, Lowin represented the company in transactions with Herbert (Adams, *Dram. Rec.*, pp. 38, 44, 47, 65). Wright in *Historia Histrionica* (1699) tells us that "before the wars Lowin used to act with mighty applause Falstaff, Morose, Volpone, . . . Mammon in *The Alchymist*, Melantius in *The Maid's Tragedy*"; that he and Taylor and Thomas Pollard at the outbreak of civil war "were superannuated"; that he played Aubrey in *Rollo, or the Bloody Brother*, at the Cockpit in 1648; and "in his latter days kept an inn, the Three Pigeons at Brentford, where he died very old, for he was an actor of eminent note in the reign of King James I, and his poverty was as great as his age" (Hazlitt's *Dodsley*, xv. 405, 409, 411). In 1647 he joined a group of the King's players in publishing a folio edition of Beaumont and Fletcher; his name is appended to the dedicatory epistle (*Works*, i. p. x). In 1652 he and Taylor published Fletcher's *Wildgoose Chase* (*Works*, iv. 407) for their "private benefit." In their dedication "To the Honour'd Few Lovers of Drammatick Poesie" they quote, with a glance at their poverty, some lines that Walter Raleigh (*Works*, ii. 395) "once spake of his Amours":

> Silence in Love betrays more Wo
> Than Words, though ne'r so Wittie:
> The Beggar that is Dumb, you know,
> Deserves a Double Pittie.

On January 28, 1648, he and other members of the King's company gave a bond to pay off an old Blackfriars debt to Michael Bowyer's heirs (Hotson, pp. 31–34).

The date of Lowin's death is uncertain; either of two burial entries may refer to him: a "John Lewin," who left a widow Martha, was buried at St. Martin's-in-the-Fields on March 18, 1659; a "John Lowen" was buried at St. Paul's, Covent Garden, on March 16, 1669 (*Variorum*, iii. 211; Collier, iii. 403). Downes (*Ros. Ang.*, p. 24), writes of Betterton's performance of Shakespeare's *Henry VIII*: "The part of the King was so right and justly done by Mr. *Betterton*, he being Instructed in it by Sir *William* [Davenant], who had it from Old Mr. *Lowen*, that had his Instructions from Mr. Shakespear himself that I dare and will aver, none can, or will come near him in this Age, in the performance of that part." Lowin, Taylor, and Swanston are praised by Snarl, who admires nothing but the things of a former age, in Thomas Shadwell's *The Virtuoso*, acted in 1676 (*Works*, i. 328):

Miranda. Methinks, though all Pleasures have left you, you may go to see Plays.

Snarl. I am not such a Coxcomb, I thank God: I have seen 'em at *Black-Fryers*. Pox, they act like Poppets now, in Sadness. I, that have seen *Joseph Taylor*, and *Lowen*, and *Swanstead*! Oh, a brave roaring Fellow, would make the House shake again! Besides, I can never endure to see Plays, since Women came on the Stage. Boys are better by half.

LYLY, JOHN.

John Lyly, the author of the popular novel *Euphues* (1578) and of various comedies, became lessee of the First Blackfriars in 1583, when the Earl of Oxford bought the lease from Henry Evans and presented it to him. He served as payee for Court performances by Oxford's troupe on January 1 and March 3, 1584 (Steele, pp. 89, 90). Later, he was Vice-Master of Paul's boys, wrote plays for them, and superintended their performances in Paul's Singing-School (Adams, *Playhouses*, pp. 109, 113–14).

MACHIN, RICHARD.

Richard Machin visited Frankfort in March, Nuremberg in April, 1600, Frankfort at Easter, 1601, and Frankfort for a third time in the autumn of the same year. During this period he was associated with a group of English players under the patronage of Maurice of Hesse. Although he was at Frankfort for Easter, 1603, as a member of the Hessian company, he had left the Landgrave's service in 1602. His appearances are recorded during 1605 at the Frankfort Easter fair, at Strassburg in May, at Frankfort again in the autumn, and in 1606 at Frankfort for Easter (Herz, pp. 38–40).

MAGET, STEPHEN.

Stephen Maget appears in Henslowe's accounts as tireman for the Admiral's men in 1596. He is possibly the Stephen who played a beggar in *Troilus and Cressida* about 1599 (*H.D.*, ii. 295; *H.P.*, p. 154).

MAGO, WILLIAM.

William Mago is named in a Protection from Arrest issued by Herbert on December 27, 1624, to twenty-one men "imploycd by the Kinges Maiesties servantes in theire quallity of Playinge as Musitions and other necessary attendantes." As a King's man he apparently played Hanno or Asolrubal in Massinger's *Believe as You List*, licensed May 7, 1631 (Adams, *Dram. Rec.*, pp. 33, 74).

He is probably the W. Mago appearing with W. Humlac in the *dramatis personae* to *The Witch of Edmonton*; and the two were presumably minor actors in the tragedy (Ford, *Works*, iii. 175). The play, not printed until 1658, may have passed from Prince Charles's men to Queen Henrietta's men about 1625, when the latter troupe was organized (Murray, i. 236*n*.). The notice on the title-page assigns the play to the Prince's men, but Ezekiel Fenn and Theophilus Bird, both of whom are mentioned in the quarto, were members of the Queen's troupe and are not traceable to the Prince's company. Thus Mago must have transferred his services at some unknown date from the King's to the Queen's men.

MAIRVIN.

Mairvin is recorded at Norwich on March 10, 1635, when his troupe, presumably the King's Revels, applied for permission to act in that town (Murray, i. 279–80).

MANNERY, SAMUEL.

Samuel Mannery played a bawd in Marmion's *Holland's Leaguer*, presented in December, 1631 (Adams, *Dram. Rec.*, p. 45), by "the high and mighty Prince Charles his servants, at the private house in Salisbury Court" (Marmion, *Works*, pp. 2, 6).

MANSELL, JOHN.

A member of the Children of Paul's in 1607 (Hillebrand, *Child Actors*, p. 112).

MARBECK, THOMAS.

With the Admiral's men in 1602 Thomas Marbeck played a nobleman, Pontus, attendant, hostage, guard, child, and captain in *1 Tamar Cam*, and a Bactrian in the Procession (*H.P.*, p. 154). The register of St. Saviour's, Southwark, records on June 26, 1603, the baptism of Roger Marbeck, son of Thomas, "a musitian" (Bentley, *T.L.S.*, Nov. 15, 1928, p. 856).

MARCUPP, SAMUEL.

A member of the Children of Paul's in 1598 (Hillebrand, *Child Actors*, p. 111).

MARCY, CHARLES.

See Charles Massey.

MARRANT, EDWARD.

Part owner of the Fortune (Warner, p. 54).

MARSHALL, CHARLES.

During 1615–16 Charles Marshall, Humphrey Jeffes, and William Parr secured a duplicate of the 1613 patent to the Palsgrave's men, organized a troupe, and traveled in the provinces. This duplicate warrant was condemned and withdrawn by order of the Earl of Pembroke on July 16, 1616 (Murray, ii. 4 ff.).

MARSTON, JOHN.

John Marston, dramatist, acquired a share in the Second Blackfriars organization in 1604, and became a regular playwright for the Queen's Revels company at that house. In 1605 the Children offended King James by acting *Eastward Hoe*, a comedy written by Marston, Chapman, and Jonson. Marston seems to have been chiefly responsible for the indiscretion, and chose flight as the surest means of escaping the King's wrath. Probably about this time he sold his share in the Second Blackfriars syndicate to Robert Keysar, and subsequently gave up his career as a dramatist for the less strenuous life of a country parson (Adams, *Playhouses*, pp. 216–18).

MARTINELLI (?), ANGELICA.

Angelica Martinelli (?), née Alberghini, appears to have been a member of a company of Italian players in England, and the wife of Drusiano Martinelli (*q.v.*). In 1580 Martinelli subscribed himself as "marito di Ma Angelica," who was formerly mistress to the Duke of Mantua's son, and, who, Chambers thinks (*Eliz.*

Stage, ii. 263), is possibly "the nimble, tumbling Angelica" mentioned in Marston's *Scourge of Villainy* (1598), Satire xi. 101 (*Works*, iii. 375). Professor Adams, however, suggests that Marston may be alluding to one of the famous apes that rode ponies at Paris Garden.

MARTINELLI, DRUSIANO.

On January 13, 1578, the Privy Council directed that "one Dronsiano, an Italian, a commediante and his companye" should be allowed to play in London (Dasent, x. 144). This "Dronsiano" is no doubt Drusiano Martinelli, son of Francisco Martinelli, of Mantua. He later became quite famous as a comedian, and in 1595 was in the service of the Duke of Mantua. His brother Tristano was even more noted as *Arlecchino* in the *commedia dell' arte* (*Eliz. Stage*, ii. 263).

MARTON, THOMAS.

With the Children of the Chapel Royal Thomas Marton appeared in Jonson's *Poetaster*, acted in 1601 (*Eliz. Stage*, iii. 365).

MARTYN, WILLIAM.

In 1572 William Martyn was the leader of a company of players at Ipswich, as shown by the following entry in the town records: "Paid to William Martyne and his companye for a plaie at the Mote Hall, 6*s*. 8*d*." He is presumably identical with "Martyn the mynstrell," who visited Ipswich with his troupe in 1569, and received 10*s*. on two occasions (*Hist. MSS. Comm.*, ix. 1. p. 249).

MASON.

"Mason among the Kings players" is mentioned in *Sir Thomas More* (*c*. 1594), IV. i. 298. Brooke (*Shak. Apoc.*, p. 437) explains the allusion by citing from Collier, i. 77, a payment on January 6, 1515: "To the Kings Players in rewarde, £3 6*s*. 8*d*. . . . To John Mason wages 8*d*. per day." Chambers (*Eliz. Stage*, iv. 33) calls attention to another reference in Collier, i. 45, showing that Alexander Mason was marshal of the royal minstrels in 1494. Nothing further is known of him.

MASON, JOHN.

As a lessee of the Whitefriars playhouse in 1608, John Mason held one half-share in the syndicate (Adams, *Playhouses*, pp. 315, 316). His play, *The Turk*, was printed in 1610 "as it hath bene diuers times acted by the Children of his Maiesties Reuels." For a sketch of his life, see Adams's edition of *The Turk*.

MASSEY, CHARLES.

Charles Massey (Massye) first appears as an Admiral's man in *Frederick and Basilea* (1597), in which he played Tamar (*H.P.*, p. 153). On November 16, 1598, be bound himself to play with Henslowe's company, the Admiral's men at the Rose. He seems to have been a sharer by March 8, 1598, when he signed the acknowledgment of the company's debt. At various subsequent dates he is found in Henslowe's records as a borrower, as a witness, and as a representative of the company in its reckonings with Henslowe. Apparently he wrote *Malcolm King of Scots* for the Admiral's men, receiving £5 for the play on April 18, 1602, and began *The Siege of Dunkirk*, for which he received £2 in advance on March 7, 1603. Neither play is extant (*H.D.*, ii. 296). Besides Tamar in *Frederick and Basilea* (1597), he also played for the Admiral's company an unspecified part in *Fortune's Tennis* (*c.* 1597–98), Zareo and Barcelis in *The Battle of Alcazar* (*c.* 1600–01), and Artaxes, an attendant, and a nobleman in *1 Tamar Cam* (1602). In the plots of all these plays he is referred to only by his Christian name (Greg, *H.P.*, pp. 153, 154; *R.E.S.*, i. 270; Chambers, *Eliz. Stage*, ii. 175). About Christmas, 1603, the Admiral's men were taken into the service of Prince Henry. As a member of the Prince's company Massey's name occurs in the coronation list of March 15, 1604; in the patent of April 30, 1606; and in the household list of 1610 (*Eliz. Stage*, ii. 186, 187, 188). The Prince died in November, 1612, and his troupe soon passed under the patronage of the Palsgrave. Massey is named in the new patent of January 11, 1613 (*M.S.C.*, i. 275). About 1613 he wrote to Edward Alleyn concerning a loan (*H.P.*, p. 64). With other members of the Palsgrave's company he appears as lessee of the Fortune playhouse on October 31, 1618, and of the new Fortune on May 20, 1622 (*H.P.*, pp. 27, 28). He dined with Alleyn on March 18, April 15, August 12, 1621, and on July 21, 1622, on which last occasion he was accompanied by his cousin Ned Collins (Warner, pp. 188, 189, 192). He is presumably the Charles Marcy or Mercy, described as player, gentleman, and yeoman, in the registers of St. Giles's, Cripplegate, from December 30, 1610, to July 20, 1625 (*Eliz. Stage*, ii. 330). He died before December 6, 1635, leaving a widow Elianor; and his interest in the Fortune passed, with that of Alleyn and others, to Edward Marrant and John Roods, as shown by a Chancery suit of November, 1637 (Warner, p. 54). On April 30, 1624, he and others of the Palsgrave's men entered into a bond to Richard Gunnell, manager of the company (Hotson, pp. 52–53).

MASSEY, GEORGE.
A joint-lessee of the new Fortune playhouse, in which he obtained a half-share on May 20, 1622 (Warner, p. 246).

MASSYE, CHARLES.
See Charles Massey.

MAXE, WILLIAM.
A member of the Chapel Royal from 1509 to 1511, and possibly longer. In 1513 he was paid 40*s.*, and is described as "late a Child of the Chapel" (*Eliz. Stage*, ii. 27*n.*; Hillebrand, *Mod. Phil.*, xviii, 244).

MAXSEY, GILBERT.
A member of the Children of Paul's in 1554 (Hillebrand, *Child Actors*, p. 110).

MAY, EDWARD.

From 1494 to 1503 Edward May belonged to Henry VII's Court Interluders, under the leadership of John English (Collier, i. 44; *Eliz. Stage*, ii. 78).

MAY, EDWARD.

Edward May played Fidelio in Marmion's *Holland's Leaguer*, presented in December, 1631 (Adams, *Dram. Rec.*, p. 45), by "the high and mighty Prince Charles his servants, at the private house in Salisbury Court" (Marmion, *Works;* pp. 2, 6). He is recorded at Norwich on March 10, 1635, when his troupe, presumably the King's Revels, applied for permission to act in that town (Murray, i. 279–80). According to the marginal notes of the Egerton MS. of *Edmond Ironside*, he acted a bailiff in the play (Boas, *Library*, 1917, viii. 233, 235).

MAY, NATHAN.

On February 27, 1615, a license was granted to William Hovell, William Perry, and Nathan May, as representatives of presumably the King's Revels company. Nothing is heard of these players in London, and their only recorded provincial appearance is at Norwich on June 17, 1615. Their license was apparently condemned and withdrawn by an order of the Earl of Pembroke on July 16, 1616 (Murray, ii. 10, 340, 343).

MAY, RANDOLPH.

Randolph May, painter, about sixty years old, of St. Leonard's, Shoreditch, appears as a witness in the lawsuit between Cuthbert Burbage and Gyles Alleyn. In his deposition of May 15, 1600, he says that "about eighteene yeares nowe paste" he was "A servant in the house Called the Theater" (Wallace, *N.U.S.*, xiii. 240). Probably he was a gatherer or a stage-attendant.

MAYCOCKE, WILLIAM.

A member of the Children of Paul's in 1594 (Hillebrand, *Child Actors*, p. 111).

MAYDESTON, JOHN.

A member of the Chapel Royal in 1423 (Hillebrand, *Mod. Phil.*, xviii. 235).

MAYLER, GEORGE.

George Mayler was a Court Interluder from 1526 to about 1540, and figures in two lawsuits during this period. In 1528–29 there was a dispute between him and Thomas Arthur (*q.v.*), his apprentice, and he is described as a glazier. About 1530 he appears as a witness in proceedings of John Rastell and Henry Walton concerning the use of certain theatrical apparel, and is noted as a merchant-tailor (Collier, i. 97, 116, 117; Chambers, *Med. Stage*, ii. 184, 187).

MEADE, JACOB.

Jacob Meade was Keeper of the Bears, by November 24, 1599 (Warner, p. 234), and partner with Henslowe in the Bear Garden (Greg, *H.D.*, ii. 38). In 1613 he and Henslowe signed a contract with the carpenter Gilbert Katherenes for the erection of the Hope, which was for some years used for both the performance of plays and the baiting of animals. Henslowe died early in January, 1616, and his interest in the Hope passed to Edward Alleyn. On March 20, 1616, Alleyn and Meade made an agreement with Prince Charles's men to continue at the Hope. Later in the same year the company left the playhouse as the result of a disagreement with Meade, after which the building seems to have been used only for baiting. There followed a dispute between Alleyn and Meade, which was not settled until September 22, 1619 (Greg, *H.D.*, ii. 66–68). Meade was buried at St. Saviour's, Southwark, on July 9, 1624 (*Eliz. Stage*, ii. 330).

MELYONEK, JOHN.

Probably Master of the Chapel Royal during 1483–85 (*Eliz. Stage*, ii. 27).

MERCY, CHARLES.

See Charles Massey.

MERETT, HENRY.

See Henry Meryell.

MERYELL, HENRY.

Henry Meryell (or Merett) was a member of the Chapel Royal in 1509 and 1511 (Hillebrand, *Mod. Phil.*, xviii. 244; Chambers, *Eliz. Stage*, ii. 27n.).

MICHAEL.

See Mighel.

MIGHEL.

The stage-directions of *Sir John van Olden Barnavelt* (ed. Frijlinck, p. clx), acted by the King's men in 1619, assign the parts of a huntsman and of a captain to one Mighel or Michael. This may have been his first name.

MILLES, TOBIAS.

See Tobias Mils.

MILS, TOBIAS.

Tobias Mils (or Mylles) was a member of Queen Elizabeth's company in 1583, as shown by a London record that gives the personnel of the troupe at this date (*Eliz. Stage*, ii. 106). Heywood mentioned him with others as having flourished before his time, i.e. before about 1594 (*Apology*, p. 43). He was buried as "one of the Queenes Maiesties players" at St. Olave's, Southwark, on July 11, 1585, where his sons, William and Toby, were baptized on January 3, 1584, and September 5, 1585, respectively (*Eliz. Stage*, ii. 330). He may or may not be identical with "one Myles," a player, mentioned in *A Booke of the Nature and Properties, as well as the Bathes in England, as of other Bathes in Germanye* (1557): "for they [the waters of Bath] drye up wounderfully, and heale the goute excellentlye (and that in a short tyme), as with diverse other, one Myles, one of my Lord Summersettes players, can beare witnesse" (Collier, i. 139). The Duke of Somerset was beheaded on January 22, 1552. Robert Cecil's secretary was named Milles, and had a son Tobias buried at Chelsea on April 9, 1599 (*Eliz. Stage*, ii. 330).

MINION, SAMUEL.

Samuel Minion is named in a license of November 28, 1634, granted to a company under the leadership of William Daniel, and known as the King's Revels (Murray, ii. 8 ff.).

MISTALE.

Mistale is recorded at Norwich on March 10, 1635, when his troupe, presumably the King's Revels, applied for permission to act in that town (Murray, i. 279–80).

MOHUN, MICHAEL.

Wright tells us in *Historia Histrionica* (1699) that Michael Mohun (or Moone) "was a boy . . . under Beeston at the Cockpit," where he acted Bellamente in *Love's Cruelty*, "which part he retained after the Restoration" (Hazlitt's *Dodsley*, xv. 404, 409). On May 12, 1637, he and other members of William Beeston's company were summoned before the Privy Council for playing during plague quarantine (*M.S.C.*, i. 392). At the closing of the playhouses in 1642 and the beginning of the Civil War, he enlisted in the King's army. He "was a captain, and (after the wars were ended here) served in Flanders, where he received pay as a major." His career at the Cockpit was continued after the Restoration. He is named in the Petition of the Cockpit Players on October 13, 1660, and the Articles of Agreement between Herbert and Killigrew on June 4, 1662 (Adams, *Dram. Rec.*, pp. 94, 113–14). His Majesty's Company of Comedians opened their new playhouse, the Theatre Royal, on May 7, 1663 (Pepys, *Diary*, iii. 107), under the management of Thomas Killi-

grew. As a member of the organization Mohun played the follow-
ing parts (Downes, *Ros. Ang.*, pp. 2 ff.): Leontius in *The Humorous
Lieutenant*; Don Leon in *Rule a Wife and have a Wife*; Volpone in
The Fox; Truewit in *The Silent Woman*; Face in *The Alchemist*;
Melantius in *The Maid's Tragedy*; Mardonius in *King and no King*;
Aubrey in *Rollo, Duke of Normandy*; Iago in *The Moor of Venice*;
Philocles in *The Maiden Queen*; Belamy in *The Mock Astrologer*;
Cassius in *Julius Caesar*; the Emperor in *The Indian Emperor*;
Maximin in *Tyrannick Love*; the old Emperor in *Aureng Zeb*;
Clytus in *Alexander the Great*; Ventidius in *All for Love, or the World
Well Lost*; the Duke of Mantua in *The Assignation, or Love in a
Nunnery*; Mythridates in *Mythridates, King of Pontus*; Matthias in
The Destruction of Jerusalem; Rhodophil in *Marriage Alamode*;
Lord Burleigh in *The Unhappy Favorite, or the Earl of Essex*; King
Edward III in *The Black Prince*; Abdemelech in *The Conquest of
Granada*; and Hannibal, in *Sophonisba, or Hannibal's Overthrow*.
Downes (*Ros. Ang.*, p. 17) says that "he was Eminent for Vol-
pone; Face in *The Alchymst*; Melantius in *The Maids Tragedy*;
Mardonius in *King and no King*; Cassius in *Julius Caesar*; Clytus in
Alexander; Mithridates, &c. An Eminent Poet [Nathaniel Lee]
seeing him Act this last, vented suddenly this Saying: 'Oh Mohun,
Mohun! Thou little Man of Mettle, if I should Write a 100 Plays,
I'd Write a Part for thy Mouth'; in short, in all his Parts, he was
most Accurate and Correct." Pepys gives three notices of him:
On November 20, 1660, he saw Beaumont and Fletcher's *Beggar's
Bush*, and for "the first time one Moone, who is said to be the
best actor in the world, lately come over with the King"; on
November 22, 1660: "Mr. Moon did act the Traitor very well,"
in Shirley's play of that title; and on February 6, 1669, he was
disappointed on seeing *Othello* "but ill acted in most parts;
Mohun, which did a little surprise me, not acting Iago's part by
much so well as Clun used to do" (*Diary*, i. 267, 270; viii. 207).
In *The Tattler*, Number 99, November 26, 1709, Richard Steele
writes of his "old friends, Hart and Mohun, the one by his nat-

ural and proper force, the other by his great skill and art, never failed to send me home full of such ideas as affected my behaviour, and made me insensibly more courteous and humane to my friends and acquaintances" (Chalmers, *British Essayists*, ii. 367). After the union of the Duke's and the King's companies in 1682, Mohun appears never to have acted again. He soon found it necessary to ask the King to help him in getting a sufficient pension from the united company, and his petition is interesting for its autobiographic quality (Nicoll, *Rest. Drama*, pp. 327–28). He died in October, 1684, and was buried in the church of St. Giles-in-the-Fields (Pepys, *Diary*, vi. 258*n*.; *D.N.B.*, xxxviii. 110).

MONKE, WILLIAM.

Samuel Monke, son of William, "a musitian," was baptized at St. Saviour's, Southwark, on June 10, 1619 (Bentley, *T.L.S.*, Nov. 15, 1928, p. 856).

MOON, PETER.

In 1562 Peter Moon was the leader of a company of players at Ipswich, as shown by an entry in the town records: "Item, to the plaiers Peter Moone and his companie, 5*s*." (*Hist. MSS. Comm.*, ix. 1. p. 248).

MOONE, MICHAEL.

See Michael Mohun.

MOORE, JOSEPH.

Joseph Moore and John Townsend are named in a license of April 27, 1611, as leaders of the Lady Elizabeth's troupe (*M.S.C.*, i. 274). On August 29, 1611, he and his fellow-actors gave Henslowe a bond of £500 to perform "certen articles" of agreement (*H.P.*, pp. 18, 111). He no doubt continued with the company, for on March 20, 1618, a new license mentions him as one of the leaders. From this date to 1631 he appears to have been active in the management of the Lady Elizabeth's troupe, especially on provincial tours. On July 16, 1616, the Earl of Pembroke issued an order for the suppression of certain theatrical organizations, and Moore brought this document to Norwich on June 4, 1617. On July 11, 1617, Townsend and Moore were paid £30 for three plays performed before King James on his journey to Scotland during the preceding March or April (Steele, p. 198). He was leader of the company at Norwich on February 8, 1619 (?); but at the next visit on April 22, 1620, Francis Wambus told the town authorities that although Moore was still a member of the troupe, he had not played during the past year, and that he was then keeping an inn at Chichester. He is named in a patent of March 20, 1622; in a bill of March 13, 1622, signed by the Lord Chamberlain; in the 1622 Herbert list of "the chiefe of them at the Phoenix" (Adams, *Dram. Rec.*, p. 63); in a warrant of June 30, 1628, appointing several of the Lady Elizabeth's (Queen of Bohemia's) players as Grooms of the Chamber (Stopes, *Jahrbuch*, xlvi. 94); and in a license of December 9, 1628. He also appears in later provincial records of visits of the company: Reading, December 24, 1629; Norwich, March 3, 1630; Coventry, June, 1630, and March 30, 1631; and Reading, August 13, 1631. By December 7, 1631, he had joined Prince Charles's men, as shown by the company's license of that date. Since his name does not appear in the cast of Marmion's *Holland's Leaguer* (December, 1631), he possibly came to the Prince's men as manager. He was no doubt admirably fitted for such a position, for he had directed during many years the affairs of the Lady Elizabeth's players. The Norwich annals mention him on November 3, 1635, and February 21, 1638. He served as payee for Court performances on December 10, 1635, March 21, 1638, and May 4, 1640 (Steele, pp. 250, 268, 275). In 1623 he lived "att the Harowe in Barbican" (Murray, i. 192, 218, 222, 243, 252, 254, 255, 259, 260; ii. 251, 340, 343, 344, 345, 346, 353, 358, 386, 387; Wallace, *Jahrbuch*, xlvi. 347; Adams, *Playhouses*, pp. 375–78).

MORE, GEORGE.

A member of the Children of Paul's in 1554 (Hillebrand, *Child Actors*, p. 110).

MORE, ROGER.

Roger More was in 1640 a hired man of Prince Charles's company. In an order of April 25, 1640, he is named as a Prince's man who is not "to be hindered or diverted in his service by being impressed, arrested, or otherwise molested, without leave first asked" (Stopes, *Jahrbuch*, xlvi. 103).

MORGAN, FLUELLEN.

Fluellen Morgan is mentioned in the examination of Richard Bradshaw's players who got into trouble at Banbury in 1633, when the town authorities became suspicious of the validity of the company's license (Murray, ii. 106 ff., 163 ff.). From the records it appears that Edward Whiting (*q.v.*) either had been or was in some way connected with Bradshaw's troupe, that he "let the commission in question to William Cooke and Fluellen Morgan, and they two went with it with a puppet-play until they had spent all, then they pawned the commission for 4*s*." Subsequently Bradshaw redeemed and bought the commission.

MORLEY, THOMAS.

A member of the Children of Paul's in 1574 (Hillebrand, *Child Actors*, p. 111).

MORRIS, MATHIAS.

Mathias Morris played Sylana, wife to Silius, in Richards's *Messallina, the Roman Empress*, printed in 1640 as "acted with generall applause divers times by the Company of his Majesties Revells."

MOTTERAM, JOHN.

A member of the Chapel Royal about 1600–01. In Henry Clifton's complaint to the Star Chamber on December 15, 1601, as to

how boys were pressed for the Chapel at Blackfriars, John Mot-
teram is named as one so taken, and is described as "a gramer
scholler in the free schole at Westminster" (Wallace, *Blackfriars*, p. 80).

MOUNFELD, JOHN.

John Mounfeld and three of his fellows who had been players
to Queen Jane before her death in 1537 are mentioned about 1538
in a Chancery suit concerning the payments for a horse hired "to
beare there playing garments" (Stopes, *Shak. Envir.*, p. 236).

MUFFORD, JOHN.

On June 10, 1590, John Mufford, "one of the Lord Beauchamps
players," was committed to prison for disobeying the order of
the mayor of Norwich that he should not play in that town
(Murray, ii. 25, 337).

MULCASTER, RICHARD.

Headmaster of the Merchant Taylors' School, 1561–86, and of
St. Paul's Grammar School, 1596–1608 (*D.N.B.*, xxxix. 275;
Eliz. Stage, ii. 19, 75 ff.).

MUNDAY, ANTHONY.

Anthony Munday, dramatist, was a player before 1582, according to an anonymous pamphlet, *A True Report of . . . M.
Campion* (1582), where it is said that he "first was a stage player"
and "did play extempore, those gentlemen and others whiche
were present, can best giue witnes of his dexterity, who being
wery of his folly, hissed him from his stage. Then being thereby
discouraged, he set forth a balet against playes, but yet (o con-
stant youth) he now beginnes againe to ruffle upon the stage."
In all probability he was a member of the troupe of players
under the patronage of the Earl of Oxford, whose "servant"
he calls himself in his *View of Sundry Examples*, 1580 (*D.N.B.*,
xxxix. 290; *Eliz. Stage*, iii. 444).

MYLDEVALE, THOMAS.

A member of the Chapel Royal in 1423 (Hillebrand, *Mod. Phil.*, xviii. 235).

MYLLES, TOBIAS.
See Tobias Mils.

NASION.
See Henry Nation.

NATION, HENRY.

A member of the Children of Paul's in 1574 (Hillebrand, *Child Actors*, p. 111). He is perhaps identical with Nasion, a legatee in the will of Sebastian Westcott, dated April 3, 1582, where he is named among the "sometimes children of the said almenerey," i.e. St. Paul's (*Eliz. Stage*, ii. 15n.).

NAVARRO, JOHN.

The leader of a company of Spanish actors in London, as shown by a warrant of December 23, 1635, "to pay £10 to John Navarro for himself and his company of Spanish players for a play before the King" (Steele, p. 253).

NED.

A clown mentioned in Nashe's *Summer's Last Will and Testament* (*Works*, iii. 233), acted in 1592 at Croydon, possibly by members of Archbishop Whitgift's household (*Eliz. Stage*, iii. 451–53). In the Prologue (line 8), Will Summers says that the play can proceed "if my cousin *Ned* will lend me his Chayne and his Fiddle." Summers later refers to him as "Ned foole" (Nashe, *Works*, iii. 258, 269): "I haue had a dogge my selfe, that would dreame, and talke in his sleep, turne round like Ned foole, and sleepe all night in a porridge pot" (line 783); "Ned fooles clothes are so perfumde with the beere he powrd on me, that there shall not be a Dutchman within 20. mile, but he'le smel out & claime kindred of him" (line 1120).

NED.

In the plot of 2 *Seven Deadly Sins,* presented by Strange's men about 1590, Ned is cast for the part of Rhodope (?) in "Sloth" (Greg, *H.P.,* p. 152; *R.E.S.,* i. 262).

NETHE, JOHN.

A London player in 1550, named in an order demanding that all plays be licensed by the King or his Council (Harrison, *England,* iv. 314).

NETHERSALL, JOHN.

A London player in 1550, named in an order demanding that all plays be licensed by the King or his Council (Harrison, *England,* iv. 314).

NEWARK, WILLIAM.

Master of the Chapel Royal, 1493–1509 (Wallace, *Evolution,* pp. 26 ff., 33).

NEWMAN, JOHN.

A lessee, with William Hunnis, of the First Blackfriars playhouse, 1581-83. In 1583 Hunnis and Newman transferred their lease to Henry Evans (Adams, *Playhouses,* pp. 107–08).

NEWTON, JOHN.

John Newton was a member of Prince Charles's troupe from 1610 to 1625. As a Prince's man he appears in the patent of March 30, 1610; in a warrant of March 29, 1615, to come before the Privy Council for playing during Lent (*M.S.C.,* i. 272, 372); in an agreement with Alleyn and Meade on March 20, 1616 (Warner, p. 50); early in 1619 as A Fasting-Day in Middleton's *Masque of Heroes* (*Works,* vii. 200); and in King James's funeral procession on May 7, 1625 (Murray, i. 161, 237).

NICHOLAS.

Apparently the name of the "Singing-boy" in Jonson's *Staple of News,* acted by the King's men in 1626 (*Works,* v. 160, 256).

In the *dramatis personae* we find: "Fiddlers, Singing-boy, Attendants, &c." A stage-direction, IV. i, reads: "Enter the Fidlers, and Nicholas." Then a character says: "Nick the boy shall sing it." Later, "Nich" sings: "As bright, &c." He is probably to be identified with the Nick who seems to have assumed two or three parts in Massinger's *Believe as You List* (ed. Croker, pp. 26, 49, 86), licensed for the King's men on May 7, 1631 (Adams, *Dram. Rec.*, p. 33).

NICK.

Nick played a lady in "Envy," and probably Pompeia in "Sloth," of *2 Seven Deadly Sins*, acted by Strange's men about 1590 (Greg, *H.P.*, p. 152; *R.E.S.*, i. 262). A Nicke also appears in the 1623 folio text of *The Taming of the Shrew*, III. i. 82, where he speaks three lines that follow the stage-direction: "Enter a Servant." The Admiral's men on December 25, 1601, bought hose for Nycke to tumble in before Queen Elizabeth (*H.D.*, i. 152). A Nicke is mentioned in a letter from Joan Alleyn to her husband on October 21, 1603 (Warner, p. 25). He has been conjectured to be identical with Nicholas Tooley (*q.v.*).

NICOLL, BASILIUS.

Basilius Nicoll, a scrivener, apparently controlled Thomas Bromley's interest in the Globe playhouse. Bromley was a minor (Adams, *Mod. Phil.*, xvii. 4 ff.).

NILL, JOHN.

A player, whose daughter Alice was baptized at St. Saviour's on August 13, 1601 (*Eliz. Stage*, ii. 331).

NORWOOD, JOHN.

John Norwood belonged to the Children of Paul's in 1598 (Hillebrand, *Child Actors*, p. 111). Apparently he was the performer of Lucio mentioned in a stage-direction of Marston's

1 Antonio and Mellida, IV. i. 29, presented by Paul's boys about 1599 (*Works,* i. 63): "Enter Andrugio, Lucio, Cole, and Norwood."

NYCKE.

See Nick.

NYCOWLLES, ROBERT.

A player, who witnessed a loan from Philip to Francis Henslowe on June 1, 1595 (*H.D.,* i. 6).

OFFLEY, THOMAS.

At an uncertain date, Thomas Offley, subsequently Lord Mayor of London, was a member of the Children of Paul's. Joseph Hunter, in *Chorus Vatum,* quotes from a biographical sketch: "This Thomas Offley became a good grammarian under Mr. [William] Lillie and understood the Latin tongue perfectly; and because he had a sweet voice he was put to learn prick-song among the choristers of St. Paul's, for that learned Mr. Lillie knew full well that knowledge in music was a help and a furtherance to all arts" (*Eliz. Stage,* ii. 16n.; *D.N.B.,* xlii. 5). William Lyly was Headmaster of St. Paul's Grammar School from about 1509 to 1522.

OSTLER, WILLIAM.

William Ostler first appears with the Children of the Chapel Royal in Jonson's *Poetaster,* acted in 1601 (*Eliz. Stage,* iii. 365). Subsequently, with Field and Underwood, he was "taken to strengthen the Kings service" (Halliwell-Phillipps, *Outlines,* i. 317). He had passed to the King's men by 1610, when he is found in the actor-list of Jonson's *Alchemist.* With this company he also acted in the following plays (Murray, i. opp. 172): *Catiline* (1611); *The Duchess of Malfi* (c. 1611), Antonio, which character was later played by Robert Benfield; *The Captain* (c. 1612); *Valentinian* (1611–14); and *Bonduca* (1613–14). He is named in the 1623 folio list of Shakespearean players. In 1611 he married

Thomasine, daughter of John Heminges. Their son Beaumont was baptized at St. Mary's, Aldermanbury, on May 18, 1612 (Collier, iii. 423). He died on December 16, 1614. That he won considerable fame is indicated by an epigram by John Davies, printed about 1611 in *The Scourge of Folly* (ed. Grosart, ii. 31):

> *To the Roscius of these times Mr. W. Ostler*
> Ostler thou tookst a knock thou would'st haüe giu'n,
> Neere sent thee to thy latest home; but O!
> Where was thine action when thy crowne was riu'n
> Sole king of actors; then wast idle? No:
> Thou hadst it for thou wouldst bee doing; thus
> Good actors' deeds are oft most dangerous:
> But if thou plaist thy dying part as well
> As thy stage-parts thou hast no part in hell.

The shares he had acquired in the Blackfriars playhouse, May 20, 1611, and in the Globe, February 20, 1612, were soon involved in a lawsuit between his widow and Heminges (Wallace, London *Times*, October 2 and 4, 1909).

OTTEWELL, GEORGE.
See George Attewell.

OTTEWELL, HUGH.
See Hugh Attwell.

OTWELL, GEORGE.
See George Attewell.

PAGE, JOHN.
With Queen Henrietta's company (Murray, i. opp. 266), John Page acted Jane, Justice Lanby's daughter, in Shirley's *Wedding* (*c.* 1626), and Lelius, in Nabbes's *Hannibal and Scipio* (1635).

PAGE, OLIVER.
A London player in 1550, named in an order demanding that all plays be licensed by the King or his Council (Harrison, *England*, iv. 314).

PALLANT, ROBERT.

In the plot of *2 Seven Deadly Sins*, acted by Strange's company about 1590, Robert Pallant is cast for several parts: a warder in the Induction; an attendant, a soldier, and Dardan in "Envy"; Nicanor in "Sloth"; and Julio (?), in "Lechery" (Greg, *H.P.*, p. 152; *R.E.S.*, i. 262). By November 26, 1602, he belonged to Worcester's men, when he authorized payment on behalf of the company. This is the only mention of him in Henslowe's *Diary* (Greg, *H.D.*, ii. 300). Early in the reign of James I Worcester's men became Queen Anne's company. As a Queen's man Pallant is named in the list of players who took part in the coronation procession of March 15, 1604; in the patent of April 15, 1609, where an obvious clerical error gives his name as "Richard"; and in the duplicate license issued on January 7, 1612, to the traveling company (*Eliz. Stage*, ii. 229; *M.S.C.*, i. 270; Murray, ii. 343). In 1612 Heywood published his *Apology for Actors*, to which Pallant contributed commendatory verses:

> *To my good friend and fellow, Thomas Heywood*
> Have I not knowne a man, that to be hyr'd
> Would not for any treasure see a play,
> Reele from a taverne? Shall this be admir'd,
> When as another, but t'other day,
> That held to weare a surplesse most unmeet,
> Yet after stood at Paul's-crosse in a sheet.
> ROBERT PALLANT.

Subsequently he was temporarily associated with the Lady Elizabeth's troupe. He is mentioned as joining the Lady Elizabeth's men in June, 1614, and a letter from Daborne to Henslowe seems to indicate that he was negotiating with the company as early as March 28, when he was "much discontented" with Henslowe's "neglect of him" (*H.P.*, pp. 82, 88). By March 20, 1616, he had transferred his services to Prince Charles's men, entering into an agreement between this company and Alleyn and Meade (Warner, p. 50). His career is quite involved, but through it all he seems to have continued technically a servant to the Queen; he attended her funeral in this capacity on May 13, 1619. He may have been with the Queen's men at Norwich on May 6, 1615, and May 31, 1617, for his name is given in the abstracts of the license in the town records (Murray, i. 196; ii. 340, 343). He was a visitor at Henslowe's death-bed on January 6, 1616 (*H.D.*, ii. 20). The register of St. Saviour's, Southwark, records the baptism of children of the player: Robert, September 28, 1605; John, August 24, 1608; Ephraim, January 1, 1611, buried October 19, 1611; Hanburye, July 3, 1614, buried July 4, 1614; and the burial on September 4, 1619, of "Robert Pallant, a man, in the church" (Bentley, *T.L.S.*, Nov. 15, 1928, p. 856). This burial entry probably refers to the player; but see Robert Pallant, "the younger."

PALLANT, ROBERT, "THE YOUNGER."

Chambers (*Eliz. Stage*, ii. 331) suggests that the R. Pallant who played the part of Cariola (a waiting-woman, and thus a minor part) in Webster's *Duchess of Malfi* was not the old actor of the same name, but one of a younger generation. The play was given by the King's men, and the actor-list is reasonably dated 1619–23 (Murray, i. opp. 172; ii. 146–48). Chambers's suggestion seems plausible when we consider that a Robert Pallant is named in a Protection from Arrest issued by Herbert on December 27, 1624, to twenty-one men "imployed by the Kinges Maiesties servantes in theire quallity of Playinge as Musitions and other necessary attendantes" (Adams, *Dram. Rec.*, p. 74). It does not seem likely that the "elder" Robert Pallant, an experienced actor and a veteran of the stage, first mentioned about 1590, would have been a mere stage-attendant or musician in 1624. The available evidence seems to favor the conjecture that the Robert Pallant with the King's men was of a younger generation, and that the "elder" player died in 1619. More recent research by G. E. Bentley (*T.L.S.*, Nov. 15, 1928, p. 856) corroborates

Chambers's view that a "younger" Pallant appeared as Cariola in *The Duchess of Malfi*. He is quite probably the Robert Pallant, son of the "elder" player, whose baptism is recorded in the register of St. Saviour's, Southwark on September 28, 1605.

PANT, THOMAS.

Thomas Pant, apprentice to Christopher Simpson of Egton, shoemaker and recusant, appears to have been a strolling player from 1607 to 1610. At Topcliffe, Yorkshire, on October 2, 1610, he was released from his indentures on complaining that he had been "trayned up for these three yeres in wandering in the country and playing of interludes" (*Eliz. Stage*, i. 304*n*.)

PARKINS.

See John Perkin.

PARLOWE, RICHARD.

See Richard Parrowe.

PARR, WILLIAM.

With the Admiral's men in 1602 William Parr was cast for several minor parts in the plot of *1 Tamar Cam*: a nobleman, a scout, an attendant, a trumpet, a guard, and a Bohar in the Procession (*H.P.*, p. 154). About Christmas, 1603, the Admiral's men were taken into the service of Prince Henry. Although Parr is not named in the patent of April 30, 1606, he apparently continued with the company after the transfer, for in 1610 he appears in a household list of the Prince's men (*Eliz. Stage*, ii. 188). The Prince died in November, 1612, and his troupe soon passed under the patronage of the Palsgrave. Parr is mentioned in the new patent of January 11, 1613 (*M.S.C.*, i. 275), and in the lease of the Fortune by the Palsgrave's men on October 31, 1618 (*H.P.*, p. 27). He dined with Edward Alleyn on March 22, 1618 (Warner, p. 169). During 1615–16 Charles Marshall, Humphrey Jeffes, and Parr secured a duplicate of the 1613 patent to the Palsgrave's company, organized a troupe, and traveled in the provinces. This duplicate warrant was condemned and withdrawn by order of the Earl of Pembroke on July 16, 1616 (Murray, ii. 4 ff.). He is last heard of as a Palsgrave's man on April 9, 1620, when certain members of the company dined with Alleyn (Warner, p. 184).

PARROWE, RICHARD.

Richard Parrowe (or Parlowe) was a member of Henry VIII's troupe of Court Interluders from 1538 to 1545 (*Eliz. Stage*, ii. 79*n*.; Collier, i. 117).

PARSELEY, RICHARD.

A London player in 1550, named in an order demanding that all plays be licensed by the King or his Council (Harrison, *England*, iv. 314).

PARSONS, THOMAS.

Thomas Parson's, Thomas Downton's boy, fetched money on behalf of the Admiral's men from Henslowe for properties on (?) April 16, 1599 (*H.D.*, ii. 301). With the Admiral's company he acted in *The Battle of Alcazar* (*c.* 1600–01), appearing as a Fury, and in *1 Tamar Cam* (1602), assuming the parts of an attendant, a Persian, a guard, a spirit, a messenger, a nurse, and an Hermaphrodite in the procession (*H.P.*, pp. 153, 154; *Eliz. Stage*, ii. 175–76).

PATESON, WILLIAM.

On March 6, 1584, William Pateson, "my lord Harbards man," belonged to the Earl of Worcester's players, and was engaged in a dispute between the players and the authorities at Leicester. Lord Herbert was Worcester's son (*Eliz. Stage*, ii. 223, 224*n*.).

PATRICK, RICHARD.

A member of the Children of Paul's in 1607 (Hillebrand, *Child Actors*, p. 112).

PATTMIE(?), EDWARD.

A member of the Children of Paul's in 1574 (Hillebrand, *Child Actors*, p. 111).

PATTRICK, WILLIAM.

William Pattrick is known as a minor actor with the King's men from 1624 to 1636. His name occurs in a Protection from Arrest issued by Herbert on December 27, 1624, to twenty-one men "imployed by the Kinges Maiesties servantes in theire quallity of Playinge as Musitions and other necessary attendantes" (Adams, *Dram. Rec.*, p. 74); in the actor-list of Massinger's *Roman Actor* (licensed October 11, 1626), as Palphurius Sura, a senator; in the marginal notes to Massinger's *Believe as You List* (licensed May 7, 1631), as a captain and probably as Demetrius; in a Ticket of Privilege granted on January 12, 1636, to the attendants "employed by his Majesty's servants the players of the Blackfriars, and of special use to them both on the Stage and otherwise for his Majesty's disport and service"; and in the "Players Pass" on May 17, 1636. In 1623 he lived "on the Banckesyde neare the Bargehouse" (Murray, i. opp. 172; Wallace, *Jahrbuch*, xlvi. 347; Stopes, *Jahrbuch*, xlvi. 99). Margaret Pattrick, daughter of William, "a player," was baptized on June 20, 1622, at St. Saviour's, Southwark (Bentley, *T.L.S.*, Nov. 15, 1928, p. 856).

PAVY, SALATHIEL.

Salathiel (or Salmon) Pavy belonged to the Chapel Royal from about 1600 to about 1603, and became one of its most famous children. In Henry Clifton's complaint to the Star Chamber on December 15, 1601, as to how boys were pressed for the Chapel at Blackfriars, Pavy is named as one so taken, and is described as "apprentice to one Peerce" (Wallace, *Blackfriars*, p. 80). His employer, "one Peerce," has been identified with Edward Pearce, Master of the Children of Paul's; but there seems to be no likelihood that the managers of Blackfriars would have committed the imprudent act of taking one of Paul's boys. He is known to have acted in two of Jonson's plays, *Cynthia's Revels* and *The Poetaster*, presented by the Children of the Chapel in 1600 and 1601 respectively (*Eliz. Stage*, iii. 363, 365). Jonson in his *Epigrams* (1616), cxx (*Works*, viii. 221), gives eloquent testimony to Salathiel's power to portray the character of old men; although he was "scarce thirteen" when he died after three years of playing:

> *An Epitaph on Salathiel Pavy, a child of*
> *Queen Elizabeth's chapel*
>
> Weep with me, all you that read
>   This little story:
> And know, for whom a tear you shed
>   Death's self is sorry.
> 'Twas a child that so did thrive
>   In grace and feature
> As heaven and nature seem'd to strive
>   Which own'd the creature.
> Years he number'd scarce thirteen
>   When fates turn'd cruel,
> Yet three fill'd zodiacs had he been
>   The stage's jewel;
> And did act, what now we moan,
>   Old men so duly,
> As, sooth, the Parcae thought him one,
>   He play'd so truly.
> So, by error to his fate
>   They all consented;
> But viewing him since, alas, too late!
>   They have repented;
> And have sought, to give new birth,
>   In baths to steep him;
> But being so much too good for earth,
>   Heaven vows to keep him.

PAVYE, WILLIAM.

With the Admiral's company one Pavy acted Boniface(?) in *Fortune's Tennis*, about 1597–98 (Greg, *H.P.*, p. 154; *R.E.S.*, i.

270). He may fairly be identified with the William Pavye whose burial is recorded on September 8, 1608, in the register of St. Bodolph Aldgate, where he is described as "one of ye princes players dwelling by the Mynoryes" (Denkinger, *P.M.L.A.*, xli. 103). This identification is quite plausible, for about Christmas, 1603, the Admiral's men were taken into the service of Prince Henry. He was apparently only a minor actor, which would account for the non-appearance of his name in the patent granted to the Prince's men on April 30, 1606. "Mres Pavie," presumably the player's widow, is mentioned in a letter from Charles Massey to Edward Alleyn, about 1613 (*H.P.*, p. 64).

PAYNE, ROBERT.

A patentee for the Children of the Queen's Revels at the Second Blackfriars, on February 4, 1604 (Adams, *Playhouses*, p. 215).

PEACOCKE, ROBERT.

A London player in 1550, named in an order demanding that all plays be licensed by the King or his Council (Harrison, *England*, iv. 314).

PEADLE, ABRAHAM.

See Abraham Pedel.

PEADLE, WILLIAM.

See William Pedel.

PEARCE, EDWARD.

Edward Pearce (Piers, Peers), who had been a Gentleman of the Chapel since 1598, resigned his place in 1600 upon his appointment to the Mastership of the Children of Paul's, which apparently he held until about 1609 (Rimbault, *Old Cheque Book*, pp. 4, 5 ff.; Adams, *Playhouses*, p. 117). For his connection with the lawsuit concerning Chapman's *The Old Joiner of Aldgate* in 1603, see Charles Sisson, "*Keep The Widow Waking*," *The Library*, N.S. (1927), viii. 41.

PEDEL, ABRAHAM.

During 1614–15 Abraham Pedel was in Germany with a group of English players in the service of John Sigismund, Elector of Brandenburg (Cohn, p. lxxxviii). Apparently he is the Abraham Peadle who visited Norwich on June 17, 1616, and June 14, 1620, with a company licensed to do "dancinge on the Roape and other feats of activity" (Murray, ii. 342, 346). By 1623 he had become an actor at the Fortune, and lived at "George Alley in Gouldinge lane." With Richard Claytone, Richard Grace, and William Stratford, "all Actors at the fortune neere Golding lane," he was summoned to appear at court to answer a bill of complaint made by Gervase Markham (Wallace, *Jahrbuch*, xlvi. 348, 350). Since in 1623 the Fortune playhouse was occupied by the Palsgrave's men, Pedel, it may be reasonably assumed, belonged to that company.

PEDEL, JACOB.

In 1597 Jacob Pedel (Behel or Biel) was in Germany, visiting Strassburg and Frankfort with a company under the leadership of Thomas Sackville (Herz, pp. 34 ff.). During 1614–15 he is again recorded on the Continent, with a troupe of English actors patronized by John Sigismund, Elector of Brandenburg (Cohn, p. lxxxviii).

PEDEL, WILLIAM.

William Pedel first appears as an English pantomimist in Holland. On November 18, 1608, he was allowed by the Council of Leyden "to exhibit various beautiful and chaste performances with his body, without using any words" (Cohn, p. lxxxiii). The Continental records again give his name during 1614–15, when he belonged to the players with John Sigismund, Elector of Brandenburg (Cohn, p. lxxxviii). By June 17, 1616, he had returned to England, where he continued his profession of "dauncing & vaulting" with "other feats of activity," and is found in provincial records as late as December 24, 1639 (Murray,

ii. 248, 253, 342, 346). This last notice, however, may refer to a younger William Peadle mentioned with his father in 1620. The family traditions seem to have been maintained by the younger Peadle, who is presumably alluded to in *Mercurius Fumigosus*, 1654 (Rollins, *Stud. in Phil.*, xviii. 315): "The lately desceased Montford, Peadle, and now Christ. Whitehead, who for agility of body, and neatness in Dancing,"

> Doth in best iudgements, as farr exceed the Turks,
> As Shakspere Haywood in his Commick Works.

The registers of St. Saviour's, Southwark, record in 1610, 1617, and 1629, children of a William Peadle, described as "tumbler" and "gentleman" (*Eliz. Stage*, ii. 332).

PEERS, EDWARD.

See Edward Pearce.

PEERS, THOMAS.

A member of the Children of Paul's in 1607 (Hillebrand, *Child Actors*, p. 112).

PENDRY, CHARLES.

A member of the Children of Paul's in 1598 (Hillebrand, *Child Actors*, p. 111).

PENN, WILLIAM.

As a member of the Children of the Queen's Revels company, William Penn appears in the actor-list of Jonson's *Epicoene*, which, according to the folio of 1616, was "Acted in the yeere 1609, by the Children of her Maiesties Revells." By March 20, 1616, he belonged to Prince Charles's men, joining his fellows in signing an agreement with Alleyn and Meade (*H.P.*, p. 90). On May 7, 1625, he took part in King James's funeral procession (Murray, i. 161, 237). Soon after his accession, Charles I took his father's players under his patronage, and several members of the old Prince Charles's company were no doubt transferred to the King's men. William Rowley is the only one of the Prince's troupe mentioned in the King's men's license of June 24, 1625; but Penn and Anthony Smith, both former Prince's men, appear in the cast of Ford's *Lover's Melancholy*, licensed for the King's troupe on November 24, 1628. The omission of their names from the 1625 patent is not explained, but conceivably their transfer occurred about this time. As a King's man Penn appears in the livery allowance of May 6, 1629; as Julio Baptista, a great scholar, in Massinger's *Picture* (licensed June 8, 1629); in the marginal notes to Massinger's *Believe as You List* (licensed May 7, 1631), where he is assigned the parts of a merchant and a jailor; as Nantolet in Fletcher's *Wildgoose Chase* (a revival, 1631); and in the "Players Pass" of May 17, 1636 (Murray, i. opp. 172). The registers of St. Bodolph Aldgate record his marriage to Sibill West on June 30, 1616; he was then of St. Leonard's, Shoreditch. Their children, Marie and William, were baptized November 21, 1617, and March 31, 1619, respectively; in 1617 he was of Houndsditch (Denkinger, *P.M.L.A.*, xli. 104). In 1623 he lived "at the George Alley in Gouldinge lane" (Wallace, *Jahrbuch*, xlvi 347), and in 1636 children of his were baptized and buried at the parish of St. Giles, Cripplegate (*Eliz. Stage*, ii. 322).

PENNYCUICKE, ANDREW.

Andrew Pennycuicke published in 1655 Robert Davenport's *King John and Matilda* (Davenport, *Works*, p. 4), which had been presented by Queen Henrietta's men, probably about 1629 (Murray, i. opp. 266). In his dedication of the play to the Earl of Lindsey, Pennycuicke writes: "It past the Stage with generall Applause (my selfe being the last that Acted *Matilda* in it) and since through the absurdity of times it hath laine obscured." This is the earliest information we have concerning him. After the closing of the playhouses in 1642 he followed the custom of certain other actors and turned publisher. In 1652 Robert Chamberlain's *Nocturnall Lucubrations* was "Printed by T. F. for the

A DICTIONARY OF ACTORS

Use and Benefit of Andrewe Pennycuicke Gent" (Hazlitt, *Hand-Book*, p. 81). He is evidently the A. P. who signed with A. T. (probably Anthony Turner) the dedication of William Heminges's *Fatal Contract* (1653), addressed to the Earl and Countess of Northampton, for there was another quarto in 1654, with a similar dedication, "Printed at London for Andrew Pennycuicke" (Hazlitt, *Coll. & Notes*, 1867–1876, p. 207). He published Ford and Dekker's *Sun's Darling* in 1656, inscribing the play to the Lady Newton; and in the following year the same play appeared with a dedication to the Earl of Southampton by Pennycuicke and Theophilus Bird, an actor (Hazlitt, *op. cit.*, p. 164). *The Hunting of the Fox*, by T. F., was printed for Pennycuicke in 1657 (Hazlitt, *op. cit.*, p. 201). In 1658 and 1659 he published Massinger's *City Madam*; the Countess of Oxford was the dedicatee of the 1658 edition (Hazlitt, *op. cit.*, p. 284).

PENTON, FABIAN.

The leader of a company of English players at Augsburg, Germany, in June, 1602 (Trautmann, *Archiv*, xiii. 317).

PEPEREL, GILES.

Possibly the boy who took the part of Iphigenia in *The Bugbears* (c. 1564–65). One of the songs in the play is headed: "Giles peperel for Iphiginia" (Bond, *Early Plays from the Italian*, pp. 83, 154).

PERCY, ROBERT.

During 1586–87 Robert Percy (Rupert Persten or Persj) was on the Continent. The Elsinore pay-roll records that he was in the Danish service from June 17 to September 18, 1586. Soon he went to the court of the Elector of Saxony, at Dresden, where he held an appointment as actor-entertainer until July 17, 1587 (Cohn, p. xxv; Herz, p. 3; Riis, *Century Magazine*, lxi. 391). Nothing is heard of him after this.

273

PERKIN, JOHN.

As one of the Earl of Leicester's men in 1572 John Perkin signed a letter addressed to the Earl requesting his continued patronage; he is named in the license granted to Leicester's players on May 10, 1574 (*M.S.C.*, i. 262, 348). Possibly he is to be identified with the Parkins, who, dressed as a fool, appeared as one of the Lord of Misrule's sons in the Christmas festivities of 1552–53 at the Court of Edward VI (Feuillerat, *Edw. & Mary*, p. 120).

PERKINS, RICHARD.

Richard Perkins is first known as a member of Worcester's company in 1602–03. He authorized payment on behalf of Worcester's men on September 4, 1602; and he borrowed 10s. from Henslowe on March 12, 1603, when accompanying that troupe on a provincial tour (*H.D.*, i. 178; ii. 301). Early in the reign of James I Worcester's men became Queen Anne's company. As a Queen's man Perkins is named in the list of players who took part in the coronation procession of March 15, 1604; in the patent of April 15, 1609; and in the duplicate license issued to the traveling company on January 7, 1612 (*Eliz. Stage*, ii. 229; *M.S.C.*, i. 270; Murray, ii. 343). With the Queen's men he acted a part, probably Brachiano, in Webster's *White Devil*. In a note appended to the first edition (1612), the playwright commends the actors and especially Perkins (*Webster*, ed. Sampson, pp. 183–84, 206):

For the action of the play, twas generally well, and I dare affirme, with the joint testimony of some of their owne quality, for the true imitation of life, without striving to make nature a monster, the best that ever became them: whereof as I make a generall acknowledgment, so in particular I must remember the well approved industry of my friend Maister Perkins, and confesse the worth of his action did crowne both the beginning and end.

He was concerned in the dispute between the Queen's men and Thomas Greene's widow, and on June 3, 1617, refused to sign an agreement with Susan Baskervile (*Eliz. Stage*, ii. 238). He may have been with the Queen's troupe at Norwich on May 6, 1615, and May 31, 1617, for his name is given in the abstracts of the license in the town records (Murray, ii. 340, 343). On October 2, 1617, he, with others of the Queen's troupe, petitioned the Sessions of Peace against the various presentments that had been issued against them for not "repayringe the Highwayes neere the Red Bull" (Jeaffreson, *Middlesex*, ii. 170). At Queen Anne's funeral on May 13, 1619, he was a representative of her London company (Murray, i. 196). On November 18, 1619, he appeared as a witness in the Smith-Beeston lawsuit. On June 27, 1620, his wife, Elizabeth, testified in the same dispute as to the whereabouts of Emanuel Read, who was then in Ireland (Wallace, *N.U.S.*, ix. 321, 335). The burial of "Elizabeth wife of Richard Perkins" is recorded in the register of St. James, Clerkenwell, on March 31, 1621 (Hovenden, iv. 151). After the Queen's death her London troupe was known as the Players of the Revels at the Red Bull. Perkins is noted in 1622 as one of the "chiefe players" of this company (Adams, *Dram. Rec.*, p. 63), and is named with Robert Lee in a warrant of November, 1622 (*M.S.C.*, i. 284). About May, 1623, the company seems to have disbanded, for on May 23 of that year John Cumber and two of his fellows pleaded to be excused from their payments to Susan Baskervile, on the ground that the other players named in the original agreement were either dead or with another organization (Murray, i. 199). Perkins evidently soon joined the King's men. As a member of the King's company he is mentioned in a livery allowance of 1623–24, and in the list of players who attended King James's funeral on May 7, 1625 (Stopes, *Jahrbuch*, xlvi. 93; Murray, i. 161, opp. 172). In 1623 he was living "att the vpper end of St. Iohns Streete" (Wallace, *Jahrbuch*, xlvi. 347). He seems to have become a member of Queen Henrietta's company at the Cockpit in Drury Lane at its formation soon after the accession of Charles I. With this organization he continued until 1637 (Murray, i.

265–67), appearing as Sir John Belfare in Shirley's *Wedding* (*c.* 1626); as Fitzwater in Davenport's *King John and Matilda* (*c.* 1629), where his "action gave grace to the play"; as Captain Goodlack in Heywood's *Fair Maid of the West*, Part I (*c.* 1630); and as Hanno, in Nabbes's *Hannibal and Scipio* (1635). He also played Barabas in a revival of Marlowe's *Jew of Malta*, by the Queen's men at the Cockpit, as shown by Heywood's prologue to the play in 1633. Heywood praises Edward Alleyn, probably the original performer of Barabas, and deprecates comparison between Alleyn and Perkins (Marlowe, *Works*, ii. 6):

> Nor is't hate
> To merit, in him ["Perkins," in the margin] who
>   doth personate
> Our Jew this day; nor is it his ambition
> To exceed or equal, being of condition
> More modest: this is all that he intends,
> (And that too, at the urgence of some friends)
> To prove his best, and, if none here gainsay it,
> The part he hath studied, and intends to play it.

From Wright's *Historia Histrionica* (1699) we learn that Perkins was among the "eminent actors" listed as "of principal note at the Cockpit" (Hazlitt's *Dodsley*, xv. 406). At the reorganization of Queen Henrietta's men about October, 1637, he joined the Revels company at Salisbury Court, as shown by Herbert's record (Adams, *Dram. Rec.*, p. 66): "I disposed of Perkins, Sumner, Sherlock and Turner, to Salisbury Court, and joynd them with the best of that company." The amalgamated company evidently retained the name of the Queen's players, and Perkins apparently continued with the troupe at Salisbury Court until the closing of the playhouses in 1642 (Adams, *Playhouses*, p. 380). He was obviously one of the managers of the company, for a warrant of December 10, 1638, states that liveries are "to be delivered to Richard Perkins for himself and the others his fellows"; on January 8, 1641, he and Anthony Turner are named in another warrant for liveries "for themselves and twelve of their fellows of the

Queen's Majesty's company of players" (Stopes, *Jahrbuch*, xlvi. 101, 103). Wright tells us that "Perkins and Sumner of the Cockpit kept house together at Clerkenwell, and were there buried . . . some years before the Restoration" (Hazlitt's *Dodsley*, xv. 411–12). He is probably the Richard Perkins whose burial is recorded in the register of St. James, Clerkenwell, on April 20, 1650 (Hovenden, iv. 284). His portrait at Dulwich is described as: "Mr. Pirkines, the actor, in a 3 quarters cloth; in a gilt frame" (Warner, p. 207). He contributed prefatory verses to Heywood's *Apology for Actors* (1612), p. 9:

> *To my loving friend and fellow, Thomas Heywood*
> Thou that do'st raile at me for seeing a play,
> How wouldst thou have me spend my idle houres?
> Wouldst have me in a taverne drinke all day,
> Melt in the sunne's heate, or walke out in showers?
>
> Gape at the Lottery from morne till even,
> To heare whose mottoes blankes have, and who prises?
> To hazzard all at dice (chance six or seven)
> To card or bowle? my humour this despises.
>
> But thou wilt answer: None of these I need,
> Yet my tir'd spirits must have recreation.
> What shall I doe that may retirement breed,
> Or how refresh my selfe, and in what fashion?
>
> To drabbe, to game, to drinke, all these I hate:
> Many enormous things depend on these.
> My faculties truely to recreate
> With modest mirth, and my selfe best to please,
>
> Give me a play, that no distaste can breed.
> Prove thou a spider, and from flowers sucke gall;
> I'le, like a bee, take hony from a weed;
> For I was never puritannicall.
>
> I love no publicke soothers, private scorners,
> That raile 'gainst letchery, yet love a harlot:
> When I drinke, 'tis in sight, and not in corners;
> I am no open saint, and secret varlet.

Still, when I come to playes, I love to sit
That all may see me in a publicke place,
Even in the stages front, and not to git
Into a nooke, and hood-winke there my face.

*This is the difference: such would have men deeme
Them what they are not; I am what I seeme.*

RICH. PERKINS.

PERKINS, WILL.

Possibly an actor whose name accidentally crept into the text of *George a Green*, printed in 1599 "As it was sundry times acted by the seruants of the right Honourable the Earle of Sussex." At line 1073 (Greene, *Plays*, ed. Collins, ii. 213), George says:

Heere, Will Perkins, take my purse,
Fetch me a stand of Ale.

PERRY, WILLIAM.

On February 27, 1615, a license was granted to William Hovell, William Perry, and Nathan May, presumably as representatives of the King's Revels company. Nothing is heard of these players in London, and their only recorded provincial appearance is at Norwich on June 17, 1615. Their license was apparently condemned and withdrawn by order of the Earl of Pembroke on July 16, 1616 (Murray, ii. 10, 340, 343). By October 31, 1617, Perry had become associated with Robert Lee, Philip Rosseter, and Nicholas Long as patentees for the Queen's Revels company, and visited Norwich on August 29, 1618. After the death of Queen Anne in March, 1619, this organization was known as the Children of the Revels to the late Queen Anne. On April 9, 1623, a confirmation of the 1617 patent was granted to the company, which visited Norwich on May 24, 1623, with Perry as manager. The troupe is recorded in provincial records until 1627, and Perry doubtless continued as its leader. By September 18, 1629, the company had apparently disbanded, for on that date Perry received a commission to organize a group of players under the title of "His Majesty's servants of the city of York" (Murray, i.

361, 362; ii. 8, 345, 347). Nothing further is known of this troupe. On November 10, 1629, Perry and Richard Weekes were granted a new license as managers of the Red Bull company, and Perry remained as leader of these players until the closing of the theatres in 1642. The provincial annals record his visits to Reading on November 30, 1629, and again in November, 1630; Doncaster, July 15, 1632; Leicester, after February 19, 1633; Coventry, before December 4, 1633; Norwich, July 3, 1633, and March, 1634; Leicester, before November 22, 1635; Canterbury, March, 1636; Doncaster, April 24, 1636(?); Norwich, May 11, 1636; and Coventry, between December, 1641, and December 7, 1642 (Murray, i. 272–78; ii. 252, 254, 257, 318, 354, 358, 386).

PERSJ, RUPERT.

See Robert Percy.

PERSONN, JOHANN.

Johann Personn was associated with a troupe of English players at the Danish Court during 1579–80 (Bolte, *Jahrbuch*, xlvi. 99 ff.).

PERSTEN, RUPERT.

See Robert Percy.

PERY, ROBERT.

A member of the Chapel Royal from 1529 to 1531 (*Eliz. Stage*, ii. 27*n*.).

PERY, WILLIAM.

A member of the Chapel Royal in 1530 (*Eliz. Stage*, ii. 27*n*.).

"PETER"(?).

Possibly a King's man. The 1623 Shakespeare folio edition of *The Taming of the Shrew*, IV. iv. 68, gives the stage-direction: "Enter Peter." Peter is perhaps Tranio's servant, who does not speak; and the name may be that of the character, not of the actor taking the part.

PETTINGTON, HENRY.

Henry Pettington is named in a Ticket of Privilege granted on January 12, 1636, to the attendants "employed by his Majesty's servants the players of the Blackfriars, and of special use to them both on the Stage and otherwise for his Majesty's disport and service" (Stopes, *Jahrbuch*, xlvi. 99).

PFLUGBEIL, AUGUST.

During 1614–15 August Pflugbeil is recorded in Germany with a group of English players in the service of John Sigismund, Elector of Brandenburg (Cohn, p. lxxxviii).

PHEN, EZEKIEL.

See Ezekiel Fenn.

PHILIP, ROBERT.

A member of the Chapel Royal in 1514 (*Eliz. Stage*, ii. 27n.).

PHILLIPP, PETER.

A member of the Children of Paul's in 1574 (Hillebrand, *Child Actors*, p. 111).

PHILLIPPE, ROBERT.

A "momer," who was buried at St. Leonard's, Shoreditch, on April 9, 1559 (Collier, *Actors*, p. 79n.).

PHILLIPS, AUGUSTINE.

Augustine Phillips played Sardanapalus in "Sloth" of *2 Seven Deadly Sins* for Strange's men about 1590 (Greg, *H.P.*, p. 152; *R.E.S.*, i. 262), and is named in the traveling license granted by the Privy Council to Strange's company on May 6, 1593 (*Eliz. Stage*, ii. 123). Subsequently, he joined the Chamberlain's men, presumably when the troupe was organized in 1594. His name occurs in the actor-lists of *Every Man in his Humor* (1598) and of *Every Man out of his Humor* (1599), both played by the Chamberlain's company. He was one of the original shareholders in the

Globe syndicate on February 21, 1599 (Adams, *Playhouses*, p. 239). On February 18, 1601, he was called to testify concerning the performance of *Richard II* by the Chamberlain's men, because the play was regarded by some persons as a means of predisposing the mind of the populace to the cause of the Earl of Essex in his attempt to dethrone Queen Elizabeth (Colllier, iii. 324). In 1603 the Chamberlain's men passed under royal patronage; Phillips is named in the patent granted to the King's company on May 19, 1603 (*M.S.C.*, i. 264). As a King's man he appears in the 1623 folio list of Shakespearean players; in the actor-list of *Sejanus* (1603); and among the actors who took part in the coronation procession on March 15, 1604. "Phillips his gigg of the slyppers" was entered in the Stationers' Registers on May 26, 1595 (Arber, ii. 298). Children of Augustine Phillips, who is described as "*histrionis,*" "player of interludes," or "player," are recorded in the registers of St. Saviour's, Southwark (Collier, iii. 322–23): Magdalen (baptized September 29, 1594), Rebecca (baptized July 11, 1596), and Awstyn or Augustine (baptized November 29, 1601; buried July 1, 1604). The register of St. Bodolph Aldgate records the burial of "A childe daughter of Augustine Phillipps, A player," on September 7, 1597 (Denkinger, *P.M.L.A.*, xli. 105). The token-books of St. Saviour's give his residence as Horse-shoe Court in 1593 and 1595, later near the Swan playhouse in Paris Garden, Montague Close in 1601, Bradshaw's Rents in 1602, and Horse-shoe Court again in 1604 (Collier, iii. 325; Rendle, *Bankside*, p. xxv). Bentley (*T.L.S.*, Nov. 15, 1928, p. 856) gives his address in 1593 as "bulhed allye." By May 4, 1605, when he made his will, he had moved to Mortlake, Surrey, where he "lately purchased . . . house and land." His will mentions his wife, Anne; his daughters, Magdalen, Rebecca, Anne, and Elizabeth; his mother, Agnes Bennett; his brothers, William and James Webb; his sister, Margery Borne, perhaps wife of William Borne, *alias* Bird (*q.v.*), with her sons, Myles and Phillipps; and his sister, Elizabeth Goughe, who had married Robert Goughe (*q.v.*) in 1603 (Collier,

iii. 327–29). His personal relations with the members of his company are reflected in legacies of £5 to "the hyred men of the company which I am of"; 30s. gold-pieces to his "fellowes" William Shakespeare and Henry Condell, and his "servaunte" Christopher Beeston; 20s. gold-pieces to his "fellowes" Lawrence Fletcher, Robert Armin, Richard Cowley, Alexander Cook, and Nicholas Tooley; and "a boule of silver of the value of fyve pounds a piece" to John Heminges, Richard Burbage, and William Sly, the overseers of the will. Samuel Gilburne "my late apprentice," received 40s. and "my mouse colloured velvit hose, and a white teffety dublet, a blacke taffety sute, my purple cloke, sword, and dagger, and my base viall." James Sands, "my apprentice," was bequeathed 40s. and "a citterne, a bandore, and a lute, to be paid and delivered unto him at the expiration of his terme of yeres in his indenture of apprenticehood." His wife Anne is appointed executrix, on condition that if she re-marries she is to have "no parte or portion of my goods or chattels." Robert Goughe is a witness to the will. Phillips died between May 4, when he made his will, and May 13, when the will was proved by his widow. The will was proved again on May 16, 1607, because Anne Phillips forfeited her right by marrying John Witter within less than two years after the death of her first husband. This marriage subsequently led to a lawsuit between Witter, who squandered his wife's estate, and Heminges and Condell, concerning Phillips's share in the Globe property (Wallace, *N.U.S.*, x. 305 ff.). Early in the reign of James I Phillips was mentioned in a notice of heraldic irregularities by William Smith, Rouge Dragon Pursuivant in the College of Heralds, who states that "Phillipps the player had graven in a gold ring armes of Sr Wm Phillipp, Lord Bardolph, with the said L. Bardolph's cote quartred, which I shewed to Mr York at a small graver's shopp in Foster Lane" (Adams, *Shakespeare*, p. 247). Heywood, *Apology for Actors* (1612), p. 43, names him among other dead players, whose "deserts" he commemorates.

PICKERING, JAMES.

James Pickering, mason, is mentioned as an unlicensed player of Bowlby, Yorkshire, in 1612 (*Eliz. Stage*, i. 305*n*.).

PICKLEHERRING.

See Robert Reynolds.

PIERS, EDWARD.

See Edward Pearce.

PIG, JOHN.

John Pig (Pyk, Pyge, or Pigge) was Edward Alleyn's boy or apprentice. A letter from Pig to Joan Alleyn, undated, but presumably written during the provincial tour of Strange's men in 1593, is preserved, in which he refers to himself as "yor petty prety pratlyng parlyng pyg." He appears as a witness on August 17, 1594, and March 27, 1599. His name occurs in the inventories of the Admiral's company in 1598: "j red sewt of cloth for pyge, layed with whitt lace." With the Admiral's men he played the title-rôle in *Alice Pierce*, about 1597; Andreo in *Frederick and Basilea*, 1597; and an unindentified part in the non-extant *Troilus and Cressida*, about 1599 (*H.D.*, ii. 303; *H.P.*, pp. 41, 115, 153, 154; Warner, p. 127).

PIGGE, JOHN.

See John Pig.

PLUMFIELD, THOMAS.

Thomas Plumfield's name appears in a warrant of May 10, 1632, appointing several of Prince Charles's men as Grooms of the Chamber (Stopes, *Jahrbuch*, xlvi. 96).

PLUMMER, JOHN.

Master of the Chapel Royal, 1444–55 (Wallace, *Evolution*, pp. 21 ff.).

POKELEY, RICHARD.

A London player in 1550, named in an order demanding that all plays be licensed by the King or his Council (Harrison, *England*, iv. 314).

POLE.

The gatekeeper at Paul's, named as a legatee in the will of Sebastian Westcott, dated April 3, 1582 (*Eliz. Stage*, ii. 16*n*.).

POLLARD, THOMAS.

Thomas Pollard appears to have begun his theatrical career with the King's men as John Shank's apprentice, as suggested by the *Sharers' Papers* of 1635 (Halliwell-Phillipps, *Outlines*, i. 316). He was evidently with the King's men from about 1617 to the closing of the playhouses in 1642, and assumed parts in the following plays presented by that company (Murray, i. opp. 172): *The Queen of Corinth* (c. 1617); Holderus and a servant in *Sir John van Olden Barnavelt* (1619; ed. Frijlinck, p. clx); *The Humorous Lieutenant* (c. 1619); Silvio in *The Duchess of Malfi* (1619–23); *The Laws of Candy* (c. 1621); *The Island Princess* (c. 1621); *The Spanish Curate* (1622); *The Maid in the Mill* (1623); *The Lover's Progress* (1623); Aelius Lamia in *The Roman Actor* (licensed October 11, 1626); *The Lover's Melancholy* (licensed November 24, 1628); Ubaldo, a wild courtier, in *The Picture* (licensed June 8, 1629); Pinac in *The Wildgoose Chase* (a revival, 1631), with the comment, "Admirably well acted"; and Berecynthus, in *Believe as You List* (licensed May 7, 1631). His name occurs in the submission for playing *The Spanish Viceroy*, without license, December 20, 1624; among the players who took part in King James's funeral procession, May 7, 1625; in the patent of June 24, 1625; and in the cloak allowance of May 6, 1629. In 1635, after the petition by him, Benfield, and Swanston, he controlled one whole share in the Globe and one-third of a share in the Blackfriars (Adams, *Mod. Phil.*, xvii. 8; Halliwell-Phillipps, *Outlines*, i. 313–

14). He is mentioned in the Epilogue to Shirley's *Cardinal*, licensed November 25, 1641 (Shirley, *Works*, v. 352; Adams, *Dram. Rec.*, p. 39):

> [*Within*] Master Pollard! where's master Pollard, for the
> epilogue?   [*He is thrust upon the stage, and falls.*
> *Epilogue* [rising]. I am coming to you, gentlemen; the poet
>   Has helped me thus far on my way, but I'll
>   Be even with him . . .

His name is appended to the dedicatory epistle of the 1647 folio of Beaumont and Fletcher's plays, published by a group of the King's players (Beaumont and Fletcher, *Works*, i. p. x). Wright in *Historia Histrionica* (1699) tells us that "before the wars . . . Pollard and Robinson were comedians . . . of Blackfriars"; that at the outbreak of civil war he was "superannuated"; that he played the Cook in *Rollo, or the Bloody Brother*, at the Cockpit in 1648; and that he "lived single, and had a competent estate, retired to some relations he had in the country, and there ended his life" (Hazlitt, *Dodsley*, xv. 405–06, 409, 411). In *A Key to the Cabinet of the Parliament* (1648), he is mentioned with two other celebrated players (Collier, ii. 38): "We need not any more stage-plays: we thank them [the Puritans] for suppressing them: they save us money; for I'll undertake we can laugh as heartily at Foxley, Peters, and others of their godly ministers, as ever we did at Cane at the Red Bull, Tom Pollard in *The Humorous Lieutenant*, Robins in *The Changling*, or any humourist of them all." On January 28, 1648, he with others of the King's company gave a bond to pay off an old Blackfriars debt to Michael Bowyer's heirs. He was dead by Easter term, 1655 (Hotson, pp. 31–34).

POPE, THOMAS.

During 1586–87 Thomas Pope was on the Continent. The Elsinore pay-roll records that he was in the Danish service from June 17 to September 18, 1586. Soon he went to the Court of the Elector of Saxony, at Dresden, Germany, where he held an appointment as actor-entertainer until July 17, 1587 (Cohn, p. xxv; Riis, *Century Magazine*, lxi. 391; Herz, p. 3). He is next heard of as playing Arbactus in "Sloth" of *2 Seven Deadly Sins* for Strange's men about 1590 (Greg, *H.P.*, p. 152; *R.E.S.*, i. 262). He is named in the traveling license granted by the Privy Council to Strange's company on May 6, 1593 (*Eliz. Stage*, ii. 123). Subsequently he joined the Chamberlain's men, presumably when the troupe was organized in 1594. With this company he played in *Every Man in his Humor* (1598) and *Every Man out of his Humor* (1599). He was joint-payee with John Heminges for the Court performances by the Chamberlain's men from November 27, 1597, to October 2, 1599 (Steele, pp. 111, 113, 116). On August 30, 1598, William Bird obtained a loan of 10s. from Henslowe "to folowe the sewt agenst Thomas poope" (*H.D.*, ii. 303). He was one of the original shareholders in the Globe organization on February 21, 1599 (Adams, *Playhouses*, p. 239). In 1600 he and John Singer, of the Admiral's company, are mentioned by Samuel Rowlands in *The Letting of Humours Blood in the Head-Vaine*, Satire iv, p. 63 (*Works*, i):

> What meanes *Singer* then?
> And *Pope* the Clowne, to speak so Boorish, when
> They counterfaite the Clownes vpon the Stage?

His name occurs in the 1623 folio list of actors in Shakespeare's plays. He had doubtless retired before the Chamberlain's troupe passed under royal patronage, for he is not mentioned in the patent granted to the King's men on May 19, 1603. The token-books of St. Saviour's, Southwark, give his residence as Blamer's Rents in 1593, Wrench's Rents in 1595, and Mr. Langley's New Rents in 1596, 1598, 1600, and 1602 (Collier, iii. 359; Rendle, *Bankside*, p. xxvi). The register of St. Botolph, Bishopsgate, records the marriage of a Thomas Pope and Elizabeth Baly on December 20, 1584 (Collier, *Actors*, p. xxxvi); but the wording of the player's will seems to indicate that he was never married (Collier, iii. 359–63). He made his will on July 22, 1603, and it was proved on February 13, 1604. He left £100 and considerable property to Suzan Gasquine, "whom I have brought up ever since she was born"; his shares in the Globe and Curtain to Mary Clark, *alias* Wood, and Thomas Bromley; to Robert Goughe and John Edmans or Edmonds (*q.v.*), "all my wearing apparel, and all my arms, to be equally divided between them"; and £20 each to his mother Agnes Webbe, and his brothers John and William Pope. Together with his fellow-actor Augustine Phillips (*q.v.*), Pope is mentioned in a complaint against heraldic irregularities: "Pope the player would have no other armes but the armes of Sr Tho. Pope, Chancelor of ye Augmentations" (Adams, *Shakespeare*, p. 248). Heywood, *Apology for Actors* (1612), p. 43, praises him with other dead players whose "deserts yet live in the remembrance of many."

POWLTON, THOMAS.

Thomas Powlton is not mentioned in the license given to Worcester's troupe on January 14, 1583, but he appears as "my lord of Worcesters man" on March 6, 1584, when the players were engaged in a dispute with the authorities at Leicester (*Eliz. Stage*, ii. 222–23).

PRICE, JOHN.

John Price, a musician, was probably with a company of English players (known as the Hessian comedians) in the service of Maurice of Hesse, when he visited Stuttgart in 1609. Subsequently he is known as a celebrated musician, especially as a flutist, at the Courts of Stuttgart, 1625, and Dresden, 1629 (Cohn, pp. xcvii*n*., cxxxviii).

PRICE, RICHARD.

A writer signing himself "Dramaticus," in *Shakespeare Society's Papers*, iv. 110, describes a copy of Dekker's *Shoemaker's Holiday* with alleged manuscript notes giving the cast of the play as produced by the Admiral's men about 1600. To Price is assigned the part of Scott. Greg discredits the list as "an obvious forgery" (*H.D.*, ii. 203).

PRICE, RICHARD.

A "Rychard Pryore" in a household list of Prince Henry's players in 1610 is presumably identical with the Richard Price named in the patent of January 11, 1613, granted to the Palsgrave's men, who had passed under the patronage of the Palsgrave after the death of Prince Henry in November, 1612 (*Eliz. Stage*, ii. 188, 190). He is known as a Palsgrave's man until 1624. With other members of the Palsgrave's company he appears as a lessee of the Fortune playhouse on October 31, 1618, and of the new Fortune on May 20, 1622 (*H.P.*, pp. 27, 29). He is named in Herbert's list of the troupe in 1622 (Adams, *Dram. Rec.*, p. 63). On April 9, 1620, he dined with Edward Alleyn (Warner, p. 184). In 1623 he lived "in White Crosse Streete" (Wallace, *Jahrbuch*, xlvi. 348). The registers of St. Giles's, Cripplegate, record children of his from 1620 to 1627, describing him as gentleman, yeoman, or player (*Eliz. Stage*, ii. 335), and record his own burial in 1627 (Malcolm, *Lond. Rediv.*, iii. 304). On April 30, 1624, he and others of the Palsgrave's men entered into a bond to Richard Gunnell, manager of the company (Hotson, pp. 52–53).

PROCTOR.

Proctor is mentioned in the plot of the non-extant *Troilus and Cressida*, an Admiral's play presented about 1599 (*Eliz. Stage*, ii. 158). In his review of Chambers's *Elizabethan Stage*, Greg (*R.E.S.*, i. 110) says that Proctor is "evidently a character, not an actor."

PRUN, PETER DE.

A company of English players under the leadership of Peter de Prun, of Brussels, visited Nuremberg in April, 1594 (Trautmann, *Archiv*, xiv. 116).

PRYNCE, RICHARD.

A member of the Children of Paul's in 1554 (Hillebrand, *Child Actors*, p. 110).

PRYORE, RYCHARD.

See Richard Price.

PUDSEY, EDWARD.

Edward Pudsey was the leader of a troupe of English players at Strassburg in June, 1628, and appears with Robert Reynolds's company in Germany during 1640 (Herz, pp. 54, 55). He is perhaps identical with the Edward Pudsey whose manuscript notebook contains Shakespearean extracts (printed by R. Savage, in *Stratford-upon-Avon Note Books*, 1888, i).·

PULHAM, GEORGE.

A "half sharer" in Queen Anne's company, "who died, one of the said Companie," shortly before Thomas Greene's death in August, 1612. His executors were given £40 by the Queen's men for his half-share (Fleay, *Stage*, p. 280; Murray, i. 193).

PYE, JOHN.

A "momer," whose son Samuel was baptized at St. Leonard's, Shoreditch, on May 28, 1559 (*Eliz. Stage*, ii. 335).

PYGE, JOHN.

See John Pig.

PYK, JOHN.

See John Pig.

PYKMAN, PHILLIP.

A member of the Chapel Royal about 1600–01. In Henry Clifton's complaint to the Star Chamber on December 15, 1601, as to how boys were pressed for the Chapel at Blackfriars, Phillip Pykman is named as one so taken, and is described with Thomas Grymes as "apprentices to Richard and Georg Chambers" (Wallace, *Blackfriars*, p. 80).

PYTCHER, CAROLUS.

A member of the Children of Paul's in 1598 (Hillebrand, *Child Actors*, p. 111).

RADSTONE, JOHN.

A London player in 1550, named in an order demanding that all plays be licensed by the King or his Council (Harrison, *England*, iv. 314).

RAINESCROFTE, THOMAS.

A member of the Children of Paul's in 1598 (Hillebrand, *Child Actors*, p. 111).

RASTELL, WILLIAM.

A partner with Edward Kirkham and Thomas Kendall in the management of the Second Blackfriars playhouse, as shown by Articles of Agreement signed on April 20, 1602 (Adams, *Playhouses*, p. 213). He died in 1608 (*Eliz. Stage*, ii. 335).

RAWLYNS, JOHN.

A London player in 1550, named in an order demanding that all plays be licensed by the King or his Council (Harrison, *England*, iv. 314).

RAYE, RALPH.

Ralph Raye borrowed £10 from Henslowe about May 13, 1594. He is described as "my lorde chamberlenes man," but whether he was an actor or a common servant is not known (*H.D.*, ii. 305).

READE, EMANUEL.

The 1679 folio of Beaumont and Fletcher names Emanuel Reade as one of the "principal actors" in *The Coxcomb* and in *The Honest Man's Fortune*, both of which were probably performed by the Lady Elizabeth's company in 1613 (*Eliz. Stage*, ii. 251). By 1616 he had joined Queen Anne's men, for in June of that year he is mentioned in the Baskervile papers as a member of the company.

On June 3 of the following year he refused to sign an agreement with Susan Baskervile (*Eliz. Stage*, ii. 237). About 1617 he took up permanent residence in Ireland, as shown by the records of the Smith-Beeston lawsuit (Wallace, *N.U.S.*, ix. 335–36); thus his name disappears from dramatic annals. On June 27, 1620, Elizabeth Perkins, wife of the well-known actor Richard Perkins, made "othe that Emanuell Reade hath made his abode in Jreland by the space of two or three yeares last past or thereaboutes with his wief & familie and about Easter last did come into England and did lye often tymes in the howse of the said xpofer Beeston & was much in his company whilest he was in England. And about Whitsontyde last the saide Emanuell Reade went againe into Jreland & at his departure he sayde that he thought he should never returne agayne into England."

READE, JOHN.

The registers of St. Bodolph Aldgate record the burial on September 13, 1600, of "A woman Chyld daughter to Jhon Read a Player." The same registers record the burial on June 14, 1608, of "Anne Reade a norse [*sic*] childe daughter to John Reade of Saviours parish in Southwarke" (Denkinger, *P.M.L.A.*, xli. 106).

READE, TIMOTHY.

Timothy Reade first appears as Cardona, Gratiana's maid, in Shirley's *Wedding*, a play acted about May, 1626, by Queen Henrietta's men at the Cockpit in Drury Lane. He is recorded at Norwich on March 10, 1635, when his troupe, presumably the King's Revels, applied for permission to act in that town (Murray, i. opp. 266, 279–80). He is one of the speakers in *The Stage-Players Complaint, in a pleasant Dialogue between Cane of the Fortune and Reed of the Friers, deploring their sad and solitary condition for the want of Imployment, in this heavie and Contagious time of the Plague in London* (1641). In *The Complaint*, Cane and Reed are brought together in the street conversing about their misfortunes. The dialogue commences thus:

Cane. Stay, Reed. Whither away so speedily? What, you goe as if you meant to leape over the Moon now! What's the matter?

Reede. The matter is plain enough. You incuse me of my nimble feet, but I thinke your tongue runnes a little faster and you contend as much to outstrip facetious Mercury in your tongue, as lame Vulcan in my feete.

In the next speeches, and for the rest of the dialogue, Cane is called *Quick* in the prefixes, and Reade, *Light,* which are perhaps the nicknames by which they were then popularly known (Hazlitt, *Eng. Drama & Stage*, p. 253). From *Perfect Occurrences of Every Daie Journall* we learn that Reade was arrested on October 6, 1647, during a performance of Beaumont and Fletcher's *A King and no King*, at Salisbury Court (Rollins, *Stud. in Phil.*, xviii. 283): "The Sheriffes of the City of *London* with their officers went thither, and found a great number of people; some young Lords, and other eminent persons; and the men and women with the Boxes, [that took monies] fled. The Sheriffes brought away *Tim Reede* the Foole, and the people cryed out for their monies, but slunke away like a company of drowned Mice without it." That he was a popular comedian is shown by two allusions to him. Edmund Gayton applauds him in *Pleasant Notes upon Don Quixot* (1654), p. 86: "when as at a Bartholmewtide, the Fights and Travels of this great *Knight-Errant* are to be seen, and himselfe represented (for these honours came after his death) to the life, by *Timotheo Reado* of *Tiveri-ae*, who was the most incomparable mimicke upon the face of the Earth." He is also praised in Thomas Goffe's *Careless Shepherdess*, published in 1656 but acted at Court about 1625–29 (Collier, *Bibl. Acc.*, iv. 93; Steele, *Plays at Court*, p. 280):

> There is ne'er a part
> About him but breaks jests.—
> I never saw Reade peeping through the curtain,
> But ravishing joy entered my heart.

READING, WILLIAM.

A London player in 1550, named in an order demanding that all plays be licensed by the King or his Council (Harrison, *England*, iv. 314). By December 25, 1559, Reading was a Court Interluder, and probably continued so until his death in 1563 (*Eliz. Stage*, ii. 83, 84; Murray, i. 3).

REASON, GILBERT.

Gilbert Reason was a member of Prince Charles's troupe from 1610 to 1625. He is named in the patent of March 30, 1610; and as leader of the traveling company, by a duplicate license of May 31, 1613. On March 30, 1616, he visited Norwich. He is mentioned in Pembroke's order of July 16, 1616, for the suppression of certain irregular provincial troupes; but he must have satisfied the requirements for a *bona fide* company, and continued to appear in the provinces. The Coventry accounts record him and his company on August 24, 1621. Any doubt as to the legality of his patent in 1616 was certainly overcome by November 20, 1622, as shown by his carrying on provincial tours the Lord Chamberlain's warrant of that date, "Comandinge to seise all patents that shall not be vnder the seale of office of the master of the Revells." He and William Eaton were payees for the Prince's men at Coventry on December 23, 1622. He is recorded at Norwich on May 31, 1623, and January 29, 1625. The provincial company under his management seems to have disbanded before May 7, 1625, by which date he was associated with the Prince's London players who took part in King James's funeral procession (Murray, i. 161, 230–33, 237, 240–42; ii. 249, 341, 347, 351).

REDFORD, JOHN.

From Thomas Tusser's autobiographical verses, printed with the 1573 edition of his *Five Hundred Pointes of Good Husbandrie* (ed. Payne and Herrtage, pp. xiii, 207), we learn that John Redford was Master of the Children of Paul's, about 1540:

> But marke the chance, my self to vance,
> By friendships lot, to Paules I got,
> So found I grace, a certaine space,
>   still to remaine:
> With Redford there, the like no where,
> For cunning such, and vertue much,
> By whom some part of Musicke art,
>   so did I gaine.

His play, *Wyt and Science* (*c.* 1530–48), is reprinted in Adams, *Chief Pre-Shakespearean Dramas*, p. 325.

REEVE, RALPH.

Ralph Reeve is known on the Continent from 1603 to 1609. For some years he was associated with Richard Machin, formerly a member of the Hessian troupe. He visited Frankfort at Easter, 1603, 1605, and 1606, and during the autumn of 1605. By 1608 he had come under the patronage of Maurice of Hesse, and had succeeded Machin as leader of the Hessian company. He continued as manager of this troupe of English players until the autumn of 1609. His appearances are recorded at the Frankfort Easter and autumn fairs of 1608 and 1609 (Herz, pp. 39–40). He had returned to England by August 10, 1611, when he visited Norwich with a company of actors, presumably the Children of the Queen's Revels. As leader of these players he presented a license that had been issued to Philip Rosseter, and affirmed that he was Rosseter. The town authorities discovered the deception, and he confessed that his name was Reeve (Murray, i. 359; ii. 339). On June 3, 1615, he and Rosseter and others are named as patentees for the erection of Porter's Hall playhouse in Blackfriars (Adams, *Playhouses*, p. 343).

RESTER.

As an Admiral's man, Rester appeared as a Cannibal in the procession of *1 Tamar Cam*, about October, 1602 (*H.P.*, p. 154).

REYNOLDS, ROBERT.

Robert Reynolds appears as a member of Queen Anne's company in June, 1616 and 1617, when he is mentioned in the Baskervile papers (*Eliz. Stage*, ii. 237, 238). The Middlesex records name him and his wife Jane in an indictment for non-attendance at church in 1616 and 1617 (Jeaffreson, ii. 120, 127). He is not otherwise known in England, but evidently attained considerable popularity in Germany under the clown-name Pickleherring. He accompanied John Green at Danzig in July, 1616, and Robert Browne at Strassburg in June and July, and at Frankfort for the autumn fair, 1618. He apparently acted Nobody in the play of *Nobody and Somebody*, to which the clown refers in his farewell speech on leaving Frankfort to go to Prague:

> Vorm Jahr war ich gering,
> Ein aus der Maszen gut Pickelharing,
> Mein Antlitz in tausend Manieren,
> Konnt ich holdselig figurieren.
> Alles was ich erbracht,
> Das hat man ja stattlich belacht,
> Ich war der Niemand kennt ihr mich?

> Last year I was a mighty good Pickleherring,
> I could twist my face in a thousand ways,
> Everything that I did gave great amusement,
> I was Nobody: do you recognize me?

By 1626–27 he had returned to Green's players, when they visited Frankfort, Dresden, and Torgau. Green now disappears from the German records, and Reynolds seems to have taken the leadership of the troupe. In the housing-list at Torgau in 1627, he is called Pickleherring. From Torgau the company journeyed to Dresden, thence to Nuremberg in July, and to Frankfort for the autumn fair of the same year (Herz, pp. 30–32, 114). During 1628 he visited Frankfort at the Easter fair; Cologne in May; Nuremberg in July; and Frankfort again for the autumn fair. He is recorded at Cologne in 1631, and is mentioned on July 11, 1640, in a letter from Elector George William, granting safe conduct to certain players in Germany (Herz, pp. 54 ff.).

REYNOLDS, WILLIAM.

William Reynolds acted Francisco, a Jesuit, in Massinger's *Renegado*, printed in 1630 as presented by Queen Henrietta's men at the Cockpit in Drury Lane (Murray, i. opp. 266).

RHODES, JOHN.

John Rhodes is named in a Protection from Arrest issued by Herbert on December 27, 1624, to twenty-one men "imployed by the Kinges Maiesties servantes in theire quallity of Playinge as Musitions and other necessary attendantes" (Adams, *Dram. Rec.*, p. 74). By 1628 he was a London bookseller (McKerrow, *Dictionary*, p. 227). He probably continued as a bookseller through the period of the Civil War and Commonwealth, and became one of the first theatrical managers of the Restoration. Downes (*Ros. Ang.*, p. 17) informs us that "In the Year 1659 . . . Mr. Rhodes a Bookseller being Wardrobe-Keeper formerly (as I am inform'd) to King Charles the First's Company of Comedians in Black-Friars; getting a License from the then Governing State, fitted up a House then for Acting call'd the Cock-pit in Drury Lane, and in a short time Compleated his Company." His troupe, which included Thomas Betterton, the greatest actor of his time, had by November 5, 1660, passed under the management of William Davenant (Adams, *Dram. Rec.*, p. 96), and subsequently became the Duke of York's men at Lincoln's Inn Fields (Nicoll, *Rest. Drama*, p. 283). Rhodes apparently organized another company, for he received payment for a Court performance of November 1, 1662, and was granted a license to travel in the provinces on January 2, 1663. His company was probably taken into the patronage of the Duchess of Portsmouth (Nicoll, *op. cit.*, pp. 278–79).

RICE, JOHN.

John Rice is described as Heminges's "boy" when he took part in the entertainment given by the Merchant Taylors in honor of

King James on July 16, 1607 (*Eliz. Stage*, ii. 321). On May 31,
1610, he was associated with Richard Burbage in a pageant on
the Thames in honor of the creation of Prince Henry as Prince
of Wales. He appeared as "Corinea, a very fayre and beautifull
Nimphe, representing the Genius of olde Corineus Queene, and
the Prouince of Cornewall, suited in her watrie habit yet riche
and costly, with a Coronet of Pearles and Cockle Shelles on her
head" (Wallace, London *Times*, March 28, 1913, p. 6). By August
29, 1611, he was a member of the Lady Elizabeth's troupe, joining
his fellow-actors in giving Henslowe a bond of £500 to perform
"certen articles" of agreement (*H.P.*, pp. 18, 111). Subsequently
he was again with the King's men. With this company he acted
a captain and Barnavelt's servant in *Sir John van Olden Barnavelt*
(ed. Frijlinck, p. clx), in August, 1619; the Marquesse of Pescara
in *The Duchess of Malfi*, at some date between 1619 and 1623;
and a part in *The False One*, about 1620. He appears as a member
of the King's company in the 1623 folio list of Shakespearean
actors; in the livery allowance of April 7, 1621; in the submission for playing *The Spanish Viceroy* without license,
December 20, 1624; at King James's funeral on May 7, 1625;
and in the patent of June 24, 1625 (Adams, *Dram. Rec.*, p. 21;
Chambers and Greg, *M.S.C.*, i. 282; Murray, i. 161, opp. 172;
ii. 146 ff.). His name does not occur in the livery allowance
list of May 6, 1629, by which date he had probably retired
and taken orders, for John Heminges, by his will dated 1630,
left 20*s.* as "a remembrance of my love" to "John Rice,
clerk, of St. Saviour's, in Southwark," and named "Mr.
Rice" as overseer of the will (Collier, iii. 319, 320, 487). A
John Rice lived in Southwark during 1615, and with an
"uxor . . . near the playhouse" in 1619, in 1621, and in 1623,
as shown by the parish token-books (*Eliz. Stage*, ii. 336;
Collier, iii. 488); he is described as "of the Bancksyde" in
the Gervase Markham lawsuit with certain players and
others during 1623 (Wallace, *Jahrbuch*, xlvi. 348).

ROBINS, WILLIAM.

William Robins (sometimes known as Robinson or Robson) appears as a member of Queen Anne's company from 1616 to 1619. He is named in the Baskervile papers of June, 1616 and 1617 (*Eliz. Stage*, ii. 237, 238), and in the list of players who attended the Queen's funeral on May 13, 1619 (Murray, i. 196). After the death of the Queen her London company was known as the Players of the Revels at the Red Bull, of which Robins is noted in 1622 as one of the "chiefe players" (Adams, *Dram. Rec.*, p. 63). He seems subsequently to have transferred his services to the provincial company, the Players of the late Queen Anne, and may reasonably be identified with the Robson named with Martin Slater and one Silvester as payees for the troupe at Coventry on October 16, 1625 (Murray, i. 188; ii. 250). Shortly after this date he must have passed to Queen Henrietta's men at the Cockpit in Drury Lane; and presumably he continued with them until the breaking up of the company in 1637. As a member of this organization he assumed the following parts (Murray, i. opp. 266): Rawbone, a thin citizen, in Shirley's *Wedding* (*c.* May, 1626); Clem, a drawer of wine under Bess Bridges, in Heywood's *Fair Maid of the West*, Part I (*c.* 1630); and Carazie, a eunuch, in Massinger's *Renegado* (printed in 1630). In Wright's *Historia Histrionica* (1699), he is mentioned as a comedian among those "of principal note at the Cockpit" (Hazlitt's *Dodsley*, xv. 406). When Queen Henrietta's company disbanded in 1637 some of the members united with the Revels company at Salisbury Court and others joined Beeston's Boys at the Cockpit; but Robins is not known to have joined either of these troupes. By 1641 he was a King's man, his name appearing in a warrant of January 22 of that year (Stopes, *Jahrbuch*, xlvi. 103). In *A Key to the Cabinet of the Parliament* (1648), he is mentioned with two other celebrated players (Collier, ii. 38): "We need not any more stage-plays: we thank them [the Puritans] for suppressing them: they save us money; for I'll undertake we can laugh as heartily at Foxley,

Peters, and others of their godly ministers, as ever we did at Cane at the Red Bull, Tom Pollard in *The Humorous Lieutenant*, Robins in *The Changling*, or any humourist of them all." In 1623 he lived "on Clarkenwell hill" (Wallace, *Jahrbuch*, xlvi. 348). Evidence seems to favor Collier's identification (*H.E.D.P.*, iii. 479) of William Robins with the Robinson who was killed at Basing House in October, 1645, while fighting for the King, although Wright in *Historia Histrionica* (1699) apparently implies that Richard Robinson (*q.v.*) was the victim of Harrison's thirst for blood. Wright says: "Robinson was killed at the taking of a place (I think Basing House) by Harrison, he that was after hanged at Charing Cross, who refused him quarter, and shot him in the head when he had laid down his arms; abusing Scripture at the same time in saying, *Cursed is he that doth the work of the Lord negligently*" (Hazlitt's *Dodsley*, xv. 409). Hugh Peters, the noted Puritan minister, executed after the Restoration, who was attending Cromwell's army as chaplain, made the following report of the episode to Parliament (Sprigg, *Anglia Rediviva*, 1647, edit. 1854, pp. 150-51): "That he came into Basing-house some time after the storm, on Tuesday the 14th of October 1645 . . . In the several rooms, and about the house, there were slain seventy-four . . . There lay dead upon the ground, major Cuffle, (a man of great account amongst them, and a notorious papist,) slain by the hands of major Harrison, (that godly and gallant gentleman,) and Robinson the player, who, a little before the storm, was known to be mocking and scorning the parliament and our army." In all probability Robins was slain during this affray of 1645. Had he been alive in 1647 his name would doubtless have been appended to the dedicatory epistle of the 1647 folio of Beaumont and Fletcher, published by a group of his fellow-actors of the King's men.

ROBINSON, JAMES.

In 1600 James Robinson was associated with Nathaniel Giles and Henry Evans in the management of the Children of the Chapel

Royal at the Second Blackfriars playhouse (Adams, *Playhouses*, pp. 205, 213).

ROBINSON, JOHN.

John Robinson is recorded at Norwich on March 10, 1635, when his troupe, presumably the King's Revels, applied for permission to act in that town. He played Saufellus, chief of counsel to Silius and Messallina, in Richards's *Messallina, the Roman Empress*, printed in 1640 as "acted with generall applause divers times by the Company of his Majesties Revells" (Murray, i. 279–81). He also contributed laudatory verses to Richards's play (ed. Skemp, p. 14):

> *To his Friend Mr. Nathanael Richards,*
> *upon his Tragedy of Messallina*
>
> If it be good to write the truth of ill
> And Vertues excellence, 'tis in thy skill
> (Respected Friend) thy nimble Scenes discover
> Romes lust-burnt Emp'resse and her vertuous Mother
> So truly to the life; judgement may see,
> (Praysing this Peece) I doe not flatter thee.
> Men here may reade Heaven's Art to chastise Lust;
> Rich Vertue in a Play, so cleare; no rust,
> Bred by the squint ey'd critickes conquering breath
> Can e're deface it; Messalina's death
> Adds life unto the Stage; where though she die
> Defam'd; true justice crownes this Tragedy.
>   Jo. ROBINSON.

His burial is recorded at St. Giles's, Cripplegate, on April 27, 1641 (Collier, iii. 478).

ROBINSON, RICHARD.

The earliest appearance of Richard Robinson is in the cast of Jonson's *Catiline*, acted by the King's men in 1611. A stage-direction in *The Second Maiden's Tragedy* (1611) shows that he played the Lady: "Enter Ladye Rich Robinson" (ed. Greg, p. 61). In *The Devil is an Ass* (1616), II. viii. 56–77, Jonson praises him for his success in impersonating women (ed. W. S. Johnson, p. 54):

> *Meere-craft.* Why this is well! The clothes we 'haue now:
> But, where's this *Lady*?
> If we could get a witty boy, now, *Ingine*;
> That were an excellent cracke: I could instruct him,
> To the true height. For any thing takes this *dottrel.*
>   *Ingine.* Why, Sir your best will be one o' the players!
>   *Mer.* No, there's no trusting them. They'll talke on't,
> And tell their *Poets.*
>   *Ing.* What if they doe? The iest will brooke the Stage.
> But, there be some of 'hem
> Are very honest lads. There's *Dicke Robinson*
> A very pretty fellow, and comes often
> To a Gentlemans chamber, a friend of mine. We had
> The merriest supper of it there, one night, ·
> The Gentlemans Land-lady invited him
> To'a Gossips feast. Now, he Sir brought *Dick Robinson,*
> Drest like a Lawyers wife, amongst 'hem all;
> (I lent him cloathes) but, to see him behaue it;
> And lay the law; and carue; and drinke vnto 'hem;
> And then talke baudy: and send frolicks! o!
> It would haue burst your buttons, or not left you
> A seame.
>   *Mer.* They say hee's an ingenious youth!
>   *Ing.* O Sir! and dresses himselfe, the best! beyond
> Forty o' your very *Ladies*!

Chambers (*Eliz. Stage,* ii. 336) suggests that he may have been the son of James Robinson (*q.v.*), and a member of the Children of the Chapel Royal at Blackfriars before joining the King's men. As a King's man (Murray, i. opp. 172) he appears in the 1623 folio list of Shakespearean players; in the patent of March 27, 1619; in the livery allowances of May 19, 1619, and April 7, 1621; in the submission for playing *The Spanish Viceroy* without license, December 20, 1624 (Adams, *Dram. Rec.,* p. 21); in King James's funeral procession on May 7, 1625; in the license of June 24, 1625 (*M.S.C.,* i. 282); and in the livery allowance of May 6, 1629. With this company he acted in the following plays (Murray, *loc. cit.*): *Bonduca* (1613–14); *The Double Marriage* (c. 1619–20); the Cardinal in *The Duchess of Malfi* (1619–23), which part was formerly played by Henry Condell; *The Wife for a Month* (1624); Aesopus, a player, in Massinger's *Roman Actor* (licensed October 11, 1626); Count Orsinio in Carlell's *Deserving Favorite* (published in 1629); Lentulus in Massinger's *Believe as You List* (licensed May 7, 1631; and La-Castre, in Fletcher's *Wildgoose Chase* (a revival, 1631). Nicholas Tooley, in his will dated June 3, 1623, bequeathed to Sara Burbage the sum of £29 13s. "which is owing unto me by Richard Robinson" (Collier, iii. 453). In 1623 he lived "att the vpper end of Shoreditch" (Wallace, *Jahrbuch*, xlvi. 347). He is alluded to in the dedication of Abraham Cowley's *Love's Riddle*, published in 1638 (Cowley, *Works*, i. 36):

> Nor has 't a part for Robinson, whom they
> At schoole, account essentiall to a Play.

Davenport's poem, "Too Late to Call Back Yesterday" (1639), is dedicated "to my noble friends, Mr. Richard Robinson and Mr. Michael Bowyer" (Bullen, *Old Plays*, New Series, iii. 311). Wright in *Historia Histrionica* (1699) says that Robinson was a comedian at Blackfriars, that he had Charles Hart (*q.v.*) as his apprentice, and that he was killed at the taking of Basing House in October, 1645 (Hazlitt's *Dodsley*, xv. 404, 406, 409). This last statement is evidently a mistake for William Robins (*q.v.*), since in 1647 Richard Robinson joined his fellow-actors in dedicating the first folio of Beaumont and Fletcher's plays; and the burial of "Richard Robinson, a player" is recorded in the register of St. Anne's, Blackfriars, on March 23, 1648 (Collier, iii. 479). He presumably married Richard Burbage's widow, Winifred, who appears as Mrs. Robinson in the *Sharers' Papers* of 1635 (Adams, *Mod. Phil.*, xvii. 7 ff.); and the burial of "Winifred, the wyfe of Mr. Richard Robinson" is entered in the records of St. Leonard's, Shoreditch, on May 2, 1642 (Stopes, *Burbage*, p. 140). The confusion of the names of Richard Robinson and William Robins was no doubt made easy by the fact that Robinson was the more popular of the two players. The mistake is incorporated in Scott's novel of *Woodstock* (1826), where Tomkins, knowing Harrison's fanatical fears, instructed Joceline how to play the part of "Dick Robison the player, whose ghost haunted Harrison." On January 28, 1648, Robinson and other members of the King's company gave a bond to pay off an old Blackfriars debt to Michael Bowyer's heirs (Hotson, pp. 31–34).

ROBINSON, THOMAS.

Thomas Robinson is known as a player with Robert Reynolds's company in Germany. He perhaps acted female parts, for in the housing-list at Torgau in 1627 he is called "Thomas die Jung-fraw." He accompanied Reynolds at Cologne in May, 1628 (Herz, pp. 31, 54).

ROBINSON, WILLIAM.
See William Robins.

ROBSON, WILLIAM.
See William Robins.

ROBYN.

A member of the Chapel Royal in 1518. Some interesting cor-respondence of 1518 informs us that Robyn was transferred from Wolsey's chapel to the Chapel Royal at the express desire of Henry VIII, who told Cornish to treat him honestly, not "other-wise than he doth his own." On April 1, 1518, Richard Pace, secre-tary to Wolsey and Henry, wrote to Wolsey: "Cornsyche doth greatly laud and praise the child of your chapel sent hither, not only for his sure and clean singing, but also for his good and crafty descant" (Brewer, *L. & P. Henry VIII*, ii. 2. pp. 1246, 1249, 1252).

ROE, WILLIAM.

A player with Robert Reynolds's company in Germany during 1640 (Herz, p. 55).

ROGERS, EDWARD.

As a member of Queen Henrietta's company at the Cockpit in Drury Lane, Edward Rogers played Milliscent, Cardona's daughter, in Shirley's *Wedding* (about May, 1626), and Donusa, niece to Amurath, in Massinger's *Renegado*, printed in 1630 (Murray, i. opp. 266).

ROGERS, WILLIAM.

William Rogers's name appears in a warrant of June 30, 1628, appointing several of the Lady Elizabeth's (Queen of Bohemia's) players as Grooms of the Chamber (Stopes, *Jahrbuch*, xlvi. 94).

ROLL, JOHN.

John Roll (or Roo) was a Court Interluder in 1530 (Collier, i. 115). He died in 1539 (*Eliz. Stage*, ii. 80).

RONNER, JOHN.

A London player in 1550, named in an order demanding that all plays be licensed by the King or his Council (Harrison, *England*, iv. 314).

ROO, JOHN.

See John Roll.

ROODS, JOHN.

Part owner of the Fortune (Warner, p. 54).

ROSE.

Rose was apparently with Prince Henry's company in 1612. On April 11, 1612, Robert Browne wrote to Edward Alleyn on behalf of one Mr. Rose, "entertayned amongst the princes men," to request his help in procuring "a gathering place for his wife" (*H.P.*, p. 63).

ROSSETER, PHILIP.

Philip Rosseter was a lessee of Whitefriars from about February, 1609, to December 25, 1614. He is named in a patent of January 4, 1610, granted to the Children of the Queen's Revels. From March, 1613, to March, 1614, he was associated with Henslowe in the management of the combined Revels and the Lady Elizabeth's companies at the Whitefriars, Swan, and Hope playhouses. On June 3, 1615, he and others are recorded as patentees for the erection of Porter's Hall playhouse in Blackfriars (Adams, *Playhouses*, pp. 317–23, 330–32, 342–47). On October 31, 1617, a license was granted to the Children of the Queen's Revels, under the leadership of Rosseter, Lee, Perry, and Long; they visited Norwich on August 29, 1618 (Murray, i. 361; ii. 345). He was one of the royal lutenists from 1604 to 1623 (*Eliz. Stage*, ii. 337), and wrote some of the music for Thomas Campion's *A Booke of Ayres* (1601). On March 1, 1620, Campion bequeathed "all that he had unto Mr. Philip Rosseter, and wished that his estate had bin farr more." He died on May 5, 1623 (*D.N.B.*, xlix. 282).

ROSSILL.

In *1 Henry IV*, acted by the Chamberlain's men at the Theatre in 1597, Poins says in the course of a speech to the Prince (I. ii. 181): "Falstaff, Harvey, Rossill, and Gadshill shall rob those men that we have already waylaid." But in the scene of the robbery (II. ii) the characters here called Harvey and Rossill are discovered to be Bardolph and Peto, which led to Theobald's suggestion that Harvey and Rossill were the actors who took the parts of Bardolph and Peto. A. Gaw (*P.M.L.A.*, xl. 531) regards Harvey and Rossill, not as actors but, as "ghost-names."

ROWLAND.

With the King's men, one Rowland seems to have acted Amilcar, Prusias, and a servant, in Massinger's *Believe as You List* (ed. Croker, pp. 26, 43, 49, 95), licensed May 7, 1631 (Adams, *Dram. Rec.*, p. 33).

ROWLEY, SAMUEL.

Samuel Rowley, actor and playwright, belonged to the Admiral's company, and is first heard of, as a witness for Henslowe, on August 3, 1597. On November 16, 1598, he bound himself to play with Henslowe's company, the Admiral's men, at the Rose

(*H.D.*, ii. 307). With the Admiral's players he acted Heraclius in *Frederick and Basilea* (1597); an unindentified part in *Fortune's Tennis* (*c.* 1597–98); an ambassador in *The Battle of Alcazar* (*c.* 1600–01); Ascalon in *1 Tamar Cam* (1602), and Crymm in the procession of the same play, appearing always as Sam (Greg, *H.P.*, pp. 153, 154; *R.E.S.*, i. 270; Chambers, *Eliz. Stage*, ii. 175). About Christmas, 1603, the Admiral's men were taken into the service of Prince Henry. As a member of the Prince's company, Rowley is mentioned in the coronation list of March 15, 1604; in the patent of April 30, 1606; and in the household list of 1610 (*Eliz. Stage*, ii. 186, 187, 188). The Prince died in November, 1612, and his troupe soon passed under the patronage of the Palsgrave. Rowley is named in the new patent of January 11, 1613 (*M.S.C.*, i. 275); but he does not appear in subsequent lists of the Palsgrave's men. He wrote several plays alone and collaborated in others, the last of which was licensed on April 6, 1624 (*Eliz. Stage*, iii. 472). He is perhaps the "Sam Rowley" referred to in *Mercurius Pragmaticus*, 1647 (Hotson, p. 15): "he [Hugh Peters, the famous divine] has a fine wit I can tell you, *Sam Rowley* and he were a *Pylades*, and *Orestes*, when he played a woman's part at the Curtaine Play-house, which is the reason his garbe is so emphaticall in the Pulpit."

ROWLEY, THOMAS.

With the Admiral's men Thomas Rowley appeared in the procession of *1 Tamar Cam*, acted in 1602 (*H.P.*, p. 154).

ROWLEY, WILLIAM.

William Rowley, player and dramatist, was a member of Prince Charles's troupe from 1610 to 1625. As a Prince's man he appears in the patent of March 30, 1610; in a warrant of March 29, 1615, to come before the Privy Council for playing during Lent (*M.S.C.*, i. 272, 372); in an agreement with Alleyn and Meade on March 20, 1616 (Warner, p. 50); early in 1619 as Plumporridge in Middleton's *Masque of Heroes* (*Works*, vii. 200); and in King James's funeral procession on May 7, 1625 (Murray, i. 161, 237). He served as payee for performances at Court by Prince Charles's men from 1610 to 1615 (Steele, pp. 163, 164, 170, 173, 180, 189). On May 18, 1615, he is recorded at Norwich with the company (Murray, ii. 340). Although technically a Prince's man until the death of King James in 1625, he appears as a King's man (Murray, i. opp. 172) in the cast of *The Maid in the Mill* (1623); in the submission for playing *The Spanish Viceroy*, without license, December 20, 1624; and in the stage-directions of *Love's Pilgrimage* and *The Chances*, both plays conjecturally dated about 1624–25. He was involved in a lawsuit as a result of the performance, probably by Prince Charles company, of *Keep the Widow Waking* at the Red Bull, 1624 (Charles Sisson, "*Keep the Widow Waking*," *The Library*, N.S., viii, 1927). He became definitely associated with the King's men in the patent of June 24, 1625 (*M.S.C.*, i. 282). This is the latest notice of his connection as an actor with any company. He dedicated his *Search for Money* (1609) to Thomas Hobbes (*q.v.*), is presumably the W. R. who contributed a couplet on the death of Thomas Greene (*q.v.*) to *Greene's Tu Quoque* (1614), and composed an elegy on his fellow-actor Hugh Attwell (*q.v.*) in 1621. He wrote plays for various companies (*Eliz. Stage*, iii. 473–75). From the documents connected with the lawsuit growing out of the performance of *Keep the Widow Waking* (*The Library*, N.S., viii, 1927) we learn that he was dead before March 24, 1625–26; and Sisson notes that in the Parish Registers of St. James, Clerkenwell, is recorded the burial of "William Rowley, housekeeper" on February 11, 1625–26.

RUSSELL, JOHN.

John Russell was a gatherer for the Palsgrave's men, about 1617. He proved dishonest, as stated in an undated letter from William Bird to Edward Alleyn (*H.P.*, p. 85):

Sir there is one Jhon Russell, that by yowr apoyntment was made a gatherer with vs, but my fellowes finding often falce to vs, haue many tymes warnd him ffrom taking the box. And he as often, with moste damnable othes, hath vowde neuer to touch, yet not with standing his execrable othes, he hath taken the box, & many tymes moste vnconsionablye gatherd, for which we haue resolued he shall neuer more come to the doore; yet for your sake, he shall haue his wages, to be a nessessary atendaunt on the stage, and if he will pleasure himself and vs, to mend our garmentes, when he hath leysure, weele pay him for that to. J pray send vs word if this motion will satisfye you; for him his dishonestye is such we knowe it will not, Thus yealding our selues in that & a farr greater matter to be comaunded by you J committ you to god. Your loving ffrend to comaund,

W. BIRDE.

He is doubtless identical with the person of the same name who occupied two rooms adjoining the Fortune, leased on June 20, 1617 (*H.P.*, pp. 28, 29), and to whom Alleyn paid £10 on August 8, 1619, as a legacy from Agnes Henslowe (Warner, p. 181).

RUTTER, WILLIAM.

In 1503 William Rutter was a Court Interluder in the service of Henry VII (*Eliz. Stage*, ii. 78).

SACKVILLE, THOMAS.

Thomas Sackville is named in a passport issued on February 10, 1592, by the Lord Admiral, giving permission for a group of players under the leadership of Robert Browne to travel on the Continent (Cohn, p. xxix). He was at Arnhem, Netherlands, in 1592, with a license from Prince Maurice of Orange-Nassau (*Eliz. Stage*, ii. 274n.). In August, 1592, the company presented *Gammer Gurton's Needle* and some of Marlowe's plays at the Frankfort autumn fair; again in 1593 Sackville is named in the Frankfort records of English players at the fair (Herz, pp. 10, 11). The company seems to have disbanded in 1593, and Sackville is not again traceable until 1597, when he appears in the records of Wolfenbüttel, the Court of Henry Julius, Duke of Brunswick-Wolfenbüttel. He is described as "Thomas Sackefiel, Princely servant at Wolfenbüttel," and had a quarrel with another English player, Edward Wakefield, in a Brunswick tavern (Cohn, pp. xxxiii-xxxv). He used the clown-name John Bouset (Herz, p. 17). During 1597 he visited Nuremberg, Augsburg, Strassburg, and Frankfort. In 1601 he (called John Bouset) was expected to join his old leader Robert Browne for the Frankfort Easter fair. From 1602 to 1617 his name frequently appears in the Brunswick household accounts; on August 30, 1602, he served as payee for the English actors. Subsequent entries show that he was concerned in transactions for the Court, and apparently continued in the service of the Duke, though not as a regular player. During this period, 1602–17, he was a merchant in Frankfort (Herz, pp. 32–36), and must have prospered, as evidenced by Thomas Coryat in 1608, when he "hastily gobled up" the following observation at Frankfort (*Crudities*, ii. 290–91):

> The wealth that I sawe here was incredible, so great that it was unpossible for a man to conceive it in his minde that hath not first seene it with his bodily eies. The goodliest shew of ware that I sawe in all Franckford saving that of the Goldsmithes, was made by an Englishman one Thomas Sackfield a Dorsetshireman, once a servant of my father, who went out of England but in a meane estate, but after he had spent a few yeares at the Duke of Brunswicks Court, hee so inriched himselfe of late, that his glittering shewe of ware in Franckford did farre excell all the Dutchmen, French, Italians, or whomsoever else.

His autograph, dated February 1, 1604, is found in an album of Johannes Cellarius of Nuremberg (Cohn, *Shak. in Germany*, Plate i, facsimiles). He died in 1628, leaving a library of theology and English literature (*Eliz. Stage*, ii. 277).

SAM.

The "b[oy?] Sam" in the plot of *The Dead Man's Fortune* (H.P., pp. 133, 152) has been rather doubtfully conjectured to be Samuel Gilburne (*q.v.*). The play was possibly acted by the Admiral's men at the Theatre about 1590 (*Eliz. Stage*, ii. 136; Greg, *R.E.S.*, i. 263).

SANDERS, WILLIAM.

William Sanders is named in a Protection from Arrest issued by Herbert on December 27, 1624, to twenty-one men "imployed by the Kinges Maiesties servantes in theire quallity of Playinge as Musitions and other necessary attendantes" (Adams, *Dram. Rec.*, p. 74).

SANDERSON, GEORGE.

George Sanderson, described as servant to Lord Goring, is recorded at Coventry on January 9, 1640, with a company composed of players from various troupes. They received a payment of 48*s*. 2*d*., under date of November 25, 1640 (Murray, ii. 52, 254).

SANDERSON, GREGORY.

Gregory Sanderson appears among the representatives of Queen Anne's London and provincial companies of players who attended her funeral on May 13, 1619 (Murray, i. 196–97). Chambers (*Eliz. Stage*, iii. 271) suggests that he may be identical with one Sands who appears in a stage-direction (line 186), "Enter 2 Lords, Sands, Ellis," of Robert Daborne's *Poor Man's Comfort* (ed. Swaen, p. 382), a play possibly acted by Queen Anne's men at the Cockpit in Drury Lane, about 1617. But there were also actors named James Sands and Thomas Sands.

SANDS, JAMES.

James Sands in 1605 was associated with the King's men as an apprentice to Augustine Phillips, who names him as a legatee in his will dated May 4, 1605 (Collier, *Actors*, p. 87): "I geve to James Sands, my apprentice, the some of fortye shillings, and a citterne, a bandore, and a lute, to be paid and delivered unto him at the expiration of his terme of yeres in his indenture of apprenticehood." William Sly, also a King's man, by his will dated August 4, 1608, left him £40 (Collier, *Actors*, p. 157). A James Sands is traceable in the Southwark token-books of 1596, 1598, and 1612 (*Eliz. Stage*, ii. 337). He may be identified with one

Sands who is mentioned in a stage-direction (line 186), "Enter 2 Lords, Sands, Ellis," of Robert Daborne's *Poor Man's Comfort* (ed. Swaen, p. 382), probably a play of Queen Anne's company at the Cockpit in Drury Lane, about 1617; but there was a player named Sanderson with the Queen's men in 1619 and possibly earlier.

SANDS, THOMAS.

Thomas Sands is recorded at Norwich on March 10, 1635, when his troupe, presumably the King's Revels, applied for permission to act in that town (Murray, i. 279–80).

SANDT, BERNHARDT.

Bernhardt Sandt visited Nuremberg in April, 1600, with a group of English players under the patronage of Maurice of Hesse (Herz, p. 38).

SAUNDERS, WILLIAM.

A member of the Chapel Royal, not later than 1517 (*Eliz. Stage*, ii. 27n.).

SAUSS, EVERHART.

Everhart Sauss is recorded at Arnhem, Netherlands, in 1592, with a company of English actors under the leadership of Robert Browne, carrying a license from Prince Maurice, of Orange-Nassau (*Eliz. Stage*, ii. 274n.).

SAVAGE, JEROME.

Jerome Savage appears to have been a member of the Earl of Warwick's company, from 1575 to 1579. With John and Lawrence Dutton he received payment for the two Court performances by that troupe during the Christmas season of 1575–76, on December 27, 1575, and January 1, 2576); and alone he was payee for a play scheduled to have been given at Court on February 2, 1579 (Steele, pp. 57, 58, 74).

SAVAGE, RAFE.

Apparently "the successor of Aaron Holland [*q.v.*] and the purchaser of his property in the Red Bull" (Charles Sisson, "*Keep the Widow Waking*," *The Library*, N.S., viii, 1927, pp. 235 ff.).

SAVEREY, ABRAHAM.

In the few notices we have of Saverey he is associated with Francis Henslowe in borrowing from Philip Henslowe and in giving bond for debts. He is described as "of Westminster, gent." on October 25, 1604, when he gave bond to Francis Henslowe and James Browne as security for payment of £10 to Joshua Speed, for which they were jointly bound (Warner, p. 235). By March, 1605, he belonged to the Lennox company. On March 1, 1605, he gave Francis Henslowe a power of attorney to recover £40 from John Garland, forfeited on a bond "for the deliuere of a warrant, which was mayd vnto me from the gratious the duke of Linox"; and on March 16, 1605, Francis gave his uncle a bond of £60 to observe an agreement that he had made with Garland and Saverey "his ffellowes, servantes to the most noble Prince the duke of Lennox." He acknowledged a debt of £1 to Philip Henslowe, payable on demand, March 11, 1606. There was an undated loan, probably in 1604, of £7 by Philip Henslowe to his nephew "to goyne with owld Garlland and Symcockes and Saverey when they played in the dukes nam at ther laste goinge owt" (*H.D.*, i. 160; ii. 308; *H.P.*, pp. 62 ff.; Warner, pp. 27, 28, 29).

SAVILL, ARTHUR.

Arthur Savill played Quartilla, a gentlewoman, in Marmion's *Holland's Leaguer*, presented in December, 1631 (Adams, *Dram. Rec.*, p. 45), by "the high and mighty Prince Charles his servants, at the private house in Salisbury Court" (Marmion, *Works*, pp. 2, 6).

SCARLETT, JOHN.

A player, whose son Richard was baptized at St. Giles's on September 1 and buried on September 19, 1605 (*Eliz. Stage*, ii. 337).

SCARLETT, RICHARD.

The registers of St. Giles's record the burial of Richard Scarlett, a player, on April 23, 1609; the baptism of his daughter Susan, on February 11, 1607; the burial of his wife Marie, on February 12, 1607 (*Eliz. Stage*, ii. 337); and the burial of a son in 1607 (Malcolm, *Londinium Redivivum*, iii. 303–04).

SCHADLEUTNER, SEBASTIAN.

In February, 1623, Sebastian Schadleutner visited Nuremberg with John Spencer (Herz, p. 52).

SCOTT, JOHN.

John Scott was a Court Interluder from 1503 to 1528 (*Eliz. Stage*, ii. 78, 80). The unusual circumstances of his death are related by a contemporary historian (*Chronicle of the Grey Friars of London*, ed. Nichols, p. 34):

Also this same yere [1528–29] John Scotte, that was one of the kynges playeres, was put in Newgate for rebukynge of the shreffes, and was there a sennet, and at the last was ledde betwene two of the offecers from Newgate thorrow London and soe to Newgat agayne, and then was delyveryd home to hys howse; but he toke soch a thowte that he dyde, for he went in hys shurte.

SEABROOKE, THOMAS.

Thomas Seabrooke's name appears in a warrant of July 2, 1629, appointing several of the Lady Elizabeth's (Queen of Bohemia's) players as Grooms of the Chamber (Stopes, *Jahrbuch*, xlvi. 95).

SEBECK, HENRY.

Henry Sebeck was leader of the Lady Elizabeth's men when they visited Norwich on June 7, 1617 (Murray, i. 253; ii. 344).

SEHAIS, JEHAN.

Jehan Sehais is known as an English player in Paris during May and June, 1598. On may 25, 1598, the Confrères de la Passion leased their theatre in Paris, the Hôtel Bourgogne, to him (Soulié, *Recherches sur Molière*, p. 153):

1598. 25 mai.—Bail fair par les maîtres de ladite confrérie à "Jehan Sehais, comédien anglois, de la grande salle et théâtre dudit hôtel de Bourgogne, pour le temps, aux réservations, et moyennant les prix, charges, clauses et conditions portées par icelui" passé par devant Huart de Claude Nourel, notaires.

On June 4, judgment was obtained against him:

1598. 4 juin.—Sentence du Châtelet donnée au profit de ladite confrérie a l'encontre desdits comédiens anglois, "tant pour raison du susdit bail que pour le droit d'un écu par jour, jouant par lesdits Anglois ailleurs qu'audit hôtel."

Chambers (*Eliz. Stage*, ii. 338) suggests that Sehais is possibly to be identified with the John Shaa (or Shaw) who witnessed a payment to Dekker by Henslowe for the Admiral's men on November 24, 1599 (*H.D.*, ii. 309).

SHAA, JOHN.
See Jehan Sehais.

SHAA, ROBERT.
See Robert Shaw.

SHAKERLEY, EDWARD.
Edward Shakerley played Gazet, servant to Vitelli, in Massinger's *Renegado*, printed in 1630 as acted by Queen Henrietta's company at the Cockpit in Drury Lane (Murray, i. opp. 266). In 1623 he lived "in Clarkenwell Close" (Wallace, *Jahrbuch*, xlvi. 347). Herbert granted him a Protection from Arrest on November 29, 1624 (Adams, *Dram. Rec.*, p. 75).

SHAKESPEARE, EDMUND.
Edmund Shakespeare, a player, and presumably the brother of the dramatist, was buried at St. Saviour's on December 31, 1607. The burial entry: "Edmond Shakespeare, a player: in the church," is expanded in the monthly accounts: "Edmund Shakespeare, a

player, buried in the church, with a forenoone knell of the great bell, 20*s*." (Collier, *Actors*, p. xiv; Adams, *Shakespeare*, pp. 395, 446).

SHAKESPEARE, EDWARD.

The register of St. Giles's, Cripplegate, records the burial of "Edward, sonne of Edward Shackspeere, Player: base borne," on August 12, 1607 (Collier, *Actors*, p. xv).

SHAKESPEARE, WILLIAM.

William Shakespeare (1564–1616) came to London about 1590. His early life in London is to a great extent a matter of conjecture; various theories have been advanced to fix his theatrical connections and to explain his dual profession of actor and playwright. The pros and cons are legion, and are too well known to call for discussion in this brief sketch. One of the most plausible explanations of his first years in London seems to be that he became associated with the Earl of Pembroke's men, with whom he no doubt acted and for whom he certainly revised several plays (Adams, *Shakespeare*, pp. 131 ff.). The closing of the playhouses on account of the plague, the traveling of Pembroke's men in the provinces, and the resultant bankruptcy of the troupe led naturally to his period of non-dramatic composition during 1592–94. He joined the Chamberlain's company on its formation early in the summer of 1594, and for this famous organization (from 1603 onwards, the King's men) his great dramas were written. On March 15, 1595, he served as joint-payee with Burbage and Kempe for two plays presented by the Chamberlain's men at Court on December 26 and 28, 1594. He is named in the patent granted to the King's men on May 19, 1603, and in the coronation list of March 15, 1604. As a player he appears in the 1623 folio list of actors in his own plays, and in the casts of *Every Man in his Humor* (1598) and of *Sejanus* (1603). This is his last appearance in the cast of any play. For a discussion of the parts he is supposed to have assumed, see Adams, *Shakespeare*, pp. 424–27. As chief playwright for the King's men and as a prominent shareholder in the Globe and the Blackfriars syndicates, he was associated with that company until his death in 1616.

SHAKSHAFTE, WILLIAM.

Possibly William Shakshafte was in 1581 a player in the service of Alexander Houghton, of Lea, in Lancashire. On August 3, 1581, Houghton wrote (*Eliz. Stage*, i. 280*n.*): "Yt ys my wyll that Thomas Houghton of Brynescoules my brother shall have all my instrumentes belonginge to mewsyckes and all maner of playe clothes yf he be mynded to keepe and doe keepe players. And yf he wyll not keppe and maynteyne playeres then yt ys my wyll that Sir Thomas Heskethe Knyghte shall haue the same instrumentes and playe clothes. And I moste hertelye requyre the said Syr Thomas to be ffrendlye unto Foke Gyllome and William Shakshafte now dwellynge with me and ether to take theyn unto his servyce or els to helpe theym to some good master."

SHANBROOKE, JOHN.

A player, who was buried at St. Giles's on September 17, 1618. The register also records his children from June 10, 1610, to June 4, 1618 (*Eliz. Stage*, ii. 338).

SHANCKE, JOHN.

See John Shank.

SHANK, JOHN.

John Shank (or Shanks—and various other spellings) in the *Sharers' Papers* of 1635 (Halliwell-Phillipps, *Outlines*, i. 314) describes himself to the Earl of Pembroke, then Lord Chamberlain, as "beeing an old man in this quality [playing], who in his youth first served your noble father, and after that, the late Queene Elizabeth, then King James, and now his royall Majestye [Charles I]." We have no further record of his connection with Pembroke's and the Queen's men; but presumably (*Eliz. Stage*,

ii. 338) he refers to his association with the Pembroke troupe about 1597–1600 and Elizabeth's traveling company during the years toward the end of her reign. He does not mention his other theatrical connections; but we know from the records that he was a member of Prince Henry's troupe in 1610, when he appears in the household list of players, and of the Palsgrave's troupe on January 11, 1613, when his name is found in the license granted to the new company that passed under the patronage of the Palsgrave after the death of Prince Henry in November, 1612 (*Eliz. Stage*, ii. 188; *M.S.C.*, i. 275). He appears to have been a resident of Rochester Yard, Southwark, in 1605 (Rendle, *Bankside*, p. xxvi); but subsequently he lived in Golden Lane, in the parish of St. Giles's, Cripplegate (Collier, iii. 482–83). The registers of St. Giles's contain records of his children and of his servants, between 1610 and 1629. In these entries he is variously described as player and as gentleman, and, in one record that may not refer to him, as chandler. The parish records are as follow: an unnamed son (buried December 31, 1610), Elizabeth (baptized February 10, 1612), an unnamed daughter (buried March 22, 1615), James (baptized August 1, 1619), John, "sonne of John Shanckes, *chandler*" (baptized February 2, 1621), Thomas (baptized November 18, 1621; buried December 1, 1621), Winifred (baptized August 3, 1623), a second Winifred (baptized May 19, 1626; buried June 16, 1629); Susan Rodes and Jane Buffington, "servants to Mr. Shancke," were buried in 1618 and 1622; and Mrs. Sarah Dambrooke and Mrs. Maryan Porter, widows, were buried "from the house of John Shancke, gentleman," in 1624. He joined the King's men between January 11, 1613, when he is named in the license to the Palsgrave's troupe, and March 27, 1619, when his name occurs in the patent to the King's company (*M.S.C.*, i. 275, 280). Thereafter until his death in 1636 he was a King's player. He is mentioned (Murray, i. 161, opp. 172) in the livery allowances of May 19, 1619, and April 7, 1621; in the submission for playing *The Spanish Viceroy*, without license, December 20, 1624 (Adams, *Dram. Rec.*, p. 21); in the list of players who took part in King James's funeral procession on May 7, 1625; in the patent of June 24, 1625 (*M.S.C.*, i. 282); in the livery allowance of May 6, 1629; and in the 1623 folio list of Shakespearean actors. With the King's men he played in *The Prophetess* (1622); in Ford's *Lover's Melancholy* (licensed November 24, 1628); and Petella, a waiting-woman, in Fletcher's *Wildgoose Chase*, a revival, 1631 (Murray, i. opp. 172). Wright in *Historia Histrionica* (1699) says that he was a comedian and played Sir Roger in *The Scornful Lady*, at Blackfriars, where Nicholas Burt (*q.v.*) was his apprentice (Hazlitt's *Dodsley*, xv. 404, 406). In the *Sharers' Papers*, 1635 (Halliwell-Phillipps, *Outlines*, i. 316), he says that he had "of his own purse supplyed the company for the service of his Majesty with boyes, as Thomas Pollard, John Thompson deceased (for whome hee payed £40), your suppliant haveing payd his part of £200 for other boyes since his comming to the company, John Honiman, Thomas Holcome and diverse others, and at this time maintaines three more for the sayd service." At the death of John Heminges in 1630, William Heminges inherited his father's interests in the Globe and the Blackfriars playhouses. Between 1633 and 1635 Shank bought from William Heminges three shares in the Globe and two shares in the Blackfriars, paying for them £506. Several of his fellow-actors resented his purchase of these shares, and testified that the transactions had been surreptitious. This led to the petition of Benfield, Swanston, and Pollard to the Lord Chamberlain for the compulsory sale to them of shares held by the larger shareholders; and Shank was directed to transfer one share in each house to the petitioners. Subsequently he affirmed that "hee did make a proposition to his fellowes for satisfaccion, upon his assigening of his partes in the severall houses unto them; but they not onely refused to give satisfaccion, but restrained him from the stage." On August 1, 1635, the Lord Chamberlain ordered the proper authorities to "sett downe a proportionable and equitable summe of money to bee payd unto Shankes for the two partes which hee is to passe unto Benfield, Swanston, and Pollard, and to cause a finall agreement and conveyances to bee settled accordingly" (Adams, *Mod. Phil.*, xvii. 7 ff.; Halliwell-Phillipps, *Outlines*, i. 312–19). On March 16, 1624, Herbert licensed for the King's men a piece entitled *"Shankes Ordinary*, written by Shankes himself," which is not extant (Adams, *Dram. Rec.*, p. 27). This was presumably a jig. That he was noted for his jigs is shown by an allusion to him in William Heminges's *Elegy on Randolph's Finger*, written about 1630–32 (ed. G. C. M. Smith, p. 14):

> Rounce Roble hoble, he that wrote so byg,
> Bass for a ballad, Iohn Shanke for a Jigg.

Shank was also the author of a song, "Now Chrecht me save, Poor Irish knave," preserved at Oxford in Ashmolean MS. 38, art. 131 (Smith, *Ibid.*, p. 26*n.*). Collier (*H.E.D.P.*, iii. 483–85) quotes this song, entitled *Shankes Song*, from an imperfect copy, with interpolations from another exemplar, and characterizes it as "obviously intended to ridicule the unfortunate Irish papists on their condition and sufferings in England, as well as on the power and influence of their priesthood." Shank is also said to be mentioned in some verses, signed "W. Turner" and dated 1662, quoted by Collier (*Ibid.*, iii. 481) from *Turner's Dish of Lenten Stuff, or a Gallimaufry*:

> That's the fat fool of the Curtain,
> And the lean fool of the Bull:
> Since Shancke did leave to sing his rhimes,
> He is counted but a gull:
> The players on the Bankside,
> The round Globe and the Swan,
> Will teach you idle tricks of love,
> But the Bull will play the man.

The verses, if genuine, were apparently, as Collier suggests, originally written much earlier than 1662, at some date when the playhouses mentioned were occupied by more or less famous companies. The first edition of Turner's book was issued about 1612, and hence "the lean fool of the Bull" was probably Thomas Greene. The register of St. Giles's, Cripplegate, records Shank's burial on January 27, 1636 (Collier, iii. 483). The John Shank of the Fortune playhouse may have been his son.

SHANK, JOHN, "THE YOUNGER."

John Shank, "the younger," is perhaps the son of the more celebrated comedian of the King's men, John Shank (*q.v.*), who died in January, 1636. He may fairly be identified with the John Shancke whose marriage to Elizabeth Martin is recorded in the register of St. Giles's, Cripplegate, on January 26, 1630 (Collier, iii. 483). This conjecture is supported by the testimony of Tobias Lisle in a Chancery suit of 1647–49 concerning the non-payment of rent for shares in the Fortune playhouse. Lisle says that " 'about 9 yeares synce' he became assignee of a half-share in trust for Elizabeth Shanckes, his interest in which, at the request of the same Elizabeth and her husband, he afterwards made over to Winifred Shanckes" (Warner, p. 246). And the date "about 9 yeares synce" is in accord with a record that "John Shaunks, actor, of the Fortune playhouse, appeared and was sworn" by the Court of High Commission on February 8, 1640. This court on February 13, 1640, referred his case to Sir Nathaniel Brent, "to ascertain his income from the playhouse and otherwise, and out of his means to allot alimony to his wife" (*S.P.D. Charles I*, 1640, pp. 393, 396). At an earlier date he was a member of the Red Bull company, as shown by a Norwich record. On June 6, 1635, he and Richard Weekes were leaders of this troupe on a visit to that town (Murray, i. 274; ii. 357). Late in 1635 the Red Bull players moved to the Fortune, where they remained until about Easter, 1640 (Adams, *Playhouses*, pp. 287–89); this accounts for Shank's appearance as a player at the Fortune in the records of the Court of High Commission, February, 1640. By December 17, 1640, he was a member of Prince Charles's company, as evidenced by a warrant of that date, appointing "John Shanke a Groom of the Chamber of the Prince in quality of Player" (Stopes, *Jahrbuch*, xlvi. 103). Doubtless he continued with this company, which occupied the Fortune from Easter, 1640, until the closing of the playhouses in September, 1642. Upon the outbreak of war he seems to have joined the army of Parliament, and yet to have remained loyal to the King, as shown by *The Perfect Diurnal*, October 24, 1642 (Collier, iii. 485–86), which tells of "one Shanks, a player," who, with a Captain Wilson and a Lieutenant Whitney, deserted from the Parliamentary army rather than fight against the King's forces. Parliament ordered that "they should all three be committed to the Gatehouse, and brought to condign punishment, according to marshal law, for their base cowardliness."

SHANKS, JOHN.
See John Shank.

SHARP, RICHARD.
Richard Sharp is known as a member of the King's company from 1618 to 1629 (Murray, i. opp. 172). He acted in *The Loyal Subject*, licensed November 16, 1618 (Adams, *Dram. Rec.*, p. 22); *The Knight of the Malta* (c. 1618); *The Mad Lover* (c. 1618); *The Humorous Lieutenant* (c. 1619); the Duchess in *The Duchess of Malfi* (1619–23); *The Custom of the Country* (c. 1619–20); *The Double Marriage* (c. 1619–20); *Women Pleased* (c. 1620); *The Little French Lawyer* (c. 1620); *The False One* (c. 1620–21); *The Laws of Candy* (c. 1621); *The Island Princess* (c. 1621); *The Prophetess* (1622); *The Lover's Progress* (1623); Parthenius, Caesar's friend, in Massinger's *Roman Actor* (licensed October 11, 1626); Ford's *Lover's Melancholy* (licensed November 24, 1628); Ferdinand, general of the army, in Massinger's *Picture* (licensed June 8, 1629); and Lysander, in Carlell's *Deserving Favorite* (published in 1629). He is also named in the submission for playing *The Spanish Viceroy*, without license, December 20, 1624; in a Protection from Arrest granted by Her-

bert, December 29, 1624 (Adams, *Dram. Rec.*, pp. 21, 75); in the list of players who took part in King James's funeral procession on May 7, 1625 (Murray, i. 161); in the patent of June 24, 1625 (*M.S.C.*, i. 282); and in the livery allowance of May 6, 1629.

SHATTERELL, ROBERT.

Wright tells us in *Historia Histrionica* (Hazlitt's *Dodsley*, xv. 404, 409) that Robert (?) Shatterell "was a boy . . . under Beeston at the Cockpit." At the closing of the playhouses in 1642 and the beginning of Civil War, he enlisted in the King's army as quartermaster in Prince Rupert's regiment. After the Restoration he continued his career at the Cockpit. He is named in the Petition of the Cockpit Players on October 13, 1660, and in the Articles of Agreement between Herbert and Killigrew on June 4, 1662 (Adams, *Dram. Rec.*, pp. 94, 96, 113–14). His Majesty's Company of Comedians opened their new playhouse, the Theatre Royal, on May 7, 1663 (Pepys, *Diary*, iii. 107), under the management of Thomas Killigrew. As a member of that organization Shatterell assumed the following parts in plays presented by the company (Downes, *Ros. Ang.*, pp. 2 ff.): Voltore in *The Fox*, Sir John Daw in *The Silent Woman*, Calianax in *The Maid's Tragedy*, Bessus in *King and no King*, Charles's man in *The Elder Brother*, Poins in *King Henry the Fourth*, and Maskal, in *The Mock Astrologer*. On March 19, 1666, Pepys records that he went "behind stage" and was greatly amused by the "sights," including "Shotrell's" wardrobe (*Diary*, v. 235). Downes (*Ros. Ang.*, p. 2) mentions also a William Shatterell, and Nicoll (*Rest. Drama*, p. 269) an Edward Shatterell, in the lists of the King's company during the early years of the Restoration. A confusion in the names of the three— possibly only two—persons seems to have resulted; but Robert is apparently the actor who began his theatrical career before the closing of the playhouses in 1642.

SHAW, JOHN.
See Jehan Sehais.

SHAW, ROBERT.

Robert Shaw (or Shaa), with several of his fellows of the Earl of Pembroke's company, is a complainant in a lawsuit during 1597 against Francis Langley, builder and owner of the Swan playhouse (Wallace, *Eng. Studien*, xliii. 340; Adams, *Playhouses*, pp. 168–74). As a result of the dissolution of the company, caused by the production of *The Isle of Dogs*, Shaw bound himself to Henslowe to play with the Admiral's men at the Rose; on October 11 his name is found in the company's accounts (*H.D.*, i. 82, 202). Thereafter until 1602 he appears in the *Diary* as authorizing payments on innumerable occasions, as borrowing money from Henslowe, as paying personal debts, as acknowledging company debts in the capacity of share-holder, and as a witness. He took a leading part in the business affairs of the troupe (*H.D.*, ii. 309). During the Christmas seasons of 1597–98 and 1598–99 he served as joint-payee with Thomas Downton for performances at Court by the Earl of Nottingham's (Admiral's) men, and during 1599–1600 he was sole payee (Steele, pp. 113, 116, 118). As an Admiral's man he played an Irish bishop in *The Battle of Alcazar*, about 1600–01 (*H.P.*, p. 153; *Eliz. Stage*, ii. 175). By February 7–13, 1602, he and Richard Jones had left the Admiral's men, and the two had received £50 at their departure (*H.D.*, i. 164). Worcester's men on September 19, 1602, paid Shaw 16*s.*, and on December 6, 1602, £17 for four cloth cloaks. Also about this time the Admiral's men paid him £2 for a play called *The Four Sons of Aymon* (*H.D.*, i. 181, 185; ii. 227). The registers of St. Saviour's, Southwark, record the baptism of John, son of Robert Shaw, "player," on April 10, 1603, and the burial of Robert Shaw, "a man," on September 12, 1603 (*Eliz. Stage*, ii. 339). This last entry in all probability refers to the player, of whom nothing more is heard.

SHEALDEN.

A player, who witnessed a loan for Henslowe on August 24, 1594 (*H.D.*, i. 76).

SHEPARD.

"Shepard that keepeth the door at playes" at Paul's is named as a legatee in the will of Sebastian Westcott, dated April 3, 1582 (*Eliz. Stage*, ii. 16*n*.)..

SHEPPARD, WILLIAM.

A player, whose son Robert was baptized at St. Helen's on November 26, 1602 (*Eliz. Stage*, ii. 339).

SHERLOCK, WILLIAM.

William Sherlock is named in the 1622 Herbert list of the Lady Elizabeth's players (Adams, *Dram. Rec.*, p. 63). He seems to have become a member of Queen Henrietta's company at the Cockpit in Drury Lane at its formation soon after the accession of Charles I. With this organization he continued until 1637 (Murray, i. 265–67), appearing as Lodam, a fat gentleman, in Shirley's *Wedding* (*c.* 1626); Brand in Davenport's *King John and Matilda* (*c.* 1629), where he "performed excellently well"; Mr. Ruffman, a swaggering gentleman, in Heywood's *Fair Maid of the West*, Part I (*c.* 1630); and as Maharaball and Prusias in Nabbes's *Hannibal and Scipio* (1635). At the reorganization of Queen Henrietta's men about October, 1637, he joined the Revels company at Salisbury Court, as shown by Herbert's record (Adams, *Dram. Rec.*, p. 66): "I disposed of Perkins, Sumner, Sherlock and Turner, to Salisbury Court, and joynd them with the best of that company." He probably continued with this company, which retained the name of the Queen's players, until the closing of the playhouses in 1642.

SIBTHORPE, EDWARD.

Edward Sibthorpe owned one-half of one share in the syndicate that in 1608 leased the Whitefriars playhouse (Adams, *Playhouses*, pp. 313–15).

SILVESTER.

At Coventry on October 16, 1625, one Silvester appeared with Martin Slater and William Robins as payees for the company known as the players to the late Queen Anne (Murray, i. 188; ii. 250).

SIMPSON, CHRISTOPHER.

A shoemaker of Egton, Yorkshire, who appears as an unlicensed player and recusant in 1610–12 (*Eliz. Stage*, i. 305*n.*).

SIMPSON, CUTHBERT.

An unlicensed player and recusant, of Egton, Yorkshire, in 1616 (*Eliz. Stage*, i. 305*n.*).

SIMPSON, JOHN.

An unlicensed player and recusant, of Egton, Yorkshire, in 1616 (*Eliz. Stage*, i. 305*n.*).

SIMPSON, RICHARD.

An unlicensed player and recusant, of Egton, Yorkshire, in 1616 (*Eliz. Stage*, i. 305*n.*).

SIMPSON, ROBERT.

A shoemaker of Staythes, Yorkshire, who is mentioned as an unlicensed player and recusant in 1612 and 1616 (*Eliz. Stage*, i. 305*n.*).

SINCKLER, WILLIAM.

Elizabeth, daughter of William Sinckler, "a musitan," was baptized at St. Saviour's, Southwark, on September 6, 1629 (Bentley, *T.L.S.*, Nov. 15, 1928, p. 856).

SINCKLO, JOHN.
See John Sincler.

SINCLAW.
See John Sincler.

SINCLER, JOHN.

John Sincler (Sincklo or Sinklo) is first known in the plot of *2 Seven Deadly Sins*, acted by Strange's men about 1590. He appeared as a keeper in the Induction, a soldier in "Envy," a captain and a musician in "Sloth," and probably as Mercury in "Lechery" (Greg, *H.P.*, p. 152; *R.E.S.*, i. 262). During 1592–93 he was possibly with Pembroke's men, for his name is found in a stage-direction of *3 Henry VI* (III. i. 1), 1623 folio: "Enter Sinklo, and Humfrey, with Crosse-bowes in their hands," which presumably refers to a production by Pembroke's men in 1592–93 or to a revival by the Chamberlain's men (*Eliz. Stage*, ii. 129–30, 200). His name also slipped in as substitute for "Player" in the folio text of *The Taming of the Shrew* (Induction, 88): "*Sincklo*. I thinke 'twas *Soto* that your honor meanes"; and here again this may point to a presentation by either the Pembroke or the Chamberlain organization (*Eliz. Stage*, ii. 199, 200). Thus we may with some reason assume that he was a Pembroke's man during 1592–93. Subsequently he joined the Chamberlain's troupe, probably at its formation in 1594. That he was a Chamberlain's man is shown by his appearance in a play acted by that company. He is found in a stage-direction of *2 Henry IV* (V. iv. 1), quarto of 1600: "Enter Sincklo and three or foure officers." When the Chamberlain's players passed under royal patronage in 1603 he became a King's man. In Marston's *Malcontent* (1604), he appears in the Induction (*Works*, i. 199). Probably he was only a hired man, for he is not mentioned in any of the formal lists of the company. After 1604 nothing further is heard of him. He is discussed at length by A. Gaw (*Anglia*, xlix. 289–303), who suggests that he was a "thin actor," that in some cases his "thinness especially fitted him for the assigned part," and concludes that "he seems in general to have been an actor of no great power, not rising high in the company throughout his connection with it, and used as a rule for supernumerary work or where . . . his physique rendered him useful for a certain effect." He is also considered by K. Elze

(*Notes on Eliz. Dram.*, pp. 163–64), who conjectures that he may
be identical with one Sinclaw mentioned as a Court fool in the
household books of the Emperor Maximilian II (1564–76): Elze
writes: "Like many others of his fellows Sincklo may have gone
to Germany when a young man; he may have been about 25 years
of age when he stood in the Emperor's service at Vienna about
the year 1570."

SINGER, JOHN.

John Singer became a member of Queen Elizabeth's troupe when
it was first established in 1583, for he is named in a London record
that gives the personnel of the company at this time (*Eliz. Stage*,
ii. 106). He was with the Queen's men at Norwich in June, 1583,
when an affray occurred between the players and one Wynsdon
and his servant (see John Bentley). Apparently he remained with
the Queen's men, for he is mentioned in a document of June 30,
1588, concerning the non-payment of subsidy by certain members
of the company (*M.S.C.*, i. 354). He may be identical with a John
Singer who owed money in 1571 to Robert Betts, a deceased
Canterbury painter; Betts had sold "certen playe-bookes" to
William Fidge and one Whetstone, possibly actors (Plomer,
Library, 1918, ix. 253). By the autumn of 1594 he had joined the
Admiral's men, with whom he remained until 1603. He is named
in Henslowe's first list of the company, December 14, 1594 (*H.D.*,
i. 5). He appears as joint-payee with Edward Alleyn and Richard
Jones for the Court performances by the Admiral's men in December and January, 1594–95 (Steele, p. 108). The Henslowe
records show him as witnessing transactions, acknowledging
company debts, borrowing various sums of money, and in one
instance as authorizing a payment on behalf of the company. At
some date after March 14, 1597, he and Thomas Towne borrowed
40*s.* from Henslowe "when they went into the countrey." On
January 13, 1603, the Admiral's men paid him £5 "for his playe
called Syngers vallentary." This is his last appearance in the

Diary (*H.D.*, ii. 310). With the Admiral's company (*H.P.*, p. 154) he played Mauritius (?) in *Fortune's Tennis* (*c.* 1600) and Assinico in *1 Tamar Cam* (1602). He probably left the Admiral's men to become an ordinary Groom of the Chamber, which office he held at Queen Elizabeth's funeral in 1603 (*Eliz. Stage*, i. 312). The register of St. Saviour's records the baptism of the following children of John Singer, "player": Thomas, August 7, 1597; William, June 17, 1599; John, September 21, 1600; Elizabeth, August 30, 1601; Jane, May 1, 1603. The token-books give his residence as "Awstens Rents" in 1597, 1598, 1599, 1601, and 1602 (Bentley, *T.L.S.*, Nov. 15, 1928, p. 856). Collier has erroneously attributed the *Quips upon Questions* (1600) of Robert Armin (*q.v.*) to Singer. In 1600 he and Thomas Pope, of the Chamberlain's men, are mentioned by Samuel Rowlands in *The Letting of Humours Blood in the Head-Vaine*, Satire iv (*Works*, i. 63):

> What meanes *Singer* then?
> And *Pope* the Clowne, to speake so Boorish, when
> They counterfaite the Clownes vpon the Stage?

Dekker, in *Gull's Horn-Book* (1609), writes: "*Tarleton, Kemp*, nor *Singer*, nor all the litter of Fooles that now come drawling be-hinde them, never played the clownes more naturally then the arrantest Sot of you all shall." Heywood, in *Apology for Actors* (written after the death of William Sly in August, 1608, and published in 1612), praises him with other dead actors whose "deserts yet live in the remembrance of many." John Taylor, in *Taylors Feast* (1638) gives an anecdote of him (*Works*, iii. 70):

Amongst all these, I my selfe did know one *Thomas Vincent* that was a Book-keeper or prompter at the Globe play-house neere the Banck-end in Maid-lane: As also I did know *Iohn Singer*, who playd the Clownes part at the Fortune-play-house in *Golding* Lane, these two men had such strange and different humours, that *Vincent* could not endure the sight or scent of a hot Loyne of Veale, and *Singer* did abhorre the smell of *Aqua vitae*: But it hapned that both these were invited to Dinner by a Widdow, (that did not well know their dyets) and as they sate at the Boord, a hot Loyne of Veale was set before *Vincent*, who presently began to change colour, and looke pale, and in a trembling manner, hee drop't in a swowne under the Table; the Widdow (being in a great amazement) made haste for an *Aqua vitae* bottle to revive him, which was no sooner opened, but the very scent sent *Singer* after *Vincent* in the like foolish traunce. But when the Veale and *Aqua vitae* were taken away, after a little time the men recover'd: *Vincent* went into another Roome, and dranke, and *Singer* call'd for the Veale, and din'd well with it.

SINKLO, JOHN.
See John Sincler.

SKINNER, RICHARD.
A Court Interluder from 1547 to about 1559 (Collier, i. 136, 165; *Eliz. Stage*, ii. 82, 83).

SLATER, MARTIN.
Martin Slater (or Slaughter) was a member of the Admiral's troupe from 1594 to 1597. He is named in Henslowe's first list of the company, December 14, 1594 (*H.D.*, i. 5). He served as payee with Edward Alleyn for the Court performances by the Admiral's men in January and February, 1596 (Steele, pp. 110, 111). Various loans to him are recorded in the Henslowe accounts, where he is often referred to simply as Martin (*H.D.*, ii. 310–11). With the Admiral's men he played Theodore in *Frederick and Basilea*, acted in 1597 (*H.P.*, p. 153). He left the Admiral's company on July 18, 1597, as shown by Henslowe's entry (*H.D.*, i. 54): "Martin Slather went for [from] the company of my lord admeralles men the 18 of July 1597." On May 16, 1598, he sold for £8 the books of five old plays to the Admiral's men, who had produced them some years earlier (*H.D.*, i. 86, 90; ii. 311; *Eliz. Stage*, ii. 167). He is presumably the Martin mentioned with Lawrence Fletcher (*q.v.*) in Scotland during 1599. He seems to have been associated with Fletcher at a time previous to their appearance in Scotland, for Henslowe records money "lent vnto Martyne to feache Fleacher" in October, 1596 (*H.D.*, i. 45). How long he remained

in Scotland is not known, but he was connected with the Earl of Hertford's players by January 6, 1603, as shown by a payment to him for a performance at Court by that company (Steele, p. 126). He was married; his wife received from Henslowe on July 22, 1604, a loan of £5 on his behalf (*H.D.*, i. 213). He was a member of a provincial company under the patronage of Queen Anne by March 7, 1606, when he is named in a patent, with Robert Lee and Roger Barfield (*Eliz. Stage*, ii. 235). In 1608 he was manager of the Children of the King's Revels at the Whitefriars playhouse, and owned one whole share in the syndicate. An ensuing lawsuit describes him as a citizen and ironmonger of London, and refers to his family as being ten in number (Adams, *Playhouses*, pp. 315, 317–18). Subsequently he returned to Queen Anne's provincial company. On July 16, 1616, the Earl of Pembroke issued an order for the suppression of certain troupes traveling in the provinces under spurious licenses. Among others in this order are mentioned Thomas Swinnerton and Slater, who had separated themselves from the Queen's company and become leaders of "vagabonds and such idle persons" (Murray, ii. 343). About April, 1618, he is named as a Queen's man in a Letter of Assistance granting John Edmonds, Nathaniel Clay, and himself permission to play as "her Maiesties servants of her Royall Chamber of Bristol." Slater did not remain long with this troupe, which seems to have been taken under the King's patronage, and is next found with a provincial company in the Queen's service. Before December 6, 1618, he visited Ludlow as leader of "the Queenes Players" (Murray, ii. 5 ff., 15, 325). On May 13, 1619, he attended Queen Anne's funeral in London. After the death of the Queen, her provincial troupe was known as the players of the late Queen Anne. Slater continued as one of their leaders, and is traceable in provincial annals until 1625. He is recorded at Coventry on December 23, 1620, and between January 24 and August 28, 1623; at Leicester on October 15, 1625; and at Coventry on October 16, 1625 (Murray, i. 188, 196, 204, 205; ii. 248, 249, 250, 316). His name is found in the Southwark token-books from 1595 to 1602; Martin Slawter, "a servant," was buried at this parish on August 4, 1625 (*Eliz. Stage*, ii. 340).

SLAUGHTER, MARTIN.
See Martin Slater.

SLAUGHTER, WILLIAM.
A "ghost-name" evolved by Fleay (*Drama*, ii. 315–16) for a supposed member of Queen Elizabeth's company (*Eliz. Stage*, ii. 108*n*.).

SLEE, JOHN.
John Slee (or Slye) and three of his fellows who had been players to Queen Jane before her death in 1537 are mentioned about 1538 in a Chancery suit concerning the payments for a horse hired "to beare there playing garments" (Stopes, *Shak. Env.*, p. 236). In 1539–40 he was a Court Interluder in the service of Henry VIII (Collier, i. 116; *Eliz. Stage*, ii. 79*n*., 80*n*.).

SLEY, WILLIAM.
See William Sly.

SLY, WILLIAM.
William Sly first appears as Porrex in "Envy" and as a lord in "Lechery" of *2 Seven Deadly Sins*, acted by Strange's men about 1590 (Greg, *H.P.*, p. 152; *R.E.S.*, i. 262). On October 11, 1594, he bought from Henslowe "a Jewell of gowld seat with a whitte safer" for 8*s*., to be paid for at the rate of 1*s*. weekly (*H.D.*, i. 29). "Perowes sewt, which Wm Sley were" is mentioned in an inventory of theatrical apparel owned by the Admiral's men of March 13, 1598 (*H.P.*, p. 120). By 1598 he belonged to the Chamberlain's company, which he presumably joined at its formation in 1594. As a Chamberlain's man he appears in the actor-lists of *Every Man in his Humor* (1598) and of *Every Man out of his Humor* (1599). In 1603 the Chamberlain's men passed under

royal patronage; Sly is mentioned in the patent granted to the King's men on May 19, 1603 (*M.S.C.*, i. 264), and he continued with this company until his death in 1608. He appears in the 1623 folio list of Shakespearean players; in the cast of *Sejanus* (1603); in the coronation list of March 15, 1604; in the Induction to *The Malcontent* (1604); and in the actor-list of *Volpone* (1605). Augustine Phillips named him as an overseer, residuary executor, and legatee in his will dated May 4, 1605 (Collier, iii. 329). The Southwark token-books record a William Sly in Norman's Rents during 1588, in Horseshoe Court during 1593, and in Rose Alley during 1595 and 1596. The register of St. Giles's, Cripplegate, gives the baptism on September 24 and the burial on October 4, 1606, of John, son of William Sly, player, "base-borne on the body of Margaret Chambers." His own burial is recorded in the register of St. Leonard's, Shoreditch, on August 16, 1608. He made a nuncupative will on August 4, 1608 (Collier, iii. 381–87; *Variorum*, iii. 476–78). He named Cuthbert Burbage and James Sands as legatees, but assigned most of his property to Robert and Sisely Browne and their daughter Jane. Robert Browne received Sly's interest in the Globe, and Sisely was appointed executrix. The will was probated on August 24, notwithstanding that it had been witnessed only by several illiterate women and disputed by a kinsman named William Sly. Although not one of the original shareholders in the Globe, Sly was admitted to a share at some date after the death of Phillips in 1605 (Adams, *Mod. Phil.*, xvii. 4; Wallace, *N.U.S.*, x. 317). Early in August, 1608, just a few days before he died, he had obtained a lease in the Second Blackfriars syndicate of a seventh share, which was surrendered by his executrix to Richard Burbage after Sly's death (Adams, *Playhouses*, pp. 224, 225*n.*). Heywood, *Apology for Actors* (1612), p. 43, praises his "deserts" with those of other dead players.

SLYE, JOHN.
    See John Slee.

SLYE, THOMAS.

Kempe was attended by "Thomas Slye my Taberer" in his dance from London to Norwich (*Nine Daies Wonder*, ed. Dyce, p. 3). Perhaps Slye was regularly attached to Kempe in connection with the latter's clownage. Both men are pictured in the woodcut prefixed to *Nine Daies Wonder*.

SMITH, ANTHONY.

Anthony Smith by March 20, 1616, belonged to Prince Charles's men, and joined his fellows in signing an agreement with Alleyn and Meade (*H.P.*, p. 91). On May 7, 1625, he took part in King James's funeral procession (Murray, i. 161, 237). Charles, soon after his accession, took his father's players under his patronage, and several members of the old Prince Charles's company were no doubt transferred to the King's men. William Rowley is the only one of the Prince's troupe mentioned in the King's men's license on June 24, 1625; but Smith played Philargus, a rich miser, in Massinger's *Roman Actor*, licensed for the King's troupe on October 11, 1626. The omission of his name from the 1625 patent is not explained, but conceivably his transfer occurred about this time. As a King's man he appears in the cast of Ford's *Lover's Melancholy*, licensed November 24, 1628; in the livery allowance of May 6, 1629; and as Gerard, in Carlell's *Deserving Favorite*, published in 1629 (Murray, i. opp. 172).

SMITH, JOHN.

John Smith appears to have been a Court Interluder from about 1547 to 1580, at an annual salary of £3 6s. 8d., and an allowance for livery (Collier, i. 138, 238; *Eliz. Stage*, ii. 82, 84; Murray, i. 3, 4.). Perhaps he is to be identified with the John Smith who took the part of the "disard" or jester in the Christmas festivities of 1552–53, at the Court of Edward VI (Feuillerat, *Edw. & Mary*, pp. 89, 90, 97, 98, 119).

A DICTIONARY OF ACTORS

SMITH, JOHN.

John Smith appears in the actor-list of Jonson's *Epicoene*, which, according to the folio of 1616, was "Acted in the yeere 1609, by the Children of her Maiesties Revells."

SMITH, LEONARD.

Leonard Smith and Jeremy Allen are recorded at Coventry on August 19, 1640, as members of an unnamed company of players. They received a payment of 20*s.* under date of November 25, 1640 (Murray, ii. 254).

SMITH, MATTHEW.

Matthew Smith is named with Joseph Moore and Ellis Worth in a license granted to Prince Charles's men on December 7, 1631 (Murray, i. 218). During the same month (Adams, *Dram. Rec.*, p. 45) he acted with this company in Marmion's *Holland's Leaguer*, appearing as Agurtes, an impostor (Marmion, *Works*, pp. 2, 6). His name occurs in a warrant of May 10, 1632, appointing several of Prince Charles's men as Grooms of the Chamber (Stopes, *Jahrbuch*, xlvi. 96). He is mentioned in the Norwich records of February 21, 1638, when the company visited that town—but this does not necessarily indicate that he was present for the entry is a mere abstract of the 1631 license (Murray, ii. 358)'

SMYGHT, WILLIAM.

A player, who witnessed a loan from Philip to Francis Henslowe on June 1, 1595 (*H.D.*, i. 6; ii. 312).

SNELLER, JAMES.

See James Kneller.

SOMERSETT, GEORGE.

George Somersett was an Admiral's man about 1600–02. He acted with that company in *The Battle of Alcazar* (*c.* 1600–01), appearing as attendant, fury, and Vinioso, and is presumably the George of the plots of *Fortune's Tennis* (*c.* 1597–98) and of *1 Tamar*

Cam (1602), in the last of which he is noted as attendant, guard, captain, child, and (in the procession) as Cathayan (Greg, *H.P.*, pp. 153, 154; *R.E.S.*, i. 270; Chambers, *Eliz. Stage*, ii. 175–76). The register of St. Giles's, Cripplegate, records the burial on September 3, 1624, of an unnamed son of John Wilson (*q.v.*), "from the house of George Sommerset, musitian" (Collier, *Actors*, p. xix). An undated and detached note mentions "a Staple for George Sommersetts Dore" (*H.P.*, p. 150).

SOTHERNE, DAVID.

David Sotherne and three of his fellows who had been players to Queen Jane before her death in 1537 are mentioned about 1538 in a Chancery suit concerning the payments for a horse hired "to beare there playing garments" (Stopes, *Shak. Env.*, p. 236).

SOULAS, JOSIAS DE.

See Josias Floridor.

SOUTHEY, THOMAS.

A Court Interluder from 1547 to about 1556 (Collier, i. 136, 165; *Eliz. Stage*, ii. 82, 83).

SOUTHYN, ROBERT.

A London player in 1550, named in an order demanding that all plays be licensed by the King or his Council (Harrison, *England*, iv. 314).

SOYLES, WILLIAM.

William Soyles is named in a Ticket of Privilege granted on January 12, 1636, to the attendants "employed by his Majesty's servants the players of the Blackfriars, and of special use to them both on the Stage and otherwise for his Majesty's disport and service" (Stopes, *Jahrbuch*, xlvi. 99).

SPARKES, THOMAS.

A joint-lessee of the new Fortune playhouse, in which he obtained a whole share on May 20, 1622 (Warner, p. 246).

SPENCER, GABRIEL.

Gabriel Spencer, with several of his fellows of the Earl of Pembroke's company, is named as complainant in a lawsuit during 1597 against Francis Langley, builder and owner of the Swan playhouse (Wallace, *Eng. Studien*, xliii. 340; Adams, *Playhouses*, pp. 168–74). He is presumably the Gabriel mentioned in a stage-direction of the Folio *3 Henry VI* (I. ii. 48), "Enter Gabriel," which possibly refers to a production by Pembroke's men in 1592–93 or to a revival by the Chamberlain's men (*Eliz. Stage*, ii. 129–30, 200). This conjecture gives the possibility that he was a Chamberlain's man previous to his connection with Pembroke's men in 1597. As a result of the dissolution of Pembroke's company, caused by the production of *The Isle of Dogs*, Spencer joined the Admiral's men under Henslowe's management at the Rose; on October 11, 1597, his name is found in the company's accounts (*H.D.*, i. 82). He is recorded in various transactions with Henslowe, who sometimes refers to him simply as Gabriel. He appears as a witness, as acknowledging company and personal debts, as borrowing money, and as making payments (*H.D.*, ii. 312–13). On May 19, 1598, he borrowed 10*s*. from Henslowe "to bye a plvme of feathers which his mane Bradshawe feched of me" (*H.D.*, i. 79). This servant was probably Richard Bradshaw (*q.v.*), also a player. Spencer was killed by Ben Jonson with a three-shilling rapier in a duel on September 22, 1598 (Jeaffreson, *Middlesex*, i. pp. xxxviii-xlii). The register of St. Leonard's, Shoreditch, records his burial on September 24, and gives his residence as Hogge Lane (Collier, *Actors*, p. xxii). On September 26 Henslowe wrote to Alleyn at the Brill in Sussex (*H.P.*, p. 48): "Now to leat you vnderstand newes J will teall you some but yt is for me harde & heavey. Sence you weare with me J haue loste one of my company which hurteth me greatley, that is Gabrell, for he is slayen in Hogesdon fylldes by the hands of Bengemen Jonson bricklayer." The Middlesex records show that Spencer had himself previously slain one James Feake, who attacked him with a copper candlestick in the house of Richard Easte, a barber, in St. Leonard's. They fought on December 3, 1596; Feake died on December 6; and the coroner's inquisition is dated December 10 (Jeaffreson, i. pp. xlv, 234). Heywood, *Apology for Actors* (1612), p. 43, calls him "Gabriel" and praises his "deserts."

SPENCER, JOHN.

John Spencer ranks with Robert Browne as one of the most prominent leaders of English actors on the Continent. Nothing is heard of him in London or in provincial records; but he was active in the Netherlands and in Germany from 1605 to 1623, and used the clown-name Hans Stockfisch (Cohn, pp. lxxviii, lxxxiii–lxxxviii, xci–xcii; Herz, pp. 44–52; *Eliz. Stage*, ii. 288–92). He was apparently in the service of the Elector of Brandenburg during 1605, and visited Leyden in January and The Hague in May. His players then passed to the Elector of Saxony, at Dresden, where they seem to have remained for some time, and played at Cologne in April, 1608. For a time he was with the Duke of Stettin, then with the Elector of Brandenburg, and by July 14, 1609, again with the Elector of Saxony, at Dresden, where his troupe continued about two years. In 1611 he again returned to the Elector of Brandenburg. His company visited Danzig and Königsberg in July and August, and accompanied the Elector to Ortelsburg and Königsberg in October and November, and during the following year, when the troupe numbered nineteen actors and sixteen musicians, gave a spectacular production, "The Turkish Triumph-comedy." Spencer's men visited Dresden in April, 1613; Nuremberg in June; Augsburg in July and August; Nuremberg again in September; Regensburg in October; and Heidelberg, where they spent the winter. They were at Frankfort for the Easter fair of 1614; at Strassburg from May to July; and at Augsburg in August. By February, 1615, they came to Cologne, where all the players, besides Spencer's wife and children, were converted to Catholicism, as a result of the seductive oratory of a Franciscan friar. Spencer is next found at Strassburg in June and July, 1615, and at Frankfort for the autumn fair of the same year; he returned to Cologne during the winter of 1615–16. By August, 1617, he was again with the Elector of Saxony at Dresden, and in the following year returned to the patronage of John Sigismund, Elector of Brandenburg, at Berlin. During 1618 the company played at Elbing, Balge, and Königsberg, under the leadership of "Hans Stockfisch." The troupe is recorded at Danzig in July, 1619. Sigismund died in December, 1619, and his successor, Elector George William, did not favor theatrical organizations. In 1620 Hans Stockfisch petitioned for certain arrears in salary, but his claim was dismissed. As a result of the Elector's disfavor and the beginning of the Thirty Years' War, Spencer no doubt fared badly. He is not heard of again until February, 1623, when he and Sebastian Schadleutner were refused permission to play at Nuremberg. Nothing further is known of him. The register of St. Saviour's, Southwark, records on June 26, 1603, the baptism of Elizabeth and Maudlin Spencer, daughters of John, "a musitian" (Bentley, *T.L.S.*, Nov. 15, 1928, p. 856).

SPENCER, WILLIAM.

On February 29, 1589, William Spencer and William Gascoigne served as payees for a performance at Court by the Admiral's men (Steele, p. 98).

SQUIRE, LAWRENCE.

Master of the Chapel Royal, 1486–93 (Wallace, *Evolution*, pp. 25 ff.).

STAKHOUSE, ROGER.

A member of the Children of Paul's in 1554 (Hillebrand, *Child Actors*, p. 110).

STEVENS, THOMAS.

During 1586–87 Thomas Stevens was on the Continent. The Elsinore pay-roll records that he was in the Danish service from

June 17 to September 18, 1586, and served as payee for the company of actors. Soon he went to the Court of the Elector of Saxony, at Dresden, Germany, where he held an appointment as actor-entertainer until July 17, 1587 (Cohn, p. xxv; Riis, *Century Magazine*, lxi. 391; Herz, p. 3).

STOCKFISCH, HANS.

See John Spencer.

STOKEDALE, EDMUND.

A London player in 1550, named in an order demanding that all plays be licensed by the King or his Council (Harrison, *England*, iv. 314).

STONE, PHILIP.

A lessee of a seventh part of the Red Bull playhouse. About 1608–09 Thomas Swinnerton (*q.v.*) sold for £50 his interest in the playhouse to Philip Stone, who transferred the share to Thomas Woodford, about 1612–13 (Wallace, *N.U.S.*, ix. 291 ff.).

STRATFORD, ROBERT.

Robert Stratford played Triphoena, wife to Philautus, in Marmion's *Holland's Leaguer*, presented in December, 1631 (Adams, *Dram. Rec.*, p. 45), by "the high and mighty Prince Charles his servants, at the private house in Salisbury Court" (Marmion, *Works*, pp. 2, 6).

STRATFORD, WILLIAM.

William Stratford is named as one of Prince Henry's players in the household list of 1610 (*Eliz. Stage*, ii. 188). The Prince died in November, 1612, and his troupe soon passed under the patronage of the Palsgrave. Stratford is mentioned in the new patent granted to the Palsgrave's company on January 11, 1613 (*M.S.C.*, i. 275), and in the lease of the Fortune by the Palsgrave's men on October 31, 1618 (*H.P.*, p. 27). In 1623 he was still with the Palsgrave's company at the Fortune, and lived "att the vpper end of White Crosse Streete"; with Richard Claytone, Richard Grace, and Abraham Pedle, "all Actors at the fortune neere Golding lane," he was summoned to appear at court to answer a bill of complaint made by Gervase Markham (Wallace, *Jahrbuch*, xlvi. 348, 350). The register of St. Giles's, Cripplegate, records the burial of a William Stratford on August 27, 1625 (Malcolm, *Lond. Rediv.*, iii. 304). On April 30, 1624, he and others of the Palsgrave's men entered into a bond to Richard Gunnell, manager of the company (Hotson, pp. 52–53).

STRETCH, JOHN.

John Stretch is recorded at Norwich on March 10, 1635, when his troupe, presumably the King's Revels, applied for permission to act in that town (Murray, i. 279–80).

STROWDEWIKE, EDMUND.

A Court Interluder from about December 25, 1559, to his death on June 3, 1568 (*Eliz. Stage*, ii. 83, 84; Murray, i. 3).

STURVILE, GEORGE.

See George Stutfield.

STUTFIELD, GEORGE.

George Stutfield (Stutvile or Sturvile) appears as "Sturvile" in a warrant of May 10, 1632, appointing several of Prince Charles's men as Grooms of the Chamber (Stopes, *Jahrbuch*, xlvi. 96). Under the name of Stutvile he is recorded at Norwich on March 10, 1635, when his troupe, presumably the King's Revels, applied for permission to act in that town. As Stutfield he played a soldier and Bostar in Nabbes's *Hannibal and Scipio*, presented by Queen Henrietta's company in 1635 (Murray, i. opp. 266, 279–80). He is also mentioned in marginal notes to the plays in the British Museum Egerton MS. 1994. He apparently acted a "spirrit" and a Triton in *The Two Noble Ladies*, a nobleman's son in *Edmond Ironside*, and probably a servant in *Richard II* (Boas, *Library*, 1917, viii. 232, 233, 235).

STUTVILE, GEORGE.
See George Stutfield.

SUDBOROUGH, THOMAS.
See Thomas Sudbury.

SUDBURY, THOMAS.
Thomas Sudbury (or Sudborough) was a Court Interluder in 1530. He died in 1546 (Collier, i. 115; *Eliz. Stage*, ii. 79*n*., 80).

SUMNER, JOHN.
John Sumner was probably with Queen Henrietta's company at the Cockpit in Drury Lane from its formation in 1625 to its dissolution in 1637. As a Queen's man he played (Murray, i. opp. 266) Marwood in Shirley's *Wedding* (*c.* 1626); Young Bruce in Davenport's *King John and Matilda* (*c.* 1629); the Duke of Florence in Heywood's *Fair Maid of the West*, Part II (*c.* 1630); Mustapha in Massinger's *Renegado* (pr. 1630); and Himulco, in Nabbes's *Hannibal and Scipio* (1635). From Wright's *Historia Histrionica* (1699) we learn that he was among the "eminent actors" listed as "of principal note at the Cockpit" (Hazlitt's *Dodsley*, xv. 406). At the reorganization of Queen Henrietta's men about October, 1637, he joined the Revels company at Salisbury Court, as shown by Herbert's record (Adams, *Dram. Rec.*, p. 66): "I disposed of Perkins, Sumner, Sherlock and Turner, to Salisbury Court, and joynd them with the best of that company." He probably continued with this troupe until the closing of the playhouses in 1642. Wright tells us that "Perkins and Sumner of the Cockpit kept house together at Clerkenwell, and were there buried . . . some years before the Restoration" (Hazlitt's *Dodlsey*, xv. 411–12). Thus he may fairly be identified with the "Jno Sumpner" whose burial is recorded in the register of St. James, Clerkenwell, on September 18, 1651 (Hovenden, iv. 288).

SUMPNER, JOHN.
See John Sumner.

SUTTON, ROBERT.

A London player in 1550, named in an order demanding that all plays be licensed by the King or his Council (Harrison, *England*, iv. 314).

SWANSTON, ELLIARD.

Elliard Swanston is first heard of as a member of the Lady Elizabeth's company in 1622, when Herbert includes him among "the chiefe of them at the Phoenix" (Adams, *Dram. Rec.*, p. 63). He had joined the King's men before December 20, 1624, when he and others of the company signed a submission for playing *The Spanish Viceroy* without license (Adams, *Ibid.*, p. 21). With the King's men he continued until the closing of the playhouses in 1642. He took part in King James's funeral procession on May 7, 1625. As a player to King Charles he appears (Murray, i. 161, opp. 172) in the patent of June 24, 1625 (*M.S.C.*, i. 282); as Aretinus Clemens, Caesar's spy, in Massinger's *Roman Actor* (licensed October 11, 1626); in the actor-list of Ford's *Lover's Melancholy* (licensed November 24, 1628); as Ricardo, a wild courtier, in Massinger's *Picture* (licensed June 8, 1629); as Count Utrante in Carlell's *Deserving Favorite* (published 1629); as Chrysalus in Massinger's *Believe as You List* (licensed May 7, 1631); and as Lugier, the rough and confident tutor, in Fletcher's *Wildgoose Chase* (a revival, 1631). On October 24, 1633, he and Lowin craved the pardon of Herbert "for their ill manners" in acting an unexpurgated version of Fletcher's *Woman's Prize, or the Tamer Tamed* (Adams, *Dram. Rec.*, pp. 20 ff.). Wright in *Historia Histrionica* (1699) tells us that before 1642 Swanston played Othello (Hazlitt's *Dodsley*, xv. 406). At some period in his career he played Bussy D'Ambois in Chapman's play of that name. He is supposed to be the "third man" referred to in the Prologue to the 1641 edition of the play as undertaking the part of Bussy (Parrott, *Trag. of Chapman*, p. 3). His characterization of Ricardo in Massinger's *Picture* is perhaps also alluded to in the Prologue, "As

Richard he was liked" (cf. Graves, *Mod. Phil.*, xxiii. 3 ff.). That he played Bussy is shown by Gayton, *Pleasant Notes upon Don Quixot* (1654), p. 25: "Insomuch that our Emperour (having a spice of self-conceit before, was soundly peppered now) for he was instantly Metamorphoz'd into the stateliest, gravest and commanding soule, that ever eye beheld. *Taylor* acting *Arbaces*, or *Swanston D'Amboys*, were shadowes to him; his pace, his look, his voice, and all his garb was alter'd." He is named in the livery allowances of May 6, 1629, April 22, 1637, March 12, 1639, and March 20, 1641 (Stopes, *Jahrbuch*, xlvi. 95, 99, 101, 104). Before 1635 he had one-third of a share in the Blackfriars syndicate, as shown by the testimony of Shank in 1635 (Halliwell-Phillipps, *Outlines*, i. 314–15): "Mr. Swanston . . . who is most violent in this business . . . receaved this last yeere above £34 for the profitt of a third part of one part in the Blackfriers which hee bought for £20 . . . and yet hath injoyed the same two or three yeeres allready." After the petition in 1635 by him, Benfield, and Pollard, he acquired another third of a share in the Blackfriars and one whole share in the Globe (Adams, *Mod. Phil.*, xvii. 8; Halliwell-Phillipps, *Outlines*, i. 313–14). From this time to the closing of the playhouses, he and Lowin and Taylor were the most important members of the King's company. They received payment for the Court performances from April 27, 1634, to March 20, 1641 (Steele, pp. 244, 249, 262, 267, 274, 276). In 1647 he joined a group of the King's players in publishing the folio of Beaumont and Fletcher's plays; his name is appended to the dedicatory epistle (*Works*, i. p. x). Wright says of him: "I have not heard of one of these players of any note that sided with the other party [the Puritans], but only Swanston; and he professed himself a Presbyterian, took up the trade of a jeweller, and lived in Aldermanbury, within the territory of Father Calamy" (Hazlitt's *Dodsley*, xv. 409). This statement is in part confirmed by a pamphlet quoted by Collier (*H.E.D.P.*, i. 488), *A Key to the Cabinet of the Parliament* (1648), where the writer asks: "What need is there of any playes? Will not these serve well enough, especially when they have gotten Hillyar Swansted, the player, to be one [a Puritan]?" In Thomas Shadwell's *Virtuoso*, acted in 1676, he and Taylor and Lowin are praised by Snarl, who admires nothing but the things of a former age (*Works*, i. 328):

Miranda. Methinks, though all Pleasures have left you, you may go see Plays.
Snarl. I am not such a Coxcomb, I thank God: I have seen 'em at *Black-Fryers*. Pox, they act like Poppets now, in Sadness. I, that have seen *Joseph Taylor*, and *Lowen*, and *Swanstead*! Oh, a brave roaring Fellow, would make the House shake again! Besides, I can never endure to see Plays, since Women came on the Stage. Boys are better by half.

Collier (*H.E.D.P.*, iii. 437*n*.) says that the registers of Aldermanbury "contain many entries of the birth of his children, beginning in 1622, and ending in 1638, after which date we hear no more of him in that parish." Leslie Hotson, in his *Commonwealth and Restoration Stage* (1928), pp. 15, 73, gives more complete information: Swanston's will was dated June 24, 1651; he died before July 3 of that year, and is described as "Eylaeardt Swanston, of St. Mary Aldermanbury, London, gent."

SWETHERTON, THOMAS.

See Thomas Swinnerton.

SWINNERTON, ABEL.

Abel Swinnerton is named in a warrant of June 30, 1628, appointing several of the Lady Elizabeth's (Queen of Bohemia's) players as Grooms of the Chamber (Stopes, *Jahrbuch*, xlvi. 94).

SWINNERTON, THOMAS.

Thomas Swinnerton (or Swetherton) was a member of Queen Anne's company from its formation late in 1603 or early in 1604. He took part in the coronation procession of March 15, 1604, and is named in both the license of April 15, 1609, and the duplicate patent granted to the traveling company on January 7, 1612

(*Eliz. Stage*, ii. 229; *M.S.C.*, i. 270; Murray, ii. 343). In 1605 he was lessee of a share, or a seventh part, of the Red Bull playhouse, presumably at that time occupied by the Queen's men. The lease entitled him also to a gatherer's place. Some three years later he sold his interest to one Philip Stone for £50 (Wallace, *N.U.S.*, ix. 294). Swinnerton was an active leader of the Queen's provincial company. He is recorded in the Norwich accounts on April 18, 1614, May 6, 1615, March 30, 1616, May 29, 1616, and May 31, 1617. Previous to this last appearance in Norwich, the Earl of Pembroke had issued an order on July 16, 1616, for the suppression of certain provincial troupes that were using questionable licenses. Among others in this order are mentioned Swinnerton and Martin Slater, who are said to have separated themselves from the Queen's company and become leaders of "vagabonds and such idle persons." On May 13, 1619, he attended Queen Anne's funeral in London. After the death of the Queen, her provincial troupe was known as the players to the late Queen Anne. Under Swinnerton's leadership the players visited Leicester in 1619 and Coventry on March 29, 1620 (Murray, i. 191, 192, 203–04; ii. 248, 313, 340, 341, 343). On March 16, 1625, Herbert granted a license to Swinnerton, Ellis Guest, and Arthur Grimes. They were in Leicester on March 6, 1626. Swinnerton is not mentioned in the company's new license of June 7, 1628, by which date he had apparently organized a troupe under his own management. He appears as the leader of such a company at Norwich on July 19, 1628, and at Leicester during the same year (Murray, ii. 101, 102, 105, 316, 317, 371). This is the last we hear of him.

SYFERWESTE, RICHARD.

On September 4, 1602, Richard Syferweste borrowed money from Henslowe "to ride downe to his felowes," who were presumably in the country. Richard Perkins, of Worcester's men, is mentioned in the same entry, which would suggest that Syferweste was also a member of Worcester's company. But Worcester's players were not on a tour at this time, for they were acting at the Rose (*H.D.*, i. 178; ii. 314).

SYMCOCKES.

The Henslowe accounts show that one Symcockes was a member of the Duke of Lennox's company of players about 1604–05. There was an undated loan of £7 by Philip to Francis Henslowe "to goyne with owld Garlland and Symcockes and Saverey when they played in the duckes nam at ther laste goinge owt" (*H.D.*, i. 160; ii. 314). The loan may be safely dated about 1604–05, for the other players concerned in the transactions are found during this period in other notices of Lennox's men.

SYMONS, JOHN.

John Symons was a tumbler. He served as payee for feats of activity and tumbling by Strange's men at Court on January 1, 1583. He appeared again at Court with feats of activity and vaulting on January 1, 1585, when the Earl of Oxford was his patron. By January 9, 1586, he had returned to Lord Strange's patronage, and was giving exhibitions at Court. He is again recorded at Court on December 28, 1587, presumably as a member of Strange's company. On December 29, 1588, and February 11, 1599, he seems to have been at Court with the Admiral's men, who were paid for activities and plays, and the Revels accounts for 1587–89 record "a paire of fflannell hose for Symmons the Tumbler." This connection, as in the other instances, was apparently only temporary, for the Nottingham accounts for 1588–89 record a payment of 20s. to "Symons and his companie, beinge the Quenes players" (*Eliz. Stage*, ii. 119; iv. 159, 161, 162; Murray, ii. 375).

T., R.

With the King's men in 1619, R. T., an unidentified actor or stage-attendant, played five minor parts in *Sir John van Olden Barnavelt* (ed. Frijlinck, p. clx): an officer, a provost, a servant, a huntsman, and a messenger.

346

TAILOR, ROBERT.

Robert Tailor belonged to the Admiral's men about 1597–1601. He acted with them in *Fortune's Tennis* about 1597–98, and appears as an attendant, a fury, and as Jonas in *The Battle of Alcazar*, about 1600–01 (Greg, *H.P.*, pp. 153, 154; *R.E.S.*, i. 270; Chambers, *Eliz. Stage*, ii. 175–76).

TARBOCK, JOHN.

John Tarbock was a patentee for the Children of the Queen's Revels at Whitefriars, on January 4, 1610 (Adams, *Playhouses*, p. 318).

TARLTON, RICHARD.

Richard Tarlton, doubtless the most popular Elizabethan comedian, is said (Fuller, *Worthies*, ii. 311) to have been born at Condover in Shropshire, where "he was in the field, keeping his Father's Swine, when a Servant of Robert Earl of Leicester . . . was so highly pleased with his *happy unhappy* answers, that he brought him to Court, where he became the most famous Jester to Queen Elizabeth." Another account of his early life is given by his fellow-actor Robert Wilson in *The Three Lords and Three Ladies of London*, published in 1590 (Hazlitt's *Dodsley*, vi. 396–98):

Simplicity. Thou wast the more fool. If thou cannot read, I'll tell thee. This is Tarlton's picture. Didst thou never know Tarlton?
Will. No: what was that Tarlton? I never knew him.
Simplicity. What was he? A prentice in his youth of this honourable city, God be with him. When he was young, he was leaning to the trade that my wife useth now, and I have used, *vide lice shirt* [*videlicet*] water-bearing. I-wis, he hath toss'd a tankard in Cornhill ere now: if thou knew'st him not, I will not call thee ingram [ignorant]; but if thou knewest not him, thou knowest nobody. I warrant, here's two crackropes knew him.
Wit. I dwelt with him.
Simplicity. Didst thou? now, give me thy hand: I love thee the better.
Will. And I, too, sometime.

Simplicity. You, child! did you dwell with him sometime?
Wit dwelt with him, indeed, as appeared by his rhyme,
And served him well; and Will was with him now and then.
But, soft, thy name is Wealth; I think in earnest he was little
acquainted with thee.
O' it was a fine fellow, as e'er was born:
There will never come his like, while the earth can corn.
O passing fine Tarlton! I would thou hadst lived yet.
Wealth. He might have some, but thou showest small wit.
There is no such fineness in the picture that I see.
Simplicity. Thou art no Cinque-Port man; thou art not wit-free.
The fineness was within, for without he was plain;
But it was the merriest fellow, and had such jests in store
That, if thou hadst seen him, thou would'st have laughed
thy heart sore.

Whatever his origin, the earliest notice of him is the "Qd.
Richard Tarlton" at the end of a ballad entitled: *A very lamentable
and Wofull Discours of the fierce fluds whiche lately flowed in Bedford-
shire, in Lincolnshire, and in many other places, with the great losses of
sheep and other cattel, the 5 of October, 1570* (Arber, i. 440). The
ballad is reprinted by Halliwell–Phillipps, *Tarlton's Jests*, p. 126,
and by Collier, *Old Ballads*, p. 78. Stow (*Annales*, ed. Howes,
1631, p. 667) gives an account of the "terrible tempest of wind
and raine" on October 5, 1570. Tarlton's ballad on the floods
consists of thirty-six stanzas, of which the first two may be taken
as representative:

> All faithful harts come waile,
>   Com rent your garments gay,
> Els nothing can prevaile
>   To turn Gods wrath away.
>
> Of waters fierce and fel,
>   And fluds both huge and hie,
> You may report and tel
>   Of places far and nye.

The Stationers' Registers accredit him with other pieces, which
are not extant: 1576, "a newe booke in Englishe verse intituled

Tarltons Toyes" (Arber, ii. 306); 1578, "Tarltons Tragical
Treatises conteyninge sundrie Discourses and pretie conceiptes
bothe in prose and verse" (Arber, ii. 323); and 1579, "Tarltons
Devise upon this vnlooked for great snowe" (Arber, ii. 346).
Also attributed to him is *Tarlton's Jigge of a horse loade of Fooles*
(*c.* 1579), taken from a manuscript in Collier's possession (Collier, *New Facts*, p. 18; Halliwell-Phillipps, *Jests*, p. xx); the jig,
however, may be regarded as one of Collier's fabrications. The
first reference to him as a player occurs about 1579 in *The Letter-
Book of Gabriel Harvey* (ed. E. J. L. Scott, p. 67), where he is mentioned with Robert Wilson in terms that suggest he was already
conspicuous as an actor: "Howe peremptorily ye have preiudishd
my good name for ever in thrustinge me thus on the stage to make
tryall of my extemporall faculty, and to play Wylsons or Tarletons parte." He became associated with Queen Elizabeth's men
when the troupe was first organized in 1583; he is named in a
London record that gives the personnel of the company at this
time (*Eliz. Stage*, ii. 106); and he continued as the talented and
popular comedian of the Queen's company until his death in 1588.
Howes (continuation of Stow's *Annales*, 1631, p. 698) speaks of
Tarlton and Wilson as "two rare men" of the Queen's players,
and says that "for a wondrous plentifull pleasant extemporall
wit," Tarlton was "the wonder of his time." He was with the
Queen's men at Norwich in June, 1583, when an affray occurred
between the players and one Wynsdon and his servant (see John
Bentley). There seems to be no likelihood that he is identical
with "one Tarlton" whose house in Paris Garden about 1585 was
under suspicion as a resort of papists (Wright, *Elizabeth*, ii. 250).
He is named in a document of June 30, 1588, concerning the non-
payment of subsidy by certain members of the Queen's company
(*M.S.C.*, i. 354). His popularity as a comedian was supplemented
by his fame as a playwright. For the Queen's players he wrote in
1585 *The Seven Deadly Sins*, a comedy that attained very great
popularity. Evidence of Tarlton's authorship is given by Gabriel

Harvey, *Four Letters* (1592), who, after telling an anecdote (*Works*, i. 194) concerning Tarlton, says that Nashe's *Pierce Penilesse* (1592) is—

not Dunsically botched-vp, but right-formally conueied, according to the stile, and tenour of Tarletons president, his famous play of the seauen Deadly sinnes: which most-deadly, but most liuely playe, I might haue seene in London: and was verie gently inuited thereunto at Oxford, by *Tarleton* himselfe, of whome I merrily demaunding, which of the seauen, was his owne deadlie sinne, he bluntly aunswered after this manner: By God, the sinne of other Gentlemen, Lechery. Oh but that, M. Tarleton, is not your part vpon the stage: you are too-blame, that dissemble with the world, & haue one part for your frends pleasure, an other for your owne. I am somewhat of Doctor Pernes religion, quoth he: and abruptlie tooke his leaue.

In *Strange Newes* (1592), Nashe alludes to Harvey's charge of plagiarism, and thus strengthens the indication that Tarlton was the author of the play (*Works*, i. 304): "Haue I imitated Tarltons play of the seauen deadly sinnes in my plot of Pierce Penilesse?" He was a great favorite with royalty and nobility. Fuller (*Worthies*, ii. 312) says: "Our Tarlton was master of his *Faculty*. When Queen Elizabeth was *serious* (I dare not say *sullen*) and out of *good humour*, he could *un-dumpish* her at his pleasure. Her highest *Favorites* would, in some cases, go to *Tarleton* before they would go to the *Queen*, and he was their *Usher* to prepare their advantagious access unto Her. In a word, *He told the Queen more of her faults* than most of her *Chaplains*, and *cured her Melancholy better* than all *of her Physicians*." That he carried his privilege too far and incurred the displeasure of the Queen is shown by an anecdote related by Bohun, *Elizabeth*, p. 352 (Disraeli, *Amenities*, p. 595; Halliwell-Phillipps, *Jests*, p. xxix):

At supper she [Queen Elizabeth] would divert herself with her friends and attendance; and if they made her no answer, she would put them upon mirth and pleasant discourse with great civility. She would then also admit Tarleton, a famous comedian and a pleasant talker, and other such like men, to divert her with stories of the town, and the common jests, or accidents; but so that they kept within the bounds of modesty and chastity. In the winter-time, after supper, she would some time hear a song, or a lesson or two plaid upon the lute; but she would be much offended if there was any rudeness to any person, any reproach or licentious reflections used. Tarlton, who was then the best comedian in England, had made a pleasant play, and when it was acting before the Queen, he pointed at Sir Walter Rawleigh, and said: See, the Knave commands the Queen; for which he was corrected by a frown from the Queen; yet he had the confidence to add that he was of too much and too intolerable a power; and going on with the same liberty, he reflected on the over-great power and riches of the Earl of Leicester, which was so universally applauded by all that were present, that she thought fit for the present to bear these reflections with a seeming unconcernedness. But yet she was so offended, that she forbad Tarleton, and all her jesters from coming near her table, being inwardly displeased with this impudent and unseasonable liberty.

He was also skilled in fencing, as evedenced by the record on October 23, 1587, when "Mr. Tarlton, ordenary grome off her majestes chamber," was admitted to the degree of Master of Fence (Halliwell-Phillipps, *Jests*, p. xi). This title was then highly regarded; accoding to *The Mountebank's Masque* (Marston, *Works*, iii. 429), "A Master of Fence is more honoutable than a Master of Arts; for good fightin was before good writing." A scrap of paper (*S.P.D. Eliz.*, ccxv. 89) records "How Tarlton played the God Lutz with a flitch of bacon at his back, and how the Queen bade them take away the knave for making her laugh so excessively, as he fought against her little dog, Perrico de Faldas, with his sword and long staffe, and bade the Queen take off her mastie; and what my Lord Sussex and Tarlton said to one another. The three things that make a woman lovely." Tarlton made his will, died, and was buried at St. Leonard's, Shoreditch, on September 3, 1588. His will (Halliwell-Phillipps, *Jests*, pp. xiii–xv), which describes him as "one of the Gromes of the Quenes Majesties chamber," leaves his property to his son Philip, and appoints as guardians for the boy Tarlton's mother,

Katharine, then a widow, his friend Robert Adams, and his fellow
William Johnson. Soon after Tarlton's death a dispute arose as to
the disposition of his property (*Eliz. Stage*, ii. 343; *D.N.B.*, lv.
370). Katharine Tarlton alleged that her son had been unduly
influenced in assigning £700 in property to Robert Adams, apparently a lawyer, and had made a second will. Another record
(*S.P.D. Eliz.*, ccxv. 90) shows that Tarlton had addressed a
death-bed petition to Walsingham, imploring him to see that
his mother and six-year-old son Philip, godson of Philip Sidney,
are not defrauded by "a sly fellow, one Mr. Adams." The Stationers' Registers record after Tarlton's death several pieces
either purporting to have been written by him, or taking advantage of his popularity to increase their sale: 1588, "a ballad
intituled Tarltons Farewell" (Arber, ii. 500); 1589, "a sorrowfull
newe sonnette, intituled Tarltons Recantacon vppon this theame
gyven him by a gentleman at the Bel savage without Ludgate
(nowe or ells never) beinge the laste theame he sange" (Arber,
ii. 526); 1589, "Tarltons repentance of his farewell to his frendes
in his sicknes a little before his deathe" (Arber, ii. 531); and 1590,
"a pleasant Dyttye Dialogue wise betwene Tarltons ghost and
Robyn Good Fellowe" (Arber, ii. 559). The first, *Tarltons Farewell*, is perhaps to be identified with "A pretie new ballad,
intituled Willie and Peggie, to the tune of Tarlton's Carroll"
(*Archiv*, cxiv. 341; *Shirburn Ballads*, ed. Clark, p. 351). Although
the ballad ends "quod Richard Tarlton," it is evidently a lament
over the famous comedian under the pseudonym of Willie. This
evidence supports the theory (*Notes and Queries*, 1885, xi. 417;
Halliwell-Phillipps, *Outlines*, ii. 394) that Tarlton is "Our pleasant Willy" mentioned by Spenser, *Teares of the Muses* (1591).

> Our pleasant Willy, ah! is dead of late:
> With whom all joy and jolly meriment
> Is also deaded, and in dolour drent.

His "caroll" is again alluded to in "A proper new ballade wherin

is plaine to be seene, how god blesseth England for love of our
Queene: Soung to the tune of Tarletons caroll" (*Archiv*, cxiv.
344). Another ballad, signed R. T., is also accredited to Tarlton
(Huth, *Ancient Ballads*, pp. lv, 377): "A prettie newe Ballad,
intytuled: The Crowe sits upon the wall, Please one and please
all." Soon after his death appeared *Tarltons Newes out of Purga-
torie. Onelye such a jest as his Jigge, fit for Gentlemen to laugh at an
houre, &c. Published by an old companion of his, Robin Goodfellow.*
The quarto has no date, but the entry in the Stationers' Registers
is dated June 26, 1590 (Arber, ii. 553). The author explains that,
withdrawing from the crowded playhouse for a walk in the
fields, he fell asleep and was visited by Tarlton's ghost, which
described Purgatory, and related eight stories to account for the
punishment of those confined there. The tales are picaresque in
nature, and are based chiefly upon Boccaccio. The writer declares
that Tarlton "was only superficially seene in learning, having no
more but a bare insight into the Latin tung," and describes him
as "one attired in russet, with a buttond cap on his head, a great
bag by his side, and a strong bat in his hand" (ed. Halliwell-Phillipps, pp. 53, 54). In 1590 appeared an answer entitled: *The Cobler
of Caunterburie, or an Invective against Tarltons Newes out of Purga-
torie. A merrier jest then a clownes Jigge, and fitter for Gentlemens
humors,* which is another collection of tales. A description of
Tarlton, quite similar to that given in *Tarltons Newes*, is found in
Henry Chettle's *Kind-Heart's Dream* (1592), where the author,
feigning a dream, says he recognized Tarlton's ghost "by his
sute of russet, his buttond cap, his taber, his standing on the toe,
and other tricks." Chettle puts into his mouth a defense of plays
and a diatribe on landlords, under the heading: "To all Maligners
of Honest Mirth, Tarleton wisheth Continuall Melancholy"
(ed. Rimbault, pp. 10, 12, 35, 56). For light upon the character
and personality of the famous comedian the most important work
is *Tarltons Jests, drawn into three parts: His Court Witty Jests; His
Sound City Jests; His Country Pretty Jests; full of Delight, Wit, and*

Honest Mirth. The earliest edition now known is that of 1611, but there is reason to believe that at least the first part dates from the latter years of the sixteenth century. On August 4, 1600, the second part was entered in the Stationers' Registers (Arber, iii. 168); and, on February 21, 1609, the book was transferred from one publisher to another (Arber, iii. 402). We cannot accept the *Jests* as authentic in every detail, but the anecdotes are no doubt partly representative of Tarlton's clownage, and contain some biographical facts that are supported by other evidence. The more important items in the *Jests* may be summarized (Halliwell-Phillipps, *Jests*, p. xxxviii; Chambers, *Eliz. Stage*, ii. 344): Tarlton was a member of the Queen's troupe (Halliwell-Phillipps, pp. 13, 27, 29, 30, 33); he played at the Bull in Bishopsgate (13, 24), the Curtain (16), and the Bell in Gracechurch Street (24); he acted both the clown (Dericke) and the Judge to Knell's Harry in *The Famous Victories of Henry the Fifth* (24); he jested before Queen Elizabeth and the nobility (5, 7, 8); he was a Protestant (6, 34, 37); he was a skilled fencer (9); he was dissipated in his life (9, 13, 32, 33, 36); he kept the Saba tavern in Gracechurch Street, where he was scavenger of the ward (15, 21, 22); his father lived at Ilford (40); his wife, Kate, was of a loose character (17, 19); he kept an ordinary in Paternoster Row (21, 26); and he had a squint eye (12) and a flat nose (28). Halliwell-Phillipps gives as a frontispiece to his edition of the *Jests* a reproduction of a portrait-drawing of Tarlton by John Scottowe in an initial letter to some verses on Tarlton's death in Harl. MS. 3885, f. 19. The portrait represents Tarlton as a short, broad-faced man with a flat nose and curly hair, wearing a cap, carrying a money-bag at his side, and playing on a tabor and a pipe. The verses claim that the drawing is a good likeness of the comedian (*Jests*, p. xliv):

> The picture here set down
> Within this letter T:
> A-right doth shewe the forme and shape
> Of Tharlton unto the.

When hee in pleasant wise
The counterfet expreste
Of clowne, with cote of russet hew
And sturtups, with the reste.

Whoe merry many made
When he appeared in sight;
The grave and wise, as well as rude,
At him did take delight.

The partie nowe is gone
And closlie clad in claye;
Of all the jesters in the lande
He bare the praise awaie.

Now hath he plaid his parte,
And sure he is of this,
If he in Christe did die to live
With Him in lasting bliss.

Wilfred Partington (*Smoke Rings and Roundelays*, pp. 9, 10) calls attention to the fact that the jest on *How Tarlton tooke tobacco at the first comming up of it* (Halliwell-Phillipps, p. 26), namely that two of Tarlton's companions, seeing smoke come from his nose, "cryed out, fire, fire, and threw a cup of wine in Tarlton's face," was published at least as early as 1611, "whereas the later variant in which Raleigh was the central figure did not appear in print until 1708." The reference to Yorick in *Hamlet*, V. i. 201, has been taken as a compliment to the memory of Tarlton. William Percy celebrates him in *Cuck-Queanes and Cuckolds Errants* (c. 1601), and has his ghost speak the prologue. The setting of the play is given as the Tarlton Inn, Colchester, of which he is referred to as the "quondam controller and induperator" (*Eliz. Stage*, ii. 345; iii. 465). No other Elizabethan actor has been the object of so many notices in contemporary and later writing, or has been remembered with such various and practical tokens of esteem. A marginal entry in Stow's *Annales* (ed. 1631, p. 698) notes: "Tarleton so beloued that men vse his picture for their signes." This

statement is borne out by Joseph Hall, *Satires* (1599), vi. 1. 204
(*Works*, xii. 279):

> · O honour, far beyond a brazen shrine,
> To sit with Tarleton on an ale-post's sign!

Also, by Ellis, *History of Shoreditch* (1798), p. 209, who says that
even as late as 1798 "His portrait, with tabor and pipe, still
serves as a sign to an alehouse in the Borough." John Oldham,
Remains (ed. 1703, p. 108), says that his picture often adorned
the jakes: "One would take him for the Picture of Scoggin or
Tarleton on a Privy-house Door, which by long standing there
has contracted the Colour of the neighbouring Excrements." He
is also honored in the title of a popular nursery song, published
in *Pigges Corantoe, or Newes from the North*, 1642 (Halliwell-Phillipps, *Nursery Rhymes of England*, pp. 12, 163):

> *Old Tarlton's Song*
> The king of France went up the hill,
> With twenty thousand men;
> The king of France came down the hill,
> And ne'er went up again.

George Wilson, *Commendation of Cockes, and Cock-fighting* (1607),
relates that there was on "the 4th day of May, 1602, at a cocke-
fighting in the citie of Norwich aforesayd a cocke called Tarleton
(who was so intituled, because he alwayes came to the fight like
a drummer, making a thundering noyse with his winges) which
cocke fought many battels, with mighty and fierce aduersaries"
(*British Bibliographer*, ed. Brydges and Haslewood, iv. 320).
Below I cite the more interesting allusions to Tarlton.

Roger Williams, *A Brief Discourse of Warre* (1590):
Our pleasant Tarleton would counterfeite many artes, but he
was no bodie out of his mirths.

Nashe, *Pierce Penilesse*, 1592 (*Works*, i. 188):
A tale of a wise Iustice. Amongst other cholericke wise Iustices,
he was one, that hauing a play presented before him and his

Towneship by *Tarlton* and the rest of his fellowes, her Maiesties seruants, and they were now entring into their first merriment (as they call it), the people began exceedingly to laugh, when *Tarlton* first peept out his head. Whereat the Iustice, not a little moued, and seeing with his beckes and nods hee could not make them cease, he went with his staffe, and beat them round about vnmercifully on the bare pates, in that they, being but Farmers & poore countrey Hyndes, would presume to laugh at the Queenes men, and make no more account of her cloath in his presence.

Nashe, *Pierce Penilesse*, 1592 (*Works*, i. 215):

Tarlton, Ned Allen, Knell, Bentlie, shall be made knowne to *France, Spaine,* and *Italie:* and not a part that they surmounted in, more than other, but I will there note and set downe, with the manner of theyr habites and attyre.

Nashe, *Strange Newes*, 1592 (*Works*, i. 319):

Not *Tarlton* nor *Greene* but haue beene contented to let my simple iudgement ouerrule them in some matters of wit.

B. R., *Greenes Newes both from Heauen and Hell* (1593), ed. Mc-Kerrow, p. 58:

In comes *Dick Tarlton*, apparrelled like a Clowne, and singing this peece of an olde song.

> If this be trewe as true it is,
>   Ladie, Ladie:
> God send her life may mend the misse,
>   Most deere Ladie.

This suddaine iest brought the whole company into such a vehement laughter, that not able agayne to make them keepe silence, for that present tyme they were faine to breake vppe.

John Harington, *Ulysses upon Ajax* (1596):

And so to Tarlton's Testament I commend you, a little more drinke, then a little more bread, and a few more clothes, and God be at your sport, Master Tarleton.

I could use Tarlton's jest upon you touching the secret of barley, who, attending one day at a great dinner on Sir Christopher Hatton, Lord Chancellor deceased, by chance, among other

pretty jests, gave him unadvisedly the lie; for which the honourable person merrily reproving him, instead of submitting himself, he thus wittily justified: My Lord, said he, is it not a custom
when a prince hath spoken any thing note worthy to say he hath
delivered it majestically? Again, when you that are *monsieurs,
my lords, excellencies, altesses,* and such like speak any thing, say
not the assistants straitways, he concluded honourably? Nay, in
every estate, if either noble, right worshipful, worshipful, gentle,
common, honest, dishonest, poor or rich, sick or whole, *et sic
ad infinitum,* speak any thing, doth not the world conclude
straight that they have spoken nobly, right worshipfully, worshipfully, gently, commonly, honestly, poorly, richly, sickly,
wholly? Nought without a lie, my Lord, quoth Dick Tarlton,
nought without a lie: he that therefore pays it with a frown or
stab, forgetteth himself.

Harington, *A new discourse of a stale subject, called the Metamor-
phosis of Ajax* (1596):

What should I speake of the great league betweene God and
man, made in circumcision? impressing a painefull *stigma* or
character in God's peculiar people, though nowe most happily
taken away in the holy sacrament of baptisme. What the worde
signified I have known reverent and learned have bene ignorant,
and we call it a very well of circumcision, and uncircumcision,
though the Remists, of purpose belike to varie from Geneva,
will needs bring in Prepuse, which worde was after admitted into
the theater with great applause by the mouth of Mayster Tarlton,
the excellent comedian, when many of the beholders, that were
never circumcised, had as great cause as Tarlton to complaine of
their Prepuse.

The Returne of Parnassus (*c.* 1597–1601), ed. Macray, p. 34:

Ingenioso. O fustie worlde! were there anie commendable passage to Styx and Acharon I would go live with Tarleton, and
never more bless this dull age with a good line. Why, what an
unmanerlie microcosme was this swine-faced clowne! But that
the vassall is not capable of anie infamie, I would bepainte him;
but a verie goose quill scornes such a base subject, and there is no
inke fitt to write his servill name but a scholeboye's, that hath
bene made by the mixture of urin and water.

Thomas Bastard, *Chrestoleros* (1598), ed. Grosart, p. 82, Epigram 39:

De Richardo Tharltono

Who taught me pleasant follies, can you tell?
I was not taught and yet I did excell;
'Tis harde to learne without a president,
'Tis harder to make folly excellent;
I sawe, yet had no light to guide mine eyes,
I was extold for that which all despise.

Meres, *Palladis Tamia* (1598), ed. Smith, *Eliz. Crit. Essays*, ii. 323:

As Antipater Sidonius was famous for extemporall verse in Greeke, and Ouid for his *Quicquid conabar dicere versus erat:* so was our Tarleton, of whome Doctor Case, that learned physitian, thus speaketh in the Seuenth Booke and seuenteenth chapter of his *Politikes: Aristoteles suum Theodoretum laudauit quendam peritum Tragaediarum actorem, Cicero suum Roscium; nos Angli Tarletonum, in cuius voce et vultu omnes iocosi affectus, in cuius cerebroso capite lepidae facetiae habitant.*

Samuel Rowlands, *The Letting of Humours Blood in the Head-Vaine* (1600), Epigram 30, p. 36 (*Works*, i):

When *Tarlton* clown'd it in a pleasant vaine,
And with conceites, did good opinions gaine
Vpon the Stage, his merry humors shop,
Clownes knew the Clowne, by his great clownish slop.
But now th' are gull'd, for present fashion sayes,
Dicke Tarltons part, Gentlemens breeches playes:
In euery streete where any *Gallant* goes,
The swagg'ring Sloppe, is *Tarltons* clownish hose.

Charles Fitzgeoffrey, *Cenotaphia* (1601), ed. Grosart, p. xx:

Richardo Tarltono

Conspicienda amplo quoties daret ora Theatro
Tarltonus, lepidum non sine dente caput,
Spectantum horrifico coelum intonat omne cachinno,
Audijt & plausus aula suprema Iovis.
Attoniti stupuere Poli stupuere polorum
Indigenae indigites coelicolumque cohors.
Hausuri ergo tuos omnes *Tarltone* lepores

Elysia in terras valle redire parant.
Id metuans, ne fors deserta Ivpiter aula
Bellerophontaeos transigat vsque dies,
Ha! crudele tibi scelus imperat *Atropos*, et tu
Tarltonvm ad *Plures*, insidiosa rapis.
Quod nisi tu peteres superos *Tarltone*, petissent
Te superi, ad blandos conflua turba jocos.

Grosart, p. xxiii, gives a translation "for the benefit of the general reader":

To Richard Tarlton

Oft in the theatre as Tarlton's face
Was seen, instinct with keenness as with grace,
A thunderous roar of laughter straight arose
From all who saw, and shook the sky's repose;
The heavens were all astonished and the host
Of native deities who crowd heaven's coast.
To enjoy the pleasantries they all prepare,
Tarlton, to quit for earth the elysian air.
Jove, fearing lest his halls being vacant made,
His lonseome days should pass in lowering shade,
A cruel crime he wreaks upon thy head:
The treacherous Fury bids thee join the Dead.
But if thou hadst not sought the gods on high,
The gods to seek thee would have left the sky,
Circling thy gracious jocularity!

T. Wright, *Passions of the Minde in generall* (1601), quoted by Dobell in his edition of *The Partiall Law*, p. 127:

Sometimes I have scene Tarleton play the clowne, and use no other breeches than such sloppes or slivings as now many gentlemen weare: they are almost capable of a bushel of wheate; and if they be of sackecloth, they would serve to carrie mawlt to the mill.

John Manningham, *Diary*, January, 1602, ed. Bruce, p. 16:

Tarlton called Burley house gate in the Strand towardes the Savoy, the Lord Treasurers Almes gate, because it was seldom or never opened.

Ashmolean MS. 38, 187 (also in *Hobson' Jests*, 1607, where the anecdote is attributed to Hobson):

A DICTIONARY OF ACTORS

Uppon on Medcalfe
I desire you all in the Lordes behalfe
To praye for the soule of poere John Calfe.

But Tarlton, the jester, noting the simplicitie of the poett, wrightes this:

O cruell death, more subtell than a fox,
Thou mightst have lett hym live to have bine an oxe,
For to have eaten both grass hay and corne,
And like his sire to have worn a horne.

Stradling, *Epigrammata* (1607):

Rich. Tarltono, Comoedorum principi. Epit.
Cujus (viator) sit sepulchrum hoc scire vis,
Inscriptionem non habens?
Asta, gradumque siste paulisper tuum:
Incognitum nomen scies.
Princeps Comoedorum tulit quos Angliae
Tellus, in hoc busto cubat.
Quo mortuo, spretae silent Comoediae,
Tragoediaeque turbidae.
Scenae decus desiderant mutae suum,
Risusque abest Sardonius.
Hic Roscius Britannicus sepultus est,
Quo notior nemo fuit.
Abi, viator: Sin te adhuc nomen latet,
Edicet hoc quivis puer.

Dekker, *Gull's Horn-Book* (1609), p. 11:

Tarleton, Kemp, nor *Singer*, nor all the litter of Fooles that now come drawling behinde them, never played the clownes more naturally than the arrantest Sot of you all shall.

Heywood, *Apology for Actors* (1612), p. 43:

Here I must needs remember Tarleton, in his time gratious with the queene, his soveraigne, and in the people's generall applause.

Humphrey King, *An Halfe-Penny worth of Wit, in a Penny-worth of Paper*, 1613 (*Bibliotheca Heberiana*, iv. 1205):

Let us talke of *Robin Hoode*
And little John in merry Shirewood,

Of Poet Skelton with his pen,
And many other merry men,
Of May-game Lords and Sommer Queenes,
With Milke-maides, dancing or'e the Greenes,
Of merry Tarlton in our time,
Whose conceite was very fine,
Whom death hath wounded with his dart,
That lov'd a May-pole with his heart.

Ben Jonson, *Bartholomew Fair* (1614), Induction 38:

Stage-Keeper. I kept the *Stage* in Master *Tarletons* time, I thanke my starres. Ho! and that man had liu'd to haue play'd in *Bartholomew Fayre*, you should ha' seene him ha' come in, and ha' beene coozened i' the Cloath-quarter, so finely! And *Adams*, the Rogue, ha' leap'd and caper'd vpon him, and ha' dealth his vermine about, as though they had cost him nothing.

The Partiall Law (*c.* 1615–30), ed. Dobell, p. 43:

Nay, that's as old as the beginning of the world, or Tarlton's Trunk-hose.

Machivells Dogge (1617):

Tell captaine Tospot with his Tarleton's cut,
His swaggering will not get him sixteene pence.

John Davies of Hereford, *Wits Bedlam* (1617):

Here within this sullen earth
Lies Dick Tarlton, lord of mirth;
Who in his grave, still laughing, gapes,
Syth all clownes since have been his apes.
Earst he of clownes to learne still sought,
But now they learne of him they taught;
By art far past the principall,
The counterfet is so worth all.

Henry Peacham, *Thalia's Banquet* (1620):

To Sir Ninian Ouzell

As Tarlton when his head was onely seene,
The Tire-house doore and Tapistrie betweene,
Set all the multitude in such a laughter,

> They could not hold for scarse an houre after.
> So, sir, I set you, as I promis'd, forth,
> That all the world may wonder at your worth.

William Vaughan, *Golden Fleece* (1626):

In the meane space, as long as like mules you claw one another, I assure you wise masterships that you shall but minister matter to Buffones of rederision, as some of your alliance sometimes felt from the mouth of Tarleton, who being upon the stage in a towne where he expected for civill attention to his Prologue, and seeing no end of their hissing, hee brake forth at last into this sarcasticall taunt:

> I liv'd not in the Golden Age,
> When Jason wonne the fleece,
> But now I am on Gotam's stage,
> Wher fooles do hisse like geese.

John Taylor, the Water Poet, *Wit and Mirth*, 1629 (*Works*, p. 353):

Dicke Tarleton said that hee could compare Queene Elizabeth to nothing more fitly than to a Sculler; for, said he, Neither the Queene nor the Sculler hath a fellow.

Henry Peacham, *Truth of our Times* (1638), p. 103 (*N. & Q.*, 1867, xii. 222):

I remember when I was a schoolboy in *London*, *Tarlton* acted a third son's part, such a one as I now speake of: His father being a very rich man, and lying upon his death-bed, called his three sonnes about him. . . . To the third, which was *Tarlton* (who came like a rogue in a foule shirt without a band, and in a blew coat with one sleeve, his stockings out at the heeles, and his head full of straw and feathers), as for you, Sirrah, quoth he, you know how often I have fetched you out of *Moorgate* and *Bridwell*, you have beene an ungracious villaine, I have nothing to bequeath to you but the gallowes and a rope. *Tarlton* weeping, and sobbing upon his knees (as his brothers) said, O Father, I doe not desire it, I trust in God you shall live to enjoy it your selfe.

Richard Brome, *Antipodes* (1638), II. ii. (*Works*, iii. 260):

> *Letoy*. Yes in the dayes of *Tarlton* and *Kempe*,
> Before the stage was purg'd from barbarisme,

> And brought to the perfection it now shines with,
> Then fooles and jesters spent their wits, because
> The Poets were wise enough to save their owne
> For profitabler uses.

Richard Baker, *Theatrum Redivivum* (1662), p. 34 (*N. & Q.*, 1880, i. 113):

For let him [Prynne] try when he will, and come himself upon the *Stage*, with all the scurrility of the Wife of *Bath*, with all the ribaldry of *Poggius* or *Boccace*, yet I dare affirm, he shall never give that contentment to Beholders as honest *Tarlton* did, though he said never a word.

William Camden, *Remains* (edit. 1674; reprint of 1870, p. 431):

Upon merry Tarlton, I have heard this:

> Hic situs est cujus vox, vultus, actio possit
> Ex Heraclito reddere Democritum.

Baker, *Chronicle* (edit. 1674), p. 500:

To make their Comedies compleat, *Richard Tarleton*, who for the Part called the Clowns Part, never had his match, never will have.

For less important allusions to Tarlton see: *A Whip for an Ape*, 1589 (*N. & Q.*, 1858, vi. 7); Thomas Nashe, *An Almond for a Parrot*, 1590 (*Works*, iii. 341); Thomas Nashe, *Pierce Penniless*, 1592 (*Works*, i. 197); Thomas Nashe, *Strange Newes*, 1592 (*Works*, i. 308); Gabriel Harvey, *Four Letters*, 1592 (*Works*, i. 168, 202); Thomas Nashe, *Terrors of the Night*, 1594 (*Works*, i. 343); Thomas Lodge, *Wits Miserie*, 1596, (*Works*, iv. 80); *The Discoverie of the Knights of the Post*, 1597; J. M., *A Health to the Gentlemanly Profession of Seruingmen*, 1598 (Graves, *Mod. Phil.*, xviii. 493); Robert Armin, *Quips upon Questions*, 1600 (*Ibid.*, p. 493); Letter from the Earl of Salisbury to the Earl of Shrewsbury, March 7, 1607 (E. Lodge, *Illustrations*, edit. 1838, iii. 231); *The Abortive of an Idle Hour*, 1620; Augustine Vincent, *A Discoverie of Errours*, 1622, address to the reader; John Taylor, the Water Poet, *Sir Gregory Nonsence* (*Works*, p. 160); R. Junius, *The Drunkard's Character*, 1638

(Graves, *Mod. Phil.*, xviii. 493); S. F., *Sportive Funeral Elegies*, 1656 (*Ibid.*, p. 493); Henry Peacham, *Worth of a Penny* (edit. 1687, p. 6).

TATTERDELL, HUGH.

Under license of November 10, 1629, Hugh Tatterdell is named as a member of the Red Bull Company that visited Reading on November 30 of the same year (Murray ii. 386).·

TAWYER, WILLIAM.

William Tawyer (or Toyer) appears as a minor actor or stage-attendant with the King's men about 1619–25, apprenticed to John Heminges. He is mentioned in a stage-direction of the 1623 folio text of *A Midsummer Night's Dream*, V. i. 128: "Tawyer with a trumpet before them." This evidently refers to a performance by the King's men between 1619 and 1623, because neither the 1600 nor 1619 quarto of the play gives Tawyer's name. He is doubtless identical with the William Toyer named in a Protection from Arrest issued by Herbert on December 27, 1624, to twenty-one men "imployed by the Kinges Maiesties servantes in theire quallity of Playinge as Musitions and other necessary attendantes" (Adams, *Dram. Rec.*, p. 74). The records of St. Saviour's note the burial in June, 1625, of "William Tawier, Mr. Heminges man" (Halliwell-Phillipps, *Outlines*, ii. 260, *note* 22).

TAYLOR.

Taylor is named in marginal notes to the plays in the British Museum Egerton MS. 1994. He had a minor part in *The Captives*, and appears as a guard and as a soldier in *The Two Noble Ladies* (Boas, *Library*, 1917, viii. 231, 232). On September 3, 1624, *The Captives* was licensed for the Cockpit company (Adams, *Dram. Rec.*, p. 29), i.e. the Lady Elizabeth's men. *The Two Noble Ladies*, "often tymes acted with approbation at the Red Bull in St. John's Streete by the company of the Revells" (Bullen, *Old Plays*, ii. 430), is assigned by Fleay to 1619–22 (*Drama*, ii. 334).

TAYLOR, JOHN.

Master of the Choir at St. Mary's, Woolnoth, 1557; Master of the Song School at Westminster, 1561–67 (*Eliz. Stage*, ii. 72, 73).

TAYLOR, JOHN.

A member of the Children of Paul's in 1594 and 1598 (Hillebrand, *Child Actors*, p. 111).

TAYLOR, JOHN.

Possibly an actor whose name accidentally crept into the text of *George a Green*, printed in 1599 "As it was sundry times acted by the seruants of the right Honourable the Earl of Sussex." At line 14 (Greene, *Plays*, ed. Collins, ii. 183), Kendall asks:

> Say, Iohn Taylour,
> What newes with King Iames?

TAYLOR, JOSEPH.

Joseph Taylor is perhaps to be identified with a person of the same name baptized at St. Andrew's by the Wardrobe in Blackfriars on February 6, 1586. He is probably the Joseph Taylor who married Elizabeth Ingle, widow, at St. Saviour's, Sothwark, on May 2, 1610; and who is recorded in the Southwark token-books as a resident of "Mr. Langley's new rents, near the playhouse" in 1607, of Austen's Rents in 1612 and 1615, as "gone" in 1617, as "near the playhouse" in 1623 and 1629, "on the Bankside" in 1631, and of Gravel Lane in 1633. The registers of St. Saviour's record the following children of "Joseph Taylor, a player": Elisabeth (baptized July 12, 1612), Dixsye and Joseph (baptized July 21, 1614), Jone (baptized January 11, 1616), Robert (baptized June 1, 1617), and Anne (baptized August 24, 1623). A Joseph Taylor is mentioned in 1623 as living "in Bishoppsgate neare the Spittle" (Collier, iii. 460 ff.; Rendle, *Bankside*, p. xxvi; Wallace, *Jahrbuch*, xlvi. 347). He first appears as a player with the Duke of York's company, and is named in the patent of

March 30, 1610. He joined the Lady Elizabeth's troupe on its formation about April, 1611. As a result of this transfer he seems to have incurred the disfavor of certain members of the Duke of York's company. Subsequently a lawsuit arose between Taylor and John Heminges, concerning some theatrical costumes that had been sold to the Duke's men on the recommendation of Taylor (Wallace, *Globe Theatre Apparel*). On August 29, 1611, Taylor and his fellow-actors of the Lady Elizabeth's troupe gave Henslowe a bond of £500 to perform "certen articles" of agreement (*H.P.*, pp. 18, 111). He served as payee for the Court performances by the Lady Elizabeth's players during 1613–14 (Steele, pp. 183, 186). The 1679 folio of Beaumont and Fletcher names him as one of the "principal actors" in *The Coxcomb* and in *The Honest Man's Fortune*, both of which were probably acted by the Lady Elizabeth's men in 1613 (*Eliz. Stage*, ii. 251). In 1614 the same company acted Jonson's *Bartholomew Fair*, in which Cokes says, V. iii: "I thinke, one *Taylor*, would goe neere to beat all this company, with a hand bound behinde him" (ed. C. S. Alden, p. 113). This is presumably an allusion to Taylor the actor; but John Taylor the Water Poet has also been suggested. During 1615 Prince Charles's troupe (formerly known as the Duke of York's troupe) and the Lady Elizabeth's troupe were more or less closely associated in their theatrical activities. On the separation of the two companies in 1616 Taylor was again a Prince's man; on March 20, 1616, he joined his fellow-actors in an agreement with Alleyn and Meade (*H.P.*, p. 91). As a member of the Prince's company he appeared early in 1619 as Doctor Almanac in Middleton's *Masque of Heroes* (*Works*, vii. 200). By May 19, 1619, he had joined the King's men, perhaps taking the place of Burbage, who had died on March 13. From this date to the closing of the playhouses in 1642 he was one of the most prominent members of the King's company. He became a distinguished actor, took over several of Burbage's famous parts, and was a leader in the management of the troupe. He is named

(Murray, i. opp. 172) in the 1623 folio list of Shakespearean players; in the livery allowances of May 19, 1619 (his earliest appearance as a King's man), and April 7, 1621; in the submission for playing *The Spanish Viceroy*, without license, December 20, 1624 (Adams, *Dram. Rec.*, p. 21); in the list of players who took part in King James's funeral procession on May 7, 1625; in the patent of June 25, 1625 (*M.S.C.*, i. 282); and in the warrants for liveries on May 6, 1629, April 22, 1637, March 12, 1639, and March 20, 1641 (Stopes, *Jahrbuch*, xlvi. 95, 99, 101, 104). He and Lowin and Swanston served as payees for the Court performances by the King's men from April 27, 1634, to March 20, 1641 (Steele, pp. 244, 249, 262, 267, 274, 276). Nicholas Tooley in his will dated June 3, 1623, instructed his executors to pay a debt of £10 for which he was surety for Taylor (Collier, iii. 453). About 1637 Taylor petitioned for "the next King's waiter's place which shall fall void in the Custom House, London" (*S.P.D. Charles I*, ccclxxvii. 13). On November 11, 1639, he was appointed to the office of Yeoman of the Revels (Cunningham, *Revels*, p. 1). Sir Henry Herbert was perhaps responsible for the appointment, for in February, 1635, he had requested King Charles to give him permission "to commend a fitt man" for the post; the King had replied: "I will not dispose of it, or it shall not be disposed of, till I heare you" (Adams, *Dram. Rec.*, p. 68). In 1635 he controlled two-sixteenths of the Globe and one-eighth of the Blackfriars, which shares he apparently acquired after the death of Condell in 1627 (Adams, *Mod. Phil.*, xvii. 7 ff.). Lowin held a similar interest in the playhouses; he and Taylor seem to have shared the business responsibilities of the King's men in their transactions with Herbert, with the Court, and in general. Taylor assumed parts in the following plays (Murray, i. opp. 172): *The Humorous Lieutenant* (c. 1619); *The Custom of the Country* (c. 1619-20); *The Double Marriage* (c. 1619-20); Ferdinand, formerly played by Richard Burbage, in *The Duchess of Malfi* (1619-23); *Women Pleased* (c. 1620); *The Little French Lawyer* (c. 1620); *The False One* (c. 1620–

21); *The Pilgrim* (*c.* 1621); *The Island Princess* (*c.* 1621); *The Laws of Candy* (*c.* 1621); *The Prophetess* (1622); *The Sea Voyage* (1622); *The Spanish Curate* (1623); *The Maid in the Mill* (1623); *The Lover's Progress* (1623); *The Wife for a Month* (1624); Paris, the Roman Actor, in Massinger's *Roman Actor* (licensed October 11, 1626); Ford's *Lover's Melancholy* (licensed November 24, 1628); Mathias, a knight of Bohemia, in Massinger's *Picture* (licensed June 8, 1629); the Duke in Carlell's *Deserving Favorite* (published 1629); Antiochus in Massinger's *Believe as You List* (licensed May 7, 1631); and Mirabel, the Wildgoose, "incomparably acted," in Fletcher's *Wildgoose Chase* (a revival, 1631). According to the testimony of Downes (*Ros. Ang.*, p. 21), Taylor repeated instructions that he received from Shakespeare for the playing of the part of Hamlet: "Hamlet being Perform'd by Mr. Betterton, Sir William [Davenant] (having seen Mr. Taylor of the Black-Fryars Company Act it, who being Instructed by the Author Mr. Shaksepear) taught Mr. Betterton in every Particle of it." The statement of Downes cannot be accepted without modification. Taylor is not known as a King's man until May, 1619; Burbage, the original Hamlet, died in March, 1619; and Shakespeare died three years earlier. That Taylor succeeded Burbage in this part we know from Wright's *Historia Histrionica* (Hazlitt's *Dodsley*, xv. 405): "Before the wars . . . Taylor acted Hamlet incomparably well, Jago, Truewit in *The Silent Woman*, and Face in *The Alchymist*." That he played Arbaces, King of Iberia, in Beaumont and Fletcher's *A King and no King* is shown by Gayton, *Pleasant Notes upon Don Quixot* (1654), p. 25: "Insomuch that our Emperour (having a spice of self-conceit before, was soundly peppered now) for he was instantly Metamorphoz'd into the stateliest, gravest and commanding soule, that ever eye beheld. *Taylor* acting *Arbaces*, or *Swanston D'Amboys*, were shadowes to him; his pace, his look, and all his garb was alter'd." We learn from Richard Flecknoe's *Enigmatical Characters* (1665) that he was also famous as Mosca, Volpone's parasite, in Jonson's *Vol-*

pone. In the *Character of One Who Imitates the Good Companion Another Way* (said to have been composed in 1654), Flecknoe writes: "He is one, who, now the stage is down, acts the parasite's part at table; and, since Taylor's death, none can play Mosca so well as he" (*Variorum*, iii. 218). He and Lowin are referred to in Alexander Gill's satirical verses on Jonson's *Magnetic Lady*, in 1632 (Jonson, *Works*, vi. 116):

> Lett Lownie cease, and Taylore feare to touch
> The loathed stage; for thou hast made ytt such.

According to Shackerley Marmion's verses prefixed to Fletcher's *Faithful Shepherdess* (1634), Taylor was instrumental in bringing about the revival of the play at Court in 1634. Herbert gives the entry, January 6, 1634 (Adams, *Dram. Rec.*, p. 53): "On Monday night, the sixth of January and the Twelfe Night, was presented at Denmark-house, before the King and Queene, Fletchers pastorall called *The Faithfull Shepheardesse*, in the clothes the Queene had given Taylor the year before of her owne pastorall." The verses by Marmion first appear in the edition of 1634 (Beaumont and Fletcher, *Works*, ii. 523):

Unto his worthy friend Mr. Joseph Taylor upon his presentment of the Faithful Shepherdesse *before the King and Queene, at White-hall, on Twelfth night last. 1633.*

> When this smooth Pastorall was first brough forth,
> The Age twas borne in, did not know it's worth.
> Since by thy cost, and industry reviv'd,
> It hath a new fame, and new birth atchiv'd.
> Happy in that shee found in her distresse,
> A friend, as faithfull, as her Shepherdesse.
> For having cur'd her from her courser rents,
> And deckt her new with fresh habiliments,
> Thou brought'st her to the Court, and made her be
> A fitting spectacle for Majestie.
> So have I seene a clowded beauty drest
> In a rich vesture, shine above the rest.
> Yet did it not receive more honour from
> The glorious pompe, then thine owne action.

Expect no satisfaction for the same,
Poets can render no reward but Fame.
Yet this Ile prophesie, when thou shalt come
Into the confines of *Elysium*
Amidst the Quire of Muses, and the lists
Of famous Actors, and quicke Dramatists,
So much admir'd for gesture, and for wit,
That there on Seats of living Marble sit,
The blessed Consort of that numerous Traine,
Shall rise with an applause to entertaine
Thy happy welcome, causing thee sit downe,
And with a Lawrell-wreath thy temples crowne.
And mean time, while this Poeme shall be read,
Taylor, thy name shall be eternized.
For it is just, that thou, who first did'st give
Unto this booke a life, by it shouldst live.

SHACK. MARMYON.

Wright in *Historia Histrionica* (1699) records that on the closing of the playhouses and the outbreak of civil war, Taylor, Lowin, and Pollard "were superannuated," and that Taylor acted Rollo, in *Rollo, or the Bloody Brother*, at the Cockpit in 1648 (Hazlitt's *Dodsley*, xv. 409). *Mercurius Anti-Britannicus*, published at Oxford on August 11, 1645, gives the note: "the Players . . . say 'twas never a good World, since the Lord Viscount Say and Seale succeeded Joseph Taylor" (Rollins, *Stud. in Phil.*, xviii. 274). In 1647 he joined a group of the King's players in publishing and dedicating Beaumont and Fletcher's plays in folio (*Works*, i. p. x). In 1652 Fletcher's *Wildgoose Chase* (*Works*, iv. 407) was published for the "private benefit" of Taylor and Lowin. Thomas Killigrew in *Parson's Wedding* (printed in 1663) alludes to Taylor (Hazlitt's *Dodsley*, xiv. 505): "*Captain.* But who should I meet at the corner of the Piazza, but Joseph Taylor: he tells me there's a new play at the Friars to-day." He, Lowin, and Swanston are praised by Snarl, who admires nothing but the things of a former age, in Thomas Shadwell's *Virtuoso*, acted in 1676 (*Works*, i. 328):

371

Miranda. Methinks, though all Pleasures have left you, you may go see Plays.

Snarl. I am not such a Coxcomb, I thank God: I have seen 'em at *Black-Fryers.* Pox, they act like Poppets now, in Sadness. I, that have seen *Joseph Taylor,* and *Lowen,* and *Swanstead!* Oh, a brave roaring Fellow, would make the House shake again! Besides, I can never endure to see Plays, since Women came on the Stage. Boys are better by half.

Taylor contributed commendatory verses to the 1629 quarto of Massinger's *Roman Actor* (*Works*, i. p. clvi):

> *To his long-known and loved Friend, Mr. Philip*
> *Massinger, upon his* Roman Actor.

> If that my lines, being placed before thy book,
> Could make it sell, or alter but a look
> Of some sour censurer, who's apt to say,
> No one in these times can produce a play
> Worthy his reading, since of late, 'tis true,
> The old accepted are more than the new:
> Or, could I on some spot o' the court work so,
> To make him speak no more than he doth know;
> Not borrowing from his flatt'ring flatter'd friend
> What to dispraise, or wherefore to commend:
> Then, gentle friend, I should not blush to be
> Rank'd 'mongst those worthy ones which here I see
> Ushering this work; but why I write to thee
> Is, to profess our love's antiquity,
> Which to this tragedy must give my test,
> Thou hast made many good, but this thy best.
>
> JOSEPH TAYLOR.

He was buried at Richmond, Surrey, on November 4, 1652 (Cunningham, *Revels*, p. 1; Hazlitt's *Dodsley*, xv. 411).

TEODOR, JACOB.

A player with Robert Reynolds's company in Germany, during 1627 at Torgau, and in May, 1628, at Cologne (Herz, pp. 31, 54).

THAIRE, WILLIAM.

See William Thayer.

THARE, JOHN.

John Thare (or Thayer) belonged to Worcester's men in 1602–03, as shown by his authorizing payments on their behalf at various dates between August 21, 1602, and January 1, 1603 (*H.D.*, ii. 314). When playing in London was suspended, owing to the illness of Queen Elizabeth, Thare must have gone at once to Germany, for he and Thomas Blackwood visited Frankfort with Robert Browne's players at the Easter fair of 1603. Thare is recorded at Ulm and at Augsburg in December of the same year (Herz, p. 42).

THAYER, JOHN.

See John Thare.

THAYER, WILLIAM.

William Thayer (or Thaire) was a member of the Children of Paul's in 1594 and 1598 (Hillebrand, *Child Actors*, p. 111).

THOMKINS, JOHN.

A member of the Children of Paul's in 1598 (Hillebrand, *Child Actors*, p. 111).

THOMPSON, JOHN.

John Thompson appears to have begun his theatrical career with the King's men as John Shank's apprentice, as evidenced by the *Sharers' Papers* of 1635. Shank had paid £40 for him. He was dead by 1635 (Halliwell-Phillipps, *Outlines*, i. 316). With the King's company he is known to have played (Murray, i. opp. 172) Julia in *The Duchess of Malfii* (1619–23); in *The Pilgrim* (*c.* 1621); in *The Maid in the Mill* (1623); in *The Lover's Progress* (1623); Domitia, wife of Aelius Lamia, in Massinger's *Roman Actor* (licensed October 11, 1626); in Ford's *Lover's Melancholy* (licensed November 24, 1628); Honoria, the Queen, in Massinger's *Picture* (licensed June 8, 1629); and Cleonarda, the King's sister, in Carlell's *Deserving Favorite* (published in 1629).

TILBERY, JOHN.

A member of the Children of the Chapel Royal on November 12, 1405 (*Cal. Pat. Rolls, Henry IV*, iii. 96).

TOBYE, EDWARD.

Edward Tobye is named in a license granted to the Children of the Revels to the late Queen Anne, on April 9, 1623 (Murray, i. 362; ii. 272–73). He possibly acted a servant in *Richard II*, as suggested by a marginal note in the Egerton MS. of the play, where "Toby" is substituted for "ser" (Boas, *Library*, 1917, viii. 233).

TOMSON, SAM.

Sam Tomson played Menester, an actor, in Richards's *Messallina, the Roman Empress*, printed in 1640 as "acted with generall applause divers times by the Company of his Majesties Revells."

TOMSONE, JOHN.

A player, who borrowed 5*s*. from Henslowe on December 22, 1598 (*H.D.*, i. 40; ii. 315).

TONY, WILL.

Will Tony seems to have acted Martin Marprelate, "attired like an ape" (cf. Fleay, *Drama*, ii. 126). Nashe, *An Almond for a Parrat* (1590), writes: "Therefore we must not measure of *Martin* as he is still allied to *Elderton* or tongd like *Will Tony*, as he was attired like an Ape on ye stage" (*Works*, iii. 354). McKerrow (*Nashe*, iv. 466) says: "I can give no information about this person. One may safely infer that he was notorious for the scurrility of his language."

TOOLEY, NICHOLAS.

Nicholas Tooley's original name appears to have been Nicholas Wilkinson. Although his name is given as Tooley in the main text of his will in 1623, he made a codicil signed Nicholas Wilkinson, *alias* Tooley, to insure the validity of the document. Thus he may be the Nicholas, son of Charles Wilkinson, whose baptism is recorded at St. Anne's, Blackfriars, on February 3, 1575 (Collier, iii. 448). He has been conjectured to be the Nick (*q.v.*) who acted in *2 Seven Deadly Sins* (*c.* 1590); who appears in the 1623 folio text of *The Taming of the Shrew*; for whom the Admiral's men bought hose on December 25, 1601; and who is mentioned by Joan Alleyn in a letter on October 21, 1603. At some period during his career he was doubtless apprenticed to Richard Burbage, whom in his will he calls his "late master." He was apparently with the King's men by May 4, 1605, when Augustine Phillips left him 20*s.* as his "fellowe." He continued with this company until his death in 1623. He acted (Murray, i. opp. 172) in *The Alchemist* (1610); *Catiline* (1611); *Bonduca* (1613–14); *The Queen of Corinth* (*c.* 1617); *The Loyal Subject* (1618); as Barnavelt's wife in *Sir John van Olden Barnavelt* (1619); in *The Custom of the Countey* (*c.* 1619–20); *The Double Marriage* (*c.* 1619–20); as Forobosco and a madman in *The Duchess of Malfi*, about 1619–23; in *Women Pleased* (*c.* 1620); *The Little French Lawyer* (*c.* 1620); *The False One* (*c.* 1620–21); *The Pilgrim* (*c.* 1621); *The Laws of Candy* (*c.* 1621); *The Prophetess* (1622); *The Sea Voyage* (1622); and *The Spanish Curate* (1622). The inclusion of his name in the actor-list of *Wife for a Month*, licensed May 27, 1624, is evidently a mistake, for he died almost a year before that date. He is named in the patent of March 27, 1619; in the livery allowances of May 19, 1619, and April 7, 1621; and in the 1623 folio list of Shakespearean players. On March 12, 1619, he witnessed Richard Burbage's nuncupative will. His own will is dated June 3, 1623 (Collier, iii. 452–56). He left various sums of money to charity and to friends, including members of the family of his "late master" Richard Burbage, the wife and daughter of Henry Condell, and Joseph Taylor; forgave debts of John Underwood and William Ecclestone; assigned £10, "over and besides such sommes of money as I shall owe unto her att my decease," to Mrs. Burbage,

375

"the wife of my good friend, Mr. Cuthbert Burbage (in whose house I doe nowe lodge), as a remembrance of my love, in respect of her motherlie care over me"; and appointed Burbage and Condell his executors and residuary legatees. The register of St. Giles's, Cripplegate, records on June 5, 1623, the burial of "Nicholas Tooley, Gentleman, from the house of Cuthbert Burbidge, Gentleman" (Collier, iii. 451).

TOSEDALL, ROGER.

Roger Tosedall is recorded at Norwich on March 10, 1635, when his troupe, presumably the King's Revels, applied for permission to act in that town (Murray, i. 279-80).

TOTTNELL, HARRY.

A player, whose daughter Joan was baptized at St. Saviour's on March 20, 1591 (*Eliz. Stage*, ii. 347), and buried October 1, 1593. A Harry Tottnell, not specified as a player, was buried there on January 28, 1593 (Bentley, *T.L.S.*, Nov. 15, 1928, p. 856).

TOWNE, JOHN.

John Towne appears to have been a member of Queen Elizabeth's company from its formation in 1583 to about 1597. In 1583 he was with the Queen's men in London; he is named in a City record that gives the personnel of the company at this time (*Eliz. Stage*, ii. 106). Again in 1588 he is mentioned in a document concerning the Queen's players, for the non-payment of 8s. 4d. subsidy (*M.S.C.*, i. 354). On May 8, 1594, he served as a witness to a loan by Philip Henslowe to the latter's nephew, Francis Henslowe, "to laye downe for his share to the Quenes players" (*H.D.*, i. 4; ii. 80), and was himself in all probabilty at this time a Queen's man. Finally, he is described as "one of Her Maiesties plears" on July 8, 1597, when Roger Clarke, "bond lace wever" of Nottingham, released him of a debt (Murray, ii. 377).

TOWNE, THOMAS.

Thomas Towne appears as an Admiral's man on December 14, 1594, in the first list of the company in Henslowe's accounts. Thereafter he is mentioned in various records of the Admiral's men, as witnessing transactions, as borrowing money from Henslowe, as paying debts, as authorizing payments on behalf of the troupe, and as acknowledging company debts. At some date after March 14, 1597, he and John Singer borrowed 40*s.* from Henslowe "when they went into the contrey." On April 7, 1599, Henslowe advanced 10*s.* to him and Richard Alleyn "to go to the corte vpon ester euen" (*H.D.*, i. 5, 104, 199; ii. 315). With the Admiral's men he acted (*H.P.*, pp. 153, 154; *Eliz. Stage*, ii. 175) Myron-hamec in *Frederick and Basilea* (1597), Stukeley in *The Battle of Alcazar* (*c.* 1600–01), and Shah, an oracle, and (in the Procession) a Tartar in *1 Tamar Cam* (1602). About Christmas, 1603, the Admiral's men were taken into the service of Prince Henry. As a member of the Prince's company Towne is named in the coronation list of March 15, 1604; in the patent of April 30, 1606; and in the household list of 1610 (*Eliz. Stage*, ii. 186, 187, 188). He appeared as "a sweeper" in Dekker's *Honest Whore*, Part I (1604), acted by the Prince's players, as shown by a stage-direction: "Enter Towne like a sweeper" (Dekker, *Works*, ii. 78). Edward Alleyn on October 28, 1608, granted him an annuity of £12, acquittances for which are recorded to January 15, 1612, where he is described as "of St. Saviour's, Southwark, gent.," and where his wife's name is given as Agnes (Warner, pp. 71, 236). He is recorded in the Southwark token-books during 1600–07. The register of the same parish records the burial of Thomas Towne, "a man," on August 9, 1612. In his will dated July 4, 1612, he mentions his wife (called Ann), his brother John, of Dunwich in Suffolk ("if he be still living),'' and leaves £3 to his fellow-actors Bird, Downton, Juby, Rowley, Massey, and Humphrey Jeffes, "to make them a supper when it shall please them to call for it" (*Eliz. Stage*, ii. 347). The Alleyn papers mention a "widdow Towne" on November 5, 1612; and a letter, about 1613, from Massey to Alleyn, shows that she received £50 from the Prince's company on the death of her husband (Warner, pp. 36, 138).

TOWNE'S BOY.

"Towne's boy" appeared as a page in *The Battle of Alcazar*, acted by the Admiral's men about 1600–01 (*H.P.*, p. 153; *Eliz. Stage*, ii. 175–76).

TOWNSEND, JOHN.

John Townsend and Joseph Moore are named in a license of April 27, 1611, as leaders of the Lady Elizabeth's troupe (*M.S.C.*, i. 274). On August 29, 1611, he and his fellow-actors gave Henslowe a bond of £500 to perform "certen articles" of agreement (*H.P.*, pp. 18, 111). On July 11, 1617, he and Moore were paid £30 for three plays given before King James on his journey to Scotland during the preceding March or April (Steele, p. 198). A new patent of March 20, 1618, mentions him as a leader of the Lady Elizabeth's players. Until 1631 he evidently shared with Moore the managerial responsibilities of the company on provincial tours. He was leader of the troupe at Norwich on May 23, 1618, and May 2, 1621. He is mentioned in a bill of March 13, 1622, signed by the Lord Chamberlain, and in the patent of March 20, 1622. The company was under his management at Norwich on May 1, 1622, and at Leicester on July 9, 1624. He and Wambus came to Norwich on September 28, 1624, and desired redress for the imprisonment of Wambus during the preceding April and May, but their request was dismissed. On December 9, 1628, the Lady Elizabeth's men were granted another patent, in which Townsend's name occurs. He accompanied the troupe to Reading on December 24, 1629, and appears as co-leader with Moore at Coventry on March 30, 1631. He is last heard of in a license of November 28, 1634, granted to a company under the leadership of William Daniel, and known as the King's Revels

(Murray, i. 243, 252, 254–9, 262; ii. 8, 193, 251, 316, 340, 344–7, 350, 370, 386). The register of St. Bodolph Aldgate records the burial on November 15, 1619, of Christopher Bodie, "Stab'd with an All," a servant to John Townsend, "a Player of Enterludes" (Denkinger, *P.M.L.A.*, xli. 106).

TOY.

Evidently the performer of Will Summer in Nashe's *Summer's Last Will and Testament* (*Works*, iii. 233, 267, 294), acted in 1592 at Croydon, possibly by members of Archbishop Whitgift's household (*Eliz. Stage*, ii. 451–53):

Will Summer. I, that haue a toy in my head more then ordinary.
Bacchus. Ho, wel shot, a tutcher, a tutcher: for quaffing *Toy*
doth passe, in cup, in canne, or glasse.
All. God Bacchus doe him right,
And dubbe him knight.
[*Here he dubs Will Summer with the blacke Iacke.*
Bacchus. Rise vp, Sir Robert Tospot.
Summer. No more of this, I hate it to the death.
The Epilogue. The great foole *Toy* hath marde the play: Good
night, Gentlemen; I go.
[*Let him be carryed away.*
Will Summer. Is't true, Iackanapes, doo you serue me so?

McKerrow (*Nashe*, iv. 436) calls attention to a reference to Toy in *Four Letters* (1592), where Gabriel Harvey (*Works*, i. 189) says of Robert Greene: "They wronge him much with their Epitaphs, and other solemne deuises, that entitle him not at the least, The second Toy of London; the Stale of Poules."

TREVELL, WILLIAM.

William Trevell owned one-half of one share in the syndicate that in 1608 leased the Whitefriars playhouse (Adams, *Playhouses*, pp. 313–15, 322). He seems to have had some connection with the playhouse in 1621, as suggested by a lawsuit between him and Thomas Woodford in 1642 (*Eliz. Stage*, ii. 347, 517).

TRIGG, WILLIAM.

William Trigg was apparently a King's man from about 1626 to the closing of the playhouses in 1642. With the King's company he played (Murray, i. opp. 172) Julia, daughter, to Titus, in Massinger's *Roman Actor* (licensed October 11, 1626); an unassigned part in Ford's *Lover's Melancholy* (licensed November 24, 1628); Corsica, Sophia's woman, in Massinger's *Picture* (licensed June 8, 1629); and Rosalura, in Fletcher's *Wildgoose Chase* (a revival, 1631). He is named in the "Players Pass" granted to certain members of the King's troupe on May 17, 1636. That he continued with the King's men and joined the royalist forces at the outbreak of civil war in 1642 is evidenced by an allusion to him in a satirical pamphlet, *Certaine Propositions Offered to the Consideration of the Honourable Houses of Parliament*, published during the latter part of 1642 (Collier, ii. 39). The fifth proposition urges the use of Biblical, rather than "profane," plots for dramas, and concludes:

It would not be amiss, too, if, instead of the music that plays between acts, there were only a Psalm sung for distinction sake. This might be easily brought to pass, if either the Court playwriters be commanded to read the Scriptures, or the City Scripture readers be commanded to write plays. This, as it would much advantage our part, so would it much disadvantage the King's; for, as by it we should gain a new place of edifying, so Captain Trigg, and the rest of the players which are now in service, would doubtlessly return to their callings, and much lessen the King's army.

TRUSSELL, ALVERY.

A member of the Chapel Royal about 1600–01. In Henry Clifton's complaint to the Star Chamber on December 15, 1601, as to how young boys were pressed as actors for the Chapel troupe at Blackfriars, Alvery Trussell is named as one so taken, and is described as "an apprentice to one Thomas Gyles" (Wallce, *Blackfriars*, p. 80).

TUCKFEILD, THOMAS.

Thomas Tuckfeild is named in a Protection from Arrest issued by Herbert on December 27, 1624, to twenty-one men "imployed by the Kinges Maiesties servantes in theire quallity of Playinge as Musitions and other necessary attendantes" (Adams, *Dram. Rec.*, p. 74). He is probably identical with the "T. Tucke" mentioned in a stage-direction (V. iii) of *The Two Noble Kinsmen*, printed in 1634 as "Presented at the Blackfriers by the Kings Maiesties servants, with great applause." He and Curtis (?) Greville appear as attendants (Brooke, *Shak. Apoc.*, p. 344).

TUNSTALL, JAMES.

James Tunstall (Dunstall or Dunstone) is named as a member of Worcester's troupe in the abstract of the license of January 14, 1583, as given in the Leicester records (*Eliz. Stage*, ii. 222). He appears as witness of transactions for Edward and John Alleyn and others on October 28, 1585, July 6 and 8, 1590, November 23, 1590, and May 6, 1591 (Warner, pp. 3, 4, 251, 253.) During 1590–91 he belonged to the Admiral's men at the Theatre, as shown by the testimony of John Alleyn in the Brayne-Burbage lawsuit (Wallace, *N.U.S.*, xiii. 127). His name occurs in the first list of the Admiral's men in Henslowe's accounts on December 14, 1594. He bought a gown from Henslowe on August 27, 1595; opened an account on October 14, 1596; and authorized payments for the company before November 28 and on December 11, 1596. He witnessed agreements for Henslowe on July 27 and August 3, 1597, which is his last appearance in the records of the Admiral's men (*H.D.*, i. 201; ii. 261). He acted a governor and a friar in *Frederick and Basilea*, presented by the Admiral's troupe about June, 1597 (*H.P.*, p. 153). The register of St. Botolph's, Bishopsgate, records on August 20, 1572, the baptism of a Dunstone Tunstall (Warner, p. 3n.). He is alluded to by Guilpin, *Skialetheia* (1598), Epigram 43 (*Works*, p. 18):

> *Clodus* me thinks lookes passing big of late,
> With *Dunstons* browes, and *Allens Cutlacks* gate.

TURNER, ANTHONY.

Anthony Turner is first known as a member of the Lady Elizabeth's company in 1622, when he is named in Herbert's list of "the chiefe of them at the Phoenix" (Adams, *Dram. Rec.*, p. 63). Possibly he is to be identified with a person of the same name mentioned in the *Middlesex County Records* (ed. Jeaffreson, ii. 185) on October 23, 1624, when recognizances were taken for the appearance of Dorothy Turner before the Session of Peace to answer "for cruelly beatinge and abusinge her husband Anthony Turner." He apparently joined Queen Henrietta's company at the Cockpit in Drury Lane at its formation soon after the accession of Charles I. With this organization he continued until 1637 (Murray, i. 265–67), appearing as Justice Lanby in Shirley's *Wedding* (*c.* 1626); as Old Lord Bruce in Davenport's *King John and Matilda* (*c.* 1629); as a kitchen-maid in the first part of Heywood's *Fair Maid of the West*, and as Bashaw Alcade in the second part (*c.* 1630); and as Piston, in Nabbes's *Hannibal and Scipio* (1635). At the reorganization of Queen Henrietta's troupe about October, 1637, he joined the Revels company at Salisbury Court, as shown by Herbert's record (Adams, *Dram. Rec.*, p. 66): "I disposed of Perkins, Sumner, Sherlock, and Turner, to Salisbury Court, and joynd them with the best of that company." The amalgamated company evidently continued to be known as the Queen's players, and Turner no doubt remained with the troupe at Salisbury Court until the closing of the playhouses in 1642. On March 6, 1640, he (by an obvious error noted as "Henry") served as payee for Court performances by the Queen's men (Steele, p. 272). On January 8, 1641, he and Richard Perkins are named in a warrant for liveries "for themselves and twelve of their fellows of the Queen's Majesty's company of players" (Stopes, *Jahrbuch*, xlvi. 103). He is presumably the A.T. who signed with Andrew Pennycuicke (*q.v.*) the dedication of William Heminges's *Fatal Contract* (1653), addressed to the Earl and Countess of Northampton. The last notice of him is found in the *Middlesex County Records* (ed.

Jeaffreson, iii. 279) on May 12, 1659, when William Wintershall (*q.v.*) and one Henry Eaton gave recognizances for his appearance on a charge of "unlawfull mainteining of Stage-playes and enterludes att the Redd Bull in St. John's Street."

TURNER, DREWE.

Drewe Turner was a member of Richard Bradshaw's company, a troupe that got into trouble at Banbury in May, 1633. The town authorities becoming suspicious of the validity of the company's license, arrested the players, and notified the Privy Council. The players appeared before the Privy Council in June, and were soon discharged "upon bond given to be forthcoming whensoever they should be called for." In the examination of the players by the Banbury officials, Turner testified on May 2, 1633, that he "has been with this company of players these twelve months," and "does nothing but drive the horse and beat the drum" (Murray, ii. 106 ff., 163 ff.).

TUSSER, THOMAS.

From Thomas Tusser's autobiographical verses, printed in the 1573 edition of his *Five Hundred Pointes of Good Husbandrie* (ed. Payne and Herrtage, pp. xiii, 207), we learn that about 1540 he was a member of the Children of Paul's:

> But marke, the chance, my self to vance,
> By friendships lot, to Paules I got,
> So found I grace, a certaine space,
>   still to remaine:
> With Redford there, the like no where,
> For cunning such, and vertue much,
> By whom some part of Musicke art,
>   so did I gaine.

Whether he acted in plays, however, does not appear.

UBALDINI, PETRUCCIO.

Petruccio Ubaldini in an undated letter to Queen Elizabeth refers to a play at Court, and was possibly associated with "Al-

fruso Ferrabolle [Ferrabosco] and the rest of the Italian players"
who received payment for a Court performance of February 27,
1576 (*M.S.C.*, ii. 147; Steele, p. 59). He was an illuminator and
man of letters in the patronage of royalty and nobility, and lived
in England from 1562 to 1586 (*Eliz. Stage*, ii. 264; *D.N.B.*,
lviii. 1 ff.).

UNDERELL.

The Henslowe accounts record a payment of 10*s*. in wages to
one Underell for Worcester's men on October 11, 1602. He was
probably a hired man of Worcester's company (*H.D.*, i. 182; ii.
316). A Thomas Underell is known as a royal trumpeter from
1609 to 1624 (*Eliz. Stage*, ii. 348).

UNDERHILL, NICHOLAS.

Nicholas Underhill is named in a Protection from Arrest issued
by Herbert on December 27, 1624, to twenty-one men "imployed
by the Kinges Maiesties servantes in theire quallity of Playinge
as Musitions and other necessary attendantes" (Adams, *Dram.
Rec.*, p. 74).

UNDERWOOD, JOHN.

John Underwood, as a member of the Children of the Chapel
Royal, acted in *Cynthia's Revels*, 1600, and in *The Poetaster*, 1601
(*Eliz. Stage*, iii. 363, 365). Subsequently, with Field and Ostler,
he was "taken to strengthen the Kings service" (Halliwell-
Phillipps, *Outlines*, i. 317). The transfer of Underwood and Field
to the King's company is also noted by Wright in *Historia Histrionica* (Hazlitt's *Dodsley*, xv. 416). He had passed to the King's
men by 1610, when he is found in the cast of Jonson's *Alchemist*.
As a King's man he assumed parts in the following plays (Murray, i. opp. 172): *Catiline* (1611); *Valentinian* (1611–14); *Bonduca*
(1613–14); *The Queen of Corinth* (*c.* 1617); *The Loyal Subject* (1618);
The Knight of Malta (*c.* 1618); *The Humorous Lieutenant* (*c.* 1619);
The Custom of the Country (*c.* 1619–20); *The Double Marriage* (*c.*

1619–20); Delio and a madman in *The Duchess of Malfi*, about 1619–23 (ed. Sampson, p. 216); *The Little French Lawyer* (*c.* 1620); *Women Pleased* (*c.* 1620); *The False One* (*c.* 1620–21); *The Laws of Candy* (*c.* 1621); *The Island Princess* (*c.* 1621); *The Pilgrim* (*c.* 1621); *The Sea Voyage* (1622); *The Maid in the Mill* (1623); *The Lover's Progress* (1623); and *The Wife for a Month* (1624). He is also named in the patent of March 27, 1619; in the livery allowances of May 19, 1619, and April 7, 1621; and in the 1623 folio list of Shakespearean players. Nicholas Tooley forgave him a debt in his will dated June 3, 1623 (Collier, iii. 454). The register of St. Bartholomew the Less, West Smithfield, records the baptism of his son John on December 27, 1610. His will, dated October 4, 1624, with a codicil dated October 10 (apparently appended after his death, from oral directions), describes him as "of the parish of Saint Bartholomew the Less, in London, gent." (Collier, iii. 444–46). He assigns his shares in the Blackfriars, Globe, and Curtain to Henry Condell and two other executors, who are directed to hold these in trust for his five children, all in their minority: John, Elizabeth, Burbage, Thomas, and Isabel. He left 11*s.* each for memorial rings for his executors and for John Heminges and John Lowin, overseers of the will. Condell in his will, dated December 13, 1627, mentions this trust in special terms, and directs his wife as executrix to discharge faithfully his duty towards Underwood's children (Collier, iii. 377). An Underwood still controlled one share in the Blackfriars in 1635 (Halliwell-Phillipps, *Outlines*, i. 313).

VAN WILDER, PHILIP.

Philip van Wilder was a royal lutenist and Gentleman of the Privy Chamber. In February, 1550, he was granted a commission to organize a troupe, presumably of young minstrels. That he was connected with such an organization even earlier than 1550 is suggested by references to "Philippe and his fellows yong mynstrels" and to his "six singing children" (*Eliz. Stage*, ii. 31).

VERNON, GEORGE.

George Vernon is known as a King's man from 1624 to 1629. His name occurs in a Protection from Arrest issued by Herbert on December 27, 1624, to twenty-one men "imployed by the Kinges Maiesties servantes in theire quallity of Playinge as Musitions and other necessary attendantes" (Adams, *Dram. Rec.*, p. 74). He is probably the "G. Ver" mentioned in the manuscript of Beaumont and Fletcher's *Honest Man's Fortune*, relicensed for the King's men on February 8, 1625 (*Eliz. Stage*, iii. 227). As a King's man he appears in the list of players who took part in King James's funeral procession on May 7, 1625; presumably as Sejeius, in Massinger's *Roman Actor* (licensed October 11, 1626); in the cast of Ford's *Lover's Melancholy* (licensed November 24, 1628); and in the livery allowance of May 6, 1629 (Murray, i. 161, opp. 172; Stopes, *Jahrbuch*, xlvi. 95). The baptism of his children is recorded in the register of St. Saviour's, Southwark: Elizabeth, July 23, 1626; Anne, July 7, 1628; and George, April 30, 1630, (Bentley, *T.L.S.*, Nov. 15, 1928, p. 856).

VINCENT.

As a musician one Vincent appears in "Sloth" of *2 Seven Deadly Sins*, acted by Strange's men about 1590 (Greg, *H.P.*, p. 152; *R.E.S.*, i. 262).

VINCENT, THOMAS.

Thomas Vincent was prompter at the Globe. He is known only in an anecdote concerning him and John Singer (*q.v.*).

VIRNIUS, JOHANN FRIEDRICH.

Johann Friedrich Virnius was in the service of the Elector of Brandenburg in 1615, when he and Bartholomeus Freyerbott visited Danzig as the Brandenburg Comedians (Bolte, p. 41).

WAKEFIELD, EDWARD.

Edward Wakefield was in Germany during 1597 and 1602. He was presumably an actor in 1597, when he engaged in a quarrel with Thomas Sackville (*q.v.*) in a Brunswick tavern. The Brunswick household accounts record a payment of 160 thalers to him on December 28, 1602 (Cohn, p. xxxiv).

WALPOLE, FRANCIS.

Francis Walpole is named as a member of Queen Anne's company, in the Baskervile papers of June, 1616, and June, 1617 (*Eliz. Stage*, ii. 237, 238).

WAMBUS, FRANCIS.

Francis Wambus (or Waymus) is known as a member of the Lady Elizabeth's troupe from 1611 to 1624. On August 29, 1611, he and his fellow-actors gave Henslowe a bond of £500 to observe "certen articles" of agreement (*H.P.*, pp. 18, 111). He is named in the license granted to the company on March 20, 1618; in the Norwich records of May 23, 1618, and April 22, 1620; in the patent of March 20, 1622; in a bill of March 13, 1622, signed by the Lord Chamberlain; and in the Norwich annals on May 10, 1623. On April 24, 1624, he visited Norwich as leader of the company. He was not permitted to play, because of a letter, dated May 27, 1623, from the Privy Council to the authorities at Norwich, which ordered them "not to suffer any players to shewe or exercise any playes within this Citty" until further notice from the Council. Wambus said that he would play in spite of the order, and was therefore committed to prison on April 26. He apparently remained in the Norwich prison until May 26, when he and William Bee (*q.v.*), who has been doubtfully identified as William Beeston (*q.v.*), were discharged by order of the Mayor, after John Townsend (*q.v.*) had agreed to pay the charges. On September 28, 1624, accompanied by Townsend, he appeared again at Norwich and asked from the authorities recompense for the imprisonment; but the request was not granted (Murray, i. 243, 252, 255–58; ii. 193, 345–50, 359–60).

WARD, ANTHONY.

As a member of the licensed troupe of four "common players of interludes," Anthony Ward is recorded at Hastings on March 25, 1603 (see John Arkinstall).

WATERS, THOMAS.

A member of the Children of Paul's in 1607 (Hillebrand, *Child Actors*, p. 112).

WAYMUS, FRANCIS.

See Francis Wambus.

WEBSTER, GEORGE.

George Webster in 1598 was a member of Robert Browne's company in the service of the Landgrave of Hesse-Cassel; he served as treasurer of the troupe on its visit to Heidelberg. He appears as leader of the Hessian comedians at Frankfort in March, and at Nuremberg in April, 1600; again at Frankfort for Easter, 1601, and during the autumn of the same year; and once more at Frankfort for Easter, 1603, although the players had left the Landgrave's service in 1602 (Herz, pp. 16, 38 ff.).

WEBSTER, JOHN.

A John Webster accompanied Robert Browne at Cassel, Germany, in August, 1596, during the visit of the Earl of Lincoln, who came from England to stand proxy for Queen Elizabeth as godmother at the christening of the Landgrave's daughter (Herz, pp. 13 ff.). He may be the dramatist.

WEDWER, WILLIAM.

A player, with Robert Reynolds's company in Germany during 1627 and 1640 (Herz, pp. 31, 55).

WEEKES, RICHARD.

On November 10, 1629, Richard Weekes (or Wickes) and William Perry were granted a license as managers of the Red Bull company. They visited Reading on November 30, 1629, and about November of the following year. On June 6, 1635, Weekes and John Shank, "the younger," were leaders of the troupe at Norwich. In March, 1636, a complaint was made against Weekes and Perry for playing at Canterbury during Lent. Weekes is last heard of at Norwich on May 11, 1636, when the company was under his management (Murray, i. 272, 274, 275; ii. 357, 358, 386).

WEND, JOHN.

A player, with Robert Reynolds's company in Germany during 1627 and 1640 (Herz, pp. 31, 55).

WESTCOTT, SEBASTIAN.

Master of the Children of Paul's from about 1557 to 1582.

WESTE, HUMPHREY.

A member of the Children of Paul's in 1594 (Hillebrand, *Child Actors*, p. 111).

WESTE, THOMAS.

A member of the Children of Paul's in 1594 (Hillebrand, *Child Actors*, p. 111).

WHEATON, ELIZABETH.

Elizabeth Wheaton was probably a gatherer or servant of some kind in the employ of the King's players. Henry Condell (*q.v.*), in his will dated December 13, 1627, left her 40s. and "that place or priviledge which she now exerciseth and enjoyeth in the houses of the Blackfryers, London, and the Globe on the Bankside."

WHETSTONE.

In 1571 one Whetstone, with William Fidge, owed Robert Betts, a deceased Canterbury painter, 35s. 4d. "for their portions in buyinge of certen playe-bookes." Whetstone may have been an actor, and is possibly to be identified with George Whetstone, the dramatist (Plomer, *Library*, 1918, ix. 252). His play, *Promos and Cassandra* (1578), is addressed to William Fleetewoode, with a dedication that is interesting for its literary criticism on "the vse and abuse of Commedies."

WHITE, JOSIAS.

As a member of Ellis Guest's company under license of June 7, 1628, Josias White is recorded at Norwich on July 2 of the same year (Murray, ii. 103).

WHITE, ROBERT.

See Robert Hunt.

WHITELOCKE, JAMES.

James Whitelocke, later Sir James and judge of the Court of King's Bench, attended the Merchant Taylors' School from 1575 to 1588 (*D.N.B.*, lxi. 117). He tells us in *Liber Famelicus* (ed. Bruce, p. 12) that he acted in plays at Court, under the mastership of Richard Mulcaster:

I was brought up at school under mr. Mulcaster, in the famous school of the Marchantaylors in London, whear I continued untill I was well instructed in the Hebrew, Greek and Latin tongs. His care was also to encreas my skill in musique, in whiche I was brought up by dayly exercise in it, as in singing and playing upon instruments, and yeerly he presented sum playes to the court, in whiche his scholers wear only actors, and I on among them, and by that meanes taughte them good behaviour and audacitye.

WHITING, EDWARD.

Edward Whiting's connection with a provincial company of players is rather obscure. From the testimony of members of Richard Bradshaw's troupe, who got into trouble at Banbury in May, 1633, we learn that Whiting was a surgeon of Nottingham, who either had been or was in some way connected with the company, and the father of Richard Whiting (*q.v.*), *alias* Johnson.

He appears to have sold his theatrical commission to Richard Bradshaw (*q.v.*), and the town authorities, suspicious of the validity of the license, brought the players to trial. He was apparently also interested in a puppet-show that became bankrupt under the management of William Cooke and Fluellen Morgan (Murray, ii. 106 ff., 163 ff.).

WHITING, RICHARD.

Richard Whiting, *alias* Johnson (see Richard Johnson), was a member of Richard Bradshaw's company, when that troupe got into trouble at Banbury in May, 1633. The town authorities becoming suspicious of the validity of the company's license, arrested the players, and notified the Privy Council. The players appeared before the Privy Council in June, and were soon discharged "upon bond given to be forthcoming whensoever they should be called for." In the examination of the players by the Banbury officials, Whiting testified on May 2, 1633, that he "has been with this company of players about half a year," that he "has acted a part with these players lately in divers places," and that Edward Whiting (*q.v.*) was his father (Murray, ii. 106 ff., 163 ff.)

WICKES, RICHARD.

See Richard Weekes.

WIGPITT, THOMAS.

A joint-lessee of the new Fortune playhouse, in which he obtained a half-share on May 20, 1622 (Warner, pp. 246–47).

WILBRAHAM, WILLIAM.

William Wilbraham played Isaac, Sir John Belfare's man, in Shirley's *Wedding* (*c.* 1626), and Bashaw Alcade in Heywood's *Fair Maid of the West*, Part I (*c.* 1630), both plays of Queen Henrietta's men, at the Cockpit in Drury Lane. On March 10, 1635, he is recorded at Norwich, as a member of presumably the King's

Revels company, when the troupe applied for permission to act in that town (Murray, i. opp. 266, 279–80). On July 7, 1640, Elizabeth Beeston, widow of Christopher Beeston, secured a loan of £150 from Wilbraham, and gave him a mortgage on the Cockpit property as security (Hotson, p. 94).

WILKINSON, JOHN.
See John Wylkynson.

WILKINSON, NICHOLAS.
See Nicholas Tooley.

WILL.
Will appears as Itys in "Lechery" of *2 Seven Deadly Sins*, acted by Strange's men about 1590 (Greg, *H.P.*, p. 152; *R.E.S.*, i 262).

WILL.
Will assumed the part of Leonora in *Frederick and Basilea*, presented by the Admiral's men in June, 1597 (*H.P.*, p. 153). Fleay (*Stage*, p. 141) conjectures that he is identical with Will Barne (*q.v.*).

WILLANS, GEORGE.
See George Williams.

WILLIAMS, GEORGE.
Under license of November 10, 1629, George Williams is named as a member of the Red Bull company that appeared at Reading on November 30 of the same year. He is probably identical with the George Willans who is recorded at Norwich on March 10, 1635, as a member of presumably the King's Revels company, when the troupe applied for permission to act in that town (Murray, i. 272, 279–80; ii. 356, 386).

WILLIAMS, JOHN.
A member of the Chapel Royal in 1509 and 1511 (Hillebrand, *Mod. Phil.*, xviii. 244; Chambers, *Eliz. Stage*, ii. 27n.)

WILLIS, RICHARD.

As a member of Ellis Guest's company under license of June 7, 1628, Richard Willis is recorded at Norwich on July 2, 1628 (Murray, ii. 103).

WILLSON, HARRY.

See Henry Wilson.

WILLY, "OUR PLEASANT."

See Richard Tarlton.

WILLYAMS, WALTER.

Walter Willyams is recorded at Norwich on March 10, 1635, when his troupe, presumably the King's Revels, applied for permission to act in that town (Murray, i. 279–80).

WILSON, GERMAINE.

A member of the Children of Paul's in 1594 (Hillebrand, *Child Actors*, p. 111).

WILSON, HENRY.

Henry Wilson is named in a Protection from Arrest issued by Herbert on December 27, 1624, to twenty-one men "imployed by the Kinges Maiesties servantes in theire quallity of Playinge as Musitions and other necessary attendantes" (Adams, *Dram. Rec.*, p. 74). He is probably identical with the Harry Willson mentioned in a stage-direction of Massinger's *Believe as You List* (ed. Croker, p. 71): "Harry Willson & Boy ready for the Song at ye Arras." The play was licensed for the King's men on May 7, 1631 (Adams, *Dram. Rec.*, p. 33).

WILSON, JOHN.

John Wilson appears to have been a performer in *Much Ado about Nothing*, at some date before 1623. The 1600 quarto of the play gives the stage-direction (II. iii. 38):"Enter Balthaser with musicke," which in the 1623 folio becomes: "Enter . . . Iacke

Wilson.'' Wilson must therefore have played Balthasar and sung
"Sigh no more, ladies, sigh no more.'' Perhaps he may be identical with John, son of Nicholas Wilson, "minstrel,'' recorded in
the baptismal register of St. Bartholomew the Less, West Smithfield, on April 24, 1585. The registers of St. Giles's, Cripplegate,
shows that he had an elder brother Adam (baptized November
18, 1582), a wife Joan (buried July 17, 1624), and an unnamed son
buried on September 3, 1624, from the house of George Somersett (*q.v.*), musician (Collier, *Actors*, pp. xvii–xix). He was apparently a city wait from about 1622 to 1641. There was
another John Wilson, born in 1595, a royal lutenist and an eminent musician. A confusion of the two persons of the same name
has naturally resulted (*Shak. Soc. Papers*, ii. 33; *D.N.B.*, lxii.
103 ff.). One of the Wilsons took part in a performance, presumably *A Midsummer Night's Dream*, given at the house of John
Williams, Bishop of Lincoln, on September 27, 1631, which offended the Puritans (Murray, ii. 148–50).

WILSON, ROBERT.

Robert Wilson belonged to the Earl of Leicester's company
in 1572 when he signed a letter addressed to the Earl requesting
continued patronage; and he is named in the patent granted to
Leicester's troupe on May 10, 1574 (*M.S.C.*, i. 262, 348). He is
presumably the Wilson referred to as Leicester's player in a letter
of April 25, 1581, from Thomas Bayly (*q.v.*), who says that he
is "willing and able to do much" in matters theatrical. That he
was a distinguished actor of the time is evidenced by an allusion
to him in Gabriel Harvey's *Letter-Book* (*c.* 1579), where he is
coupled with Tarlton (ed. E. J. L. Scott, p. 67): "howe peremptorily ye have preiudishd my good name for ever in thrustinge me thus on the stage to make tryall of my extemporall
faculty, and to play Wylsons or Tarletons parte.'' He was also
a playwright, as shown by a reference to him about 1580 by
Thomas Lodge in his *Defence of Poetry, Musick, and Stage Plays*, a

reply to Stephen Gosson's *Schoole of Abuse*. Lodge (*Works*, i. 43) accuses Gosson of plagiarism in his play of *Catiline's Conspiracies*, not extant, and declares that he prefers Wilson's *Shorte and Sweete*, a lost play supposedly on the same theme. Lodge characterizes this play by Wilson as "a peece surely worthy prayse, the practise of a good scholler." Wilson became associated with Queen Elizabeth's men when the troupe was first organized in 1583; he is named in a London record that gives the personnel of the company at this time (*Eliz. Stage*, ii. 106). Howes (continuation of Stow's *Annales*, edit. 1631, p. 698) tells of the establishment of the Queen's troupe of twelve players, among whom are "two rare men," Tarlton and Wilson, and the latter is noted "for a quicke delicate refined extemporall wit." Wilson served as payee for the Court performances by the Queen's men during the Christmas season of 1584–85 (Steele, pp. 91, 92). His name does not appear in the list of the Queen's men in 1588, by which date he may have left the company—but this list is possibly incomplete. Meres, in *Palladis Tamia* (1598), also couples him with Tarlton (*Eliz. Crit. Essays*, ed. Smith, ii. 323); after praising Tarlton for "extemporall verse," he continues: "And so is now our wittie Wilson, who for learning and extemporall witte in this facultie is without compare or compeere, as, to his great and eternall commendations, he manifested in his challenge at the *Swanne* on the Banke side." Heywood mentions him with other actors as having flourished before his time, i.e. before about 1594 (*Apology*, p. 43). At an uncertain date, but earlier than 1594, he had doubtless retired from the regular stage, though making occasional appearances in extemporal performances, and turned to the writing of plays (*Eliz. Stage*, ii. 349). He is taken to be the author ("R. W.") of *The Three Ladies of London* (1584), of *The Three Lords and Three Ladies of London* (1590), and of *The Cobbler's Prophecy* (1594), "by Robert Wilson, Gent." He collaborated in a number of plays now lost, as shown by the Henslowe accounts of the Admiral's men, chiefly during 1598 (*H.D.*,

ii. 320–21; *Eliz. Stage*, iii. 516). He is also mentioned in 1598 with his collaborators, as "the best for Comedy amongst vs," by Meres, *Palladis Tamia* (Smith, *op. cit.*, ii. 320). The last notice of him in the Henslowe records occurs in a letter from Robert Shaw to Henslowe, on June 14, 1600 (*H.P.*, pp. 55 ff.). He is probably the "Robert Wilson, yoman (a player)," whose burial is recorded in the parish of St. Giles's, Cripplegate, on November 20, 1600 (Collier, *Actors*, p. xviii). Thus far this sketch takes no account of the theory that there were two Elizabethan dramatists by the name of Robert Wilson—a moot question that has for many years troubled historians of the stage. The *Dictionary of National Biography* (lxii. 123–25) and other more or less reputable modern works include as playwrights both an "elder" and a "younger" Robert Wilson (for various conjectures, see Fleay, *Drama*, ii. 276–85; Collier, *Actors*, p. xviii; Baldwin, *M. L. N.*, xli. 34). According to the most careful scholarship of the present day, we may now discard the twofold theory, since there seems to be no adequate proof for supposing two dramatists by the name of Robert Wilson, and the so-called "younger" Wilson is not known to have been connected with the stage (Chambers, *Eliz. Stage*, ii. 350; Greg's review of *The Elizabethan Stage*, in R. E. S., i; and I. Gourvitch, *Notes and Queries*, cl. 4 ff.).

WILSON, WILLIAM.

William Wilson appears to have been a stage-attendant, gatherer, or minor actor, at the Fortune playhouse about 1617 (J. Q. Adams, "An 'Hitherto Unknown' Actor of Shakespeare's Troupe?" *M.L.N.*, 1919, xxxiv. 46). Before November 2, 1617, he wrote to Edward Alleyn, requesting his help in touching the benevolence of Thomas Downton, Edward Juby, and other members of the company at the Fortune, on the plea that he was to be married at an early date. The register of St. Saviour's, Southwark, is said to record that "William Wilson was married . . . to Dorothea Seare, on Sunday, Nov. 2, 1617." The letter, which has been handled by at least two London booksellers during the present century, is here given in somewhat modernized form:

To my most deare and especeall good frend
Mr Edward Alleyn at Dulwich . . .

Right worshipfull, my humble dutie rememberd—hoping in the Almightie of your health and prosperety, which on my knees I beseeche him long to contyneue, ffor the many favors which I haue from tyme to tyme received my poor abillety is not in the least degree able to give you satisfaction, vnless as I and myne haue byn bounden to you for your many kyndnes soe will wee duringe life pray for your prosperety. I confess I haue found you my cheifest frend in midest of my extremeties, which makes me loath to presse or request your favor any further, yet for that I am to be married on Sunday next, and your kindnes may be a great help and furtherance vnto me towards the raisinge of my poore and deserted estate, I am enforced once agayne to entreat your worships furtherance in a charitable request, which is that I may haue your worships letter to Mr. Downton and Mr. Edward Juby to be a meanes that the Company of players of the Fortune maie either offer at my wedding at St. Saviors church, or of their owne good natures bestowe something vpon me on that day. And as ever I and myne will not only rest bounden vnto your worship but contyneually pray for your worships health with encreas of all happynes longe to contyneue. In hope of your worships favor herin, I humbly take my leave. Resting
Your worshipps during life to be commanded,

WILLIAM WILSON.

WINTER, RICHARD.

Richard Winter was possibly a player at Canterbury about 1571. He owed money to Robert Betts, a deceased Canterbury painter, with whom William Fidge and one Whetstone (who seem to have been actors) also had accounts (Plomer, *Library*, 1918, ix. 253).

WINTERSELL, WILLIAM..

See William Wintershall.

WINTERSHALL, WILLIAM.

Wiliam Wintershall (or Wintersell) is mentioned with William Cartwright, junior, by Wright in *Historia Histronica* (1699), as belonging to the company at Salisbury Court (Hazlitt's *Dodsley*, xv. 404). Wintershall does not appear with Cartwright in the Norwich list of the King's Revels on March 10, 1635, which possibly justifies the assumption that he did not become a fellow-actor with Cartwright until the amalgamation of Queen Henrietta's men and the King's Revels company at Salisbury Court about October, 1637 (cf. Murray, i. 267–68). If so, he was probably a Queen's man at Salisbury Court from 1637 to the closing of the playhouses in 1642. Nothing further is heard of him until May 12, 1659, when the *Middlesex County Records* (ed. Jeaffreson, iii. 279) show that he and one Henry Eaton gave recognizances for the appearance of Anthony Turner (*q.v.*) on a charge of "unlawfull mainteining of Stage-playes and enterludes att the Redd Bull in St. John's Street." After the Restoration he joined the company formed out of "the scattered remnants" of players belonging to several of the older houses during the reign of Charles I. He is named in the Petition of the Cockpit Players on October 13, 1660, and in the Articles of Agreement between Herbert and Killigrew on June 4, 1662 (Adams, *Dram. Rec.*, pp. 94, 96, 113–14). His Majesty's Company of Comedians opened their new playhouse, the Theatre Royal, on May 7, 1663 (Pepys, *Diary*, iii. 107), under the management of Thomas Killigrew. As a member of this organization Wintershall assumed the following parts (Downes, *Ros. Ang.*, 2 ff.): the King in *The Humorous Lieutenant*; Sir Amorous in *The Silent Woman*; Subtle in *The Alchemist*; the King in *The Maid's Tragedy*; Gobrias in *A King and no King*; the King in *King Henry the Fourth*; Don Alonzo in *The Mock Astrologer*; Odmar in *The Indian Emperor*; Arimant in *Aureng Zeb*; Pelopidus in *Mythridates, King of Pontus*; Polydamus in *Marriage Alamode*; King John of France in *The Black Prince*; and Bomilcar, in *Sophonisba, or Hannibal's Overthrow*. Downes says of him (*Ros.*

Ang., p. 17): "Mr. Wintersel, was good in Tragedy, as well as in Comedy, especially in Cokes in *Bartholomew Fair;* that the Famous Comedian Nokes came in that part far short of him." Pepys praises him under date of April 28, 1668 (*Diary*, vii. 384): "To the King's house, and there did see *Love in a Maze*, wherein very good mirth of Lacy, the clown, and Wintersell, the country-knight his master." He is said to been "an excellent judicious Actor and the best Instructor of others." He died in July, 1679 (Downes, *Ros. Ang.*, ed. Knight, p. xxx). Leslie Hotson, in *The Commonwealth and Restoration Stage* (1928), pp. 52–53, has recently brought to light the records of a Chancery suit in 1654 between Wintershall and Andrew Cane, the actor. Cane, on April 30, 1624, with other members of the Palsgrave's company, entered into a bond to Richard Gunnell, manager of the Palsgrave's men. Gunnell died intestate, leaving his widow, Elizabeth, with two daughters, Margaret and Anne. The widow administered the estate. Later she married one John Robinson, who may be the actor. About 1641 she made her will, leaving the estate to her two daughters. Margaret had married Wintershall, Ann had married William Clarke. Upon the death of Anne, the Wintershalls laid claim to this "unadministered principal debt" of £40, secured by the bond dated April 30, 1624. The outcome is not known.

WODERAM, RICHARD.

Richard Woderam appears to have been the leader of Oxford's men at Ipswich in 1586–87, as suggested by a payment of 10*s.* to "Richard Woderam for the Erle of Oxfordes plaiers" (Murray, ii. 292). Chambers (*Eliz. Stage*, ii. 101*n.*) suggests that he is "more likely to have been an agent of the Corporation than a member of the company."

WOOD, MARY.

See Mary Clarke.

WOOD, RICHARD.

The register of St. Bodolph Aldgate records on April 18, 1613, the baptism of "Roger Wood, sonne to Richard Wood, a Stage-player in Houndsditch" (Denkinger, *P.M.L.A.*, xli. 107).

WOOD, WILLIAM.

The register of St. Bodolph Aldgate records on September 27, 1615, the baptism of "Abraham Wood, sonne to William Wood, a Player of Interludes in Houndsditch" (Denkinger, *P.M.L.A.*, xli. 107).

WOODFORD, THOMAS.

Thomas Woodford, described as a London merchant, was in some way interested in the Children of Paul's about 1600. Shortly after Christmas, 1600, he purchased from Chapman for twenty marks the play *The Old Joiner of Aldgate*, which was acted by the Children of Paul's under their new master, Edward Pearce, in 1601. In the lawsuit that followed the performance of the play, we have in 1603 "depositions by Woodford and Pearce that are of great interest" (Charles Sisson, *The Library*, N.S., viii, 1927, pp. 40 ff.). He was a lessee of Whitefriars about 1607–08, and in February, 1608, sold his interest to David Lording Barry. He seems to have had some connection with the playhouse in 1621, as suggested by a lawsuit between him and William Trevell in 1642 (Adams, *Playhouses*, pp. 311–14, 332; Chambers, *Eliz. Stage*, ii. 350, 515–17). He was also interested in other theatrical enterprises. In 1613 and 1619 he was engaged in disputes with Aaron Holland in the Court of Requests concerning a seventh part and profits therefrom in the Red Bull (Wallace, *N.U.S.*, ix. 291 ff.). Sisson writes in *The Library*, N.S., viii, 1927, p. 235: "I have found a later record of a case in the Court of Chancery in 1623–4 which concludes the story of his relation with the Red Bull, and recapitulates the incidents of his long struggle with Thomas Woodford, which he finally won." He appears as a wit-

ness in the case of Witter against Heminges and Condell in 1619–
20, but his interest, if any, in the Globe is not known (Wallace,
N.U.S., x. 74).

WOODS, JOHN.

John Woods appears as leader of a troupe of English players
in Holland during 1604. On September 30, 1604, the Council of
the city of Leyden gave his company permission to play at the
approaching fair "certain decent pieces for the amusement of the
people" (Cohn, p. lxxvii).

WOORTH, ELLIS.
See Ellis Worth.

WORTH, ELLIS.

Ellis Worth belonged to Queen Anne's men before June, 1615,
when he is mentioned in the Baskervile papers as a member of
the company. He is also named in agreements with Susan Baskervile in June, 1616 and 1617 (*Eliz. Stage*, ii. 237–38). On October 2,
1617, he with others of the Queen's company petitioned the
Sessions of Peace against the various presentments that had been
issued against them for not "repayringe the Highwayes neere the
Red Bull" (Jeaffreson, *Middlesex*, ii. 170). He is presumably the
Ellis who appears in a stage-direction (line 186), "Enter 2 Lords,
Sands, Ellis," of Robert Daborne's *Poor Man's Comfort* (ed. Swaen,
p. 382), probably a play of Queen Anne's company at the Cockpit
in Drury Lane, about 1617. On May 13, 1619, he attended Queen
Anne's funeral as a representative of her London company. After
the death of the Queen her London troupe was known as the
Players of the Revels at the Red Bull; in 1622 Worth is noted as
one of "the chiefe players" in this company (Adams, *Dram. Rec.*,
p. 63). By May, 1623, the company seems to have disbanded, for
on May 23 of that year Worth and two of his fellows pleaded to
be excused from their payments to Susan Baskervile, on the
ground that the other players of the original agreement were

either dead or with another troupe; and in 1626 the court dismissed the plea of Worth and Blaney, the two surviving plaintiffs. He is mentioned in connection with a lawsuit growing out of the presentation at the Red Bull in 1624 of *Keep the Widow Waking*, but he deposed that he had nothing to do with the play, and had never seen it acted (Charles Sisson, "*Keep the Widow Waking*," *The Library*, N.S., viii, 1927). Worth was a member of Prince Charles's company by December 7, 1631, when a license was granted to him, Joseph Moore, and Matthew Smith (Murray, i. 196, 199, 218). During the same month (Adams, *Dram. Rec.*, p. 45) he acted with this company in Marmion's *Holland's Leaguer*, appearing as Ardelio, a parasite (Marmion, *Works*, pp. 2, 6). He is named in a warrant of May 10, 1632, appointing several of Prince Charles's players as Grooms of the Chamber (Stopes, *Jahrbuch*, xlvi. 96). On December 10, 1635, he served as joint-payee for performances at Court by the Prince's men (Steele, p. 250). He is mentioned in the Norwich records of February 21, 1638, when the company visited that town; but this does not necessarily mean that he was present, for the entry is a mere abstract of the 1631 license (Murray, ii. 358). The register of St. Giles's, Cripplegate, records the baptism of his daughter Jane on July 19, 1613, and of his son Elizeus on March 12, 1629; in these two records he is described as gentleman and player, respectively (*Eliz. Stage*, ii. 350).

WRIGHT, JOHN.

John Wright played Millescent, daughter to Agurtes, in Marmion's *Holland's Leaguer*, presented in December, 1631 (Adams, *Dram. Rec.*, p. 45), by "the high and mighty Prince Charles his servants, at the private house in Salisbury Court" (Marmion, *Works*, pp. 2, 6).

WYLKYNSON, JOHN.

A record of the Court of Aldermen, of London, for May 27, 1549, states: "John Wylkynson, coriour, who comenly suffreth &

meynteyneth interludes & playes to be made and kept within his dwelling house, was streyghtly commandid no more to suffer eny suche pleyes there to be kept, vpon peyne of imprysonement" (Harrison, *England*, iv. 313).

YOUNG, JOHN.

John Young, mercer, and three of his fellows who had been players to Queen Jane before her death in 1537 are mentioned about 1538 in a Chancery suit concerning the payments for a horse hired "to beare there playing garments" (Stopes, *Shak. Env.*, 236). On the death of John Roll in 1539 he became a Court Interluder, with wages of £3 6s. 8d. a year. In 1546, at the death of Thomas Sudbury, he was allowed an "annuity" of the same amount. During 1540–42 he was receiving also a payment of 1d. a day. He was probably a Court Interluder until about 1553, and was still alive in 1569–70, when he drew an annuity of £3 6s. 8d. as "agitator comediarum." In one entry he is described as "Maker of Interludes, Comedies, and Playes." He is presumably the "right worshipful esquire John Yung," to whom William Baldwin's *Beware the Cat* (1553) is dedicated (Chambers, *Eliz. Stage*, ii. 80n., 82, 84n.; Collier, *H.E.D.P.*, i. 132, 134, 148, 149, and *Bibl. Acc.*, i. 54).

YOUNG, JOHN.

John Young acted Haver, lover of Mistress Jane, in Shirley's *Wedding* (c. 1626), and Leister, in Davenport's *King John and Matilda* (c. 1629), both plays of Queen Henrietta's men at the Cockpit in Drury Lane. On March 10, 1635, he is recorded at Norwich, as a member of, presumably, the King's Revels company, when the troupe applied for permission to act in that town (Murray, i. opp. 266, 279–80).

YUNG, JOHN.
    See John Young.

BIBLIOGRAPHY

BIBLIOGRAPHY

A., R., *The Valiant Welshman*. By R. A. Gent. Edited by J. S. Farmer, 1913. (*Tudor Facsimile Texts*.)

Adams, J. Q. *Chief Pre-Shakespearean Dramas*. Boston, 1924.

Adams, J. Q. *Dramatic Records of Sir Henry Herbert, Master of the Revels, 1623–1673*. New Haven, 1917. (*Cornell Studies in English*, iii.)

Adams, J. Q. "*Every Woman in her Humor* and *The Dumb Knight*." *Modern Philology* (1913), x. 413.

Adams, J. Q. "An 'Hitherto Unknown' Actor of Shakespeare's Troupe?" *Modern Language Notes* (1919), xxxiv. 46.

Adams, J. Q. "The Housekeepers of the Globe." *Modern Philology* (1919), xvii. 1.

Adams, J. Q. Introduction to his edition of John Mason's *The Turke*, Louvain, 1913. (*Materialien*, xxxvii.)

Adams, J. Q. *A Life of William Shakespeare*. Boston, 1923.

Adams, J. Q. "Lordinge (*alias* 'Lodowick') Barry." *Modern Philology* (1912), ix. 567.

Adams, J. Q. *Shakespearean Playhouses*. Boston, 1917.

Adams, J. Q. "William Heminge and Shakespeare." *Modern Philology* (1914), xii. 51.

Adams, W. D. *A Dictionary of the Drama*. Vol. i, A–G. London, 1904. (See Northup, *Register*, pp. 121–22.)

Aldington, R. `A Book of 'Characters.'* London, [1924]. (*Broadway Translations*.)

Alexander, W. *Poetical Works of Sir William Alexander*. 3 vols. Glasgow, 1870–72.

Allot, R. *Englands Parnassus*. Edited by C. Crawford. Oxford, at the Clarendon Press, 1913.

Andrews, C. E. *Richard Brome: A Study of his Life and Works.* New Haven, 1913. (*Yale Studies in English*, xlvi.)

Arber, E. *A Transcript of the Registers of the Company of Stationers of London, 1554–1640 A.D.* 5 vols. Privately Printed. London, 1875–77; Birmingham, 1894.

Arber, E. *The Return from Parnassus.* Westminster, 1895.

Armin, R. *The Italian Taylor, and his Boy.* Reprinted, London, 1810.

Armin, R. *A Nest of Ninnies.* Edited by J. P. Collier. Printed for the Shakespeare Society. London, 1842.

Armin, R. *Works of Robert Armin, Actor.* Edited by A. B. Grosart. Printed for the Subscribers, 1880. (*Occasional Issues of Unique or Very Rare Books*, xiv.)

Ashbee, E. W. *Occasional Fac-simile Reprints.* Printed for Subscribers Only. London, 1868–72.

Aubrey, J. *"Brief Lives," Chiefly of Contemporaries, set down by John Aubrey, between the Years 1669 & 1696.* Edited from the Author's MSS. by Andrew Clark. 2 vols. Oxford, at the Clarendon Press, 1898.

Baddeley, J. J. *An Account of the Church and Parish of St. Giles, without Cripplegate, in the City of London.* London, 1888.

Baker, G. P. *The Development of Shakespeare as a Dramatist.* New York, 1907.

Baker, H. B. *Our Old Actors.* London, 1881.

Baker, R. *A Chronicle of the Kings of England.* London, 1764.

Baldwin, T. W. "Nathaniel and Nathan Field." *Times Literary Supplement*, May 27, 1926, p. 355.

Baldwin, T. W. "Nathaniel Field and Robert Wilson." *Modern Language Notes* (1926), xli. 32.

Baldwin, T. W. *The Organization and Personnel of the Shakespearean Company.* Princeton University Press, 1927.

Barksted, W. *The Poems of William Barksted, One of the Servants of His Majesty's Revels.* Edited by A. B. Grosart. Printed for the

Subscribers, 1876. (*Occasional Issues of Unique or Very Rare Books*, iii.)

Barry, L. *Ram Alley*. (Reprinted in Hazlitt's *Dodsley*, x. 265.)

Bastard, T. *Poems, English and Latin, of the Rev. Thomas Bastard, M.A.* (*1566–1618*). Edited by A. B. Grosart. Printed for the Subscribers, 1880. (*Occasional Issues of Unique or Very Rare Books*, xiii.)

Bateson, M. *Records of the Borough of Leicester, 1509–1603*. Cambridge, at the University Press, 1905.

Beaumont and Fletcher. *Works of Francis Beaumont and John Fletcher*. Edited by A. Glover and A. R. Waller. 10 vols. Cambridge, at the University Press, 1905–12.

"Ben Jonson Convicted of Felony." *Athenæum*, March 6, 1886, p. 337.

Bentley, G. E. "Shakespeare's Fellows." *Times Literary Supplement*, November 15, 1928, p. 856.

Biographia Dramatica: Historical and Critical Memoirs, and Original Anecdotes, of Dramatic Writers and Some of the Most Celebrated Actors. Compiled to 1764 by D. E. Baker, continued to 1782 by I. Reed, and to 1811 by S. Jones. 3 vols. in 4. London, 1812.

Birch, T., and R. F. Williams. *Court and Time of James the First*. 2 vols. London, 1849.

Boas, F. S. "A Seventeenth Century Theatrical Repertoire." *Library* (1917), viii. 225.

Bolle, W. "Das Liederbuch Ms. Rawlinson Poet. 185." *Archiv für das Studium der neueren Sprachen und Literaturen* (1905), cxiv. 326.

Bolte, J. *Das Danziger Theater im 16. und 17. Jahrhundert*. Hamburg, 1895.

Bolte, J. "Englische Komödianten in Dänemark und Schweden." *Shakespeare Jahrbuch* (1888), xxiii. 99.

Bolte, J. "Englische Komödianten in Münster und Ulm." *Shakespeare Jahrbuch* (1900), xxxvi. 273.

Bond, R. W. *Early Plays from the Italian*. Oxford, at the Clarendon Press, 1911.

Bourgeois, A. F. "John Webster a Contributor to Sir Thomas Overbury's 'Characters.' " *Notes and Queries* (1914), x. 3, 23.

Boyle, R. "Daborne's Share in the Beaumont and Fletcher Plays." *Englische Studien* (1889), xxvi. 352.

Brewer, A. *Anthony Brewer's "The Love-sick King."* Edited by A. E. H. Swaen. Louvain, 1907. (*Materialien*, xviii.)

Brewer, J. S. *Letters and Papers, Foreign and Domestic, of the Reign of Henry VIII*. Arranged and catalogued by J. S. Brewer, and (later) J. Gairdner and R. H. Brodie. 21 vols. London, 1862–1910.

Brinkley, R. F. "Nathan and Nathaniel Field." *Modern Language Notes* (1927), xlii. 10.

Brinley, R. F. *Nathan Field, the Actor-Playwright*. Yale University Press, 1928.

Brome, R. *Dramatic Works of Richard Brome*. 3 vols. London, 1873.

Brooke, C. F. T. *The Shakespeare Apocrypha*. Oxford, at the Clarendon Press, 1918.

Bruce, J. "Who was 'Will, my Lord of Leycester's Jesting Player'?" *Shakespeare Society's Papers*, i. 88. London, 1844.

Brydges, E., and J. Haslewood. *The British Bibliographer*. 4 vols. London, 1810–14.

Bullen, A. H. *Old English Plays*. 4 vols. Privately Printed. London, 1882–85. New Series. 3 vols. London, 1887–90.

Burgon, J. W. *Life and Times of Sir Thomas Gresham*. 2 vols. London, [1839].

Byrne, M. St. C. *Elizabethan Life in Town and Country*. London, 1925.

C., I. *The Two Merry Milke-Maids*. Edited by J. S. Farmer, 1914. (*Tudor Facsimile Texts*.)

Calderwood, D. *History of the Kirk of Scotland by Mr. David Calderwood*. Edited by T. Thomson. 8 vols. Printed for the Woodrow Society. Edinburgh, 1842–49.

BIBLIOGRAPHY

Calendar of State Papers and Manuscripts, Relating to English Affairs, Existing in the Archives and Collections of Venice, and in other Libraries of Northern Italy. Edited by R. Brown, and (later) G. C. Bentinck, H. F. Brown, and A. B. Hinds, 26 vols. London, 1864–1925.

Calendar of State Papers, Domestic Series, of the Reigns of Edward VI, Mary, and Elizabeth. 7 vols. Edited by R. Lemon and (later) M. A. E. Green. London, 1856–71.

Calendar of State Papers, Domestic Series, of the Reign of James I. 4 vols. Edited by M. A. E. Green. London, 1857–59.

Calendar of State Papers, Domestic Series, of the Reign of Charles I. 23 vols. Edited by J. Bruce, and (later) W. D. Hamilton and S. C. Lomas. London, 1858–97.

Calendar of State Papers, Domestic Series, of the Reign of Charles II, 1663–1664. Edited by M. A. E. Green. London, 1862.

Calendar of State Papers, Scottish Series, 1509–1603. Edited by M. J. Thorpe. 2 vols. London, 1858.

Calendar of the Patent Rolls, Henry IV. 4 vols. London, 1903–09.

Cambridge History of English Literature. Edited by A. W. Ward and A. R. Waller. 14 vols. New York, 1907–17. ("The Drama to 1642," vols. v and vi.)

Camden, W. *Remains Concerning Britain.* London, 1870.

Campion, T. *Works of Dr. Thomas Campion.* Edited by A. H. Bullen. London, 1889.

Cargill, A. "Shakespeare as an Actor." *Scribner's Magazine* (1891), ix. 613.

Castelain, M. *Ben Jonson: l'homme et l'oeuvre.* Paris, 1907.

Cecil Manuscripts. Calendar of the Manuscripts of the Marquis of Salisbury, Preserved at Hatfield House, Hertfordshire. Parts i–xiv. London, 1883–1923. (*Historical Manuscripts Commission.*)

Chalmers, A. *British Essayists.* 38 vols. London, 1823.

Chalmers, A. *Works of the English Poets from Chaucer to Cowper.* 21 vols. London, 1810.

Chalmers, G. *An Apology for the Believers in the Shakspeare-Papers*. London, 1797.

Chalmers, G. *A Supplemental Apology for the Believers in the Shakspeare-Papers*. London, 1799.

Chambers, E. K. "A Jotting by John Aubrey." Malone Society's *Collections*, i. 341.

Chambers, E. K. "Court Performances before Queen Elizabeth." *Modern Language Review* (1906–07), ii. 1.

Chambers, E. K. "Court Performances under James the First." *Modern Language Review* (1908–09), iv. 153.

Chambers, E. K. "Elizabethan Lords Chamberlain." Malone Society's *Collections*, i. 37.

Chambers, E. K. *The Elizabethan Stage*. 4 vols. Oxford, at the Clarendon Press, 1923.

Chambers, E. K. "Four Letters on Theatrical Affairs." Malone Society's *Collections*, ii. 145.

Chambers, E. K. *The Mediæval Stage*. 2 vols. Oxford, at the Clarendon Press, 1903.

Chambers, E. K. "Nathaniel Field and Joseph Taylor." *Modern Language Review* (1908–09), iv. 395.

Chambers, E. K. Review of Greg's edition of *Henslowe's Diary*. *Modern Language Review* (1909), iv. 407.

Chambers, E. K. "Two Early Player-Lists." Malone Society's *Collections*, i. 348.

Chambers, E. K. "William Kempe." *Modern Language Review* (1908–09), iv. 88.

Chambers, E. K., and W. W. Greg. "Dramatic Records from the Privy Council Register, 1603–1642." Malone Society's *Collections*, i. 370.

Chambers, E. K., and W. W. Greg. "Dramatic Records of the City of London. The Remembrancia." Malone Society's *Collections*, i. 43.

Chambers, E. K., and W.W. Greg. "Royal Patents for Players." Malone Society's *Collections*, i. 260.

Chandler, F. W. *The Literature of Roguery.* 2 vols. Boston, 1907.

Chapman, G. *Tragedies of George Chapman.* Edited by T. M. Parrott. London, 1910.

Chettle, H. *Kind-Heart's Dream; Containing Five Apparitions with their Invectives against Abuses Reigning.* Edited by E. F. Rimbault. Reprinted for the Percy Society. London, 1841.

Chetwood, W. R. *A General History of the Stage, from its Origin in Greece down to the Present Time.* London, 1749.

Clark, A. *Shirburn Ballads, 1585-1616.* Oxford, at the Clarendon Press, 1907.

Clark, R. "Condell and Heminge." *Notes and Queries* (1896), x. 109, 265.

Cohn, A. "English Actors in Germany." *Athenæum,* June 25, 1859, p. 842.

Cohn, A. "Englische Komödianten in Köln (1592-1656)." *Shakespeare Jahrbuch* (1886), xxi. 245.

Cohn, A. "Old English Actors in Germany." *Athenæum,* July 13, 1850, p. 738.

Cohn, A. *Shakespeare in Germany in the Sixteenth and Seventeenth Centuries.* London, 1865.

Cohn, A. "Shakespeare on the Early German Stage." *Athenæum,* January 4, 1851, p. 21.

Collier, J. P. *A Bibliographical and Critical Account of the Rarest Books in the English Language.* 4 vols. New York, 1866.

Collier, J. P. *The Alleyn Papers.* Printed for the Shakespeare Society. London, 1843.

Collier, J. P. *Fools and Jesters: with a Reprint of Robert Armin's "Nest of Ninnies."* Printed for the Shakespeare Society. London, 1842.

Collier, J. P. *History of English Dramatic Poetry.* 3 vols. 1831. Second Edition, London, 1879. (For Actors, see iii. 255-488.)

Collier, J. P. "John Wilson, the singer in *Much Ado about Nothing,* a musical composer in Shakespeare's plays." *Shakespeare Society's Papers,* ii. 33. London, 1845.

Collier, J. P. *Memoirs of Edward Alleyn*. Printed for the Shakespeare Society. London, 1841.

Collier, J. P. *Memoirs of the Principal Actors in the Plays of Shakespeare*. Printed for the Shakespeare Society. London, 1846.

Collier, J. P. *New Facts Regarding the Life of Shakespeare*. London, 1835.

Collier, J. P. *Old Ballads, from Early Printed Copies of the Utmost Rarity*. Printed for the Percy Society. London, 1840.

Collier, J. P. "Original History of 'The Theatre,' in Shoreditch, and Connexion of the Burbadge family with it." *Shakespeare Society's Papers*, iv. 63. London, 1849.

Collier, J. P. "Richard Field (the printer of Shakespeare's *Venus and Adonis* and *Lucrece*), Nathaniel Field, Anthony Munday, and Henry Chettle." *Shakespeare Society's Papers*, iv. 36. London, 1849.

Cook, D. *A Book of the Play*. 2 vols. London, 1876.

Cooke, J. *Greene's Tu Quoque, or the City Gallant*. (Reprinted in Hazlitt's *Dodsley*, xi. 173.)

Corbet, R. *Poems of Bishop Corbet*. (In A. Chalmers, *English Poets*, v. 551. London, 1810.)

Coryat, T. *Coryat's Crudities*. 2 vols. Glasgow, 1905.

Courthope, W. J. *A History of English Poetry*. 6 vols. London, 1895–1910.

Cowley, A. *Complete Works in Verse and Prose of Abraham Cowley*. 2 vols. Edited by A. B. Grosart. Printed for Private Circulation, 1881.

Creizenach, W. *Die Schauspiele der englischen Komödianten*. Berlin, [1889].

Creizenach, W. *English Drama in the Age of Shakespeare*. Translated by Miss Cecile Hugon from the 4th vol. of Creizenach's *Geschichte des neueren Dramas*. London, 1916.

Creizenach, W. *Geschichte des neueren Dramas*. 5 vols. Halle, 1893–1916.

Crüger, J. "Englische Komoedianten in Strassburg im Elsass." *Archiv für Litteraturgeschichte* (1887), xv. 113.

Cunningham, P. "Did General Harrison kill 'Dick Robinson' the player?" *Shakespeare Society's Papers*, ii. 11. London, 1845.

Cunningham, P. *Extracts from the Accounts of the Revels at Court in the Reigns of Queen Elizabeth and King James I.* Printed for the Shakespeare Society. London, 1842.

Cunningham, P. "Plays Acted at Court, Anno 1613 (from the Accounts of Lord Harrington, Treasurer of the Chamber to King James I)." *Shakespeare Society's Papers*, ii. 123. London, 1845.

Cunningham, P. "The Whitefriars Theatre, the Salisbury Court Theatre, and the Duke's Theatre in Dorset Gardens." *Shakespeare Society's Papers*, iv. 89. London, 1849.

D., T. *The Bloodie Banquet.* London, 1639. Edited by J. S. Farmer, 1914. (*Tudor Facsimile Texts.*)

Daborne, R. *The Poor Man's Comfort.* Edited by A. E. H. Swaen. *Anglia* (1898–99), xxi. 373.

D'Ancona, A. *Origini del Teatro Italiano.* 2 vols. Torino, 1891.

Daniel, S. *Complete Works in Verse and Prose of Samuel Daniel.* Edited by A. B. Grosart. 5 vols. Printed for private circulation only, 1885–96.

Dasent, J. R. *Acts of the Privy Council of England.* New Series. 34 vols. London, 1890–1925.

Davenant, W. *Dramatic Works of Sir William D'Avenant.* Edited by J. Maidment and W. H. Logan. 5 vols. Edinburgh, 1872–74.

Davenport, R. *Works of Robert Davenport.* Edited by A. H. Bullen. London, 1890. (*Old English Plays*, New Series, iii.)

Davies, J. *Complete Works of John Davies of Hereford.* 2 vols. Edited by A. B. Grosart. Printed for Private Circulation, 1878.

Davies, T. *Dramatic Miscellanies.* 3 vols. Dublin, 1784.

Day, J. *Works of John Day.* Edited by A. H. Bullen. Privately Printed, 1881.

Dekker, T. *A Knight's Conjuring: Done in Earnest, Discovered in Jest.* Edited by E. F. Rimbault. Reprinted for the Percy Society. London, 1842.

Dekker, T. *Dramatic Works of Thomas Dekker.* 4 vols. London, 1873.

Dekker, T. *The Gull's Horn-Book.* (*Temple Classics.*)

Dekker, T. *Non-Dramatic Works of Thomas Dekker.* Edited by A. B. Grosart. 5 vols. Printed for Private Circulation Only, 1884–86.

Denkinger, E. M. "Actors' Names in the Register of St. Bodolph Aldgate." *Publications of the Modern Language Association of America* (1926), xli. 91.

Dibdin, J. C. *Annals of the Edinburgh Stage, with an Account of the Rise and Progress of Dramatic Writing in Scotland.* Edinburgh, 1888.

Dictionary of National Biography. Edited by L. Stephen and S. Lee. 63 vols. London, 1885–1900. Supplement, 3 vols., 1901. Index and Epitome, 1903. Errata, 1904. Second Supplement, 3 vols., 1912. Index and Epitome, 1913.

Disraeli, I. *The Amenities of Literature.* A new edition, edited by his son, the Earl of Beaconsfield. London, [n.d.].

Disraeli, I. *Calamities and Quarrels of Authors.* London, 1865.

Dobson, A. *Collected Poems of Austin Dobson.* London, 1898.

Doran, J. *Annals of the British Stage.* Edited by R. W. Lowe. 3 vols, London, 1888.

Doran, J. *Annals of the English Stage, from Thomas Betterton to Edmund Kean.* 2 vols. New York, 1865.

Downes, J. *Roscius Anglicanus, or, an Historical Review of the Stage from 1660 to 1706. A Fac-simile Reprint of the Rare Original of 1708.* With an Historical Preface by Joseph Knight. London, 1886.

Dramaticus. "On the Profits of Old Actors." *Shakespeare Society's Papers*, i. 21. London, 1844.

Dramaticus. "Players who Acted in the *Shoemakers' Holiday*, 1600, a Comedy by Thomas Dekker and Robert Wilson." *Shakespeare Society's Papers*, iv. 110. London, 1849.

Drayton, M. *Works of Michael Drayton, Esq.* 4 vols. London, 1753.

Drew, T. *The Life of the Dutches of Suffolke*. [London], 1631.

Duncker, A. "Landgraf Moritz von Hessen und die englischen Komödianten." *Die Deutsche Rundschau* (1886), xlviii. 260.

Dunlop, J. C. *History of Prose Fiction*. Revised by H. Wilson. 2 vols. London, 1888. (*Bohn's Standard Library*.)

Ellis, H. *History and Antiquities of the Parish of Saint Leonard, Shoreditch*. London, 1798.

Elze, T. "John Spencer in Regensburg." *Shakespeare Jahrbuch* (1879), xiv. 363.

Elze, K. *Notes on Elizabethan Dramatists*. Halle, 1889.

"Englische Komödianten in Deutschland." *Shakespeare Jahrbuch* (1909), xlv. 311.

Este. "Shakespeare's 'Two Friends.' " *Notes and Queries* (1895), viii. 425.

Evelyn, J. *Diary and Correspondence of John Evelyn, F. R. S.* Edited by W. Bray. 4 vols. London, 1857.

Eyre, G. E. B., and C. R. Rivington. *A Transcript of the Registers of the Worshipful Company of Stationers; from 1640–1708 A. D.* 3 vols. London, Privately Printed, 1913–14.

Fellowes, E. H. *English Madrigal Composers*. Oxford, at the Clarendon Press, 1921.

Fellowes, E. H. *English Madrigal Verse (1588–1632)*. Oxford, at the Clarendon Press, 1920.

Feret, C. J. "Condell and Heminge." *Notes and Queries* (1896), x. 265.

Feuillerat, A. *Documents Relating to the Office of the Revels in the Time of Queen Elizabeth*. Louvain, 1908. (*Materialien*, xxi.)

Feuillerat, A. *Documents Relating to the Revels at Court in the Time of King Edward VI and Queen Mary*. Louvain, 1914. (*Materialien*, xliv.)

Field, N. *A Woman is a Weathercock*. (Reprinted in Hazlitt's *Dodsley*, xi. 1.)

Field, N. *Amends for Ladies*. (Reprinted in Hazlitt's *Dodsley*, xi. 87.)

Fitzgeoffrey, C. *Poems of the Rev. Charles Fitzgeoffrey (1593–1636).* Edited by A. B. Grosart. Printed for the Subscribers, 1881. (*Occasional Issues of Unique or Very Rare Books*, xvi.)

Fitzgerald, P. *A New History of the English Stage, from the Restoration to the Liberty of the Theatres, in Connection with the Patent Houses.* 2 vols. London, 1882.

F., F. J. "Tarlton, Allen, and Burbage." *Notes and Queries* (1880), i. 113.

Fleay, F. G. *A Biographical Chronicle of the English Drama, 1559–1642.* 2 vols. London, 1891.

Fleay, F. G. *A Chronicle History of the Life and Work of William Shakespeare, Player, Poet, and Playmaker.* New York, 1886.

Fleay, F. G. *A Chronicle History of the London Stage, 1559–1642.* London, 1890.

Fleay, F. G. "On the Actor Lists, 1578–1642." *Transactions of the Royal Historical Society* (1881), ix. 44.

Fleay, F. G. *Shakespeare Manual.* London, 1876.

Flecknoe, R. "A Short Discourse of the English Stage." (Attached to *Love's Kingdom*, 1664.) Reprinted in Hazlitt, *English Drama and Stage*; also in Spingarn, ii. 91.

Flood, W. H. C. "Queen Mary's Chapel Royal." *English Historical Review* (1918), xxxiii. 83.

Ford, J. *Works of John Ford.* Edited by W. Gifford and A. Dyce. 3 vols. London, 1895.

"A Four-Text Hamlet." *New Shakespeareana* (1901), i. 14.

Fuller, T. *History of the Worthies of England. First Printed in 1662.* A New Edition, with a few explanatory notes, by John Nichols. 2 vols. London, 1811.

Furness, H. H. *A New Variorum Edition of Shakespeare.* Philadelphia, 1871—.

Furnivall, F. J. *Robert Laneham's Letter.* Re-publisht for the New Shakspere Society. London, 1890.

G., G. M. *The Stage Censor, an Historical Sketch, 1544-1907.* London, 1908.

Gaw, A. "Actors' Names in Basic Shakespearean Texts, with Special Reference to *Romeo and Juliet* and *Much Ado*." *Publications of the Modern Language Association of America* (1925), xl. 530.

Gaw, A. "John Sincklo as One of Shakespeare's Actors." *Anglia* (1926), xlix. 289.

Gayley, C. M. *Representative English Comedies*. 3 vols. New York, 1912–14.

Gayton, E. *Pleasant Notes upon Don Quixot*. London, 1654.

Genest, J. *Some Account of the English Stage, from the Restoration in 1660 to 1830*. 10 vols. Bath, 1832.

George a Green. Edited by F. W. Clarke and W. W. Greg. *Malone Society Reprints*, 1911.

Gildersleeve, V. C. *Government Regulation of the Elizabethan Drama*. New York, 1908. (*Columbia University Studies in English*.)

Glapthorne, H. *Plays and Poems of Henry Glapthorne*. 2 vols. London, 1874.

Glapthorne, H. *The Lady Mother*. Edited by A. H. Bullen. London, 1883. (*Old English Plays*, ii. 101.)

Goedeke, K. "Aufführungen durch Berufsschauspieler." *Grundrisz zur Geschichte der deutschen Dichtung aus den Quellen* (1886), ii. 524.

Gosson, S. *The School of Abuse*. Reprinted for the Shakespeare Society. London, 1841.

Gourvitch, I. "Robert Wilson; 'The Elder' and 'The Younger.'" *Notes and Queries* (1926), cl. 4.

Gower, G. W. G. L. *Registers of St. Peter's, Cornhill*. London, 1877. Part ii, 1879. (*Harleian Society*.)

Grabau, C. "Englische Komödianten in Deutschland." *Shakespeare Jahrbuch* (1909), xlv. 311.

Graves, T. S. "Notes on Elizabethan Plays." *Modern Philology* (1915), xxiii. 1.

Graves, T. S. "Ralph Crane and the King's Players." *Studies in Philology* (1924), xxi. 362.

417

Graves, T. S. "Some Allusions to Richard Tarleton." *Modern Philology* (1921), xviii. 493.

Graves, T. S. "Tricks of Elizabethan Showmen." *South Atlantic Quarterly* (1915), xiv. 138.

Graves, T. S. "Women on the Pre-Restoration Stage." *Studies in Philology* (1925), xxii. 184.

Gray, Austin K. "Robert Armine, the Fool." *Publications of the Modern Language Association of America* (1927), xlii. 673.

Gray, C. H. *Lodowick Carliell*. Chicago, 1905. (This includes a reprint of Carlell's *Deserving Favorite*.)

Green, J. R. *A Short History of the English People*. 2 vols. (*Everyman's Library*.)

Greene, R. *Plays & Poems of Robert Greene*. Edited by J. C. Collins. 2 vols. Oxford, at the Clarendon Press, 1905.

Greenstreet, J. "Blackfriars Theatre in the Time of Shakespeare." *Athenæum*, August 10, 1889, p. 203.

Greenstreet, J. "Documents Relating to the Players of the Red Bull, Clerkenwell, and the Cockpit in Drury Lane, in the Time of James I." *New Shakspere Society's Transactions*, 1880–86, p. 489.

Greenstreet, J. "Whitefriars Theatre in the Time of Shakspere." *New Shakspere Society's Transactions*, 1887–92, p. 269.

Greg, W. W. *Collections*. Malone Society, 1907–23.

Greg, W. W. "The Evidence of Theatrical Plots for the History of the Elizabethan Stage." *Review of English Studies* (1925), i. 257.

Greg, W. W. *Henslowe's Diary*. 2 vols. London, 1904–08.

Greg, W. W. *Henslowe Papers*. London, 1907.

Greg, W. W. "Nathaniel and Nathan Field." *Times Literary Supplement*, April 15, 1926, p. 283; June 3, 1926, p. 374.

Greg, W. W. "The Elizabethan Stage. A Review." *Review of English Studies* (1925), i. 97.

Greg, W. W. *Two Elizabethan Stage Abridgements: "The Battle of Alcazar" & "Orlando Furioso."* The Malone Society, 1922.

Grove, G. *A Dictionary of Music and Musicians*. Edited by J. A. F. Maitland. 5 vols. New York, 1904–10.

Guilding, J. M. *Records of the Borough of Reading*. 4 vols. London, 1892–96.

Guilpin, E. *Skialetheia*. (In *Unique or Very Rare Books*, ed. Grosart, vi. 1878.)

Hall, J. *Works of Joseph Hall, D. D.* Edited by P. Hall. 12 vols. Oxford, 1837–39.

Hallen, A. W. C. *Registers of St. Botolph, Bishopsgate*. 3 vols. Issued to Subscribers Only, 1889–95.

Halliwell-Phillipps, J. O. *A Calendar of the Shakespearean Rarities, Drawings and Engravings, Preserved at Hollingbury Copse, near Brighton*. For Special Circulation and for Presents only. London, 1887.

Halliwell-Phillipps, J. O. "Dispute between the Earl of Worcester's Players and the Corporation of Leicester in 1586, from the Records of that City." *Shakespeare Society's Papers*, iv. 145. London, 1849.

Halliwell-Phillipps, J. O. *Illustrations of the Life of Shakespeare*. London, 1874.

Halliwell-Phillipps, J. O. *Life of William Shakespeare*. London, 1848.

Halliwell-Phillipps, J. O. *Ludus Coventriae*. Printed for the Shakespeare Society. London, 1841.

Halliwell-Phillipps, J. O. *Nursery Rhymes of England, Collected Principally from Oral Tradition*. Printed for the Percy Society. London, 1842.

Halliwell-Phillipps, J. O. *Outlines of the Life of Shakespeare*. 2 vols. London, 1907.

Halliwell-Phillipps, J. O. "Richard Burbage as a Sea Monster." *Athenæum*, May 19, 1888, p. 641.

Halliwell-Phillipps, J. O. *"Tarlton's Jests" and "News out of Purgatory": with Notes, and Some Account of the Life of Tarlton*. Printed for the Shakespeare Society. London, 1844.

Halliwell-Phillipps, J. O. *The Marriage of Wit and Wisdom, to Which are Added Illustrations of Shakespeare and the Early English Drama.* Printed for the Shakespeare Society. London, 1846.

Halliwell-Phillipps, J. O. *Tinker of Turvey, or, Canterbury Tales: An Early Collection of English Novels.* London, 1859.

Halliwell-Phillipps, J. O. *Visits of Shakespeare's Company of Actors to the Provincial Cities and Towns of England, Illustrated by Extracts Gathered from Corporate Records.* Brighton, 1887.

Harris, C. "English Comedians in Germany before the Thirty Years' War: the Financial Side." *Publications of the Modern Language Association of America* (1907), xxii. 446.

Harrison, W. *Harrison's Description of England.* Edited by F. J. Furnivall. Publisht for the New Shakspere Society. London, 1877–78. (Additions by Mrs. C. C. Stopes. *Shakespeare Library.* London, 1908.)

Harvey, G. *Letter-Book of Gabriel Harvey, A. D. 1573–1580.* Edited by E. J. L. Scott. Printed for the Camden Society, 1884.

Harvey, G. *Works of Gabriel Harvey, D. C. L.* Edited by A. B. Grosart. 3 vols. Printed for Private Circulation Only, 1884–85.

Hawkins, F. *Annals of the French Stage from Its Origin to the Death of Racine.* 2 vols. London, 1884.

Hawkins, J. *A General History of the Science and Practice of Music by Sir John Hawkins.* 3 vols. London, 1875.

Hazlitt, W. C. *Collections and Notes, 1867–1876.* London, 1876.

Hazlitt, W. C. *English Drama and Stage under the Tudor and Stuart Princes, 1543–1664.* Printed for the Roxburghe Library, 1869.

Hazlitt, W. C. *A General Index to Hazlitt's Handbook and his Bibliographical Collections (1867–1889).* By G. J. Gray.

Hazlitt, W. C. *Hand-Book to the Popular, Poetical, and Dramatic Literature of Great Britain, from the Invention of Printing to the Restoration.* London, 1867.

Hazlitt, W. C. *A Select Collection of Old English Plays. Originally Published by Robert Dodsley in the year 1744.* 15 vols. London, 1874–76.

Hazlitt, W. C. *Shakespeare Jest-Books.* 3 vols. London, 1864.

Hebel, J. W. *The Plays of William Heminges.* Ithaca, New York, 1920. (An unpublished doctoral thesis in the Library of Cornell University.)

Heber, R. *Bibliotheca Heberiana: Catalogue of the Library of Richard Heber, Sold by Auction, 1834–1837.* 13 parts in 4 vols. [London, 1834–37.]

"Heminge and Condell." Shakespeare *Jahrbuch* (1897), xxxiii. 258.

Heminges, W. *The Fatal Contract.* London, 1653.

Heminges, W. *The Jewes Tragedy von William Hemings.* Edited by H. A. Cohn. Louvain, 1913. (*Materialien*, xl.)

Heminges, W. *William Hemminge's Elegy on Randolph's Finger.* Edited by G. C. Moore Smith. Stratford-upon-Avon, 1923.

Henderson, W. A. "Shakespeare's 'Two Friends.' " *Notes and Queries* (1896), ix. 55.

Herbert, J. F. "Additions to 'The Alleyn Papers.' " *Shakespeare Society's Papers*, i. 16. London, 1844.

Herford, C. H., and P. Simpson. *Ben Jonson: the Man and his Work.* 2 vols. Oxford, at the Clarendon Press, 1925.

Herz, E. *Englische Schauspieler und englisches Schauspiel zur Zeit Shakespeares in Deutschland.* Leipzig, 1903.

Heywood, T. *An Apology for Actors.* Reprinted for the Shakespeare Society. London, 1841.

Heywood, T. *The Captives; or, the Lost Recovered.* (Bullen, *Old English Plays*, iv. 99.)

Heywood, T. *Dramatic Works of Thomas Heywood.* 6 vols. London, 1874.

Heywood, T. *The Fair Maid of the West* (Parts I and II). Edited by J. P. Collier. Printed for the Shakespeare Society. London, 1850.

Heywood, T. *Gunaikeion, or Nine Bookes of Various History concerninge Women.* London, 1624.

Heywood, T. *"A Woman Killed with Kindness"* and *"The Fair Maid of the West."* Edited by K. L. Bates. Boston, 1917. (*Belles-Lettres Series.*)

Hillebrand, H. N. *The Child Actors.* (*University of Illinois Studies in Language and Literature*, xi, Nos. 1 & 2, February-May, 1926.)

Hillebrand, H. N. "Early History of the Chapel Royal." *Modern Philology* (1920), xviii. 233.

Hillebrand, H. N. "Sebastian Westcote, Dramatist and Master of the Children of Paul's." *Journal of English and Germanic Philology* (1915), xiv. 568.

Historical Manuscripts Commission. *Reports*, i–xix. London, 1870–1926.

Hotson, Leslie. *The Commonwealth and Restoration Stage.* Harvard University Press, 1928.

Hovenden, R. *Registers of St. James, Clerkenwell.* 6 vols. London, 1884–94. (*Harleian Society.*)

Hughes, C. *Shakespeare's Europe: Fynes Moryson's Itinerary.* London, 1903.

Hughes, W. "Tarleton, the Sign of 'The Tabor,' and St. Bennet's Church." *Notes and Queries* (1905), iii. 55.

Hunter, J. *Hallamshire. The History and Topography of the Parish of Sheffield in the County of York.* A New Edition by A. Gatty. London, 1869.

Huth, H. *Ancient Ballads and Broadsides.* London, 1867. (*Philobiblon Society.*)

Ingleby, C. M. *A Complete View of the Shakspere Controversy Concerning the Authenticity and Genuineness of Manuscript Matter Published by Mr. J. Payne Collier.* London, 1861.

Ingleby, C. M. "A Literary Craze: 'Our Pleasant Willy.'" *Notes and Queries* (1885), xi. 417.

Ingleby, C. M. *Shakespeare, the Man and the Book.* 2 vols. London, 1877–81.

Ingleby, C. M. *Shakspere Allusion-Books*, Part I. Published for the New Shakspere Society. London, 1874.

Ingram, J. H. *Christopher Marlowe and his Associates*. London, 1904.

Jackson, J. E. "The Earl of Leicester's Players." *Notes and Queries* (1867), xi. 350.

Jeaffreson, J. C. *Middlesex County Records*. 4 vols. Published by the Middlesex County Records Society. [London, 1886–92.]

Jonas, M. *Shakespeare and the Stage*. London, 1918.

Jonson, B. *Bartholomew Fair*. Edited by C. S. Alden. New Haven, 1905. (*Yale Studies in English*, xxv.)

Jonson, B. *Ben Jonson's Conversations with William Drummond of Hawthornden*. Edited by R. F. Patterson. London, 1923.

Jonson, B. *Cynthia's Revels*. Edited by A. C. Judson. New Haven, 1912. (*Yale Studies in English*, xlv.)

Jonson, B. *The Devil is an Ass*. Edited by W. S. Johnson. New Haven, 1905. (*Yale Studies in English*, xxix.)

Jonson, B. *Epicoene*. Edited by A. Henry. New Haven, 1906. (*Yale Studies in English*, xxxi.)

Jonson, B. *Works of Ben Jonson*. Edited by W. Gifford and F. Cunningham. 9 vols. London, 1875.

Jordan, T. *Poeticall Varieties*. London, 1637.

Jusserand, J. J. *Shakespeare in France under the Ancien Régime*. New York, 1899.

Kelly, W. *Notices Illustrative of the Drama and Other Amusements of Leicester*. London, 1865.

Kempe, W. *Kemps Nine Daies Wonder: Performed in a Daunce from London to Norwich*. Edited by A. Dyce. Printed for the Camden Society. London, 1840.

Killigrew, T. *Parson's Wedding*. (Reprinted in Hazlitt's *Dodsley*, xiv. 369.)

Kirke, J. *The Seven Champions of Christendome*. London, 1638.

A Knack to Know a Knave. (Reprinted in Hazlitt's *Dodsley*, v. 503.)

Könnecke, G. "Neue Beiträge zur Geschichte der englischen Komödianten." *Zeitschrift für vergleichende Litteraturgeschichte* (1887–88), N. F., i. 85.

Lacy, J. *Dramatic Works of John Lacy, Comedian.* Edited by J. Maidment and W. H. Logan. Edinburgh, 1875.

Langbaine, G. *An Account of the English Dramatick Poets.* Oxford, 1691.

Lawrence, W. J. "Early French Players in England." *Anglia* (1909), xxxii. 61.

Lawrence, W. J. "Elizabethan Players as Tradesfolk." *Modern Language Notes* (1926), xli. 363.

Lawrence, W. J. *Elizabethan Playhouse and Other Studies.* Stratford-upon-Avon, 1912. Second Series, 1913.

Lawrence, W. J. "Found: a Missing Jacobean Dramatist." *Times Literary Supplement*, March 23, 1922, p. 191.

Lawrence, W. J. "John Honeyman, the Caroline Actor-Dramatist." *Review of English Studies* (1927), iii. 220.

Lawrence, W. J. "John Kirke, the Caroline Actor-Dramatist." *Studies in Philology* (1924), xxi. 586.

Lawrence, W. J. "The King's Revels Players of 1619–1623." *Modern Language Review* (1919), xiv. 416.

Lawrence, W. J. "The Mystery of Lodowick Barry." *Studies in Philology* (1917), xiv. 52.

Lawrence, W. J. "On the Underrated Genius of Dick Tarleton." *London Mercury* (1920), ii. 66.

Lee, S. *Life of William Shakespeare.* London, 1922.

Lee, S. *Shakespeare and the Modern Stage.* New York, 1906.

Lee, S. "Shakespeare in Oral Tradition." *Nineteenth Century* (1902), li. 201.

Lee, S. L. "The Date of the *Tragedy of Sir John Van Olden Barnavelt.*" *Athenæum*, January 19, 1884, p. 89.

"Lists of the Players of K. James I at his death, March 27, 1625; and of the Comedians of K. Charles I." *New Shakspere Society's Transactions, 1877–79,* Appendix ii.

Lodge, E. *Illustrations of British History, Biography, and Manners, in the Reigns of Henry VIII, Edward VI, Mary, Elizabeth, and James I.* 3 vols. London, 1838.

BIBLIOGRAPHY

Lodge, T. *Complete Works of Thomas Lodge*. 4 vols. Printed for the Hunterian Club, 1883.

London Prodigall. (Reprinted in Brooke, *Shakespeare Apocrypha*, p. 191.)

Look about You. Edited by W. W. Greg. *Malone Society Reprints*, 1913.

Lowe, R. W. *A Bibliographical Account of English Theatrical Literature*. London, 1888.

Lyly, J. *Complete Works of John Lyly*. Edited by R. W. Bond. 3 vols. Oxford, at the Clarendon Press, 1902.

Lyly, J. *Endymion*. Edited by G. P. Baker. New York, 1894.

Macaulay, G. C. *Francis Beaumont*. London, 1883.

Machin, L. (and G. Markham). *The Dumb Knight*. (Reprinted in Hazlitt's *Dodsley*, x. 107.)

Machyn, H. *The Diary of Henry Machyn, Citizen and Merchant-Taylor of London, from A. D. 1550 to A. D. 1563*. Edited by J. G. Nichols. Printed for the Camden Society. London, 1848.

MacMichael, J. G. "Tarlton, the Sign of 'The Tabor,' and St. Bennet's Church." *Notes and Queries* (1905), iii. 73.

Madden, D. H. *Shakespeare and His Fellows*. London, 1916.

Malcolm, J. P. *Londinium Redivivum*. 4 vols. London, 1803–07.

Malone, E. *Plays and Poems of William Shakespeare*. 21 vols. London, 1821. (The Variorum Edition, edited by Boswell. For Actors, see iii. 182–223; additions by Chalmers, iii. 464–517.)

Manly, J. M. "Children of the Chapel Royal and Their Masters." *Cambridge History of English Literature*, vi. 314.

Manly, J. M. *Specimens of the Pre-Shakespearean Drama*. 2 vols. Boston, 1897.

Manningham, J. *Diary of John Manningham, of the Middle Temple, and of Bradbourne, Kent, Barrister-at-Law, 1602–1603*. Edited by J. Bruce. Westminster, 1868.

Mantzius, K. *A History of Theatrical Art in Ancient and Modern Times*. Authorized Translation by Louise von Cossel. Vol. iii, "The Shakespearean Period in England." London, 1904.

Marlowe, C. *Works of Christopher Marlowe*. Edited by A. H. Bullen. 3 vols. Boston, 1885.

Marmion, S. *Dramatic Works of Shackerley Marmion*. Edited by J. Maidment and W. H. Logan. London, 1875.

Marston, J. *Works of John Marston*. Edited by A. H. Bullen. 3 vols. Boston, 1887.

Mason, J. *The Turke*. Edited by J. Q. Adams. Louvain, 1913. (*Materialien*, xxxvii.)

Massinger, P. *Believe as You List*. Edited by T. C. Croker. Printed for the Percy Society. London, 1849.

Massinger, P. *Plays of Philip Massinger*. Edited by W. Gifford. 4 vols. London, 1813.

McKerrow, R. B. *A Dictionary of Printers and Booksellers in England, Scotland, and Ireland, and of Foreign Printers of English Books, 1557–1640*. Printed for the Bibliographical Society. London, 1910.

Meeting of Gallants at an Ordinaire. Edited by J. O. Halliwell-Phillipps. Reprinted for the Percy Society. London, 1841.

Meissner, J. *Die englischen Comödianten zur Zeit Shakespeares in Oesterreich*. Wien, 1884.

Meissner, J. "Die englischen Komoedianten in Oesterreich." Shakepeare *Jahrbuch* (1884), xix. 113.

A Member of Both Societies. "On Massinger's *Believe as You List*, a newly discovered manuscript tragedy, printed by the Percy Society." *Shakespeare Society's Papers*, iv. 133. London, 1849.

Mentzel, E. *Geschichte der Schauspielkunst in Frankfurt am Main*. Frankfurt, 1882.

Meres, F. *Palladis Tamia. Wits Treasury, Being the Second Part of Wits Commonwealth* (Reprinted, in part, in G. G. Smith, *Elizabethan Critical Essays*, ii. 308.)

Meyer, C. F. "Englische Komödianten am Hofe des Herzogs Philipp Julius von Pommern-Wolgast." Shakespeare *Jahrbuch* (1902), xxxviii. 196.

Middleton, T. *Works of Thomas Middleton*. Edited by A. H. Bullen. 8 vols. London, 1885–86.

Monaghan, J. "Falstaff and His Forebears." *Studies in Philology* (1921), xviii. 353.

Munro, J. *Shakespere Allusion-Book*. 2 vols. London, 1909.

Murray, H. "Shakepeare's 'Two Friends.'" *Notes and Queries* (1895), viii. 470.

Murray, J. T. *English Dramatic Companies, 1558–1642*. 2 vols. London, 1910.

Nabbes, T. *Works of Thomas Nabbes*. Edited by A. H. Bullen. 2 vols. London, 1887. (*Old English Plays*, New Series, i–ii.)

Nairn, J. A. "Boy-Actors under the Tudors and Stuarts." *Transactions of the Royal Society of Literature* (1914), xxxii. 61.

Nashe, T. *Works of Thomas Nashe*. Edited by R. B. McKerrow. 5 vols. London, 1904–10.

Neilson, W. A. *Chief Elizabethan Dramatists, Excluding Shakespeare*. Boston, 1911.

Nero and Other Plays. Edited by H. P. Horne, H. Ellis, A. Symons, and A. W. Verity. London, 1888. (*Mermaid Series*.)

Nettleton, G. H. *English Drama of the Restoration and Eighteenth Century* (1642–1780). New York, 1923.

New Shakspere Society. *Transactions, 1874, 1875–76, 1877–79, 1880–86, 1887–92*. London, Publisht for the Society.

Nichols, J. *Progresses and Public Processions of Queen Elizabeth*. 3 vols. London, 1788–1805.

Nichols, J. *Progresses, Processions, and Magnificent Festivities of King James the First*. 4 vols. London, 1828.

Nichols, J. G. *Chronicle of the Grey Friars of London*. Printed for the Camden Society, 1852.

Nicholson, B. "Kemp and the Play of *Hamlet*—Yorick and Tarlton—a Short Chapter in Dramatic History." *New Shakspere Society's Transactions, 1880–1886*, p. 57.

Nicoll, A. *A History of Restoration Drama, 1660–1700*. Cambridge, at the University Press, 1923.

Nicoll, A. "Some Notes on William Beeston." *Times Literary Supplement*, November 22, 1923, p. 789.

Northup, C. S. *A Register of Bibliographies of the English Language and Literature*. New Haven, 1925. (*Cornell Studies in English*, ix.)

Oldham, J. *Remains of Mr. John Oldham in Verse and Prose*. London, 1703.

Oliver, D. E. *The English Stage, Its Origins and Modern Developments*. London, [1912].

O'Neill, J. J. "Elizabethan Players as Tradesmen." *Times Literary Supplement*, April 8, 1926, p. 264.

Ordish, T. F. *Early London Theatres*. London, 1894.

Overbury, T. *Miscellaneous Works in Prose and Verse of Sir Thomas Overbury, Knt.* Edited by E. F. Rimbault. London, 1890.

Overend, G. H. "On the Dispute between George Maller, Glazier and Trainer of Players to Henry VIII, and Thomas Arthur, Tailor, his Pupil." *New Shakspere Society's Transactions*, 1877–79, p. 425.

"*Partiall Law*," a Tragi-comedy by an Unknown Author (*circa 1615–30*). Edited by B. Dobell. London, 1908.

Partington, W. *Smoke Rings and Roundelays*. New York, 1925.

Peacham, H. *Worth of a Penny*. London, 1687.

Penley, B. S. *The Bath Stage*. London, 1892.

Pepys, S. *Diary of Samuel Pepys*. Edited by H. B. Wheatley. 9 vols. London, 1893–99.

Phillips, E. *Theatrum Poetarum Anglicanorum*. First published in 1675. With *Additions* by Sir Egerton Brydges. Canterbury, 1800.

"*Pilgrimage to Parnassus*" *with the two parts of the "Return from Parnassus." Three Comedies Performed in St. John's College, Cambridge, A.D. MDXCVII–MDCI.* Edited by W. D. Macray. Clarendon Press, 1886.

Planché, J. R. *A Cyclopedia of Costume*. 2 vols. London, 1876–79.

"Plays and Players." *Athenæum*, January 23, 1869, p. 132.

Plomer, H. R. "Plays at Canterbury in 1570." *Library* (1918), ix. 251.

Plomer, H. R. "Richard Cowley the Actor: Witnesses to His Will." *Notes and Queries* (1906), vi. 369.

Poel, W. "Some Notes on Shakespeare's Stage and Plays." (Reprinted from the *Bulletin of the John Rylands Library*, April–September, 1916.) Manchester, 1916.

Pollard, A. W. "Authors, Players, and Pirates in Shakespeare's Day." *Library* (1916), vii. 73.

Pollard, A. W. *Fifteenth Century Prose and Verse*. Westminster, 1903. (*An English Garner.*)

Pollard, A. W. *Shakespeare Folios and Quartos*. London, 1909.

Pollard, A. W., and G. R. Redgrave. *A Short-Title Catalogue of Books Printed in England, Scotland, and Ireland, and of English Books Printed Abroad, 1475–1640*. London. The Bibliographical Society, 1926.

Quirinus. "Tarleton, the Sign of 'The Tabor,' and St. Bennet's Church." *Notes and Queries* (1905), iii. 7.

R., B. *Greenes Newes Both from Heauen and Hell*. Edited by R. B. McKerrow. London, 1911.

Raleigh, W. *Works of Sir Walter Raleigh, Kt*. Edited by T. Birch. 2 vols. London, 1751.

Rawlins, T. *The Rebellion*. (Reprinted in Hazlitt's *Dodsley*, xiv. 1.)

Rendle, W. "Graves at St. Saviour's, Southwark." *Athenæum*, August 21, 1886, p. 252.

Rendle, W. "The Bankside, Southwark, and the Globe Playhouse." (In F. J. Furnivall's edition of *Harrison's Description of England*, Part II, Book iii.)

Richards, A. E. *Studies in English Faust Literature*, i. *The English Wagner Book of 1594*. Berlin, 1907.

Richards, N. *Messallina*. Edited by A. R. Skemp. Louvain, 1910. (*Materialien*, xxx.)

Rigal, E. *Le théâtre français avant la période classique (fin du xvie et commencement du xviie siècle)*. Paris, 1901.

Riis, J. A. "Hamlet's Castle." *Century Magazine* (1901), lxi. 388.

Rimbault, E. F. "Autobiographical Notices of Henry Peacham." *Notes and Queries* (1867), xii. 221.

Rimbault, E. F. "Martin Marprelate Rhymes." *Notes and Queries* (1858), vi. 6.

Rimbault, E. F. *The Old Cheque-Book, or Book of Remembrance, of the Chapel Royal, from 1561 to 1744.* Printed for the Camden Society, 1872.

Ritson, J. *Bibliographica Poetica: A Catalogue of Engleish Poets, of the Twelfth, Thirteenth, Fourteenth, Fifteenth, and Sixteenth Centurys, with a Short Account of Their Works.* London, 1802.

Roach, J. *Roach's New and Complete History of the Stage, from Its Origin to Its Present State.* London, 1796.

Rollins, H. E. "The Commonwealth Drama: Miscellaneous Notes." *Studies in Philology* (1923), xx. 52.

Rollins, H. E. "A Contribution to the History of the English Commonwealth Drama." *Studies in Philology* (1921), xviii. 267.

Rollins, H. E. "William Elderton: Elizabethan Actor and Ballad-Writer." *Studies in Philology* (1920), xvii. 199.

Rose, W. *Doctor John Faustus.* London, [1925]. (*Broadway Translations.*)

Rowlands, S. *Complete Works of Samuel Rowlands.* 3 vols. Printed for the Hunterian Club, 1880–86.

Rowley, W. *A Search for Money.* Edited by J. P. Collier. Reprinted for the Percy Society. London, 1840.

Russell, W. C. *Representative Actors.* London, [1875].

Rutland MSS. The Manuscripts of the Duke of Rutland Preserved at Belvoir Castle. 4 vols. London, 1888–1905. (*Historical Manuscripts Commission.* Vols. i–iii are appendices to the 12th and 14th Reports; vol. iv was issued separately.)

S., H. T. "A Shakesperean Actor's Letter." *Athenæum*, September 19, 1903, p. 392.

Savage, R. *Shakespearean Extracts from "Edward Pudsey's Booke."* *Stratford-upon-Avon Note Books* (1888), i. .

Schelling, F. E. *Elizabethan Drama, 1558–1642.* 2 vols. Boston, 1908.

Schelling, F. E. *English Drama.* London, 1914.

Schelling, F. E. *English Literature During the Lifetime of Shakespeare.* New York, 1910.

Scott, E. J. L. "Elizabethan Stage." *Athenæum,* January 21, 1882, p. 103.

Second Maiden's Tragedy. Edited by W. W. Greg. *Malone Society Reprints,* 1909.

Shadwell, T. *Dramatick Works of Thomas Shadwell, Esq.* 4 vols. London, 1720.

Shakespeare, W. *Comedies, Tragedies, Histories and Poems.* 3 vols. (*Oxford Edition.*)

Shakespeare, W. *Shakspere's King Henry the Fourth, Part II: The Quarto of 1600, a Facsimile in Photo-Lithography.* Edited by W. Griggs and H. A. Evans. London, 1882.

Shakespeare Society's Papers. 4 vols. London, Printed for the Shakspeare Society, 1844–49.

Shakespeare's England: An Account of the Life and Manners of His Age. 2 vols. Oxford, at the Clarendon Press, 1916.

Sharers' Papers. "A Collection of Papers relating to Shares and Sharers in the Globe and Blackfriars Theatres, 1635." (Halliwell-Phillipps, *Outlines,* i. 312–19.)

Sharp, R. F. *A Short History of the English Stage, from Its Beginnings to the Summer of the Year 1908.* London, 1909.

Sheavyn, P. *The Literary Profession in the Elizabethan Age.* Manchester, 1909. (*Manchester University English Series,* i.)

Shirley, J. *Dramatic Works and Poems of James Shirley.* Edited by W. Gifford and A. Dyce. 6 vols. London, 1833.

Simpson, P. "Actors and Acting." *Shakespeare's England,* ii. 240.

Simpson, R. *The School of Shakspere.* 3 vols. New York, 1878.

Sir Thomas More. Edited by W. W. Greg. *Malone Society Reprints,* 1911.

Sisson, Charles. "*Keep the Widow Waking,* a Lost Play by Dekker." *The Library,* N.S. (1927), viii. 39, 233.

431

Small, R. A. *The Stage-Quarrel between Ben Jonson and the So-called Poetasters.* Breslau, 1899.

Smith, G. G. *Elizabethan Critical Essays.* 2 vols. Oxford, at the Clarendon Press, 1904.

Smith, J. *Works of Captain John Smith.* Edited by E. Arber. Birmingham, 1884.

Smith, S. A., and E. A. Fry. *Index of Wills Proved in the Prerogative Court of Canterbury, 1584–1604.* London, 1901. (*Canterbury Wills*, iv.)

Smith, W. "Italian and Elizabethan Comedy." *Modern Philology* (1908), v. 555.

Soulié, E. *Recherches sur Molière et sur sa famille.* Paris, 1863.

Spenser, E. *Complete Poetical Works of Edmund Spenser.* Edited by R. E. Neil Dodge. Boston, 1908. (*Student's Cambridge Edition.*)

Spingarn, J. E. *Critical Essays of the Seventeenth Century.* 3 vols. Oxford, at the Clarendon Press, 1908–09.

Sprigg, J. *Anglia Rediviva; England's Recovery: being the History of the Motions, Actions, and Successes of the Army under the immediate conduct of his excellency Sir Thomas Fairfax, Kt., Captain-General of all the Parliament's Forces in England. Compiled for the public good by Joshua Sprigg, M. A. (1647).* Oxford, at the University Press, 1854.

Steele, Mary S. *Plays & Masques at Court during the Reigns of Elizabeth, James, and Charles.* New Haven, 1926. (*Cornell Studies in English*, x.)

Stevenson, W. H. *Records of the Borough of Nottingham.* Edited by W. H. Stevenson and W. T. Baker. 5 vols. London, 1882–1900.

Stocks, H. *Records of the Borough of Leicester, 1603–1688.* Cambridge, at the University Press, 1923.

Stopes, C. C. *Burbage and Shakespeare's Stage.* London, 1913.

Stopes, C. C. "The Burbages and the Transportation of 'The Theatre.'" *Athenæum*, October 16, 1909, p. 470.

Stopes, C. C. "Burbage's 'Theatre.'" *Fortnightly Review* (1909), xcii. 149.

Stopes, C. C. " 'The Queen's Players' in 1536." *Athenæum*, January 24, 1914, p. 143.

Stopes, C. C. *Shakespeare's Environment*. London, 1918.

Stopes, C. C. "Shakespeare's Fellows and Followers." Shakespeare *Jahrbuch* (1910), xlvi. 92.

Stopes, C. C. *William Hunnis and the Revels of the Chapel Royal*. Louvain, 1910. (*Materialien*, xxix.)

Stopes, C. C. "William Hunnis, Gentleman of the Chapel Royal." *Athenæum*, February 21, 1891, p. 249; March 21, 1891, 376.

Stork, C. W. *William Rowley*. Philadelphia, 1910. (*University of Pennsylvania Publications*, xiii.)

Stow, J. *A Survey of London by John Stow*. Edited by C. L. Kingsford. 2 vols. Oxford, at the Clarendon Press, 1908.

Stow, J. *Annales, or a Generall Chronicle of England begun by John Stow: Continued and Augmented with Matters Forraigne and Domestic, Ancient and Moderne, unto the end of this present yeere, 1631, by Edmund Howes, Gent.* London, 1631.

Straparola, G. F. *Le Piacevoli Notti*. Venetia, 1562.

Strunk, W., Jr. "The Elizabethan Showman's Ape." *Modern Language Notes* (1917), xxxii. 215.

Stuart, J. *Extracts from the Council Register of the Burgh of Aberdeen (1398-1625)*. 2 vols. Aberdeen, 1844-48. (*Spalding Club*.)

Suckling, J. *Works of Sir John Suckling, in Prose and Verse*. Edited by A. H. Thompson. London, 1910.

Swinburne, A. C. *The Age of Shakespeare*. London, 1908.

Tailor, R. *The Hog Hath Lost his Pearl*. (Reprinted in Hazlitt's *Dodsley*, xi. 423.)

Tannenbaum, S. A. "*The Booke of Sir Thomas Moore*." New York, Privately Printed, [1927].

Taylor, J. *Works of John Taylor, the Water-Poet, Comprised in the Folio Edition of 1630*. Printed for the Spenser Society, 1869.

Taylor, J. *Works of John Taylor, the Water-Poet, not Included in the Folio Volume of 1630*. 5 collections. Printed for the Spenser Society, 1870-78.

Thaler, A. "The Elizabethan Dramatic Companies." *Publications of the Modern Language Association of America* (1920), xxxv. 123.

Thaler, A. "Minor Actors and Employees in the Elizabethan Theater." *Modern Philology* (1922), xx. 49.

Thaler, A. *Shakspere to Sheridan*. Cambridge, Harvard University Press, 1922.

Thaler, A. "The Traveling Players in Shakspere's England." *Modern Philology* (1920), xvii. 121.

Thaler, A. "Was Richard Brome an Actor?" *Modern Language Notes* (1921), xxxvi. 88.

The Queen, or The Excellency of Her Sex. Edited by W. Bang. Louvain, 1906. (*Materialien*, xiii.)

Thoms, W. J. "English Actors in Germany." *Notes and Queries* (1859), viii. 21.

Thoms, W. J. "Old English Actors in Germany." *Athenæum*, August 25, 1849, p. 862.

Thornbury, G. W. *Shakspere's England*. 2 vols. London, 1856.

Thorndike, A. H. *The Influence of Beaumont and Fletcher on Shakspere*. Worcester, 1901.

Thorndike, A. H. *Shakespeare's Theater*. New York, 1916.

Tofte, R. *Alba*. Edited by A. B. Grosart. Printed for the Subscribers, 1880.

Tomlins, T. E. "Origin of the Curtain Theatre, and Mistakes Regarding It." *Shakespeare Society's Papers*, i. 29. London, 1844.

Tomlins, T. E. "Three New Privy Seals for Players in the Time of Shakespeare." *Shakespeare Society's Papers*, iv. 41. London, 1849.

Tragedy of Sir John Van Olden Barnavelt. Edited by A. H. Bullen. London, 1883. (*Old English Plays*, ii. 201.) Edited by Wilhelmina P. Frijlinck. Amsterdam, 1922.

Trautmann, K. "Englische Komoedianten in München." *Archiv für Litteraturgeschichte* (1884), xii. 319.

BIBLIOGRAPHY

Trautmann, K. "Englische Komoedianten in Nürnberg bis zum Schlusse des Dressigjährigen Krieges." *Archiv für Litteraturgeschichte* (1886), xiv. 113.

Trautmann, K. "Englische Komödianten in Rothenburg ob der Tauber." *Zeitschrift für vergleichende Litteraturgeschichte* (1894), N. F., vii. 60.

Trautmann, K. "Englische Komoedianten in Stuttgart und Tübingen." *Archiv für Litteraturgeschichte* (1887), xv. 211.

Trautmann, K. "Englische Komoedianten in Ulm." *Archiv für Litteraturgeschichte* (1885), xiii. 315; (1887), xv. 216.

Trevelyan Papers. 3 vols.: i and ii ed. J. P. Collier; iii ed. W. C. and C. E. Trevelyan. Printed for the Camden Society, 1857, 1863, 1872.

Tusser, T. *Fiue Hundred Pointes of Good Husbandrie by Thomas Tusser.* Edited by W. Payne and S. J. Herrtage. Published for the English Dialect Society. London, 1878.

"Twenty-six Players of Shakespeare's Company." *New Shakspere Society's Transactions,* 1880–86, p. 85*.

Waldron, F. G. *Shakespearean Miscellany.* London, 1804.

Waldron, F. G., Dibdin, &c. *A Compendious History of the English Stage, from the Earliest Period to the Present Time.* London, 1800.

Wallace, C. W. *Children of the Chapel at Blackfriars, 1597–1603.* Lincoln, Nebraska, 1908.

Wallace, C. W. *Evolution of the English Drama up to Shakespeare, with a History of the First Blackfriars Theatre.* Berlin, 1912.

Wallace, C. W. "First London Theatre, Materials for a History." *Nebraska University Studies* (1913), xiii.

Wallace, C. W. "Gervase Markham, Dramatist." Shakespeare *Jahrbuch* (1910), xlvi. 345.

Wallace, C. W. *Globe Theatre Apparel.* Privately Printed, 1909. (Described in London *Times,* November 30, 1909, p. 12.)

Wallace, C. W. "A London Pageant of Shakespeare's Time." London *Times,* March 28, 1913, p. 6.

435

Wallace, C. W. "Shakespeare and His London Associates as Revealed in Recently Discovered Documents." *Nebraska University Studies* (1910), x. 261.

Wallace, C. W. "Shakespeare in London." London *Times*, October 2, 1909, p. 9; October 4, 1909, p. 9.

Wallace, C. W. "Shakspere's Money Interest in the Globe Theater." *Century Magazine* (1910), lxxx. 500.

Wallace, C. W. "The Swan Theatre and the Earl of Pembroke's Servants." *Englische Studien* (1910–11), xliii. 340.

Wallace, C. W. "Three London Theatres of Shakespeare's Time." *Nebraska University Studies* (1909), ix. 287.

Ward, A. W. *A History of English Dramatic Literature to the Death of Queen Anne.* 3 vols. London, 1899.

Warner, G. F. *Catalogue of the Manuscripts and Muniments of Alleyn's College of God's Gift at Dulwich.* Published for the Governors, 1881.

W., D. V. "English Comedians in the Netherlands." *Notes and Queries* (1853), vii. 114, 360.

Webster, J. *Dramatic Works of John Webster.* Edited by W. Hazlitt. 4 vols. London, 1857.

Webster, J. *"The White Devil" and "The Duchess of Malfy."* Edited by M. W. Sampson. Boston, 1904. (*Belles-Lettres Series.*)

Weever, J. *Epigrammes in the Oldest Cut and Newest Fashion.* 1599. Edited by R. B. McKerrow. London, 1911.

Wewitzer, R. *A Brief Dramatic Chronology of Actors on the London Stage, from the Introduction of Theatrical Entertainments into England, to the Present Time.* London, 1817.

Whetstone, G. *Promos and Cassandra.* Edited by J. S. Farmer. (*Tudor Facsimile Texts*, 1910.)

Whitaker, T. D. *History and Antiquities of the Deanery of Craven in the County of York.* Edited by A. W. Morant. Leeds, 1878.

Whitelocke, J. *Liber Famelicus of Sir James Whitelocke, a Judge of the Court of King's Bench in the Reigns of James I and Charles I.* Edited by J. Bruce. Printed for the Camden Society, 1858.

Wilkins, G. *Miseries of Enforced Marriage*. (Reprinted in Hazlitt's *Dodsley*, ix. 465.)

"Will Kemp." Shakespeare *Jahrbuch* (1887), xxii. 255.

Wilson, F. P. "Ralph Crane, Scrivener to the King's Players." *Library* (1926), vii. 194.

Wilson, J. D. "The *Hamlet* Transcript, 1593." *Library* (1918), ix. 217.

Wilson, R. *The Cobler's Prophecy*. Edited by A. C. Wood. *Malone Society Reprints*, 1914.

Wilson, R. *Three Ladies of London*. Edited by J. S. Farmer. (*Tudor Facsimile Texts*, 1911.)

Wilson, R. *Three Lords and Three Ladies of London*. (Reprinted in Hazlitt's *Dodsley*, vi. 371.)

Witkowski, G. "Englische Komödianten in Leipzig." *Euphorion* (1908), xv. 441.

Wits Recreations. London, 1640. [Reprinted, without date (not earlier than 1817), with *Musarum Deliciæ* (1656) and *Wit Restor'd* (1658), in 2 vols., by the publisher, John Camden Hotten, London.]

Wood, A. à. *Athenæ Oxonienses by Anthony à Wood*. Edited by P. Bliss. 4 vols. London, 1813–20.

Wood, A. I. P. *Stage History of Shakespeare's "King Richard the Third."* New York, 1909.

Wright, J. *Historia Histrionica. An Historical Account of the English-Stage; showing the Ancient Uses, Improvement, and Perfection of Dramatic Representations, in this Nation. In a Dialogue of Plays and Players.* 1699. (Reprinted in Hazlitt's *Dodsley*, xv. 399.)

Wright, L. B. "Animal Actors on the English Stage." *Publications of the Modern Language Association of America* (1927), xlii. 656.

Wright, L. B. "Will Kemp and the 'Commedia dell' Arte.'" *Modern Language Notes* (1926), xli. 516.

Wright, T. *Political Ballads Published in England during the Commonwealth*. Printed for the Percy Society. London, 1841.

Wright, T. *Queen Elizabeth and Her Times*. 2 vols. London, 1838.

Wülcker, R. P. "Englische Schauspieler in Kassel." Shakespeare *Jahrbuch* (1879), xiv. 360.

Young, W. *History of Dulwich College, with a Life of the Founder, Edward Alleyn, and an Accurate Transcript of His Diary, 1617–1622*. 2 vols. London, 1889.